Exploring Employee Relations

Mike Leat

OXFORD AUCKLAND BOSTON JOHANNESBURG MELBOURNE NEW DELHI

Butterworth-Heinemann
Linacre House, Jordan Hill, Oxford OX2 8DP
225 Wildwood Avenue, Woburn, MA 01801-2041
A division of Reed Educational and Professional Publishing Ltd

A member of the Reed Elsevier plc group

First published 2001

British Library Cataloguing in Publication Data
Leat, Mike
    Exploring employee relations
    1. Personnel management   2. Industrial relations
    I. Title
    658.3

ISBN 0 7506 4396 X

Typeset by Avocet Typeset, Brill, Aylesbury, Bucks
Printed and bound in Great Britain

FOR EVERY TITLE THAT WE PUBLISH, BUTTERWORTH-HEINEMANN
WILL PAY FOR BTCV TO PLANT AND CARE FOR A TREE.

Contents

Preface

In this book I seek to achieve a number of different objectives and paramount among these is to provide students with a text which demonstrates that the subject is alive and relevant to their world in the new millennium and which they can work through on their own, hence the decision to provide, at the end of each chapter, commentaries on the various activities and questions posed throughout the text. In this sense the text is student-centred and written in a style that is student friendly though not at the expense of analytical rigour. Working through the various activities is intended to facilitate the development of critical and analytical skills and attributes as well as knowledge and understanding. As is indicated by the title the intention is that through this work students will both be able and encouraged to explore employee relations.

The book has been structured into parts and chapters convenient for use with a twelve-week semester programme and additional questions, issues and discussion topics convenient for seminar use are incorporated into a separate tutor resource pack

The central focus of the book is the employment relationship and this is located in a multilayered contextual framework, with perhaps more emphasis upon international influences and developments than has been the norm for texts on employee relations in the UK.

The intended audience are those who, for whatever reason, find themselves confronted for the first time with a module or study programme on employee or industrial relations and the author envisages that the book is suitable for those studying at undergraduate, postgraduate and professional levels. A particular eye has been kept upon the requirements of personnel practitioners studying for the CIPD professional education scheme.

In addition, the book contains a fairly extensive bibliography, glossary and detailed list of contents.

I would like to thank all those colleagues and students who collectively and over more years than I care to detail have contributed to the development of the author's views and understandings as reflected in the text. Thanks are also expressed to all those authors and copyright holders who have given their permission to reproduce items in this work.

I would also like to acknowledge the contribution made by my children through their forbearance, understanding and good humour and to those who have kept me company while writing, particular among these latter and in no order of importance must be Beethoven, Van Morrison, Miles Davis, Schubert and Shostakovich.

Finally, I would like to thank my mother who died while this book was in preparation and whom I shall always remember with the greatest of affection and gratitude and to whom this book is dedicated.

Mike Leat

Part One
Introduction

Chapter 1

Employee relations and the employment relationship

Chapter Outline

- ■ Definitions of employee relations
- ■ The employment relationship
- ■ A psychological contract?
- ■ Forms of attachment, compliance and commitment
  Compliance
  Commitment
- ■ Conflict, cooperation and perspectives
  Unitarism
  Pluralism
  Radical/Marxist
- ■ A legal contract and the relevance of ideology
- ■ The quality of employee relations
- ■ An industrial relations system
  Processes
  Criticisms of the Dunlop model
- ■ An analytical framework

Introduction

'Employee relations' is a term that has only in relatively recent years become commonly used to indicate a particular area of subject matter. Prior to this it is likely that you would have found the term 'industrial relations' in more common use. The question of whether there are genuine differences attached to the meanings and uses of these two terms forms part of the discussion in this first chapter. Also we examine briefly the issues of the nature of the employment relationship, whether it is characterized by conflict or consensus, the significance of perspective and the relevance of the notion of a psychological contract. You are also introduced to the questions of what constitutes good industrial or employee relations, what does quality mean, what does it look like and, perhaps even more relevant, whether we can actually measure it in any meaningful sense. The relevance of perspective to that debate is also illustrated. Finally in this first chapter we introduce the notion of an industrial relations system and its limitations as a theory of industrial relations and, in this context, outline an analytical framework that centres upon the employment relationship and which also provides an explanation for the structure and contents of this book.

Objectives

After studying this chapter you will be able to:

- Discuss the main differences of view as to the subject matter of both employee and industrial relations and the differences between them
- Identify the relevance of contexts to the employment relationship
- Analyse the employment relationship in terms of the form of power available to employers and the nature of employee involvement
- Examine the nature of the employment relationship in terms of compliance or commitment
- Distinguish between the notions of employee involvement and commitment
- Demonstrate the significance of perspective to our understanding of the employment relationship
- Decide whether you think the employment relationship is essentially a conflictual one
- Explain the concept and relevance of a psychological contract
- Examine the meaning of quality in employee relations and explain the relevance of perspective
- Discuss the appropriateness of the many possible indicators of the quality of employee relations and the relevance of perspective
- Critically examine the notion of an industrial relations system in the context of the development of an adequate theory of employee relations and discuss its relevance to analysis and comparison of employee relations in different environments

Definitions of employee relations

There are debates and differences of view as to the meaning of each of the two terms, employee and industrial relations. Some people argue that there are identifiable differences between them, that there are differences of a substantive nature that justify the use and maintenance of each term, while others argue that the concepts and phenomena described are to all intents and purposes interchangeable. Blyton and Turnbull (1994: 7–9) discuss this in seeking to explain why they have chosen to use the term 'employee' as opposed to 'industrial'. They begin by arguing that they see no hard and fast distinction between the two, the difference being in the tendency of each to focus the subject inside different boundaries, but in reviewing various contributions to the debate they do state some of the more common views.

They point out that **industrial relations**:

- became inevitably associated with trade unions, collective bargaining and industrial action
- had too strong a tendency to view the world of work as synonymous with the heavy extractive and manufacturing sectors of employment, sectors that were dominated by male manual workers working full-time and which are in decline in nearly all developed economies.

Using the term **employee relations** enables them to adopt a broader canvas and to:

- encompass the now dominant service sector, in which more than 70 per cent of the labour force are employed, and the changes in the composition of the labour force such as more women working and more part-time, temporary and fixed-term contracts
- include non-union as well as union scenarios and relationships.

Nevertheless, Blyton and Turnbull do not go as far as some others in that they choose to continue to focus their study of employee relations upon the **collective** aspects of the employment relationship. They suggest that in this they are maintaining a distinction between employee relations and those other areas of study: personnel management and human resource management, each of which, they suggest, focuses upon the individual as opposed to the collective elements of the relationship.

There is therefore a sense in which the difference between the two terms/concepts can be viewed as a reflection of a distinction between **individualism** and **collectivism**. This distinction is also relevant to our discussion of managerial styles in Chapter 8.

Marchington and Wilkinson (1996: 223) also discuss this 'difference' and they suggest that the term employee relations has emerged for three main reasons:

- usage, fashion and slippage
- it is increasingly used by personnel practitioners to describe that part of personnel and development concerned with the regulation of relations (collective and individual) between employer and employee
- there are actual and real differences of focus, with employee relations tending to focus upon management and management issues alone and on contemporary rather than historical practices; the way things are as opposed to the way things were.

They state that they have chosen to use the term employee relations principally for the second of these three reasons, though they also acknowledge that they use the terms interchangeably.

A comparison of these two views indicates that both:

- seek to argue that use of the term **employee relations** makes it easier to encompass change in the employment relationship, its environment and in the make up of the labour force
- both explanations would appear to allow the term **employee relations** to encompass union and non-union relations.

However, where Blyton and Turnbull are keen to maintain a collective focus and see this as the basis of a continuing distinction between employee relations and both personnel and human resource management where they suggest the focus is upon the individual and the individual employment relationship, Marchington and Wilkinson see employee relations encompassing both individual and collective relations.

Another point of difference is that Marchington and Wilkinson seem to endow the term employee relations with a managerial focus, suggesting as they do that there is a tendency for the subject matter of employee relations to be dominated by a concern with managerial issues and a managerial perspective rather than being concerned with all parties and interests in the employment relationship.

Arguably, another point of similarity is that both views tend to see employee relations as a wider concept than industrial relations, and the former can encompass the latter.

If we move on now to concentrate upon the **nature** of employee relations, rather than whether and how it may be different from industrial relations, we can see a number of the above points reflected in the following two attempts at definition:

The Institute of Personnel Management (renamed the Institute of Personnel and Development (IPD) after merger), in its Professional Education Scheme syllabus of 1993, defines **employee relations** as:

that part of personnel management that enables competent managers, through the development of institutions, procedures and policies, to reconcile within acceptable limits to the organization the interests of employers as the buyers of labour services and those of employees as the suppliers of labour services

and Farnham (1993: 4) who suggests that employee relations are:

concerned with the interactions between the primary parties who pay for work and those who provide it in the labour market (employers and employees), those acting as secondary parties on their behalf (management or management organizations and trade unions) and those providing a third party role on employment matters (state agencies and EC institutions).

Here we see the IPD effectively staking a claim to the work associated with what they perceive as the management function of employee relations and there are clear links with this definition and the explanations given by Marchington and Wilkinson for the increased usage of the term.

Both these attempts at definition imply the potential for conflict between the interests of buyers and sellers of labour and the need for these different interests to be reconciled; the IPD more explicitly than Farnham.

In this book we use the term employee relations to encompass the reconciliation of conflict inherent within the employment relationship the focus is upon collective elements of this relationship and the collective regulation of the relationships between employers and employees. We seek to take account of change and use the term to encompass both trade union and non-union relationships and environments. We do not use the term in a manner which presents the subject matter as part of a management function but, in the later sections on styles and procedures, we do emphasize the managerial perspective on the matters under consideration.

The employment relationship

In this section we examine some of the more important issues and debates surrounding the employment relationship. In particular we examine the concept of a psychological contract, the extent to which the employment relationship is characterized by compliance or commitment, conflict and/or cooperation, the relevance of perspective and the notion of control of the labour process.

No employment relationship occurs in a vacuum and it is important to realize that there is a range of contexts within which it occurs and which, to varying degrees, impinge upon the relationship.

A psychological contract?

As we see in one of the later chapters the employment relationship is to some extent circumscribed by the legal environment and context and that, at the level of the individual, there is a legally enforceable contract between employee and employer. It has also been suggested that the employment relationship can be perceived as a psychological contract.

Schein (1988) is largely responsible for this notion of a psychological contract and his suggestion was that between employer and employee there exists an implicit contractual relationship which is derived from a series of assumptions on the part of employer and employee about the nature of their relationship. These assumptions that comprise the psychological contract are not legally enforceable but they constitute a set of reciprocal arrangements and form the basis for a series of expectations which may have a considerable degree of moral force.

The main assumptions are:

- that employees will be treated fairly and honestly
- that the relationship should be characterized by a concern for equity and justice and that this would require the communication of sufficient information about changes and developments
- that employee loyalty to the employer would be reciprocated with a degree of employment and job security
- that employees' input would be recognized and valued by the employer.

Underlying this notion of a psychological contract we can also detect assumptions about what people look for in terms of returns and satisfactions from work and indeed there is an element of prescription in that Schein can be interpreted as specifying the way in which employees should be treated.

In this particular instance it is pretty clear that these underlying assumptions are essentially consistent with the sets of individual needs identified many years ago by American researchers such as Roethlisberger and Dickson (1939), Maslow (1943) and Herzberg (1966) and which encompass equity and justice, security and safety, recognition of worth and input and self-fulfillment. This model of a psychological contract, where fulfilled, provided the means for employees to derive intrinsic as well as extrinsic satisfactions and rewards from their work.

There is certainly some evidence from the UK that many employees do seek these rewards from work, for example Guest's (1995) study in which more than 70 per cent of those questioned felt that 'the opportunity to use their initiative and abilities whilst at work, in effect to be stretched in terms of problem solving and creativity' were either essential or very important.

More recent evidence from the 1998 Workplace Employee Relations Survey (WERS) (Cully *et al.*, 1998) also throws some light upon the extent to which employees are deriving the benefits and satisfactions implied by this notion of a psychological contract. The survey addressed this issue as part of an attempt to ascertain the extent to which employees in the UK were satisfied with their job/work. They compiled a measure of job satisfaction that took into account employees satisfaction with four different components:

- influence (the level of autonomy and control) over the job
- a sense of achievement derived from meeting the challenge presented by work
- respect from managers in terms of recognition for a job well done, and
- pay.

The conclusions of the researchers were that, overall, a majority of employees were satisfied (54 per cent), however:

- employees tended to be least satisfied with pay
- managers tended to be more satisfied than other occupational groups
- older workers tended to be more satisfied than younger workers
- part-time workers were more satisfied than full-time workers.

The researchers comment that 'a significant minority of employees feel that the overall deal they have – their implicit or psychological contract – is a poor one'. Other findings relevant to this concept are that 65 per cent of the employees surveyed said that they felt a loyalty to the organization that they worked for and job satisfaction levels appear to be positively associated with employees feeling that they are consulted about change in the workplace. They also found a positive association between job satisfaction and employee commitment.

In another survey, Guest and Conway (1999) found that the psychological contract remains healthy, with about two-thirds of those surveyed feeling that their employers have substantially kept their promises and commitments to them.

Forms of attachment, compliance and commitment

Compliance

Central to an understanding of the employment relationship is the question of attachment or involvement, how is it achieved and what is the nature of the relationship? We do not intend to examine the issue of motivation, you should have covered this already elsewhere in your studies and, to a minor extent, the comments above about a psychological contract should have reminded you of some of the literature on the subject.

Kinds of power	Kinds of involvement		
	Alienative	*Calculative*	*Moral*
Coercive	1	2	3
Remunerative	4	5	6
Normative	7	8	9

Figure 1.1 Sources of power and involvement. *Source:* Adapted from Etzioni (1975)

Some years ago Etzioni (1975) suggested that employees were engaged with, attached to or involved with employing organizations in a number of different ways and with differing degrees of intensity. He described the employment relationship in terms of the nature of this compliance. He divided compliance into two elements: the form of power wielded by the employer to achieve control and the nature of the employee's involvement. As can be seen from **Figure 1.1** Etzioni identified three different sources and forms of power that could be utilized by employers and three different forms of involvement. Together this provides the possibility of nine different combinations of power and involvement, nine different types of compliance.

The three different forms of involvement can be perceived to represent different degrees of negative or positive feelings. There were three ideal or congruent combinations of these two elements that were more effective than the others. For example, if the nature of the employee's involvement with work was essentially calculative, instrumental or extrinsic then the ideal or matching form of power that the employer should use would be remunerative. Where the nature of the employee's involvement is alienative or highly negative the appropriate form of power may well be coercive. If the nature of the employee's involvement was highly positive or moral, meaning that they identify with or share the values and purposes of the organization, then the ideal form of power that the employer should use would be normative, implying the allocation or withholding of symbolic rewards such as prestige and recognition.

However, these days in the UK, the term 'compliance' is not perceived as encompassing a range of forms of attachment, as was the case with Etzioni's use of the term. It is used as a comparative descriptor of a form of attachment that is less positive and intense than commitment, a form of attachment that is commonly achieved and maintained through the administration of rules and bureaucratic controls. In this latter context compliance results in reactive behaviour and a concern with rights and rules.

Commitment

In terms of the Etzioni model or typology the term 'commitment', as used in the UK in the 1990s, refers to moral involvement, employees positively identifying with and sharing the values and purposes of the organization. The kind of attachment that we tend to associate with membership of voluntary associations or perhaps with employment in public-sector service and caring organizations, such as the National Health Service, than with membership of the more common private-sector and profit-making employing organizations.

Commitment is portrayed as an internalized belief leading to constructive proactivity by employees; it leads to employees 'going one step further' (Legge, 1995: 174).

Both here and with compliance above assumptions are being made between forms of attachment and consequential behaviour and it may well be that the form of attachment between employees and the organization is discernible from the behaviour that can be seen.

It has also been suggested that distinctions can sometimes be drawn between attitudinal and behavioural commitment.

- Attitudinal commitment is the form depicted above and which would be compatible with Etzioni's moral involvement: commitment in terms of a sharing of values and attitudes, a psychological bond to an organization, an affective attachment.
- Behavioural commitment is demonstrated by a willingness to exert effort beyond the requirements of contract and/or by a desire to remain a member of an organization.

Mowday *et al.* (1982) have suggested that there may well be a reciprocal relationship between these two forms, with attitudes influencing behaviour and *vice versa.* An assumption of such a relationship underlies much of the interest in the concept of commitment in recent years. However, care is needed here in that whilst it may be that the extra effort or desire to remain with the organization are indications that the individual does have positive attitudinal commitment to the organization, there are other possible explanations such as there being little or no alternative employment available.

Commitment of an attitudinal nature has been at the centre of much of the prescriptive literature on human resource management (HRM) over the last fifteen years, from Beer *et al.* (1984) onwards, and in terms of the UK literature perhaps most famously by Guest (1987) who identified employee commitment as one of four outcomes that HRM should try to develop, but not for its own sake. Employee commitment became a desirable HRM outcome because of an assumption that attitudinal commitment would yield certain specified and desirable behaviours and, through these, certain desirable organizational outcomes, such as better quality of product or service or lower labour turnover or greater efficiency.

Employers have been exhorted by academics, popular and otherwise, and by politicians to pursue measures and policies aimed at securing this commitment and, in their turn, employers have exhorted their employees to take on and share the organization's objectives and values, often emphasizing as they did so their view that employee and employer interests were essentially the same. Alternative perceptions of the nature of the employment relationship and the realism of this view are pursued in the following sections on conflict and perspective.

It is not difficult to perceive the attractions to management of this concept. Implicit to this attractiveness is an assumed relationship between commitment and desired behaviours and, in particular, that committed employees will work harder, be more productive and innovative and exhibit a greater concern with the quality of their output and customer satisfaction. These assumptions also underlie much of the clamour from employers and politicians in recent years for employees to be more involved in their organizations.

Unfortunately we have further confusion around the meanings attached to words. The use of the word 'involvement' here does not denote a range of forms of attachment on the part of employees, as was the case in the Etzioni typology. Here, the term is used more narrowly to describe initiatives and techniques that make the employee feel more a part of the organization, as for example might be achieved by and through effective communications policies or through the organization of social events and clubs.

Employee involvement (EI) initiatives have become popular in the UK, primarily because it is assumed that EI initiatives will encourage employees to be more content and satisfied in their work; it is assumed that this will yield employee commitment, and satisfied and committed employees are harder working, etc. In the context of the pressures for organizations to be more productive and competitive, and if you believe that helping employees to feel more a part of the organization will encourage them to work harder, then such initiatives are justified. The 1998 WERS findings lend support to a belief in an association between the measures designed to engender employee commitment and levels of job satisfaction but not to the belief that satisfied workers are more productive.

In addition to commitment being a prescribed desirable outcome of the softer HRM models there has been much debate about how it is to be achieved. There is a degree of coincidence between measures that are thought to enhance employee satisfaction, involvement and commitment; in other words, the same measures hopefully will achieve all of these objectives. Examples include team working, team briefing, quality circles and problem-solving groups, the advent of development-led appraisal, multi-skilling and job rotation, enlargement and enrichment programmes. The increased frequency and incidence of practices of this kind have often implied and required changes in the way that employees are managed, the mechanisms used, the way work is organized and, thereby, the nature of the employment relationship.

In Chapter 2 we will come across many of these innovations again and we will examine further the extent to which we can confirm that changes along these lines have occurred and the extent to which there is evidence of the coherent planning and introduction of such change programmes.

The popularity and frequency of these initiatives seems to have occurred in the absence of conclusive evidence of the relationships between involvement, commitment and improved performance that have been assumed. Legge (1995: 184) sums this up as follows

> As it is, presently there has still been relatively little research on the link between a cluster of EI ... policies and organizational commitment so conclusions must be tentative (Guest, 1992) ... There is evidence that employees generally welcome such initiatives, but there is no consistent evidence of their impact upon motivation, performance or industrial relations outcomes (Kelly and Kelly, 1991)

and

> Further, with a few special case exceptions, no relationship has been found between use of EI initiatives and company and plant performance ...

The 1998 WERS does represent the kind of further research that is necessary but, unfortunately, the first findings do not contain evidence on the productivity of employees. However, these findings confirm that many organizations say that they are using a range of the techniques and programmes that are commonly seen as encouraging employee involvement (and thereby commitment) and, as was noted above, there was evidence that a majority of employees expressed themselves both satisfied and committed. In this survey commitment was measured by the employees' responses to questions concerned with whether they share the goals and values of the organization, their sense of loyalty to the employer and whether they were proud to tell people who they worked for. Referring back again to the Etzioni typology, the notion of commitment pursued by the WERS research seems more or less synonymous with the notion of moral involvement, the sharing of objectives and values.

Legge (1995) addresses all of these issues and debates in more depth than is possible in this chapter and you should try to read her Chapter 6 entitled 'HRM: from Compliance to Commitment' in which she reviews much of the research evidence and literature.

It is worth pointing out that some of the literature treats the terms 'employee involvement' and 'employee participation' synonymously, whereas others insist upon a conceptual difference. Marchington *et al.* (1992) and Hollinshead and Leat (1995) provide further discussion of the concepts of involvement and participation and the extent to which they coincide. This is also an issue that is taken up later in Chapter 9.

Activity 1

Re-read the material concerned with Etzioni's typology and then apply it to some of your own experiences. Think of some of the organizations (not necessarily work organizations) to which you have been or are attached and try to identify in your own mind the nature of the compliance relationship in each case. Try also to decide whether the form of compliance is one of those that Etzioni argued were congruent and effective.

Conflict, cooperation and perspective

In addition to the debates referred to above about the nature of the employment relationship in terms of forms of attachment and the means by which management achieve control, there has also been considerable debate about the extent to which the fundamental nature of the employment relationship is one of, and is characterized by, conflict or cooperation. Central to this debate is the issue of perspective, or frame of reference.

Students should be aware that conflict in this context refers to difference and is not to be regarded as synonymous with or be confused with industrial action. Often, in the media and elsewhere the term 'industrial conflict' is used as an alternative description for strikes and other industrial action; this is not the intention here. Industrial action is unlikely unless there is conflict and so it is reasonable to view such action as a symptom of conflict, but conflict exists in many situations that are not characterized by industrial action and there are many other potential symptoms such as poor performance, absenteeism, high stress and anxiety levels and labour turnover.

Students also often have difficulty with this notion of **perspective** and tend to confuse it with a system or form of organization so that, for example, they talk and write about 'unitaristic' organizations. It is important to appreciate that a perspective is an approach or way of looking at something, not the thing itself. We each have values and views and these have been determined through the process of socialization and informed by our experience. The perspective that we each have will mean that we approach issues, concepts and events with a particular orientation that will influence our interpretation and understanding of what we see and experience. Our view and understanding of the nature of employing organizations and the employment relationship will be subject to these influences.

Fox (1966) used the term 'frame of reference' and this may help in enabling you to understand the nature of a perspective. Initially Fox identified two particular and relevant frames of reference, the unitarist and pluralist. Subsequently and additionally a third, radical or Marxist, variant has been distinguished and contrasted with the others. These are not the only perspectives on the fundamental nature of the employment relationship and on whether it is characterized by conflict: Nicholls (1999) adds a feminist perspective which perceives capitalism and employee relations in terms of patriarchy and male domination of women. However, these three perspectives do represent distinctly different viewpoints on these issues and are indicators of the range of potential perspectives.

Unitarism

This perspective perceives employing organizations as peopled by individuals and groups that have common interests, objectives and values, and that are harmonious and integrated. Management's right to manage is legitimate and rational and management (representing the organization and the interests of capital) should be the single focus of employee loyalty as well as the sole source of legitimate authority within the organization. Unsurprisingly, therefore, this perspective tends to be associated with, and is often promoted by, management since it supports management's interests. Frequently this perspective has been characterized as the 'Team' or 'One big happy family' approach.

From the unitarist perspective conflict between labour and management is viewed as being both unnecessary and avoidable. Where conflict does occur it is argued that this is not because it is inherent to the capitalist system or even because groups have legitimate differences between their aspirations and interests; it occurs because of poor communication, because the parties to the relationship lack understanding of the extent to which their interests are coincident, because the conflict has been deliberately created by saboteurs or because individual personalities clash. The perspective argues that conflict is irrational and pathological, it should not occur; if and where it does, management has the legitimate right to manage, to control; employees owe loyalty and therefore conflict resolution ought not to be an issue.

In this context the employment relationship is likely to be perceived to be characterized by cooperation rather than by conflict with management or other representatives of capital adopting autocratic or paternalist approaches to the exercising of their authority. Cooperation between the interests of capital and labour should be normal in this scenario.

Managements with this perspective will often try to persuade their employees that they do not need a trade union to represent them and that management will look after them; indeed these managements often try to create circumstances at work which tend to reinforce this message. Examples of companies in which this attitude has dominated would certainly include big names such as Marks & Spencer, IBM and Hewlett Packard. There was a Channel 4 film made a few years ago on Hewlett Packard called *The Gilded Cage* and if you can view a copy you will see an example of this perspective and its implications. Management style in organizations in which this management perspective dominates tends to be perceived as being on a continuum between the extremes of autocracy and paternalism. Also, do not imagine that this is a perspective that is peculiar to and reserved for managements in private-sector organizations.

Pluralism

This perspective assumes that employing organizations are made up of individuals and groups with different interests, values and objectives. Each group is likely to develop its own leadership and source of loyalty. The various interests and objectives of one group are likely to conflict with those of others and, while this will include the interests of labour versus the interests of capital, conflict will not be exclusive to these interests. It is common, for example, that there are conflicts within organizations between different groups of employees, between different functions as well as between labour and capital. For example, it is not unusual for the finance function within an organization to come into conflict with other functions or departments over issues such as the determination of budgets and expenditure plans, and it is not uncommon for groups of employees to come into conflict over issues such as the 'ownership' of particular work or tasks and the rates of pay received by each of the groups. These latter conflicts arguably used to be more common than they are these days but they do still occur; one of the major arguments against the introduction of a minimum wage is that it may well provoke conflicts between groups of employees, with those lowest paid appearing to benefit as the minimum rate of pay is higher than their current earnings, whereas those on higher rates of pay are unaffected. It is suggested that there could be conflicts between groups of employees over the maintenance or not of existing pay differentials.

In the context of this perspective management is likely to be confronted by a workforce that does not necessarily accept their right to manage and who owe loyalty to other sources and interests. Management have a very different role in this context, the task facing them is not to exercise their unilateral right to manage, whether this takes an autocratic or paternalistic form, now there is an emphasis upon securing the agreement of the other interests to decisions. As Flanders (1970: 172) put it: 'the paradox, whose truth managements have found it difficult to accept, is that they can only regain control by sharing it'.

Management's job, therefore, is not to try to insist upon a right to manage unilaterally but to manage and resolve the conflict and to do this via mechanisms that emphasize the achievement of consensus and that involve representation and participation from the various interests concerned.

This is a perspective that argues that the most potential lies in joint approaches to conflict resolution.

Collective bargaining is one such mechanism and, in this context, the formation of trade unions is a realistic and rational response on the part of the labour resource, since they, through their collective strength, are able to provide employees with a counter to the otherwise unfettered power of the employer. The absence of collective organization on the part of the workforce leaves it weak and open to exploitation.

Radical/Marxist

From this perspective organizations employing labour do so only in order to exploit it. The purpose of capitalism is to make surplus value/profit from the employment of resources in the labour process, and it is in this sense that it is argued that labour is exploited, since this surplus value accumulates to capital (rather than to labour). Profit is made from employing labour for a price less than the value of its product.

The labour process is the term used to describe the process whereby labour is added to capital and technology to produce goods and services which are then exchanged for others. It is the process through which labour potential is converted into actual.

This perspective also views industrial organizations as microcosms of the wider society and the frictions in that wider society are likely to be also reflected and present in the organization. Underlying the Marxist perspective is an assumption that power in capitalist society is unfavourably weighted in favour of the owners of the means of production and not with the owners and sellers of the labour resource. This is a perspective that uncompromisingly predicts a fundamental and continuing conflict of interest between labour and capital and the conflict is likely to be about who should control the labour process as well as about the price of labour. Such conflict is inevitable and, unlike in the pluralist perspective, is not amenable to resolution through mechanisms that emphasize compromise and sharing of power. This is a perspective that does not accept the conclusion of Flanders quoted above.

The nature and depth of this endemic conflict is such that compromise and resolution via peaceful means is not a realistic option. If labour compromises it will inevitably do so on capital's terms and therefore to its own disadvantage; collective bargaining in the context of this perspective is to be avoided since it is a means by which capital secures a continuation of the status quo. The only means by which this capitalist status quo can be overcome is through thoroughgoing revolution and the replacement of control by capital with control by labour, the replacement of capitalism with a dictatorship by the proletariat; the long-term solution is in the overthrow of the capitalist system. In this struggle trade unions are to be expected and are desirable as the armies of the working class in what will inevitably be a class war leading to the creation of a socialist economy.

It is important to realize and remember that these three perspectives are 'ideal types' and that organizational reality may well encourage the adoption of hybrid perspectives. Of the three viewpoints, the unitarist tends to be most popular with employers and governments and other interests that have a liberal and individualist ideology, whereas the pluralist tends to be the most common among employee representatives and governments of a liberal collectivist (or corporatist) persuasion. The Marxist or radical approach is relatively unpopular and uncommon in the UK though there are other European countries in which it has a stronger presence and tradition, such as in France and Italy where there are still relatively strong Marxist trade union confederations and political alliances. In the mid-1990s France experienced a number of large-scale and militant strikes and other forms of industrial action and these were partially protest against right-wing government policies and also partly a Marxist response to the global pressures upon business to be more and more competitive, more and more efficient.

Edwards (1995: 15) argues a realistic compromise that neither of these ideal types can be relied upon exclusively and that the employment relationship is accurately and realistically perceived as one characterized by both conflict and cooperation. In this he expresses similar conclusions to those of Gospel and Palmer (1993) who in their introductory chapter argue that 'Conflict and cooperation therefore coexist within organizations ... Cooperation and conflict must both be expected'. Edwards characterizes the employment relationship as one of **structured antagonism**, a relationship that is both contradictory and antagonistic. The contradiction is due to management needing both to control the labour resource and also to tap into and release its creativity, and it is inevitably antagonistic because employers have to exploit labour in order to create surplus value and thereby profit. It is this deeper antagonism or conflict of interest that needs to be structured in order to facilitate the day to day production of goods and services through the labour process. He suggests that cooperation may have benefits for employees and, indeed, that the parties may share some interests, but this should not disguise the fact that ultimately the purpose of employing labour is to exploit it.

Activity 2

Re-read the accounts of the three perspectives and then answer the following:

1 Which of the three perspectives perceive conflict as something that is inevitable within employing organizations?
2 What are the implications of each of the perspectives for the appropriate means through which conflict is to be resolved?
3 If there is an inherent and inevitable conflict between the interests of employees and employers what is the nature and root of that conflict?

Activity 3

It is important to realize your own views and values and therefore your own perspective on the employment relationship and so take a few more minutes now to think through which of the viewpoints referred to above as perspectives seem to you to be the more realistic and with which you find yourself agreeing. Don't worry if you find yourself in agreement with elements of differing perspectives, as we said earlier these three perspectives are somewhat idealized and hybrid viewpoints are common. Write down now what you think and keep it so that later on as you work your way through this book you can come back to your current views and see if they have changed as you have progressed.

Activity 4

Re-examine the subsections on commitment, and on perspective and conflict and work out for yourself whether there is any coincidence between the notion of employee commitment as is prescribed as a desirable human resource management outcome and the three perspectives detailed.

A legal contract and the relevance of ideology

As already noted, the employment relationship does not occur in a vacuum. There are a range of different contexts that provide the backdrop and within which the interests of labour and capital are reconciled. Amongst others there are economic and business contexts, demographic and labour force contexts, cultural, legal, political, ideological and technical contexts and we deal with the majority of these in various of the later chapters (see also the final sections of this chapter where we discuss the notion of an industrial relations system and develop an analytical framework).

There is a legal environment and dimension to the employment relationship (see Chapter 5). As a unit of labour is hired, a legally binding contract is created; the terms of the contract may be the product of individual or collective agreement, derived from works rules, custom and practice or they may be determined legislatively.

The earliest legally enforceable obligations and responsibilities of the parties to the relationship between each other were implied and derived from common law but more recently the legal context has become more explicit as governments and the European Union has enacted or adopted legislation that specifies rights and obligations. Over the years, governments have taken different approaches to the question of legal regulation of this relationship, and where governments have intervened in order to regulate it has usually been to protect one or other party from exploitation by the other; examples would include legislation to protect women and children at work.

There is also an ideological dimension to this intervention and, therefore, to the context within which the employment relationship exists. For example, governments are much less likely to intervene to protect either party if they believe in:

- the efficiency of the market
- the rationality of individuals and their capacity to look after their own interests through the process of exchange that precedes the formation of the contract
- that there is a rough equality of bargaining power between the parties.

The UK general election of 1979 heralded the return to power of a government that shared such a **liberal individualist** ideology and we have seen since then not only a greater unwillingness on the part of government to regulate the employment relationship but also a determination to deregulate intervention to:

- eliminate or reduce legislative protections for employees
- reduce the legislative limits upon the freedoms of employers
- reduce the bargaining power of trade unions as the representatives of those employee interests.

This contrasted with the **liberal collectivist** values and beliefs of previous post-war governments that had in the main:

- placed less reliance upon the efficiency of the market and the ability of individual units of labour to look after their own interests
- acknowledged an imbalance in the bargaining power of employers and employees that was in favour of employers
- placed greater emphasis upon the need for employees to have access to the assistance of a collective organization and a regulatory legal framework.

The traditional preference had been for the parties to the relationship, both individual and collective, to be left as far as possible to voluntarily sort out their differences and agree the rules comprising the regulatory framework, but where such **voluntarism** was perceived not to result in the desired degree of fairness governments were prepared to intervene legislatively to achieve what they regarded as a fair outcome.

Intervention of a legislative nature began in earnest in the early 1960s beginning with the Contracts of Employment Act 1963 and the Redundancy Payments Act 1965.

These legal and ideological contexts are not pursued much further in this chapter, we are concerned here more with the nature of the employment relationship than with the way in which it may be regulated and what the ideology behind the currently dominant attitudes towards legal regulation may be. However, it is unlikely that we can ignore these contexts completely since developments in the nature of the relationship since 1979 have to some extent been facilitated and encouraged by government. Government sought to deregulate labour markets so as to create the circumstances in which labour could be utilized more flexibly and thereby free employers of the legal chains that previously bound their ability to be innovative, become competitive and employ more labour.

It is as yet too early to assess the impact that the Labour government, elected in 1997, will have upon these contexts and indeed upon the employment relationship. Early signs are mixed in that the government has indicated a commitment to the trade unions to provide them with the right to gain recognition rights in certain circumstances where a sufficient proportion of employees want it, even though the employer may not, and the introduction of a statutory minimum wage. Yet they have also expressed their determination to maintain the labour market flexibilities perceived as essential to the achievement and maintenance of competitiveness in the global economy.

Activity 5

Take a few minutes now to jot down the main features of both the Liberal Individualist and Liberal Collectivist ideologies as they impinge upon the employment relationship. Having done this, try to determine the main differences between them.

The quality of employee relations

This notion of quality is one that has bothered analysts for some time, since there is a lack of satisfactory indicators; the quantitative indicator most commonly used or referred to is that of the incidence of strikes. As a measure of quality this has a number of drawbacks since peace can be bought by employers giving in to the demands of employees and, in such circumstances, it might be difficult to justify the assertion that relations are good. As with other possible quantitative indicators, such as labour turnover or absenteeism rates, it may be that they do indeed give some measure of quality but it may also be that they indicate some other phenomenon entirely. For example, as in Japan where taking such action has generally been perceived to imply a loss of face for both employer and employee, the relative absence of strikes in such circumstances is reflective of cultural phenomena rather than the quality of employee relations. Another example may be where the rate of unemployment in an economy is high and the degree of employment security low an absence of strike action and/or low labour turnover rates may be indicative of fear rather than of good employee relations.

Nevertheless, this particular measure (the rate and incidence of strike action) is commonly used as an indicator of quality in international and comparative work and many comparative texts contain chapters that are concerned to compare the strike statistics in one country with those of another and from which implications are drawn about relative quality. It is interesting that these works commonly go into detail not only about the shortcomings of this as a measure but also about the difficulties of ensuring that like is compared with like, since countries tend to collect data differently and indeed apply different parameters on the data. An example of this may be that in some countries the minimum duration or numbers involved may be very different from those used elsewhere as the threshold above which strikes are counted and below which they are not.

Governments and the media tend to use this particular measure and in the UK over the last fifteen years it has been common for the government to point to the decrease in the incidence of strikes and days lost through strike action as evidence of an improvement in the quality of employee relations. To some extent this is understandable since the figures tend to be available and the audience may well be a largely uncritical one. **Figure 1.2** demonstrates that while such an assumption is not explicitly stated the implication of the article is that lots of strikes indicate bad employee relations.

The taking of strike action depends upon factors such as:

- it being allowed by the law
- culture–value systems and attitudes
- the existence and power of effective collective employee organizations
- the degree of employment security afforded employees
- the potential costs to the employees
- the availability of other means by which employees can both demonstrate and purge their dissatisfaction.

So we can see that a low incidence of strike activity may have relatively little to do with the quality of employee relations, it may simply be the result of such action being outlawed and/or employees finding alternative means of venting their frustrations or mitigating their dissatisfaction, such as absenteeism, labour turnover, working to rule, withdrawing cooperation or banning overtime, each of which may also be indicators of quality.

Once again we can trace the relevance of perspective. As implied earlier, it isn't only the difficulty of knowing whether what you are actually measuring is or is not what you want to measure, there is also the problem that perceptions of 'good' can vary quite considerably from one person to another and between the various interests and actors. If we return to our three stereotypes of perspective, the unitarist, pluralist and the radical/Marxist, we can identify for each what might constitute 'good' for each and thereby illustrate some of the range of viewpoints on this matter.

European tradition offers better way to ease industrial conflict

Briefing

Charlotte Denny
....

THE Conservatives are often credited with radically reforming industrial relations in Britain and introducing a productivity "miracle" in industry. The panegyrics are usually accompanied by warnings about the dangers of importing European-style rigidities into UK labour markets now that the Government has signed up to the Social Chapter.

A more realistic assessment of the impact of Thatcherite labour laws is provided in this month's National Institute Economic Review (NIER) which says that changes in the wider economic environment caused more of the shift in industrial relations than the new laws intended to break union power.

This power has been substantially eroded in Britain since 1980 when half the workforce were union members. By 1995 the proportion had dropped to just under a third. Strikes have also been on the wane — 440 working days for every 1,000 employers were lost on average each year between 1981-1985 compared to just 24 a decade later.

But the same pattern is observable in other industrialised countries which have not adopted *laissez-faire* employment legislation. Britain was the 11th most unionised OECD country in 1995 — one down on the ranking it held in 1980. Its place in the chart of industrial unrest has dropped — but there is not much to separate countries with low levels of strikes.

The researchers conclude that union membership has been in retreat in Britain as in the rest of the industrialised world due to more competition in product markets — the result of increasing trade with low wage econo-mies — and high unemployment. The Conservative government's drive to deregulate the labour market was a secondary cause.

Where Britain is unique in Western Europe is the rapid drop in the proportion of workers covered by collective wage agreements; 83 per cent were covered in 1980 compared with 48 per cent in 1994, among the lowest in Western Europe.

Economic research suggests that while trade and technology have led to rising pay inequality throughout the industrialised world, the low paid fare worst in countries where unions and statutory wage protection are weak.

Between one eighth and one quarter of the growth of earning inequality in Britain is attributed to the decline in bargaining coverage and the removal of protection for the low paid over this period.

The researchers acknowledge that the new laws have contributed significantly to economic performance in a few highly publicised industries where the removal of closed shops allowed firms to get rid of uncompetitive practices. But in most industries the key factors in improving performance were increased product market competition and better management.

The new laws cemented the adversarial style that has always characterised British labour-management relations. The old assumptions of a fundamental conflict were strengthened by draconian new powers available to employers and the courts.

Europe offers a different tradition of industrial relations involving institution support for labour-management co-operation. The central issue now, according to the NIER, is whether the Government will join the European mainstream in acknowledging a role for collective employee representation and statutory support for minimum employment standards.

Figure 1.2 *Source: The Guardian*, 21 July 1997 p. 17

Unitarist. The unitarist is likely to see peace, as indicated by the absence of overt conflict behaviour, as evidence of good employee relations. They are likely to similarly view as evidence of good employee relations: management control/prerogative, the absence of alternative sources of employee loyalty within the organization, and the effective use of labour as indicated by rising productivity and diminishing unit costs.

Pluralist. The pluralist is likely to concentrate upon the existence of effective mechanisms for conflict resolution as evidence of good employee relations. These mechanisms should be joint, demonstrating management's recognition of and willingness to resolve conflict through shared decision making and compromise. Employees with this perspective are likely to also refer to the existence and recognition of effective trade unions as additional criteria to be met if employee relations are to be considered good.

Radical/Marxist. The Marxist is much more likely to be concerned with issues of control of the labour process. Shared decision making through agreed procedures are much less likely to be accepted as evidence of good employee relations since the Marxist viewpoint is likely to see these mechanisms as means through which management secure the maintenance of the status quo. Industrial peace is also likely to be viewed negatively since, on the one hand, it is probably evidence that management have secured effective control and, on the other, this viewpoint is one that promotes the belief that revolution is necessary to wrest control from the owners of capital and the trade unions are to be the armies of the working classes in this struggle.

Activity 6

1 Determine for yourself the criteria that you might consider acceptable as an indicator of the quality of employee relations and write them down.
2 Now write a short essay in which you discuss the arguments for and against the suggestion that strike statistics are an adequate/appropriate measure/indicator of the quality of employee relations.

An industrial relations system

We move on now to examine one of the most important contributions to the study of industrial relations (and subsequently employee relations since the former is encompassed by the latter), this being the notion of an industrial relations system as devised by J.T. Dunlop in 1958.

Many would argue that this constitutes the major American contribution to the literature and theory of industrial relations. Dunlop thought that he was developing a general theory of industrial relations when he devised this notion of an industrial relations system, which he saw as a subsystem on its own rather than as part of a wider economic system, though it will partially overlap and interact with the economic and political systems. The outline of this concept is depicted in **Figure 1.3**. For Dunlop, the **outputs** or **outcomes** of the system are a body of both **procedural and substantive rules** and the purpose of the system framework is to facilitate the analysis and explanation of these rules, their formulation and administration.

The distinction between procedural and substantive rules is one that students often find difficult and it is important to realize that the procedural rules that are referred to as an output of the system comprise both the rules that govern the determination of the substantive rules, the 'how' that explains rule determination, as well as the procedures that govern the application of the rules in particular situations. These procedures can be seen as the rules of governance, the rules that are created (by different processes) to govern the interaction of the parties engaged in the rule-making process as well as to determine and act as a point of reference for decisions concerning the application of substantive rules.

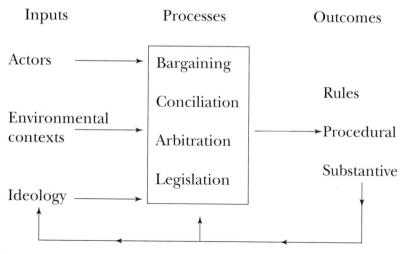

Figure 1.3 *Source:* Adapted from Dunlop (1958)

An example of the first type of procedure might be a recognition and negotiating procedure agreed between employer and employee representatives that spells out the detail of how the parties will interact with a view to the joint determination of rates of pay, hours of work, etc. Such a procedure may include details as to when and where, as well as who, is to participate in the negotiations. There may be a number of stages agreed, so that if the parties fail to agree initially it is clear how the matter is to be progressed without the need for recourse to industrial action. Commonly such procedures will also lay out a number of options for dealing with the matter if the parties cannot agree among themselves, such as provision for referral to conciliation or arbitration (see Chapter 5, section on ACAS, for the distinction between these two processes).

An example of the second type of procedural rule might be agreed procedures governing the detailed application of an agreed increase in pay (substantive) in and to a complex grading system and also encompassing procedures to deal with grievances and appeals raised as a result of the application of the pay increase. The substantive rule in this example would be the increase in the rates: this is the matter of substance.

If the rules are the outcomes of the system they are the product of a range of inputs and the utilization of particular processes for the determination of the rules and for the resolution of conflict. There are a considerable variety of processes available and they vary from one country or other scenario to another, as do the precise nature of the environmental contexts, combination of actors and ideology that Dunlop identifies as making up the inputs to the system. If we look at the **inputs** identified in **Figure 1.3** it is clear that Dunlop perceived three categories of independent variable falling into this category, **actors**, **contexts** and **ideology**. Each of these needs a little explanation and elaboration.

Actors. There are three main actors in the system:

- A hierarchy of non-managerial employees and their representative collective institutions, the trade unions and similar associations, which may be competitive with each other.
- A hierarchy of managers and their representatives which will encompass managerial and employers' associations.
- Various third-party agencies, including government agencies, for example the Advisory, Conciliation and Arbitration Service (ACAS).

Each of these are dealt with at some length in later chapters.

Contexts. There are also three main areas of environmental context:

- Technology. As was noted in the earlier Unit on the changing nature of work, the technological context has significant implications for and impact upon the interactions within the system and the outcomes; for example, the technology available at any one time will impact upon the production process and the organization of work, this influences the nature of skills, quantity, location and dispersal of labour demand.
- Market or budgetary influences. Product markets are particularly important to the interactions and outcomes. Recent years have demonstrated this with many arguing increased international competition in product markets as one of the major influences in the drive for flexibility of labour and the development of models of the flexible firm.
- The locus and distribution of power in the wider society, outside but impinging upon the industrial relations system. Having said that, it is also the case that the distribution of power outside the system tends to be reflected in the system. It is suggested that this distribution of power will have a particular impact upon the state's third-party agencies, again such as ACAS and Industrial Tribunals. An example may be that after a long period of uninterrupted rule by one particular political party it is likely that the power distribution reflected by and in this dominance will also be reflected in the make-up and disposition of the hierarchies of such agencies.

Ideology. The third category of input identified by Dunlop is ideology, by which is meant a collection of assumptions, values, beliefs and ideas that, shared by all the parties, will have the effect of binding the system together and rendering it stable. The hallmark of a mature industrial relations system is that the ideologies held by the main actors are sufficiently congruent to serve the purpose of allowing common ideas to emerge about the role of the actors within the system.

The most commonly quoted illustration of this is the assertion that at the time that Dunlop was writing there was in the UK an ideology of 'voluntarism' that fitted this stereotype. The voluntarism ideology was essentially that the employees and managers and their respective representative institutions should be left to resolve problems, difficulties and conflicts on their own without the intervention of government and particularly without the intervention of the law. At the time, this view/belief was shared by all three main actors and presumably Dunlop would have cited the UK as an example of a mature system. Subsequent events illustrate that mature and stable systems do not necessarily remain stable in the face of changing beliefs and values. Over the last twenty or thirty years in the UK the notions and institutions associated with voluntarism have been largely rejected and dismantled. The country was governed by those of a liberal individualist rather than a liberal collectivist/voluntarist persuasion and there was a determination to alter the perceived locus and distribution of power in favour of both government and the interests of capital. However, with the return in 1997 of a Labour government with a Parliamentary majority that seems big enough to warrant optimism about two successive terms in government, we may see the gradual emergence of a new consensus between the actors, a new ideology that is shared and which, in terms of the Dunlop model, may herald the emergence of a newly mature system. It is difficult at this early stage to identify what the focus of such a shared ideology might be but there are early signs that all the parties seem concerned to emphasize notions of shared interests and 'partnership', though whether this will be sufficient as a base for such a shared ideology is doubtful and at this stage it is not even clear that the term means the same to the various parties.

See **Figure 1.4**, in which there is reference to partnership, 'escape from the ideological divides of the past' and 'The new industrial consensus – over training and education, economic stability, the competitive challenge and the importance of the European Union' and in the final paragraph there is reference to 'an emerging common ground'.

Processes

As with any system the inputs are converted into the outputs through some process or other. Dunlop identified a number of processes through which this might happen and, at the time that he was writing, the dominant process in the UK was collective bargaining, a process through which, as you will see in the next section, the parties seek to resolve conflict and determine jointly agreed rules, both substantive and procedural. Other processes that might apply include the unilateral determination by either of the main actors, management and employees, the use of third parties either through the process known as conciliation or that known as arbitration, or the government might intervene and determine rules via the mechanism of legislation, a process that has recently been used a great deal more than was the norm in the days when Dunlop was writing.

CBI chief hails new 'intelligent dialogue'

Seumas Milne
Labour Editor

ADAIR Turner, CBI director general, yesterday set the seal on the new love-in between the main employers' organisation and the Trades Union Congress with a genial speech that hailed the two bodies' substantial areas of common ground, and "escape from the ideological divides" of the past.

As delegates from leftwing unions such as the Rail Maritime and Transport union, left the hall in protest at only the second-ever TUC address by a CBI leader, Mr Turner warmly embraced the partnership offered by the TUC's "new unionism" approach.

Combined with the enthusiastic support for trade union rights by the Archbishop of Canterbury — and in contrast to the critical tone of the Prime Minister — such a positive endorsement of the TUC's new platform by the CBI will add to the impression that trade unionism is being welcomed back into the mainstream of public life.

But while embracing what he called the "valid, legitimate and valuable" role unions could play in industry, Mr Turner said the issue of labour flexibility remained contentious, and warned that the CBI continued to oppose Labour plans for a statutory right to union recognition.

Echoing the words of Tony Blair on Tuesday, he told delegates: "We don't think that partnership is best fostered when one partner feels they have been forced to deal with the other — and we remain concerned that contests over recognition could sour rather than foster good relations."

Earlier in the week, John Cridland, CBI human resources director, warned that the issue of statutory union recognition, "more than the minimum wage, more than the social chapter, may lead to conflict rather than partnership".

But Mr Turner said yesterday that the CBI accepted that a recognition law was going to happen, and pledged that it would seek "to achieve a precise implementation which minimises the danger of conflict and which creates a workable set of rules".

He said the TUC and CBI were a long way from the "fundamental disagreements characterising British political debate 10 or 20 years ago".

The new national industrial consensus — over training and education, economic stability, the competitive challenge and the importance of the European Union — was already reflected at corporate and workplace level.

"Many companies have indeed worked with trade unions," he went on, "and been able increasingly to do so because of the forward-looking attitudes your phrase 'new unionism' encompasses."

Mr Turner said there was no desire on the part of the CBI to "recreate the formal corporatist structures of the 1960s and 1970s", nor the national collective bargaining structures of the past.

But intelligent dialogue based on an emerging common ground could now become a reality.

Figure 1.4 *Source: The Guardian*, 11 September 1997

Criticisms of the Dunlop model

The Dunlop system has been widely criticized. Dunlop appears to have thought that he was devising a general theory of industrial relations and much of the criticism of him and his systems model has been grounded in assertions of failure in this respect; that is that he did not produce such a theory, the model lacks analytical rigour and does not facilitate the analysis and explanation of industrial relations in a dynamic context, it merely facilitates description and the organization of facts. Another specific but related criticism is that therefore the model is too static.

Further criticisms have been made that: the systems approach tends to reinforce the status quo through its uncritical approach to the existing relationships and interactions and, perhaps most importantly, to the existing disposition of power within society and in the employment relationship. Those of a radical persuasion are most likely to be critical on these grounds. The system as devised and depicted by Dunlop is consistent with the pluralist position in that it tends to emphasize the joint resolution of conflict through the application of agreed procedures and the achievement of consensus, the outcomes being further rules geared towards the perpetuation of the status quo rather than the radical and revolutionary change that is favoured by the radical perspective. The whole emphasis of the Dunlop position is the achievement of stability and maturity through shared values/ideologies, whereas the emphasis of the radical position is upon change and, where appropriate, radical and revolutionary change.

One of the common current uses of the Dunlop model is as a framework that facilitates analysis and comparison, in particular students and others find it a useful template or checklist for the analysis and comparison of different companies, industries or countries. Much of the literature that seeks to compare industrial or employee relations in one country with those in another uses the systems framework as the structural base for both analysis and comparison (see, for example, Hollinshead and Leat, 1995, and Bamber and Lansbury, 1993).

Activity 7

Think about this systems model and then write down the advantages and value of the model. Having done this you should then write another list in which you identify the limitations or disadvantages.

An analytical framework

What is proposed in this section is not intended as a theory of employee relations but as a template or framework within which we can locate the various actors and influences. It should facilitate both the analysis of employee relations in a particular country and the comparative analysis of employee relations across national boundaries, as well as providing the newcomer to the subject with an idea of the content and focus of the study of employee relations. This framework also provides the reader with a convenient guide to and picture of the contents of this book.

At the centre of the framework (**Figure 1.5**) is the employment relationship, a relationship between buyers and sellers of labour that has both a psychological and legal dimension to it: both a legally enforceable and a psychological contract. The nature of the relationship is variously perceived, for example some see it as a relationship dominated by the inherent conflicts of interest between the parties whereas others perceive it as a relationship that is, or at least should be, dominated by cooperation. It is also a relationship that is secured through different modes and forms of involvement and attachment, ranging from an alienative to a moral involvement and from compliance to commitment as the base for the ongoing attachment of the parties.

The employment relationship and the interaction between the parties can be perceived to produce a number of different employee relations outcomes within the organization. At one level, these outcomes can be perceived purely in terms of whether they are processes, procedures or practices but, at another, they can be seen to be mechanisms for securing the objectives of the parties whether, for example, this be the resolution of conflict between them, employee participation and involvement in decision making or control of the labour process, the handling of grievances and management of discipline or the pursuit and achievement of equal opportunities. These are shown in the model of organizational level outcomes that then form part of the organizational context.

The relationship occurs within many different contexts and is variously constrained and influenced by them. These contexts can be differentiated on a number of different grounds and here we differentiate between international, national and organizational contexts. Throughout the framework there are two-way interactions between the various layers of context, the international context exerts influence upon the national context and thereby upon the organizational context and the employment relationship itself, yet the interations within the employment relationship produce outcomes which become part of the organizational context which may then impact upon the national context. Reasonably one might expect the strength or intensity of the outwardly directed influences to be less than those of an inward direction.

At the organizational level influences include the values, beliefs, expectations and objectives of the parties who may operate as individuals and as

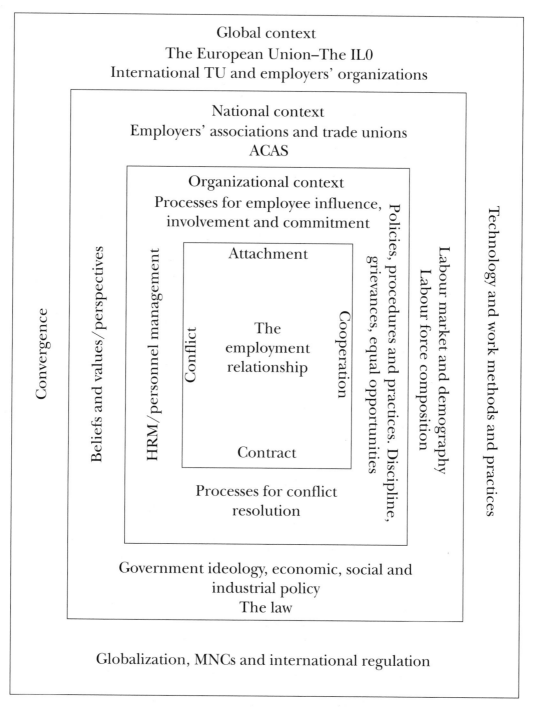

Figure 1.5 Employee relations framework

members of a collective organization or group. As we have noted earlier, the emphasis of the study of employee relations in this book and this model is on the collective dimension rather than on the individual. These values and beliefs may be indicative of national culture as well as influencing the objectives, strategies and style of the parties and the culture of the organization. In the model we have not included their influence upon all of the parties at this organizational level but the influence can be seen through the approach and style adopted by management as for example may be distinguished by their preferences for personnel or human resource management. At the level of the organization activity will be organized according to a particular formula and within particular structural forms and these influence the interactions within the employment relationship.

Outside the organization there are two levels of context in this model, the international and national. Outside the level of the nation there are a number of international contexts that can be seen to be influential. Perhaps the most important of these is associated with global capital, its objectives and its activities, encompassing the multinational enterprise and its ability to invest and locate around the world. For the UK, the European Union (EU) forms an important element of the international context. There are also international associations and federations of employers and employee organizations and there is at least one influential international regulatory organization, the International Labour Organization (ILO). Last, but by no means least, is the influence of technology and technological change, an influence upon the employment relationship that has long been international in its impact.

At the national level we have the influence of the values, beliefs and attitudes that can be perceived to constitute the national culture. At this level also we have the nature of the dominant form of economic activity, government and its ideology, and the policies and priorities pursued by government in its role as economic regulator. The government also has an influential role in the determination of the legal context. Additionally at this level of context we have to consider the structure of industrial and economic activity, the composition and structure of the labour force, demographic circumstances and trends, the distribution of power in society and the history and traditions of the country. The supply of labour will be influenced by the nature of the education and training regimes that dominate. We have also incorporated at this level the other two dominant collective actors or participants in employee relations, management and its objectives and attitudes and the trade unions, their objectives, recent problems and internal debates about how to survive.

The remainder of the book is structured in parts consistent with this model or framework, so that we work from the outside in, from the international to the national to the organizational. Inevitably, as in any text, it is impossible to be comprehensive but the contents chosen do reflect the author's perceptions of relative importance.

Activity 8

Have another look at the newspaper article (**Figure 1.4**) and ask yourself whether there is a distinct perspective implied in the views expressed by Turner.

Summary

So far we have examined different interpretations and meanings attached to the term 'employee relations' and in so doing have touched upon differences between employee and industrial relations.

You have learned that the employment relationship does not occur in a vacuum and indeed that there are a range of different contexts that together comprise the overall environment. You have also been introduced to the notion of a psychological contract between employee and employer.

The employment relationship is characterized by a range of potential and different forms of attachment, some of which may imply employee commitment to the values of the organization and some of which acknowledge more instrumental or calculative motives.

There are also a number of perspectives upon this relationship and in particular we have examined three such perspectives, each of which has implications for the way in which the issues of conflict and/or cooperation between labour and capital are perceived. Integral to this is the question of whether these two sets of interests can coincide.

The quality of employee relations is difficult to quantify and the criteria by which it may be assessed are influenced by perspective.

We have examined the notion of an industrial relations system and the various criticisms of it and have proposed an analytical framework that centres upon the collective dimensions of the employment relationship and provides a template for comparative analysis. It also acts as an indicator of the subject matter of the study of employee relations and the structure and contents of this book.

Activity Answers

Activity 2

1 Both the pluralist and radical perspectives consider conflict inevitable, for different reasons and with different implications, but in both instances there is an assumption of inevitability. The unitarist, on the other hand, is likely to argue that there is no such inevitability and indeed that conflict should be avoidable, it may occur but where and when it does it is because labour does not realize that it has common interests with the employer, or it is due to stupidity or sabotage.

2 The implications for conflict resolution are: the unitarist perspective considers that management has the unilateral right to manage, the right to decide issues within the organization. Therefore, within the context of

this perspective, employees should be loyal to management and should where necessary comply with management's legitimate decisions. Put very simply, this perspective argues that conflict is resolved in accordance with the wishes and decisions of management, they know best the interests of the organization and employees should accept that.

The pluralist perspective argues the case of joint or shared decision making so that all interests are accommodated in the decisions made. The pluralist perspective therefore leads to the development of appropriate joint mechanisms such as joint consultation and collective bargaining, concepts that we explain and discuss in more detail in the later unit dealing with employee relations.

The radical perspective tends to see the conflicts between labour and capital as so fundamental that they are not amenable to temporary or joint resolution. The solution, if you regard it as one, is victory by one side or the other. The only effective solution is either unilateral control by management or, and to someone with this perspective preferably, unilateral control by labour.

3 In the main there are three distinct views on this issue, no one is right and the others wrong, it really is a matter of which, to you, seem to be realistic and, like many other people, you may find that your view does not fit cleanly into one of these stereotypes:

- There is no such inevitability, employers and employees have common interests and cooperation is not only possible but desirable.
- Conflict between employers and employees is inevitable in a capitalist system and the subject matter of that conflict is control: control of the labour process and the employment relationship, management seek to control the labour resource and, in its own self-interest, labour will resist.
- Conflict between employers and employees is inevitable in a capitalist society and the conflict is about the price of labour, both parties in seeking to pursue their own self interest will inevitably come into conflict with the other.

Activity 4

Commitment in this context refers to circumstances in which employees share the values and objectives of the organization, indeed it is this that employees should be committed to, this is the objective of the exhortation and mechanisms that managements use. Sometimes this commitment will be indicated by certain forms of behaviour. This is consistent with the unitarist perspective but not really with either of the other two. In the context of pluralism you might realistically expect cooperation but arguably not commitment. The radical viewpoint argues against such commitment and no doubt would view employees adopting managements' values and objectives as a betrayal of the interests of labour.

Activity 5

The two ideologies or sets of beliefs do have common features, both accept that the market mechanism is the primary means through which resource allocation decisions should be made in a capitalist economy. However, the former places much more reliance upon an unregulated market as the sole mechanism through which individuals and employers buy and sell labour, thereby determining its allocation between different uses. The liberal collectivist view is not that the market doesn't work but that unless regulated the reality is that it will work to the benefit of one side at the expense of the other. In particular the liberal collectivist view perceives advantage to lie with the buyer of labour, that the employer has greater bargaining power than individual units of labour and that equity and justice are best served through allowing employees to form and be represented by collectives in their dealings with employers as the buyers of the labour resource.

The liberal individualist places reliance upon the individual contract of employment freely entered into by both parties and common law whereas the liberal collectivist acknowledges the value of the collective agreement as the base for reconciling differences between the parties and is more prepared to intervene legislatively to regulate the relationship between them.

Activity 6

1 There are many possible indicators, among which may be: the incidence or absence of strikes, the existence of conflict resolving mechanisms that provide for the joint resolution of conflicts, the recognition and presence of trade unionism, the extent to which employees or employers control the labour process, the incidence of labour turnover and/or absenteeism, the levels of employee satisfaction, stress, loyalty and commitment to the organization, and even the levels of productivity.
2 Your answer should include some if not all of the following:

- strike statistics are an appropriate indicator since people do not take such action unless they are unhappy with employee relations in their organization
- strike statistics may have their drawbacks as an indicator of quality but they are the best one we have and we know they are available in most countries: this is the only way we have of undertaking meaningful international comparisons
- strike statistics are not an appropriate or adequate indicator of the quality of industrial relations because:
  - peace can be bought
  - strikes may be politically motivated and therefore not an indicator of employee relations quality
  - striking may be inconsistent with work-related values and cultural norms in a particular country

- strikes may be outlawed
- trade unions may be outlawed or very weak
- the economic circumstances may militate against such action
- there are many other means by which employees can both demonstrate and purge their dissatisfaction, which may at the same time cost them less
- the statistics collected may not be accurate, comprehensive or comparable.

Activity 7
Examples of some possible values/limitations:

- A very useful framework for organizing data and facts which can then form a base for comparing one set of circumstances with another.
- The model is not a theory and does not facilitate analysis or explanation and therefore its use is limited.
- The emphasis in the model upon the joint resolution of conflict through the process of collective bargaining and the production of rules and regulations, which are then used as the framework for future relations between the parties, is of value because it emphasizes the conflict of interest and the possibilities of orderly resolution through agreed procedures.
- This emphasis upon the orderly resolution of conflict through joint procedures is a limitation since it reinforces managerial prerogative and the status quo of power relationships and thereby harms the prospects of the revolution necessary if workers are to gain the control of the labour process that they are entitled to.

The performance of this task has hopefully reinforced in your own mind the relevance of perspective since you probably found yourself saying that whether a particular feature of the model is of value or a limitation depends upon your perspective.

Activity 8
I would argue that there are clear signs of a modified or pragmatic unitarism: we do not see it in its purest of forms since trade unions are recognized as able to perform a valid, legitimate and valuable role, but there is an implication that management should have the right to deny employees recognition of their chosen representatives, that fostering good relations is not likely to be the outcome of forcing employers to deal with the trade unions against their will even if this is the wish of their employees. The employer representative does not appear to appreciate the irony of this view when it is placed against what might understandably be the view from the employee side on the same issue, i.e. that employers cannot expect to encourage partnership if they refuse to deal with the

employees' chosen representatives and insist on dealing with employees as individuals against their wishes. There are clearly two sides to the issue.

References

Bamber, G. and Lansbury, R.D., 1993. *International and Comparative Industrial Relations.* 2nd Edition. Routledge, London.

Beer, M., Spector, B., Lawrence, P.R., Quinn Mills, D. and Walton, R., 1984. *Managing Human Assets.* Free Press, New York.

Blyton, P. and Turnbull, P., 1994. *The Dynamics of Employee Relations.* Macmillan, Basingstoke and London.

Cully, M., O'Reilly, A., Millward, N., Forth, J., Woodland, S., Dix, G. and Bryson, A., 1998. *The Workplace Employee Relations Survey : First Findings.* DTI, ACAS, ESRC, PSI, London.

Dunlop, J.T., 1958. *An Industrial Relations System.* Holt, New York.

Edwards, P., 1995. The employment relationship. In Edwards, P. (ed.) *Industrial Relations: Theory and Practice in Britain.* Blackwell, Oxford

Etzioni, A., 1975. *A Comparative Analysis of Complex Organizations.* Free Press, New York.

Farnham, D., 1993. *Employee Relations.* IPM, London.

Flanders, A., 1970. *Management and Unions.* Faber, London.

Fox, A., 1966. *Industrial Sociology and Industrial Relations.* Royal Commission Research Paper No. 3. HMSO, London.

Gospel, H. and Palmer, G., 1993. *British Industrial Relations.* 2nd Edition. Routledge, London.

Guest, D., 1987. Human resource management and industrial relations. *Journal of Management Studies* 24(5): 503–521.

Guest, D., 1992. Employee commitment and control. In Hartley, J.F. and Stephenson, G.M. (eds), *Employment Relation.* Blackwell, Oxford.

Guest, D., 1995. Why do People Work? A Presentation to the IPD National Conference. Cited in Marchington, H. and Wilkinson, A. (1996).

Guest, D.E. and Conway, N., 1999. Fairness at Work and the Psychological Contract. IPD, London.

Herzberg, F., 1966. *Work and the Nature of Man.* World Publishing. Staples Press, London.

Hollinshead, G. and Leat, M., 1995. *Human Resource Management: An International and Comparative Perspective.* Pitman, London.

Kelly, J. and Kelly, C., 1991. Them and Us: social psychology and the new industrial relations. *British Journal of Industrial Relations* 29(1): 25–48.

Legge, K.,1995. *Human Resource Management : Rhetorics and Realities.* Macmillan, Basingstoke.

Marchington, M. and Wilkinson, A., 1996. *Core Personnel and Development.* IPD, London.

Marchington, M., Goodman, J., Wilkinson, A., and Ackers, P., 1992. *New*

Developments in Employee Involvement. Employment Department Research Series No. 2, HMSO, London.

Maslow, A., 1943. A theory of human motivation. *Psychological Review* 50: 370–396.

Mowday, R.T., Steers, R.M. and Porter, L.W., 1982. *Employee–Organization Linkages: The Psychology of Commitment, Absenteeism and Turnover.* Academic Press, New York.

Nicholls, P., 1999. Context and theory in employee relations. In Hollinshead, G., Nicholls, P. and Tailby, S. (eds), *Employee Relations.* Financial Times, Pitman, London.

Roethlisberger, F.J. and Dickson, W.J., 1939. *Management and the Worker.* Harvard University Press, Cambridge, Massachusetts.

Schein, E., 1988. *Organizational Psychology.* Prentice Hall, Englewood Cliffs, NJ.

Wilkinson, A., Marchington, M., Ackers, P. and Goodman, J., 1992. Total Quality Management and employee involvement. *Human Resource Management Journal* 2(4): 1–20.

Part Two

The Global Context

Chapter 2

The nature of work

Chapter Outline

- Taylorism – scientific management – Fordism
- Disadvantages of Fordism and the emergence of Post-Fordism
- The flexible firm
- Other competitive production strategies
- Job re-design and the search for commitment, flexibility and quality
- Commitment, intrinsic satisfaction, involvement and functional flexibility
- Japanization? Quality, involvement and commitment as competitive advantage
- The quality circle
- Total Quality Management (TQM)
- Just-in-Time (JIT)
- Incidence and impact of the new production strategies – perceptions and conclusions
- Chapter summary

Introduction

In Chapter 1 we examined the nature of the employment relationship. In this chapter we examine the nature of work and how it has changed in recent years. We examine the scale and nature of recent developments, perceptions of their impact, the inter-relationship between the nature of work and the employment relationship, and associated developments.

It seems reasonable enough to assume that there will be some degree of inter-relationship between the nature of work and the nature of the employment relationship. Certainly it has been argued in recent years that the information technology revolution and new globally competitive product markets have impacted significantly upon the nature and organization of work and that these developments have been accompanied by identifiable and common change in the nature of the employment relationship.

We pay particular attention to the recently popular thesis that organizations need to be flexible, need to be able to compete on the grounds of quality and need a labour force that is committed if they are to compete in the new global marketplace. Guest's (1987; see Chapter 8) normative model or theory of HRM identifies, and in some respects prescribes, quality, flexibility and commitment as desirable outcomes. It is argued that these competitive imperatives have imposed upon companies and thereby their workforce new forms of work organization and new work practices.

We examine models of the flexible firm and flexible specialization and we look also at the influence of Japanese companies, their approaches and practices. In examining these 'developments' you should try to bear in mind their relevance for the issues that we examined in the first chapter, that is, whether these new forms of organization etc., assuming that they exist, impact upon the employment relationship and if so how. We will return therefore to the issues of commitment or compliance and conflict or cooperation.

In order to contextualize our discussion of new forms of work organization and practices we start with a brief introduction to the form of production system and work organization that supposedly dominated in Western economies for much of the twentieth century, this being the system characterized by mass production and often referred to as Fordist. In describing this form of system we must identify the underlying principles which owe much to the work of F.W. Taylor (1911) and which are frequently collectively referred to as Taylorism and 'scientific management'.

Objectives

After studying this chapter you will be able to:

- Identify the principles of Taylorism and assess the extent to which particular work situations demonstrate them
- Distinguish between Fordist and a number of other production regimes
- Assess the relevance of the principles of scientific management to production strategies today
- Identify the main features of the flexible firm model, apply the model to work situations and examine whether the features of the model do or might apply
- Distinguish between a number of different forms of job design/redesign and how they may each contribute to the goals of quality and commitment

- Define the concepts of Total Quality Management and Just in Time and assess how they might each contribute to the goals of quality and commitment
- Assess and discuss the implications of changing systems of work organization for employees and for the employment relationship
- Discuss the relevance of perspective to an assessment of the impact of these new forms of work organization.

Taylorism – scientific management – Fordism

It is often suggested that, prior to the intervention of Taylor, work was typified by the craftsman exercising his skills in the conception and planning of a job as well as in its execution. This no doubt presents a somewhat idealized view, however for the purposes of contrasting pre- and post-Taylorist scenarios it is useful. Taylor's great contribution was to attempt to apply the principles of scientific analysis to work and its organization. He placed great emphasis upon measurement and time and conceived the idea that there was a 'one best way' of organizing work, one way that would yield greater efficiencies in terms of time and costs than any other. He assumed that the nature of man's motivation was essentially instrumental, that man could and would be motivated by the prospect of earning more. Armed with these beliefs Taylor began the process of measurement and experimentation that led to the development of the means whereby the labour process could be designed and so organized to facilitate the mass production of standardized products. This was achieved through the design and fragmentation of work into a large number of small tasks, each of which required very little skill and were performed by units of labour on a repetitive basis. Each of the tasks was to be as simple as possible and the belief was that with experience labour would become more and more proficient at the individual constituents of the process and efficiency would improve almost without end. Responsibility for the design, planning, organizing and control of the process of production was to be divorced from the labour engaged in the production process and performed by others. This contributed in large measure to the development of the management functions, and formed a basis for the development of a managerial elite or cadre.

Where possible the machine, the technology, should control the pace of the production and, as labour became more and more proficient, the speed of the machine could be increased and the rate of production enhanced. As long as pay was linked to performance or output the labour would accept these conditions since they would be content providing they earned more. Labour would also become cheaper if it were possible to break down jobs into a number of smaller tasks which could be performed repetitively, since it would be possible to use largely unskilled units that required relatively little training to perform the simplified tasks.

The effectiveness of these principles was enhanced further by the technological developments that facilitated the emergence of the conveyer belt and assembly line. It was when all these came together that capital really had the opportunity to engage in mass production.

One of the major disciples and champions of these techniques and principles was Henry Ford, the automobile manufacturer, and it is because of this that such production systems have often been referred to as **Fordist.** The development of large-scale manufacture facilitated by the work of Taylor must be seen as part of the process of industrialization and urbanization that has characterized developing economies in the twentieth century. Large-scale manufacture required plenty of labour and in the early days that labour had to live close to the place of work, given the absence of quick and cheap transport.

Mass production of standardized products also requires mass markets for standardized products and the labour employed in the resulting factories became part of these markets as their own living standards improved. In the post-war period there was a fit between the pursuit of full employment as an economic policy priority and the creation of the necessary mass markets for the output of these production systems.

In the industrial and employment circumstances created by mass production trades unions also flourished. Large numbers of semi-skilled and unskilled labour were employed on fragmented and standardized tasks, the pace of work was controlled by the technology, the working conditions were often noisy and dangerous and the collective common interests of the employees were apparent. Pressures were generated for the standardization of terms and conditions of employment. Logistically, trades unions have tended to revel in circumstances of this kind.

There is a programme in the BBC series *The People's Century* that illustrates effectively and at length the development of Fordist production systems and their implications.

In recent years there have been some outspoken critics of Fordist production systems. Chief among these is probably Braverman (1974). It is alleged that such systems have caused a general de-skilling of the labour force, a degradation and cheapening of the labour resource and they have been influential in the exploitation of labour and its input into the labour process. In terms of the radical perspective, these twentieth-century mass-production strategies and processes have facilitated capital's control over both the labour process and the price of labour. Braverman argued that the process of de-skilling and degradation was as applicable to non-manual clerical and administrative tasks and their labour as it was to manual production work. This is arguably illustrated in the magazine article on call centres (**Figure 2.1**) which suggests that the principles of scientific management continued in the UK in the latter part of the 1990s and that they are being extended into white-collar and service sectors; indeed, towards the end of

When the social history of the 1990s comes to be written, the rise of the call centre may well merit a chapter to itself. Call centres are transforming everyday life, offering a huge and growing range of sales, marketing and information services. From mortgages and car insurance to airline tickets and mobile phones, there are now few types of goods and services that cannot be obtained over the phone.

The number of people employed in call centres in Europe is expanding at a rate of 40 per cent a year, according to strategic management consultancy Datamonitor[1]. In the UK, which dominates the European call-centre market, this growth has been driven by the financial services sector. Prominent among the financial companies that use call centres are Direct Line and First Direct, which were set up in the late 1980s to provide motor insurance and retail banking services. Followed by a host of imitators (see graphs 1 and 2, page 25), these pioneers have now expanded into other areas.

Call centres are not only taking over some of the traditional functions of high-street shops, banks and other service providers; they are also having a profound effect on employment. The Datamonitor research found that one in 250 of the European working population now works full- or part-time in a call centre. This figure is set to increase to one in 10 by the year 2001. In the UK, 1.1 per cent of the workforce are employed in call centres, and this figure is likely to rise to 2.2 per cent by 2001.

New centres and the expansion of existing premises are regularly being announced. First Direct, which handled 10 million calls in 1996 at two sites in Leeds has just opened a new centre in Birmingham and plans a further opening (probably in Glasgow) in 1998. The Co-operative Bank officially opened its second centre at the Stockport Pyramid, Greater Manchester, in December. Matrixx Marketing is expanding its Newcastle site to cater for American Express customers across Europe and

London Electricity is taking on 150 more customer service staff at its base in Sunderland.

Four out of 10 people working in call-centres are based in telemarketing and telesales, including direct response advertising, but more than half of all jobs involve the care of existing customers. In developed markets such as the UK, it is customer service and information helplines that are expected to fuel future growth. The success of these helplines and, indeed, of all "direct" operations, clearly depends upon the quality, commitment and motivation of their staff. But in the rush to set up call centres – many of which operate 24 hours a day, seven days a week – employers have sometimes neglected the people management issues raised by this method of providing services.

With rows of operators crammed together in front of computer screens using highly standardised procedures, call centres have been likened to production lines, or even to battery farms. Such comparisons may seem far-fetched, but there are undoubtedly problems associated with the unrelenting pressure of work and the tight control that managers often exercise.

This degree of control has been made possible by advances in information and telecommunications technology. Central to these technologies is the automated call distribution system (ACD), which eliminates the need for a central switchboard and operator. As well as speeding up work by putting calls directly through to the "agents", as call-centre staff are often known, the ACD can monitor the length of calls, completion times and whether calls lead to sales.

The information generated by this system can then be used to determine individuals' pay. A report from Bifu[2], the financial services union, pointed out last year: "Performance-related pay is made easier by ACD systems, because all work can be monitored in detail electronically and customer calls can be taped. Employees can be easily subjected to arbitrary quantitative, as well as qualitative,

15

Figure 2.1 *Source: People Management*, 6 February 1997, pp. 22–27. Reproduced with permission of the author: Anat Arkin

performance criteria."

But the mechanistic use of quantitative performance criteria can be counterproductive. "The call centre provides management with the ultimate opportunity for control. But there's quite a lot of evidence that the more you control, the less you get in terms of quality," says Simian Roncoroni, director of the L&R Group, a consulting and training business that has developed a new certificate in call-centre management for the Institute of Direct Marketing (IDM).

Roncoroni argues that quality is generally higher in mature operations that exercise a "benign" form of control over agents, while pushing responsibility as far down the line as possible. The IDM's qualification aims to assist this process by giving team leaders, line managers and supervisors the skills to manage small groups of people. The certificate programme includes modules on selecting and developing call-centre staff and managing their performance. There is also a module on "Staying sane in the call centre", which examines the causes of stress and ways of coping with the problem.

Stress levels are thought to be higher in call centres than in more conventional office environments. So, too, are staff turnover rates. A Bifu official says that these are often at "factory levels". According to unpublished research by the Decisions Group, which operates centres on behalf of clients including American Express, Microsoft and Sony, both problems are linked to electronic performance monitoring and the role of ACD systems in controlling the pace of work.

"What we have found is that there is a hugely significant relationship between levels of perceived control over the pace of work and people's job satisfaction and stress." says Kevin Hook, principal consultant at the Decisions Group. "As you would expect, if people have low control over their jobs, they experience high levels of stress and low levels of job satisfaction, so there is a very big problem in call centres generally."

He adds that the problem is worse in organisations that use some form of

scripting system to tell agents what they can say to callers, and in those where staff breaks are scheduled. The longer agents work in these highly controlled environments, the more likely they are to experience stress and burnout, he believes (see graph).

Please hang up and try again

Hook says that giving individuals greater autonomy can reduce stress and staff turnover without affecting productivity. But he stresses that this approach succeeds only where a degree of trust has

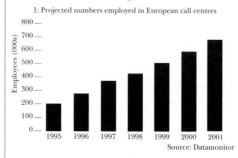
1: Projected numbers employed in European call centres
Source: Datamonitor

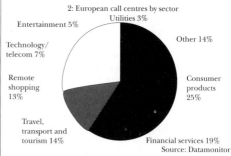
2: European call centres by sector
Source: Datamonitor

3: Burnout in call centres
NB Based on interviews with 566 call centre employees in 11 centres. Satisfaction scale runs from 11 to 55.   Source: The Decisions Group

16

Figure 2.1 (*continued*)

developed between the agents and those who manage them. Without that trust, people will use greater autonomy as an excuse to avoid working,

Disaffected agents can find ways of avoiding work even in the most tightly controlled environments. Hook describes tricks that include taking a call and saying nothing so that the caller hangs up, or letting the caller hang up first and remaining on the line so that no one else can get through. "If a degree of trust hasn't built up, agents will find some way of subverting or bucking the system," he says.

While stress cannot be eliminated entirely from call centres – or from any other kind of workplace, for that matter –

Hook believes that organisations can make these environments less stressful through the use of self-directed teams. "But it takes a degree of effort and orientation from the management to want that to happen. And in most call centres, the attitude is that human resources are expendable."

There are of course, exceptions. Recognising the inherent problems or motivating staff in call centres, the AA recently retrained its agents to take more than one type of call. Insurance sales staff can now handle membership inquiries, for example, while people who usually provide traffic and weather information can also handle emergency breakdown calls.

Top pay for women but no top positions

Call centres, rare in the prosperous south-east of England, tend to be concentrated around cities such as Glasgow, Newcastle and Leeds. Research by Ranald Richardson and J Neill Marshall of the University of Newcastle's Centre for Urban and Regional Development Studies[3] found that labour costs and the availability of skilled workers are the main factors determining their location, although financial incentives also play a part.

But in spite of the attraction of low labour costs, a strategy of "creaming off " the best workers means that those employed in provincial call centres tend to be better paid than other clerical workers in the locality.

The researchers point out that new telecommunications technologies mean that companies can direct calls from one telephone number to a range of destinations, allowing them to create "virtual single sites" as far as customers are concerned. If one centre is busy, the customer is immediately switched by the system to another site. By spreading production over several sites, providers can also reduce the effects of technical hitches and industrial action.

While call centres are bringing new and often well-paid jobs into areas of high unemployment, Richardson and Marshall found that career opportunities for their mainly female employees are strictly limited. A report by the Equal Opportunities Commission supports this finding. Referring to a telephone bank, the report concludes that the reorganisation of banking to reduce costs has increased opportunities for women in clerical and junior management roles. But its author, Angela Coyle, says: "This form of reorganisation in banking and the restructuring of personnel has stopped at senior management work, where some of the expected organisational barriers to gender equality are in evidence."

These barriers include the expectation that managers should work long hours in order to manage operations over several shifts. While flexible working patterns have been developed to attract women to lower-grade positions in the bank's call centre. Coyle argues that the problem of managing a 24-hour operation has not been addressed.

17

Figure 2.1 (*continued*)

This system clearly gives the company greater flexibility. But Penny Hardie, head of call-handling training, claims that the new system is also popular with staff. "They find it motivating and rewarding to be able to take a variety of calls," she says.

As well as multi-skilling its call handlers, the AA has also changed the role of the team managers in its call centres. They now concentrate on developing and coaching their staff by sitting next to them, listening to them and guiding them through their calls. Hardie believes that this "coaching culture" is also helping to motivate staff, with call handlers welcoming the attention they receive and team managers valuing their new responsibilities.

Other companies are looking at whether they can do without team managers or supervisors. First Direct tested the concept of self-managed teams at one of its three call centres last year, and is now taking stock of this experiment. Chris Hancock, who heads the bank's call-centre operations, sees self-managed teams

CASE STUDY

BT and union find it's good to talk

New technology means that BT's customers can now talk to telephone operators in parts of the country as diverse as Enniskillen, Glasgow, Manchester and Swansea.

Staff in such call centres handle fault notification, bill inquiries, operator assistance, directory inquiries and telemarketing. BT has about 11,000 full-time equivalent employees (FTEs) dealing with calls from domestic customers, and 8,000 FTEs handling business clients. This demarcation has produced different management styles that have recently come under attack from the Communication Workers' Union (CWU).

The union has accused managers in ST's personal communications division of attempting to "manage by fear". They claim that managers set unrealistic targets, particularly for staff dealing with fault notification and bill queries, in terms of the average length of the calls and the percentage of calls answered. They also criticise the company for overusing outside agency staff.

"There is a balance between quality and quantity," says Jeannie Drake, CWU deputy general secretary. "They want every single customer answered in x seconds, but if you are giving quality of service to the customer, your throughput may drop."

BT denies that it is putting undue pressure on employees. It agreed to take part in a joint working party with the CWU to look at the issue. At its first meeting last December, Neil Furner, BT's industrial relations manager for personal communications, took the unusual approach of leading a brainstorming session using the total quality management problem-solving model. Rather than have an adversarial meeting, the idea was to have an open and honest debate where all opinions were respected.

Furner collated and sent the ideas generated by the meeting to all the participants. "If you had walked into that meeting, I don't think you would have been able to say: 'That is union over there and that is management over here,'" he says.

The next step is the establishment of focus groups comprising randomly selected customer service staff to listen to their concerns. Subsequently, structured face-to-face interviews will be arranged to canvass the views of a handful of customer service managers.

Furner hopes that this partnership approach will produce a successful outcome for both sides. "We are looking to the CWU to add value to what we are doing, rather than them trying to stop us from what we want to do and us trying to sideline them," he says.
Mike Thatcher

18

Figure 2.1 (*continued*)

as a possible option for employees who want to pursue a career in the call centre rather than moving on to other parts of the business. "It's all about providing a range of options which are focused very much on what we can deliver for our people as well as for our shareholders and customers, " he says.

Within the context of these self-managed teams, First Direct has also been experimenting with team-based assessment. Elsewhere in the organisation, bonus payments for call-centre staff are influenced by individual assessments, which in turn are based partly on the monitoring of their calls.

First Direct uses a variety of methods to monitor average call duration and other aspects of employees' performance. These range from managers sitting next to "banking representatives" to listen in on calls, to remote monitoring, where the person taking the call does not know that somebody is listening. The company also encourages peer-group monitoring, where banking representatives give feedback to each other.

Hancock says call monitoring plays a key role in enabling First Direct to deliver a "world-class" service to customers, and believes that it does not have a demotivating effect on employees. "There are two reasons for that," he says. "One is that it's not something we overcook; the other is that, generally, the feedback will at least be constructive."

Hancock also says that staff turnover is not a problem at First Direct. This could be due to the many opportunities for career progression offered by an organisation, which started life in 1989 with a workforce of 230, that now employs nearly 3,000 people.

First Direct selects its banking representatives mainly for their communication skills, rather than for their previous experience of financial services. Other call-centre employers look for empathy with the customers and the ability to think quickly. These are the two key selection criteria for the Customer Contact Company (C3), which designs and manages call centres for direct businesses.

Tony Collins, C3's managing director, says that staff in the call centres run by his firm are expected to provide customers with all the information they need without having to refer calls to someone else. "To do that, we believe you have to disseminate information downwards," he says. "You can't have managers, because managers hold and block information."

Instead of managers, C3's call centres have "Strategists", whose job it is to direct the business. While these may sound suspiciously like managers, Collins stresses that they do not listen to calls or set targets for individuals. Instead, the agents themselves monitor each other's calls. They also receive group, rather than individual, bonuses.

This relatively anarchic approach may not be feasible in the largest call centres, but it seems to have produced impressive results in smaller direct businesses. Tony Collins cites the example of Sun Alliance Investments On-Line, which C3 set up with the Continuum Direct software company. It now generates about 20 per cent of its parent company's investment business, although it employs only 30 people.

Kieran Hedigan, Continuum Direct's general manager, describes the call centre as a fun place to work. "It's organised chaos," he says. "It would appear to be very free and easy, but in fact there's a hard core of discipline running through the operation, although people are encouraged to think for themselves."

The production-line model, it seems, is not the best way to ensure success.

1 *Call Centres in Europe 1996–2001:* Vertical Market Opportunities, Datamonitor, 1996

2 *At the Other End of the Telephone: New Technology in Retail Banking and General Insurance,* Bifu, 1996.

3 Ranald Richardson and J Neill Marshall, "The growth of telephone call centres in peripheral areas of Britain: evidence from Tyne and Wear" *AREA*, 1996.

4 Angela Coyle, *Women and Organisational Change*, Equal Opportunities Commission, research discussion series No 14, 1995.

19

Figure 2.1 (*continued*)

CASE STUDY

Don't bank on previous experience

Applicants seeking work at the Co-operative Bank's new call centre in Stockport, Greater Manchester (pictured), may have been surprised that qualifications or previous related experience were not deemed to be relevant in the recruitment process for team members.

The bank wanted to encourage applications from a wide range of candidates, including older workers and long-term unemployed people. It believed that the best way to achieve this was to set tests that would concentrate on analysing telephone skills and verbal and numerical reasoning.

"We wanted to get a good spread of people to reflect the local community. One of the reasons we put in written tests was because we weren't asking for A-levels or GCSEs," says Sue Bland, the bank's employment policy manager.

About 8,000 people responded to advertisements placed in local newspapers. Of these, 2,500 completed application forms, and 700 shortlisted candidates undertook the telephone skills assessment. Four hundred were interviewed and, by the time of the official launch last December, 185 team members had been recruited.

The centre is based in the Stockport Pyramid, a distinctive 120ft-high blue-glass building close to the M63 motorway. One-fifth of those employed by the bank are over 40, and one-third are men – a much higher proportion than in most call centres.

More than one in three new recruits had formerly been unemployed, including 8 per cent who had been out of work for more than six months. These people came forward thanks to an initiative organised with the Employment Service, which gave pre-selection training.

The Co-operative Bank now has two call centres operating 24 hours a day. Its site at Skelmersdale, Lancashire, employs 850 people, and the Stockport Pyramid will eventually house 425 occupants. It is estimated that both sites received more than seven million calls from customers last year.   *Mike Thatcher*

20

Figure 2.1 (*continued*)

1999 call centre staff in BT took industrial action in protest at these conditions.

The Braverman critique of Fordist production systems and their implications for the labour resource has itself been subject to criticism, in particular that it is both an over-simplification and inaccurate to suggest the dominant concern of management is the exploitation of labour and the creation of surplus value through processes that are concerned to de-skill, etc.

We have already mentioned some of the disadvantages of Fordist systems, that they tend to result in bored and alienated labour forces, but there are other problems associated with mature Fordism which are arguably inherent. These systems require massive investment in plant and technology to facilitate the production of large numbers of standard items relatively cheaply and, once installed, this plant and equipment is relatively fixed and inflexible, it is not common for these production systems to be amenable to change and of course the labour also tends to be relatively fixed in terms of what they can do.

Disadvantages of Fordism and the emergence of Post-Fordism

The advantages of Fordist systems when confronted with mass markets for standardized products become disadvantages the moment you want to change the product; both the technology and the labour tend to be highly specialized. The massive fixed overheads that are generated by these systems also pose problems if competition emerges from parts of the world where labour and other materials may be cheaper. Arguably the greatest threat to the viability of these systems occurs if and when the customer changes their requirements, for example when they decide that they want something a little different from the man next door, they develop a desire for customization. As living standards improve it seems that people tend to become more discriminating and less prepared to have the same as everyone else; they not only want something different they also want something better.

Other disadvantages emerge from the degree of specialization and the separation of tasks and functions. Unskilled and semi-skilled labour engaged in the production process are not required, or able, to exercise control over quality and the technology also often does not lend itself to inspection prior to the end of the process; so this function is either not performed or performed by expensive specialist quality inspection and control functions. As the size of the operation increases there is also a tendency for the overhead element, owing to the employment of specialist management and administration, to become a greater burden.

In response to these disadvantages the appropriateness of Fordism as the dominant form for organizing production has been questioned. The increasing demand by customers for customization and quality, allied to competition on both price and quality from developing economies, has encouraged employers to vary the nature of production systems to something which is more flexible and in which quality can more easily and cheaply be achieved.

Flexibility in this context needs to include both the technology and the labour and, in the latter case, the flexibility requirement may apply to both the quantity and qualitative capacity of the labour input. The demand for large quantities of relatively unskilled labour characteristic of Fordist systems has been replaced by a demand for labour that is multi-skilled and flexible, that is familiar with the new technologies and does not need external supervision.

The technological innovations, for example, that have enabled the development of robotics and vastly improved systems for controlling activity at a distance have also had relatively significant implications for the demand for labour. As noted above it is not just a matter of a different type and quality of labour that is required, these technological developments have also had an impact upon the quantitative element of demand. There are industries in which the number of jobs available and the numbers employed have been significantly reduced.

In the 1980s it was manufacture and traditional heavy capital goods industries that were in the forefront of these changes and, in many instances, employment in these industries has been decimated. In the 1990s the industries on the receiving end of such changes have tended much more to be in the service sector, the public utilities (such as electricity supply, telecommunications and water supply) and services and private-sector industries such as banking, insurance and finance. The latter sector lost tens of thousands of white-collar jobs in the 1990s and examples of this and some of the implications are referred to in the article in **Figure 2.1**. It is debatable whether job losses in one sector are replaced by jobs created in another.

In addition to a de-skilling of clerical work these changes have also contributed to the process sometimes referred to as de-layering, whereby whole layers of management disappear in response to the new technologies. As the numbers employed fall, the numbers of managers required to provide direct face-to-face decision making assistance and supervision declines. This trend is exacerbated by the enhanced capacity that the new technologies provide to control from a distance. Decisions and control previously made and exercised by human beings are now undertaken by computer.

Many of the amended and new work practices that have been introduced in recent years, and which are discussed later in this section, should properly be seen as management responses to these changed technological, market and competitive circumstances and requirements. However, it is also the case, as we also see later, that many of these innovations may have been introduced in an incoherent and piecemeal fashion; it seems that much of their potential may not have been realized and their objectives often not achieved.

Many of the new circumstances and requirements associated with Post-Fordist production strategies and systems are also encapsulated within the model of the flexible firm outlined below.

To ensure that you understand the differences between Fordist and Post-Fordist production regimes and before you go on to read about the 'flexible firm', take a few minutes now to read again the preceding section and then devise for yourself lists of the characteristics of each. To help, you could compare the regimes on the grounds of:

- the type of products that each system might be appropriate for
- the type of labour required
- the nature of the technology implied.

The flexible firm

By the early 1980s the developments outlined above, allied to changes in the political and regulatory environments, had encouraged developments in the organization of work and the demand for labour that were arguably summed up in the model of the 'flexible firm' that was devised by Atkinson (1984; **Figure 2.2**). This model has to some extent become an ideal, a blueprint, in Western economies, for the successful firm of the 1980s and 1990s. It constitutes a form of organization that satisfies the requirements of the employer in the context of newly global and competitive markets. It is arguable the extent to which it is a model of organization that provides much scope for the satisfaction of employee needs, such as needs for security, recognition, relationships, high earnings or self-actualization (these are adapted from the needs identified by writers such as Maslow (1943) and Herzberg (1966) and are intended only as examples of the sorts of needs that employees might have – they are not intended to constitute a definitive list).

The basic model of the flexible firm is depicted in **Figure 2.2** and from this you can detect the important distinctions between the primary and secondary labour markets, core and peripheral workers and the different dimensions of flexibility, functional and numerical. In this context, functional means a flexibility of task and/or skill, the ability to do different things. The core group needs to be functionally flexible and numerical flexibility is primarily derived from the selective use of labour in the secondary labour markets.

The flexible firm

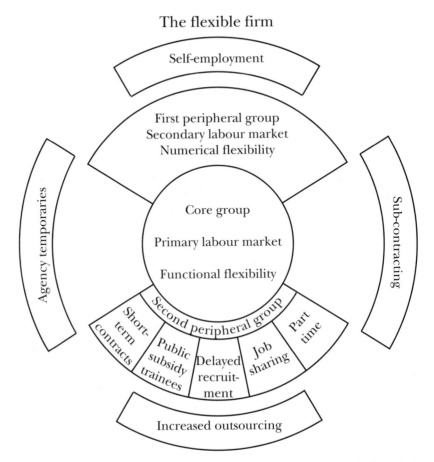

Figure 2.2 *Source:* Atkinson (1984). Reproduced with permission of the author

The core group benefits from security of employment and demand for the skills that they possess, the organization might even be prepared to invest in the training and development of this group.

In the peripheral groups, both first and second, where the emphasis is upon numerical rather than task flexibility, labour may be given the status of employees but this labour is likely to be both less skilled and more vulnerable than that in the core group. The part-time, temporary and relatively unskilled are likely to be used just as any other resource and effectively discarded when no longer required. It is extremely unlikely that the labour in this group would be developed by the employer and, of course, many of them will not have the means to finance their own development. Other means of achieving this flexibility don't involve the granting of employment contracts and rely on mechanisms such as sub-contracting and the use of agency staff.

The increased use of part-time and female labour is characteristic of recent labour market and labour force developments that are not a central issue in this chapter. Nevertheless, it is the case that the great majority of jobs/employment created in the 1990s was of a part-time nature and some 80 per cent of part-time jobs are performed by women (see DfEE Skills and Enterprise Network, 1955. *Labour Market Quarterly Report*, August p. 3, Sheffield). Nevertheless there are two distinct periods in the 1990s: the periods 1990–1994 and 1994–1997. In the former, full-time jobs declined as a percentage of the total, for both men and women. However, in the second period there was a positive annual change in both full- and part-time jobs for both men and women, though the rate of annual increase in part-time jobs has exceeded the rate of increase in full-time jobs (European Commission, 1999: 42–43).

In addition to the greater use of part-time contracts to achieve the numerical flexibility that organizations argue they need, there are also some indications beginning to emerge that core workers themselves have become more flexible in this numerical sense, working more flexible hours on an as-needed basis from week to week. Large organizations in particular seem prone to utilize this technique for dealing with fluctuations in demand. Contracts may stipulate a certain number of hours to be worked per week but the reality may well be greater flexibility than the contract would indicate.

The use of agency, 'less skilled' and peripheral workers is also apparent in some of the para-professional sectors of education and health, with cost-cutting and efficiency pressures encouraging the use of only partially qualified classroom helpers and health service assistants to undertake some of the less demanding activities previously regarded as part of the role of the teacher or nurse. These staff are quite commonly employed only on short-term contracts, for example classroom helpers being employed for one term at a time.

A peculiar public-sector development driven by government belief in the efficiency of the market and the private sector (see discussion in Chapter 5) has been the process known as compulsory competitive tendering (CCT) whereby services have been hived off from public provision to be purchased by the public sector but actually provided by the private sector. The impact of this practice in many public-sector organizations has been significantly to reduce the number of employees in the core groups, with many individuals previously in the core group being effectively shifted into peripheral and external service provision and contracting categories. We do need to bear in mind that while there may be little or no security in the external market there may be both high levels of skill and good pay; the providers of many professional services fall into this category.

The 1998 WERS (Cully *et al.* 1998) investigated the issue of workplace flexibility and distinguished between numerical and functional flexibility. On the subject of numerical flexibility they sought information on the contracting-out of particular services, the current use of particular forms of non-standard contracts and the variation in their use over the preceding five years. The findings were that around 90 per cent of workplaces contract out at least one service, the average figure was four services. The most popular included:

- building maintenance
- cleaning
- transporting documents or goods
- training
- security.

The incidence of this practice didn't seem to vary much between the private and public sectors but in the public sector it was more likely that catering would be contracted out whereas in the private sector it was more likely that recruitment and security would be contracted out.

One-third of the managers interviewed said that, five years previously, the services now contracted out would have been performed by employees of the organization and, of these workplaces, one-third were using contractors of whom at least some were former employees; this was considerably more common in the public sector than in the private sector. See the comment above on CCT.

In examining non-standard employment (temporary or agency staff, fixed term contractors and part-time) there was evidence of an increase in their use over the preceding five years, with the greatest increase occurring in the use of part-time employees and contractors. However, overall, the incidence of the use of these forms of employment was not as great as one might have imagined and the data indicate that some 72 per cent and 56 per cent of workplaces were not using temporary agency workers or fixed term contracts, respectively. The evidence does seem to confirm an increasing use of professionals as temporary staff and on fixed-term contracts.

We have already begun to voice concerns or reservations about the value to, and impact of, the flexible firm for and upon labour: if you are in the core you may well benefit but outside the core life may be very unpredictable, characterized by uncertainty and high levels of anxiety and stress.

Marchington and Wilkinson (1996: 30) identify a number of reservations and concerns about the flexible firm model:

1 They cite the views of Pollert (1988) that the flexible firm model has the tendency to fuse together description, prediction and prescription into what becomes a self-fulfilling prophecy. Writings on the subject tend to veer between describing flexible practices in the workplace, predicting that the model is the ideal design for the future and prescribing that if organizations want to be successful in the future this is the model that they should take as the blueprint. They also point out Legge's (1995) concerns that the model has been 'talked up' because it was consistent with government ideology concerning the efficiency of the market, the need for markets therefore to be deregulated and organizations to be lean.

2 They note the doubts expressed by commentators and analysts that flexibility, particularly functional flexibility, is as common or extensive as the proponents of the model and deregulation would have us believe. They refer to surveys by ACAS (1988) and by Beatson (1995) which indicate that the introduction of flexibility in terms of working practices was not as extensive as some proponents might lead us to believe, Beatson came to the conclusion that 'full blown flexibility is a rarity'. Marchington and Wilkinson (1996) comment that there are often gaps between the rhetoric and the reality. The 1998 WERS findings are consistent with those above in that they do not find that functional flexibility is widespread. It is interesting and perhaps to be expected that they find negative associations between the use of non-standard workers, particularly the use of temporary agency workers, and the proportion of employees trained to be functionally flexible.

3 They point out that there are reasons to doubt the benefits claimed for flexibility and they suggest that there may well be costs that are not realized or acknowledged. They cite studies that have cast doubts on the productivity, attendance rates, levels of commitment, quality of work and loyalty of employees employed on a flexible basis. They also note that core workers may well be disaffected by witnessing events around them, particularly when they see friends and colleagues losing their jobs through rationalization and redundancy. It is suggested that in such circumstances core worker commitment and feelings of security may well be damaged and that the nature of their attachment to the organization may revert from commitment to compliance.

The Confederation of British Industry (CBI) (see Chapter 8) in 1997 reported the findings of a survey which demonstrated that absenteeism rates were rising and it was estimated that the overall absenteeism figures indicated that the cost of absenteeism per employee reached the figure of £530 per annum in 1996. White-collar sickness absence had risen to an average of 7.9 days per employee in 1996 compared with 6.1 days in 1994. A CBI spokesperson blamed much of the absence upon low morale and stress attributable to restructuring and rationalization.

Activity 2

Look back at the model of the flexible firm and compile lists of the advantages and disadvantages from both the employer/manager and employee/labour viewpoints.

Other competitive production strategies

Consistent with the work that casts doubt upon the extensiveness of the introduction of the flexible firm model is the work of Regini (1995) who found that a range of competitive and production strategies were being adopted by managements in Europe and that by no means all of these were consistent with the models of Post-Fordist production that emphasize competition on the basis of quality, product differentiation and customization, and flexibility of response.

In all, Regini identifies five ideal types of strategy, each of which can be seen to embody a different pattern of human resource utilization, only some of which are similar to that depicted in the flexible firm model referred to above. These are:

1 **Diversified quality production**. Here, the intent is to compete on both quality and product diversification thereby avoiding competition on price with low wage economies. Often this takes the form of a high level of customization of the product and requires the kind of labour resource that is a mix of high and broad-based skills, that is adaptive, willing and able to learn new tasks rapidly and is capable itself of contributing to innovation and product development.

2 **Flexible mass production**. The strategy is to mass-produce a number of different goods thereby competing in a number of different markets and to do so on price if necessary. Production can be extensively automated and the organization tends to require a mix of labour, low and unskilled at the production end and highly skilled middle-management, marketing, sales and technical staff.

3 **Flexible specialization**. Here the emphasis is upon the organization's ability to adapt to changes in demand and Regini suggests that this strategy is more common amongst small firms. The requirements of labour include both functional and numerical flexibility allied to broadly based social and interactive skills.

4 **Neo Fordist**. The suggestion is that, even in the developed economies of Europe in the late twentieth century and in an era supposedly Post-Fordist, there are in fact still in existence many firms that operate in a largely traditional Fordist fashion, relying upon Taylorist techniques of organizing production and work practices with the traditional emphasis upon the fragmentation of the work and the de-skilling of the labour input. The requirement of such systems is for labour that is unskilled and is not required to be functionally flexible.

5 **Traditional small firm**. These organizations seek to compete on price but not through obtaining the economies that may come from scale and mass production; they can compete only by keeping down their costs, including their labour costs. Many survive only because they operate in product markets that make few demands upon the skills of the labour resource thereby enabling the employment of cheap unskilled labour.

Each of these competitive and production strategies impose their own demand features upon the labour market in terms of types, levels and mixes of skill and only some require labour that is flexible.

Examine each of the competitive production strategies identified by Regini and in each case identify whether there is a requirement for the labour resource to be flexible, whether this flexibility is of a functional or numerical nature and comment upon the appropriateness of the flexible firm model to each of these production scenarios.

Having discussed developments and change at the level of the firm it is time to look more closely at some of the apparently more common specific changes in work organization and practices/techniques.

Job re-design and the search for commitment, flexibility and quality

In most instances, as has been noted earlier, changes to working practices and the way in which work is organized and jobs designed have been introduced and motivated by the desire to compete more effectively. It is important that we don't forget that this has often been perceived in terms of reducing labour costs by cutting down the quantity and quality of labour input and, as noted earlier, technological innovation and development has often assisted this process. We must not forget, as the work of Regini clearly suggests, that the nature of change and response to market pressures has by no means always been to try to achieve HR outcomes such as commitment, quality and functional flexibility. Competition continues on the basis of price rather than, or at least as well as, on the quality of the product.

Nevertheless, in this section we are concerned to identify and describe some of the major developments claimed for industry in the UK in the arena of work and its nature and design; the more interesting innovations have tended to be introduced in order, ostensibly, to achieve one or more of these desirable HR outcomes.

Commitment, intrinsic satisfaction, involvement and functional flexibility

Some organizations have pursued change in job design and working practices oriented towards enhancing the intrinsic satisfactions that employees derive from their experience at work, assuming both that they have such needs and that satisfied employees will contribute more to the organization. Some of these schemes have been directed at adding variety and scope for achievement while others have been more concerned to enhance employee involvement or participation in the task-related decision making process.

There certainly is evidence that employees do seek these rewards from work and Guest's (1995) study supports the contention. One of the categories supported by more than 70 per cent of those questioned as being essential or very important was: 'the type of work which they are doing, the opportunity to use their initiative and abilities whilst at work, in effect to be stretched in terms of problem solving and creativity'. Whether designing work to give employees the opportunity to gain these intrinsic satisfactions then results in higher levels of **commitment** is another matter, despite the fact that many such schemes, and perhaps those associated with Japanization more than others, have been referred to as High Commitment Management.

As noted earlier (Chapter 1) commitment is a concept that is difficult to measure and attitudinal commitment more so than behavioural commitment. There may be a relationship between them so that measuring behaviour may give an indication of attitudinal commitment but this is by no means certain and, in any event, whether you believe that it is realistic to envisage employees sharing the values and objectives of their employing organization will depend in part upon your perspective (see Chapter 1) and their (the employees) needs.

It is also important to realize that designing jobs and work processes so as to facilitate employees achieving intrinsic satisfactions may yield more satisfied and even more productive employees, but only if their other needs are also being met. The Guest (1995) survey referred to above, others before it and most recently the WERS 1998 (see Chapter 1), demonstrate that employees consider extrinsic factors such as pay, working conditions and job security equally as important as the intrinsic satisfactions and presumably employers seeking a satisfied workforce need to design the wider context of work to facilitate the satisfaction of these needs too. The WERS data indicate that pay may be a potent source of dissatisfaction and it may well be that what some would argue is a relatively low overall satisfaction level (54 per cent) can be ascribed in part to this dissatisfaction with an extrinsic feature of the job.

The most common of the experiments in job design that fall into this category are: job rotation, job enlargement and enrichment and the creation of autonomous (or semi-autonomous) teams and it is these that we look at first.

Job rotation

The essence of this mechanism is the simple rotation of employees between jobs of a similar skill level so as to alleviate boredom. The employee still only undertakes one job at a time. One might automatically think of assembly line production systems as lending themselves to this kind of re-design but there are other circumstances in which this can be practised; the obvious danger is that you simply swap one boring job for another that is equally as boring.

Job enlargement

This is where tasks of a similar skill level and nature to the existing job are added so that the job is enlarged in a horizontal sense. The level of responsibility remains the same but the number of tasks being undertaken increases. This widening of the job can relieve the repetitiveness of a highly fragmented and specialized process and thereby arguably yield benefits for the employee in terms of interest and boredom relief. However, the counter view is that you may actually make the situation worse, in that with one repetitive and boring task the employee may become so proficient that they can effectively switch off and obtain relief, with two or more such tasks it may require sufficient concentration to prevent this relief giving escape and thereby breed resentment and even more dissatisfaction.

Job enrichment

Here the enlarging of the job is vertical rather than horizontal so that responsibility is added to the job; for example, a production operator may be given also the responsibility for inspecting quality, ordering materials, devising and implementing maintenance schedules on the machinery or possibly even responsibility of a supervisory nature. Commonly enrichment of this kind occurs when organizations are seeking to de-layer or reduce the number of different skill and responsibility levels within the organization. It is sometimes suggested that reductions in the number of tiers of management may provide opportunities for enlargement of this nature in the jobs lower down.

Autonomous work groups

Here the principles of both enlargement and enrichment are themselves enlarged so that a group of employees become collectively responsible for a wider range of tasks, often a complete job, and also for the kind of responsibilities that were previously performed by supervisors such as the scheduling of the work and determining the pace at which the work is performed.

Apparently teamworking has been introduced into most modern automobile plants and common characteristics include the assumption by the team of responsibility for the quality of the team's output. Each team is required to deliver the car in perfect condition to the next team in the production process. The extent to which these teams actually are autonomous, or even semi-autonomous, varies considerably. The team size typically is between five and fifteen people, this was the size stipulated for example in the agreement reached by Vauxhall in 1992 and which provided for the teamwork started in the 'door module section' to be gradually extended throughout the plant.

In each of these mechanisms a measure of functional flexibility is achieved even if it is not the major motivation or prime objective.

Scepticism about the extent to which managements have devolved responsibility to teams and the genuineness of claims that these teams are in any real sense autonomous is furthered by the 1998 WERS data. These show that while it was claimed by management in 65 per cent of workplaces that the majority of employees (in the largest occupational group) worked in formally designated teams only 5 per cent said that the members of the team **had** to work together, were given responsibility for specific services or products, jointly decided how the work was to be done, and appointed their own leaders.

In a sense these schemes have been dealt with in an order reflecting an increasing degree of re-design of traditional systems and work practices, the changes in the latter being of a more fundamental and profound nature than in the earlier ones, and it would be unwise to overestimate the frequency with which these more profound experiments may have been tried in the UK.

The more profound the re-design the greater the impact upon management. In theory it would seem that an enhancement of employee autonomy is integral to many of these initiatives and changes of this kind are likely to have implications for management style, the degree of control that management remains able to exert and the mechanisms through which they seek to do so.

Activity 4

Take another look at each of these four specific re-design techniques and work out for yourself the extent to which they are each consistent with the assumptions underlying the principles of Taylorism.

Japanization? Quality, involvement and commitment as competitive advantage

Many organizations have sought to copy others who appear to have been more successful in confronting the challenges of the global economy and

changing product markets. Often in the UK
at copying the perceived methods of Japane
ity and employee involvement and commit/
petitive advantage. Consequently w
experimenting with 'quality circles' and
groups, cell/team working, Total Quality
continuous improvement, and Just-in-T
and systems.

The quality circle

This is probably the most famous technique associated with 'Japanization'
and became popular in the UK and some other parts of Europe in the 1970s
and 1980s. The popularity of this concept in Europe was linked to the perceived need for European manufacturers to compete on the grounds of nil-
defects. Quality circles (QCs) are intended to contribute to the process of
reducing defects and the need for repair. They comprise relatively small
numbers of employees (six to ten) meeting voluntarily on a regular basis to
identify, examine and resolve quality or other operational problems concerned with their own work and immediate environment. Their remit may
be primarily to deal with quality problems but they are commonly also
expected to both devise ways of reducing costs and means for improving the
design of work. These groups rarely have the authority to implement their
own recommendations and, as the problems are resolved, there is a danger
that there may be a loss of momentum. Generally they are centred around
a particular part of the production process. The formation and active and
successful operation of such groups is not quite as easy as it may at first seem
and experience has tended to reinforce the view that these groups need to
be both guided and led; it is quite common for the participants to also need
training and some access to resources. As with many of the other mechanisms referred to here it is important that management are seen to take
note and implement at least some of the recommendations of such groups;
the effective continuation of problem-solving groups, whether quality circles or others, tends to depend upon evidence that their work is valued.

It was noted that these groups were popular in the late 1970s and
into the 1980s but it is also the case that their popularity has waned, perhaps
in part because organizations have introduced one or more of the
more comprehensive approaches that we will deal with in the following
paragraphs.

The success of these QCs has been the subject of debate over the years
with some commentators acting as protagonists and others openly critical.
They certainly were introduced into hundreds of companies and some success was claimed in terms of quality improvements, improvements in job satisfaction and employee involvement etc. However, whatever the momentum
behind the movement in the early and mid-1980s, by the end of the decade

and into the 1990s their popularity had declined. The 1998 WERS does not provide evidence of the incidence of QCs on their own but some 42 per cent of the workplaces surveyed said that they used problem-solving groups of various types, the QC being an example.

Much of the criticism of the adoption and application of the concept in Europe has focused upon ambiguity about the true purpose of such schemes, with the view being expressed by some (Batstone and Gourley, 1986: 117–129) that the true purpose of these experiments was not so much to secure improvements in quality and employee involvement, and thereby employee satisfaction, as to provide a means whereby management were able to circumvent and bypass the traditional collective mechanisms of industrial relations and develop a more individual relationship with their employees. In Japan with its very different culture and industrial relations traditions these were not issues.

Another explanation for the relative lack of success and longevity of QCs was that, because they were voluntary, they gave the impression that a concern for quality improvement was voluntary and therefore not crucial to the success of the organization. As time went by and the degree of conviction that quality was integral to competitive advantage increased, alternative and more comprehensive approaches were required.

Total Quality Management (TQM)

This approach encompasses a number of the techniques typically associated with Japanese organization. The essence of the approach is a comprehensive and continuous search for improvement, the production of goods and services with 'zero defects', which involves most employees and knows few boundaries in terms of organizational activity; as noted above it was the advent of this approach that probably contributed to the demise of the more partial QCs. In many respects it is an approach that seeks/needs to generate a culture of quality throughout the organization. See **Figure 2.3**, an article published in *The Guardian* (20 February 1999) 'Mind the quality and feel the width' which, perhaps most importantly of all, shows that the process of improvement should never stop.

The driver for this attention to TQM should be the customer and this should include internal as well as external customers. Internally the customer is/are the employees involved in the next stage of the process, this may be the next individual or team in the assembly process, the next person to receive a report or the recipient of advice from a service function internal to the organization such as the line manager who has asked the personnel officer for advice on whether it would be fair to dismiss someone in a particular set of circumstances.

The focus of improvements in quality should be the employees doing the job, a fear of failure should be replaced with a search for failure: if people are blamed for failure they are unlikely to take risks, they are unlikely to

A braking systems group, programmed for success, goes from strength to strength after overall shake-up

Mind the quality and feel the width

WHAT do you do for an encore when your factory is making products with zero defects, when all your deliveries are on time and when you have won awards and accolades from your grateful customers? The answer, it seems, is that you do the same, but a lot more, and better.

LucasVarity's light vehicle braking systems division — now subsumed into LucasVarity Automotive — is a worldwide business with leading technology in anti-lock braking. It is widely seen as the jewel in LucasVarity's crown and the prime reason why first Federal Mogul, and then TRW, chipped in with monster bids to buy the whole group last month.

The division's total quality programme has brought it considerable praise from customers. Last year, having been chosen to be one of 182 "suppliers of the year" out of General Motors' 30,000 worldwide suppliers, the braking systems group was then further honoured by being named "Corporation of the Year", the top award. It's taken the Volkswagen Formel Q award and the Chrysler Role Model award too.

But it wasn't always so. Pam Broomall, director of quality systems for the braking business, based at Livonia, Michigan, says less than three years ago, the then Kelsey-Hayes division of Varity took a long hard look at itself and "decided we had a long way to go". Its critical self-analysis was backed by surveys of customers, staff and suppliers.

Kelsey-Hayes, which had 16 plants of its own worldwide, engaged a quality consultant, Quest, to help draw up a total quality programme. The plan had barely started when the 16 plants became 23, plus some joint ventures, with the merger of Varity and Lucas.

With factories making different products and at different stages of adherence to both internal and external quality standards, it's necessarily been very much a local effort,

AWARD-WINNER: LucasVarity's Pontypool plant   *Picture: Jeff Morgan*

with project teams tackling individual ideas at shopfloor level. The programme also takes in wider aspects of manufacturing and business processes where they affect productivity, cost and delivery.

For example, the Pontypool plant in Wales won an internal LucasVarity award last year for a project that reduced excessive tooling costs and downtime on a brake caliper machining cell. Production was increased from 700 to 1,000 pieces per shift; scrap was cut from 20 parts per shift to zero; and tooling costs were cut from £35,000 a year to £650.

Despite the local approach, a feature has been the degree to which the whole staff up to top managers has been involved. Most of the effort has been kept in-house using specially trained facilitators to guide teams through projects. Suppliers and customers have also been brought in to join teams. In every project, says Broomall, the essence is that there should be some form of measurable improvement, and a system of scorecards, measuring factors such as warranty claims, parts per million returned and delivery schedules, is central to that. Some of the scores are impressive. The GM award cited fac-

tories that were achieving zero defects, 100 per cent on-time deliveries and all "plant issues" dealt with inside 24 hours; warranty claims for parts delivered to Chrysler have fallen by 30 per cent a year for three years.

So what comes next? Broomall says the total quality process never ends. "If you've got 100 per cent on-time deliveries, maybe the customer would actually like them quicker." The emphasis is on five key areas: suppliers; deliveries to customers; lean manufacturing; providing as much or as little as customers want; and batch sizes. There is also the intention to bring technology improvement into the magic circle alongside quality, cost and delivery performance — to find a measure for innovation and to reward it.

"You just get everyone involved, commitment from the top, and then you don't change direction, so people know where they are," says Broomall. And will the dislocation of potential takeovers make any difference? "Not at all. It's just business as usual."

John Pullin is editor of Professional Engineering

Figure 2.3 *Source: The Guardian,* 20 February 1999

search for failures and put them right but are more likely to try to hide them (Marchington and Wilkinson, 1996: 353–354).

The formation of cells or teams and the devolution of some additional responsibilities to these semi-autonomous teams are commonly part of this overall approach, as may be the formation of quality circles and other problem-solving groups concerned with issues of wider impact than can be dealt with by a QC, these other groups may be cross-functional. An example of this kind of initiative is shown in **Figure 2.4**. Here we see a development that seems to encompass some of the elements of staff suggestion schemes, quality circles, problem solving and cross-functional teams. The customer-driven nature of such initiatives and programmes and the implications for employees are illustrated in the 'Guiding Principles' governing a programme initiated within Ford in the UK and quoted in Storey (1992: 57):

- quality comes first
- customers are the focus of everything we do
- continuous improvement is essential to our success
- employee involvement is our way of life
- dealers and suppliers are our partners
- integrity is never compromised.

TQM programmes then are likely to include an emphasis upon employee involvement as the means through which the search for continuous improvement is to be achieved.

Just-in-Time (JIT)

The essence of the JIT approach and appropriate systems is to eliminate waste and superficially this may have little to do with either flexibility or quality. However, there are interdependent relationships between these concepts and systems.

The basic theory of JIT is that at all stages of the production of a good or the provision of a service consideration should be given to minimizing the time between the product or a raw material being needed and its acquisition. So that systems should be designed which result in the final product being produced just before it is required in the marketplace, sub-assemblies are produced just before final assembly and bought components are acquired just before they are needed. This enables the company to respond more quickly to market demand and it confirms demand as the driver of the production process. This contrasts with traditional Fordist systems in which vast quantities of standardized products are made and may be stockpiled until they are sold.

In JIT systems the production time is reduced to a minimum, the various contributions to the final product are performed and acquired at the last reasonable moment and the likelihood is that the system will be geared towards and capable of satisfying the demand for relatively small batches of differentiated goods and services. It is a system therefore which places an emphasis upon both quality and flexibility. The materials, labour and sub-assembly processes have to be of the right quality and a premium is placed upon this by the shortness of the timescale, if materials are only acquired just before they are needed they have to be of the desired quality or else the system fails. In the 1998 WERS 29 per cent of the workplaces surveyed indicated that they had a JIT system of inventory control in place.

If the object is to respond to market demand and to undertake relatively short production runs, given that the demand in the market is for customized or variated products, then both the labour and machinery must be flexible. Quality, ideally TQM, and flexibility are crucial to the effective operation of these schemes and they are very vulnerable to failure or shortcomings in either.

These organizational and technical systems give purchasers considerable power. For example, big companies such as Ford and BT who are likely to be the major customer of any supplier of components can exert great pressure upon the supplier to deliver on time a product of the desired quality.

From an employee relations perspective these systems place an emphasis upon trust since the relationships between management and employees is one of high dependency as the system operates without stocks at both ends of the process.

These same constraints place similar pressures upon the efficiency and effectiveness of the entire system and arguably act as the impetus for the application of continuous improvement, the approaches that are at the base of TQM.

Both TQM and JIT imply comprehensive change within organizations, the emphasis of the former is upon cultural change whereas the latter is more directly concerned with organizational and technical systems. There is, however, likely to be an inter-relationship since massive change such as is associated with the introduction of JIT is likely to imply cultural change as a pre-requisite to its successful implementation. Many of the other initiatives that have been discussed in this section can more easily be introduced on a piecemeal basis and it may be that the more comprehensive the change the more profound will be the impact upon the nature of the employment relationship. Again, as with many of the more fragmented initiatives in the arena of job design, it would appear necessary that employees gain autonomy in decision making with respect to many production issues if these comprehensive systems of zero defects are to work effectively.

By actively encouraging ideas for improvement from employees at every level, Ford hopes to capture knowledge which will allow it to retain its competitive edge. David White reports

Focusing on value of teamwork

THE big idea is something every organisation is looking for: to get ahead of rivals and stay in the lead.

The Ford Motor Company, fighting fierce competition worldwide, has come up with a way of generating many small ideas which it hopes will add up to the big one.

Its business leadership initiatives scheme uses team-working to create forums where ideas that will have a direct impact on the company's profits can be submitted by managers. The strategy is based on a simple duce, capture and put in to practice any suggestion from managers that has the potential to improve the way the company does business. Staff from every division and job are brought together in cross-functional teams to spend three days thinking about what Ford does and how it can do it better.

Everyone is encouraged to have their say — not only in terms of their own ideas but in appraising those of others. Each team decides collectively on one suggestion and then has 90 days to use the varied talents and creativity among staff by giving them the opportunity to come up with the ideas that shape the company.

Nearly 300 Ford managers in Britain have taken part in the initiative's process since its launch almost a year ago, coming up with 10 projects aimed at "adding value to the business".

These have ranged from ways of reducing the cost of providing warranties with vehicles through improved quality control systems on assembly lines to encouraging more

and observable truth: even the most casual conversation between staff working for the same company almost always turns to ways of putting the firm to rights. Many of the ideas will be either impractical (sack the accountants) or unlawful (shoot the managing director), but a few might be world beaters.

No one knows how many brilliant ploys suggested during informal chats are lost. Day-to-day responsibilities usually mean there is no time to refine or even remember inspirational thinking undertaken on the spur of the moment.

Ford's initiatives plan aims to pro-

of its members to convert it into a working proposition.

Every project is sponsored by an executive with enough seniority to ensure that team members are given the time and resources in between their usual work to think through all aspects of the chosen idea to ensure it has the best possible chance of succeeding.

Ford's scheme has been championed from the very top — by the company's president and chief executive, Jacques Nasser. He defines the philosophy behind it as "encouraging everyone to act like owners" — in other words, to increase motivation

school visits to the company's heritage centre at its Dagenham plant in Essex by making the displays more relevant to the needs of the national curriculum. Pupils (the car and van buyers of the future) can learn about the techniques of mass production pioneered by Henry Ford along with the present use of computer-aided design techniques.

But how does the team-working approach to generating ideas work in practice? Nigel Nicholson, a professor of organisational behaviour at the London Business School, acknowledges the potential benefits of the scheme, but says it can create

Team working should not be limited to the manufacturing sector — a point Mike Sweeney, professor of operations management at Cranfield School of Management, emphasises. "It can be successfully applied to any activity where people are working towards a common goal," he says.

"Team working can unite and motivate staff performing every function in a company or organisation by giving them 'ownership' of the ideas they come up with.

"The mix of different expertise brought together can also identify potential problems associated with ideas and solutions that people with similar training doing the same job can miss." His tips for successful outcomes include ensuring that teams do not become so big that too many conflicting suggestions are generated and that one person should act as a "facilitator" to help 'bring out' the potential of the group.

A final word from Ford. It believes that the initiatives scheme — now extended to its operations worldwide — gives substance to the mantra to which many other companies pay only lip service: "Staff are our most important asset."

risks as well as opportunities. "Ideas and decisions emerging from teams can be a way of avoiding individual responsibility when suggested courses of action do not work out as planned," he says.

"There is also evidence that the most original and practical ideas come from individuals thinking them out on their own rather than being produced through group discussions."

He believes the strength of teams is in refining ideas and in the collective weight they can bring to increase the chances of suggestions being implemented.

"Team members should come up with their own ideas before meeting as a group," he says. "Each idea should then be considered collectively — with each member using their specialist knowledge to support, add to ... or criticise. In this way, everyone contributes and agreement is usually reached on an idea or solution to a problem that has been made stronger for being modified."

Joanne Sheehan, a corporate affairs manager, was part of the team whose project is credited with play-

ing a key role in the successful launch of the Ford Focus car. "Our team came from every part of the company, from finance to fleet sales," she says, "but we had no difficulty in agreeing on an idea connected with the Focus. We all knew that as a volume-produced car, its success was vital.

"Our team was convinced that the car was a winner both technically and stylistically and that the key to translating this into sales was in ensuring that the dealers shared this enthusiasm which they could pass on to potential customers," she adds.

There was brisk discussion of how this could be achieved, with final agreement that the training on new models for dealers which was traditionally undertaken by external consultants should be carried out in-house by Ford staff. This was deemed to be the most certain way of transferring 'ownership' of all the Focus could offer to those selling it.

"We devised and put into effect a training programme which covered not only technical specifications, but explained why the car had been designed in they way it had and the advantages this gave drivers and

passengers," says Ms Sheehan. "We wanted dealers to be able to match what the Focus offered to the individual needs of customers."

Every project is evaluated after being implemented — in the case of the Focus plan, feedback from dealers identified their new-style training as a key factor in boosting sales. Ms Sheehan is convinced that bringing together staff from every function within the company is the key to creative thinking.

"Cross-functional teams are used throughout Ford," she says. "It is part of the culture and no one on our team had any problem with working together — in fact, the mix of approaches led to fresh thinking and high levels of motivation."

Professor Nicholson singles out one aspect of the Ford initiative for particular praise. "The belief within a team that a well-thought-out idea will be adopted — or at least tried out — is vital if enthusiasm, motivation and effort is to be maintained. It is a need that Ford has recognised by using senior executives to sponsor the search for new ideas and ensure they are given serious consideration."

Figure 2.4 *Source: The Guardian, 27 March 1999*

Activity 5

How do each of these three 'techniques' associated with Japanization contribute to the achievement of quality and commitment?

Incidence and impact of the new production strategies – perceptions and conclusions

There are at least three different sets of views and conclusions about the incidence and impact of the comprehensive and culture-changing approaches to the challenge of competitiveness in the global market (such as TQM and JIT) and it is possible to tentatively associate each with one of the 'ideal' perspectives that we examined in Chapter 1.

There is one group, quite likely to be imbued with a unitarist perspective, of avid proponents who tend to greet these schemes with such a degree of messianic zeal that one wonders about the veracity of their claims (e.g. Wickens, 1987 and Jones, 1990 on Nissan at Sunderland); another group one can refer to as the pluralists, the relative neutrals including many academic researchers (e.g. Hill, 1991; Storey, 1992; Oliver and Wilkinson, 1992; and Wilkinson *et al.* 1992); and thirdly there are those of a more radical persuasion (e.g. Turnbull, 1988 and Garrahan and Stewart, 1992) who are perhaps likely to be suspicious of the initiatives.

The claims of the proponents have already been aired in outlining the theories behind the various initiatives. We are more interested at this stage in trying to ascertain the extent to which it seems that these claims are realistic and being realized, what other effects the schemes may have and indeed whether any of these other effects or implications may be consistent with or counter productive to the claims made for these programmes.

Legge (1995) summarizes the conclusions of the neutrals as evidence of much enthusiasm amongst managers, variable success in implementation and the suspicion that in all but a few companies the magnitude of the cultural change and the time over which the enthusiasm and commitment needs to be maintained combine to mitigate effective implementation. These latter programmes require fundamental change, take a long time to introduce and implement and there is the suspicion that the notorious short-termism of British business is not suited to these kinds of change programmes. As she describes it, a lack of stamina associated with endemic short-termism.

The radical perspective views these initiatives as having both very different objectives and effects to those claimed by the proponents. Observers with this perspective or outlook are likely to view these strategies as the means through which the pressure upon labour is intensified and labour is further exploited. Parker and Slaughter (1988) coined the term 'management by stress' to describe the consequences for labour of these initiatives. Teamworking and an emphasis upon zero defects are perceived as mechanisms through which both a culture of blame is introduced (rather than eradicated as the theory proclaims is essential – see above) and there is more effective control of the labour resource through peer surveillance. If this interpretation of events and their impact is adopted the outcome is likely to be far from the production of an involved, satisfied and committed workforce.

- So we have very different interpretations of the impact of these changes upon the nature of work and the employment relationship. The supporters of the various schemes are likely to claim that compliance is being replaced with/by commitment; conflict by cooperation; dissatisfaction and alienation with satisfaction; and control with involvement, autonomy and discretion. On the other hand, the more radical view is that changes are being introduced that are motivated by management's and capital's desire for increased competitiveness, productivity and profit and that they result in the intensification of labour use and exploitation
- the intensification of management control through means that are often insidiously based in peer surveillance as well as the never-ending search for faults and the apportionment of blame
- these systems, through the continuous search for improvement, place unacceptable levels of stress and anxiety upon the labour resource.

What is presented as employee involvement and participation is in fact no more than a sham designed to give employees the opportunity to acquiesce to pre-ordained management decisions.

It is very difficult to ascertain which of these perspectives may be closest to the 'truth' of the nature of the employment relationship at the turn of the Millennium since most research is undertaken in specific organizations and is therefore to some extent inevitably measuring the impact of organization-specific policy mixes. There are some wider surveys of employee attitudes and feelings about work. O'Brien (1992) has summarized the results of a number of surveys in various countries that seek to identify the degree of employee commitment to work by asking whether the employee would continue in work if they were to win the lottery or similar. The results indicate that British workers had the lowest levels of commitment in this context, though it must be added that over two-thirds of those asked indicated that they would continue to work in such circumstances, however the reasons given seem to reflect the deriving of social and esteem satisfactions as well as work being important as a means of structuring time.

Undy and Kessler (1995; cited in Marchington and Wilkinson, 1996) conducted a survey for the IPD which lends support to those who argue that the new techniques result in intensification, exploitation and stress. In this survey two-thirds of the sample felt they now had to work harder than when they first joined their employing organization, and while nearly two-thirds said that they felt 'a lot' of loyalty to fellow employees only 40 per cent felt 'a lot' of loyalty to their employing organization. Even fewer, only 26 per cent, felt similar levels of trust in the organization. Arguably these are not the responses one might expect if there had been a widespread introduction of initiatives successful in enhancing employee commitment to the values and objectives of the organization, and those of a Marxist or radical perspective may well interpret them as confirming their interpretation of events over the last ten to fifteen years. Others may well argue that the degrees of exploitation and stress would be even greater in the more traditional Fordist regimes replaced by the new systems and mechanisms.

Geary (1995), in his review of the evidence and assessment of the impact of these new work structures upon employees' working lives, presents a fairly depressing picture of the extent to which these working lives have in any real sense been improved. He concludes that the dominant impacts have included:

- increased stress and effort levels
- little significant upskilling, with task specialization and gendered divisions of work remaining pretty much as they were
- little increase in employees' control of the work process and its organization, managements have remained opposed to extending employees autonomy and to any other moves that might impair their ability to define the content of acceptable work behaviour
- more assertive managements that have been successful in gaining greater control over the labour process
- little or no lasting impact upon employees' commitment to the organization and its objectives and no significant improvements in the extent to which employees trust their managements
- no change in the fundamentally conflictual nature of the employment relationship.

An interpretation that would appear consistent with the following comments from an article in *The Guardian* (6 October 1999) concerned with allegations of institutional racism at Ford's Dagenham factory, in which an association is suggested between increasing competitive pressures, lean production approaches, management bullying of employees and enhanced employee stress:

Even Ford's press releases sound fretful. They announce continued cost efficiencies and agreed performance milestones and more flexible and lean operating practices. It is not that far from here to the term the unions increasingly use: bullying.

In the summer of 1999 there were a number of reports published which provide evidence of anxiety and stress levels among workers. It is not possible to argue that these levels have increased as a result of the introduction and implementation of new production strategies in the search for quality, flexibility and competitiveness but there is a possible association, as Parker and Slaughter, Undy and Kessler and Geary, above, concluded. In addition to anxiety and stress being linked to the increasing intensification of work brought on by new production strategies, high stress and anxiety levels were also being linked to the long-hours culture that was said to pervade the UK (see also Chapter 4 on the EU Working Time Directive) and to increasing insecurity.

A survey conducted by ICM and reported in *The Guardian* (2 September 1999) found that two-thirds of the respondents suffered from workplace stress and links were drawn between long hours, intensified workloads, targets and deadlines as contributing to the stress levels.

Another report of a survey funded and published by the Joseph Rowntree Foundation in August 1999, and undertaken by the Centre for Business Research at Cambridge University, found that anxiety and stress had risen in both public and private sectors and this was linked to increased concerns about job security and work intensification resulting from the increased pressures to achieve competitiveness and consequential reductions in staffing levels. More than 60 per cent of the employees surveyed argued that the pace of work and the effort that they have to put into their work had increased over the preceding five years. The biggest increase in insecurity was among professional workers and this was consistent with the findings in an earlier survey (Felstead *et al.*, 1998) that managers and professionals were experiencing significant increases in both job and employment insecurity. The Cambridge researchers also found that there was a lack of trust among workers and a sense of a loss of control over the pace of work. Interesting in the light of the discussion earlier (Chapter 1) on perspectives and the issue of conflict between the interests of employees and employers was the finding that only 26 per cent of workers surveyed felt that employees and employers were on the same side and 44 per cent felt that management could be expected to look after employees' best interests 'only a little' or 'not at all'. The Rowntree report and that of Felstead *et al.* both make it clear that there is a negative association between insecurity, stress and anxiety and general mental and physical health and well being and also that stress and anxiety are demotivating.

Summary

Overall we have sought to identify and describe some of the more important changes to working practices, the nature and organization of work and in the nature of the employment relationship in the 1980s and 1990s. In particular we have considered forms of job re-design and some of the innovations that have been attributed to the impact of Japanese companies in Europe. These changes have in most cases been motivated by the desire of companies to be efficient and competitive in the global market. There is a degree of inter-relationship between them and we need to bear in mind that change tends to be prompted, in this case by the radical changes ongoing in the global marketplace and the imperative that companies must be competitive. It is important to be aware and bear in mind the fact that an assessment of the motives for and impact of these developments is inevitably influenced by the perspective of the observer and their perceptions of whether the employment relationship is one characterized by conflict or cooperation, or both.

Activity 6

Read the article in **Figure 2.1** on call centres which illustrates many of the points and arguments made in this unit. It describes the extension of many of these developments, and to some extent the problems caused, into the service sector. Now, using this article, consider the following questions:

1 Identify the elements and implications of Taylorism illustrated in the article.
2 Identify which, if any, of the new job design initiatives are illustrated.
3 Consider the extent to which there is evidence that management are seeking to enhance employee commitment and quality.
4 Is there any evidence of the flexible firm model?

Activity Answers

Activity 1

Fordist regimes are appropriate to the satisfaction of demand for very large numbers of standardized products, exemplified by the apparent statement by Henry Ford that 'you can have any colour you want as long as it's black'. The technology employed tends to be large scale and fixed and not capable of being used for the production of goods that are not standardized and is often not amenable to modification. The labour tasks tend to be highly fragmented and repetitive as each element of the process is broken down into its constituent parts, each part of the process being performed repetitively by labour that need have no other skill.

Post-Fordist regimes are geared to the production of customized or variegated goods on a small batch basis. It is a regime that facilitates the satisfaction of consumers desires for something different and something that may be customized to their own specific requirements. The technology therefore needs to be adaptable, it may still be relatively fixed in a physical sense but it must to some extent be flexible in terms of the functions that can be performed. Labour in this regime needs also to be more flexible and it may well require several skills and the ability to learn others. It may also be that labour in this regime has more autonomy and a greater role in the planning of the process.

Activity 2

From the employer's perspective the flexible firm model provides the obvious advantage of flexibility of both a functional and numerical nature. It provides a means by which employment responsibilities can be minimized as fewer of the labour resources used are in this category; the use of short-term contracts, agency staff and sub-contractors enables the 'employer' to avoid or ignore many legal obligations and associated costs. The costs associated with the implementation of best practice personnel policies in areas such as training, staff development, sick leave and pay and holiday entitlements can also be avoided in respect of much of the labour resource used. The main downside risks and potential costs are concerned with the availability of appropriate labour resources as and when needed and the price that they may have to pay, a premium may be placed on planning and scheduling work to be undertaken by outside labour, the quality of the work may suffer when the labour can walk away from the site at the end of the job and where there is little or no continuity in service provision.

From the viewpoint of labour it depends to some extent whether your skills and expertise are sufficiently in demand to warrant your inclusion in the core group, though even here there may be a price to pay in terms of contentment and feelings of security if you are surrounded by an environment of insecurity. Generally, those in the peripheral groups have less security, possibly experience greater levels of stress as a result and probably experience less satisfaction of other needs such as those for recognition, meaningful relationships, high earnings or self-actualization. Those who have highly marketable and perhaps professional skills and qualifications may well not suffer in this way and indeed may well gain from an enhancement of their ability to control their own work lives.

Activity 3

1 Diversified Quality Production. There is a requirement for functionally flexible labour that is multi-skilled and able to learn and innovate. It is likely that the flexible firm model would be appropriate to this strategy.
2 Flexible Mass Production. It is unlikely that the model would have much applicability in this scenario.
3 Flexible Specialization. Both numerical and functional flexibility are required, the model is relevant.
4 Neo Fordist. There is little need for flexibility if this is the strategy adopted.
5 Traditional Small Firm. There may be some requirement for numerical flexibility to cope with quantitative fluctuations in demand but not for functional flexibility.

Activity 4

None of them are consistent with the principles of Taylorism, in fact they have all been described as representing the antithesis of Taylorism and the principles of scientific management. In each case, though to varying extents and in different ways and directions, fragmented jobs are to some extent being recomposed by these mechanisms and in some instances the separation of the tasks of planning, controlling etc., from those of execution that was fundamental to Taylorism is being diluted.

Activity 5

QC. The quality circle is collectively concerned to examine and find solutions for specific quality problems in the area of work that the members are concerned with. This involvement in the resolution of identifiable and relevant problems is thought to build commitment.

TQM. The basis of TQM is the continuous search for improvement and the development of a culture of zero defects and self- or peer inspection. A fear of failure should be replaced with a search for failure. Everyone is a customer of someone else and the use of teams and peer pressure may achieve a feeling of commitment to the group and eventually to the organization as a whole.

JIT. If materials are only acquired just before they are needed they have to be of the desired quality or else the system fails. The emphasis upon the shortness of the timescale and the consequential mutual dependency also places a premium upon trust and it is felt that this evident mutual dependency contributes to feelings of commitment.

Activity 6

1

- Control of the pace of work by the technology – electronic monitoring etc.
- Fragmentation of tasks and jobs
- Evidence of deskilling and degradation of work
- Feelings of alienation, low trust and evidence of stress, low levels of job satisfaction, absenteeism and labour turnover
- Evidence of employees seeking to circumvent the existing control systems
- Payment linked to activity levels.

2 There is some evidence of managers thinking in terms of job enlargement as a means to relieve some of the problems, with schemes designed to give employees a wider range of calls to answer. There is also evidence of the introduction of self-directed teams and of coaching rather than supervising.

3 To be honest there is relatively little evidence that management are really concerned with employee commitment; the view is expressed that in most call centres battery farm conditions apply and that the management attitude is 'that human resources are expendable'. However, there are chinks of light as indicated already in the answer above and there is also reference in the article to the importance of communication, the importance of constructive feedback, help-lines and more benign forms of control. All of these could have an impact upon employee quality and

commitment. There is also reference made to the view that control and quality may be opposite sides of the same coin, that in pursuing the one you may harm the other.

4 There is some evidence of the need for numerical flexibility and the development of flexible working patterns to provide 24-hour cover but not much else.

References

ACAS, 1988: *Labour Flexibility in Britain.* Occasional Paper No.41. HMSO, London.

Atkinson, J., 1984. Manpower strategies for the flexible organization. *Personnel Management* August, pp. 28–31.

Batstone, E. and Gourley, S., 1986. *Unions, Unemployment and Innovation.* Blackwell, Oxford.

Beatson, M., 1995. *Labour Market Flexibility.* The Employment Department, Research Series No. 48, Sheffield.

Braverman, H., 1974. *Labour and Monopoly Capital.* Monthly Review Press, New York.

Cully, M. *et al.,* 1998. *The 1998 Workplace Employee Relations Survey: First Findings.* DTI, ACAS, ESRC, PSI. Crown Copyright, London.

DfEE Skills and Enterprise Network, 1999. *Labour Market Quarterly Report,* August, Sheffield.

European Commission, 1999. *Employment in Europe 1998,* Luxembourg.

Felstead, A., Burchell, B. and Green, F., 1998. Insecurity at Work. *New Economy* 5 (3), pp. 180–4.

Flanders, A., 1970. *Management and Unions.* Faber and Faber, London.

Fox, A., 1966. *Industrial Sociology and Industrial Relations.* Royal Commission Research Paper No. 3. HMSO, London.

Garrahan, P. and Stewart, P., 1992. *The Nissan Enigma: Flexibility at Work in a Local Economy.* Cassell, London.

Geary, J.F., 1995. Work practices: the structure of work. In Edwards, P. (ed.), *Industrial Relations: Theory and Practice in Britain.* Blackwell, Oxford.

Guest, D., 1987. Human resource management and industrial relations. *Journal of Management Studies* 24(5): 503–521.

Guest, D., 1995. Why do people work? A Presentation to the IPD National Conference and cited in Marchington and Wilkinson (1996).

Herzberg, F., 1966. *Work and the Nature of Man.* Staples Press, London.

Hill, S., 1991. How do you manage a flexible firm: the Total Quality Model. *Work, Employment and Society* 5(3): 397–415.

Jones, A.K.V., 1990. Quality management the Nissan way. In Dale, B. and Plunkett, J. (Eds), *Managing Quality.* Philip Allan. pp. 44–51.

Legge, K.,1995. *Human Resource Management: Rhetorics and Realities.* Macmillan, Basingstoke.

Marchington, M. and Wilkinson, A., 1996. *Core Personnel and Development.* IPD, London.

Maslow, A., 1943. A theory of human motivation. *Psychological Review* 50: 370–396.

O'Brien, G., 1992. Changing meanings of work. In Hartley, J. and Stephenson, G. (Eds), *Employment Relations.* Blackwell, pp. 44–66, Oxford.

Oliver, N. and Wilkinson, B., 1992. *The Japanisation of British Industry: New Developments in the 1990s.* Blackwell, Oxford.

Parker, M. and Slaughter, J., 1988. *Choosing Sides: Unions and the Team Concept.* Labour Notes, Boston.

Pollert, A., 1988. The flexible firm: fixation or fact. *Work, Employment and Society* 2 (3): 281–306.

Regini, M., 1995. Firms and institutions: the demand for skills and their social production in Europe. *European Journal of Industrial Relations* 1 (2): 191–202.

Storey, J., 1992. *Developments in the Management of Human Resources – An Analytical Review.* Blackwell, Oxford.

Taylor, F.W., 1911. *Principles of Scientific Management.* Harper, New York.

Turnbull, P., 1988. The limits to Japanisation – just-in-time, labour relations and the UK automotive industry. *New Technology, Work and Employment* 3(1): 7–20.

Undy, R. and Kessler, I., 1995. The changing nature of the employment relationship. Presentation to the IPD national conference. Harrowgate.

Wickens, P., 1987. *The Road to Nissan.* Macmillan, Basingstoke.

Wilkinson, A., Marchington, M., Ackers, P. and Goodman, J., 1992. Total Quality Management and employee involvement. *Human Resource Management Journal* 2(4): 1–20.

Chapter 3

Globalization, multinational corporations and employee relations

Chapter Outline

- ■ Introduction

- ■ Globalization

- ■ Multinational corporations
  Definition
  Scale and nature of multinational activity and FDI
  FDI – advantages and disadvantages
  MNCs – approaches to the management of employee relations
  MNCs and national systems
  MNCs and the trade unions

- ■ International trade union organization
  Global organizations
  Sectoral federations
  The European Trade Union Confederation (ETUC)

- ■ International regulation and control of MNC activities
  Organization for Economic Cooperation and Development (OECD)
  The International Labour Organization (ILO)

- ■ Chapter summary

The latter part of the twentieth century witnessed a massive expansion in the extent to which business has become international and commonly this is encompassed within, or referred to in terms, of 'Globalization'. There has been:

- a significant expansion of international trade, development of more global product markets and enhanced pressures of international competition
- the liberalization of trade across national borders through the removal of tariff barriers, the extension of free trade agreements, such as those that paved the way for the development of the European Union (EU) and the North American Free Trade Agreement (NAFTA)
- the cross-national integration of production within multinational corporations (MNCs) as well as an expansion in the number and influence of MNCs, whether this be through joint ventures, cross-national acquisitions and mergers or other forms of foreign direct investment(FDI).

The new information transfer and communications technologies have contributed significantly to these developments and to our awareness of them. A consequence of these developments has been that employment and the employment relationship in the UK has become increasingly subject to external influence, from forces and developments originating outside the UK. This can be seen in many different initiatives discussed in other chapters, for example:

- the drive for flexibilities at work
- the concern with quality and the implementation of new techniques and work methods often borrowed or adapted from companies or practices originating in other countries
- the deregulation of the institutions of the labour market driven along often by exhortations from government and others that this is the only way back to international competitiveness and more employment and prosperity.

There has also been much discussion of the impact that the process of globalization and perhaps the attitudes and activities of MNCs in particular may have upon and for national systems of regulation of the employment relationship. Some argue that the economic power of the MNC in the new era of free trade and free movement of capital is such that national systems of regulation of the employment relationship are becoming less and less viable.

In this chapter we concentrate upon the influences deriving from the scale, activity and influence of multinational organizations.

Some UK businesses are clearly major players in global markets and have significant holdings and interests overseas. The UK is also a base for many foreign-owned multinational organizations and their presence in the UK, allied to a greater awareness of foreign events, cultures and practices, can be detected as having the potential for influence upon the policies, procedures, practices and outcomes of employee relations in the UK. This may be only internal to the organization concerned but it may also be that the influence of MNCs extends more widely into aspects of the national system of employee relations, irrespective of the wider issue of whether differentiated national systems are doomed.

We concentrate upon the inward nature of the interaction between the international environment and UK employee relations rather than any outward influences that UK employee relations traditions and practices may have throughout the rest of the world; however these latter have been substantial over the years and can be seen to be influential still. We will also examine briefly some of the international trade and regulatory institutions and also the international trade union movement; trades unions being perceived by some as the main potential source of a countervailing power to that of multinational capital.

Objectives

Learning objectives

After studying this chapter you will be able to:

- Understand and explain the constituents of globalization
- Explain the options open to MNCs in the approach they adopt to managing employee relations in different national systems
- Appreciate that potentially there is a two-way interaction between MNCs and national systems
- Identify and discuss the difficulties faced by the trades unions and other regulatory bodies in influencing the employee relations strategies of MNCs
- Discuss the influences for and the prospects of the convergence of employee relations within MNCs and across national borders.

Globalization

This term is probably used over-frequently and we intend to try to avoid it in this chapter; however, we feel it incumbent upon us to give you at least some idea of what it means or includes. Ohmae (1990) suggested that it was a term that related to the emergence of a borderless world or interlinked economy in which globalized production chains, product markets, corporate structures and financial flows to all intents and purposes would make the nation state and national boundaries largely irrelevant. An international restructuring of product markets, production and financial markets.

Ford saves Bridgend jobs

Nicholas Bannister Chief
Business Correspondent

The immediate uncertainty over 1,400 jobs at Ford's Bridgend plant in south Wales was removed yesterday when the car company disclosed plans to consolidate its European engine production facilities.

Under the plan, Bridgend will become the sole European maker of the Zetec-SE four cylinder engine which powers the Fiesta and Focus models. It will also continue to build V8 engines for Jaguar.

Ford, which has invested $350m (£216m) in Bridgend over the past three years, is to spend a further $30m increasing the plant's capacity from 400,000 to 700,000 engines.

Until now, production of the Zetec-SE engine has been shared between Bridgend and Ford's plant in Valencia, Spain.

The Valencia plant is to make a new family of Ford engines expected to be available from the end of 2002. Ford is planning to invest about $250m to convert the plant to make the new engine, in a move which will provide longer job security than at Bridgend.

Ford's Cologne plant in Germany will be the third leg of its European engine manufacturing operations. It will be the main source of the 4 litre V6 engine for the Explorer model.

Sir Ken Jackson, general secretary of the AEEU engineering union, said: "This lifts the clouds of uncertainty over Bridgend's future. I am proud of the high level of productivity our members have achieved there. This is their reward."

Nick Scheele, chairman of Ford of Europe, said: "Ford is focused on optimising operational efficiencies by fully exploiting the production capacities of our modern European manufacturing plants.

"Consolidation and improved efficiency allow us to maximise return on investment and to optimise our fixed cost structure."

Ford came under strong political pressure to ensure that engine manufacturing at Bridgend was not brought to a premature close.

Figure 3.1 *Source: The Guardian*, 13 November 1999

Figure 3.1 demonstrates this notion of integrated production chains and shows how Ford has organized its engine production within Europe with different engines being developed and built in plants in several countries. The manufacture and acquisition of other components and assembly of the finished car are undertaken elsewhere within the Ford Europe complex. The anxieties and insecurities associated with the possibility of the company using the exit option (see below) are also demonstrated, as is the relevance of interaction between industrial and political interests.

From the perspective of the interests of labour and the impact upon employee relations, Hyman (1999) suggests that it is the cross-national integration of production within MNCs that poses the biggest threat, given their ability to move operations across frontiers if confronted with a disliked regulatory regime or to take advantage of differences in labour supply, costs etc. Hyman cites also an International Labour Organization (ILO) annual review of the state of labour movements worldwide, which suggests that there are three main elements of globalization that may be perceived to be particularly threatening to both employees and their representatives and also to national systems of employment regulation:

● the internationalization of financial markets

- the liberalization of trade across national boundaries which has facilitated the shift of low-skilled manufacturing from the developed to the developing countries
- the growing ability of MNCs to use the 'exit option' as a means of avoiding unwanted regulation or to threaten governments and employees in order to obtain beneficial regulation or tax incentives, development grants etc.

See **Figure 3.2** for an example: Glaxo cutting back its activities in the UK subsequent to a decision that a particular drug that it produces should not be available through the NHS.

We look in a later section at the options that MNCs may have when seeking to influence government or trade unions and also at whether trade unions show signs of being able to counter such initiatives.

Multinational corporations

Definition

There are many organizations that trade internationally but which do not fall into the category of a MNC. Also, many terms are used to refer to multinational organizations including **global**, **transnational**, and **international** as well as **multinational**. Some observers (for example Bartlett and Ghoshal, 1989) have sought to assign specific meanings to each of these and to distinguish between them. However, in this chapter we will use the term 'multinational' as the generic and we will use a very simple definition sufficient for our purposes:

MNCs are enterprises which in more than one country own or control production or service facilities and activities that add value. (Leat, 1999)

It is the dimension of ownership and control of value-adding activity in more than one country that sets the MNC apart from the organization that simply trades internationally, perhaps by appointing an agent to sell their goods or services internationally or increasingly directly via the Internet. It is also this element of ownership or control which tends to bring with it the challenge of managing employee relations in different national contexts and poses for the organization's management both the problems and opportunities associated with international human resource management.

Glaxo job cuts after row over flu drug

David Brindle, Social Services Correspondent

The drugs manufacturer Glaxo Wellcome announced 1,700 job losses yesterday, just 24 hours after the government's new assessment body for NHS treatments dismissed the company's appeal against rejection of its anti-flu inhaler.

Glaxo, which has issued thinly-veiled warnings about its future in Britain in view of the row over the flu drug, denied that the announcement was anything other than coincidence. However, the job cuts will serve as a sharp and timely reminder of the importance of the pharmaceuticals industry as the health secretary considers whether to endorse the verdict of the assessors, the national institute for clinical excellence (Nice).

Glaxo has been pinning great hopes on the influenza drug, Relenza, which is said to reduce the symptoms to the equivalent of a common cold. The company has been struggling to achieve its performance targets.

Although Britain is not a big market globally, the company is angry at being rebuffed in its home country — especially as the Relenza ruling is Nice's first and the entire assessment process is being watched closely by other countries.

On Monday, Nice turned down Glaxo's appeal against assessment that the drug should not be made available this winter on the NHS because its effectiveness was not proven, specifically among elderly and other vulnerable patients, the groups most at risk from flu.

Yesterday, the company declared its intention to shed more than a fifth of its 8,250 manufacturing jobs in Britain. About 1,500 jobs would go at Dartford in Kent and 200 at Speke on Merseyside. The cuts are part of a four-year programme to slim Glaxo's worldwide manufacturing workforce from 21,400 to 18,000, making its 54 plants more effective and saving £370m a year by 2003.

Sir Richard Sykes, the company's chairman, said the proposals arose from a year-long review and were vital to sustaining and strengthening their competitive position in the rapidly changing global pharmaceutical industry.

A Glaxo spokesman said: "It was always the plan to announce this round about now. It's quite a coincidence, but nothing more than that."

Unions representing Glaxo workers, however, said they had been in talks with the company and the announcement had come out of the blue. Roger Lyons, general secretary of the technical union, MSF, said: "This has come as a shock to us. We are saddened that there has been no effective consultation."

Roy Lilley, a leading NHS commentator, said that the timing of the announcement was unfortunate but could be just clumsiness.

"Behind this lies the real issue that Glaxo Wellcome is not doing well," Mr Lilley said. "It has lost Zantac [its hugely successful ulcer drug that has run out of patent] and it just doesn't have any big drugs coming in. It's facing a difficult future."

Frank Dobson, the health secretary, has received Nice's final report on Relenza. A department of health spokesman said that the report would be studied and an announcement made "shortly".

Glaxo's share price was last night up 20p at £16.10.

Figure 3.2 *Source: The Guardian*, 6 October 1999

Scale and nature of multinational activity and foreign direct investment (FDI)

The United Nations Conference on Trade and Development (UNCTAD), in its 1999 report, suggests that there were in 1998 more than 60,000 MNCs and that they have between them some 500,000 local partners. They estimate that together they account for approximately 25 per cent of total world output.

Ietto-Gillies (1997) suggested that 80 per cent of world trade is attributable to MNCs (even though he uses the term 'transnational') and all foreign direct investment (FDI). There is a close association between the growth in the number and activity of MNCs and FDI. The scale of the expansion in FDI on a global basis can be detected from comparing annual data on FDI flows which, according to UNCTAD (cited in European Commission, 1998. Employment in Europe, 1997: 125; UNCTAD, 1999; see also **Figure 3.3**) rose from just a few billion dollars in the 1970s to $250 billion in 1990, $350 billion in 1995 and to $644 billion in 1998, with a prediction that the figure for 1999 might top $800 billion.

FDI can take a number of forms, the most significant being the total or partial acquisition of existing operations in other countries, which may themselves already be operating as an MNC, or the establishment of a completely new operation in another country, commonly referred to as investment of a greenfield nature. It is the acquisition of interests in existing operations through merger and amalgamation that seems to be largely responsible for the massive rate of increase in FDI in the late 1990s. As European Commission (1999: 125) point out, much (perhaps as much as 80 per cent) FDI takes the form of a change in the ownership of existing assets from resident to non-resident and, in particular, in the ownership of shares in companies rather than some form of tangible asset.

Figure 3.4 demonstrates the scale of the merger frenzy in the latter years of the twentieth century and makes the point that much of this restructuring of ownership is across national boundaries and that it tends to be concentrated in a relatively small range of industries including high tech and telecoms, financial services, oil and chemicals and pharmaceuticals.

The UNCTAD report confirms the UK as one of the major recipients of FDI and states that inward FDI in 1998 was $63.1 billion, an increase of 71 per cent over the figure for 1997, and this represented 27 per cent of the total FDI into the EU of $230 billion.

FDI – advantages and disadvantages

Governments and the citizens of a country can demonstrate different attitudes towards the proposition of a MNC setting up in that country or acquiring ownership of a home-country company; some countries, for example Japan, have been particularly resistant to the notion whereas

Foreign direct investment and employment

Foreign direct investment (FDI) is closely associated with the growth of multinational enterprises and their spread across the global economy. From a few billion US dollars in the 1970s, FDI flows had increased to around $250 billion in 1990 and to $350 billion in 1996. This, however, represents only around 20% of the capital of $1.4 trillion, estimated by the UN, which multinationals mobilised for the needs of their foreign affiliates, which together produced an estimated $7 trillion of goods and services in 1995, more than the total value of world exports. Indeed, over the past 10 years or so, the growth of global sales by foreign affiliates of multinationals has exceeded that of exports by 20–30%. Although FDI flows are still small, therefore, in relation to exports (only around 5%), the amount of production they support is now larger, resulting in around a third or so of total exports being estimated to be traded between branches of the same firm.

Both trade and direct investment are, therefore, interrelated parts of the same globalisation process. Indeed, most empirical research has underlined the complementary nature of the two rather than direct investment displacing exports. FDI often paves the way for a change in the composition of products being sold in the foreign market and can result in an increase, rather than a reduction, in exports from the home country. Though exports of final goods might decline as these are produced abroad, exports of intermediate goods to service the foreign branch might well increase. Equally, investment might take the form of the establishment of service and marketing facilities to support the growth of exports in the foreign market. Alternatively, foreign subsidiaries may be set up to produce lower-cost inputs for the final stage of production in the home market, which may be the only viable way of the company concerned remaining competitive. In this regard, FDI flows from developed to developing countries, which are still a small part of the total, but on which a good deal of blame for the loss of low skill-skilled jobs is often focused, can also increase exports of machinery, capital goods and services from the home economy to offset further any direct job losses.

Accordingly, the most commonly-levelled criticism of FDI, that it leads to the relocation of production and to job losses, is often the reverse of the truth. Indeed, the establishment of production abroad may be a means of safeguarding, or even expanding, jobs in the home economy. In addition, the investment in developing countries, as well as in the transition economies in Central and Eastern Europe, may well contribute significantly to their economic growth, which, through trade linkages, may ultimately benefit the home country and increase the level of employment that can be sustained.

The misconceptions about the effect of FDI on employment often stem from a lack of understanding about what it involves. A common tendency is to regard all inward FDI as 'greenfield' investment, and an addition to the stock of domestic capital, and outward FDI as a loss of domestic investment, or a leak of domestic savings, leading to the relocation of industry abroad. In fact, most FDI flows (possibly 80%) consist of changes in the ownership of assets from residents to non-residents rather than of additions or subtractions from the stock of domestic capital. Moreover, for the European Union, inward and outward FDI during the 1990s fluctuated between 5% and 9% of gross domestic capital formation and, though there was a net outflow, this amounted at most to 3% of domestic investment in any year.

A final consideration is that FDI increasingly involves the development of service activities which very often can only be exported by establishing a physical presence in the foreign market. Although these are likely to increase employment there, there is no reason why this should be at the expense of jobs at home. Indeed, ultimately, it should favour domestic employment because of the additional income generated by the company concerned.

Figure 3.3 *Source:* European Commission, 1999. *Employment in Europe 1998.* p. 125

Purchase power

Alex Brummer

The pattern of corporate ownership is changing dramatically as the clock races towards the end of the century. Open markets (globalisation, if you like) are showing in a huge number of mergers — many of them across nation-state boundaries — which is radically reshaping capitalism. Once decisions in Detroit affected investment and jobs in Dagenham and Luton. Now such decisions may be taken anywhere from Munich to Stockholm, from Philadelphia to Pretoria.

In the first six months of this year, completed mergers and acquisitions reached $409bn in value, up from $243bn in the same period in 1998. It's as if half the total wealth of Britain changed hands in half a year. Britain was a big participant. British companies bought assets worth $139bn — making them responsible for 48% of cross-border deals, according to KPMG Corporate Finance. The graphic shows who has recently been buying in Britain; a parallel table would show British companies reaching out to American, Swedish and French enterprises, such as British Steel's $2.3bn merger with Dutch Hoogovens.

There have been other periods of large-scale corporate agglomeration, but none on this scale or so international in nature. The end of the last century saw John D Rockefeller establishing Standard Oil of New Jersey and a near monopoly on world oil supply. In the latter part of the 1980s there was a merger bubble as corporate financiers discovered cheap finance through leveraged and managed buyouts using junk bonds — high-interest bearing securities.

This time merger mania is also partly built on paper. Because share markets are so strong companies have been able to use those high values to pay for other corporations. It is a trend which has now spread to continental Europe — once impervious to the equity markets. The French banks Paribas, Société Générale and BNP are currently engaged in an intricate dance, and oil companies Total and Elf are seeking to absorb each other. This is part of a French effort to create national champions which can compete with the likes of Exxon-Mobil (the biggest merger so far at $87bn) and BP Amoco.

Secondly, there exists an enormous pool of cheap finance, partly as a result of a period of low inflation. Investment banks Morgan Stanley and Merrill Lynch have become masters at using debt to create deals. The banks come to companies with a target, cash, price and the deal. The recent three-way battle here for control of the Allied Domecq pub estate of 3,200 houses was given extra spice by the fact that the smallest participant in the deal, Punch Taverns (which has just withdrawn), was able to call upon the financing skills of the American investment banks.

It's not just the availability of finance. More and more deals are cross-border, some 1,100 in the last three months alone. It is focused in distinct areas: the "third industrial revolution" of high-tech and telecoms; oil; chemicals and pharmaceuticals and financial services. Much of the activity has been focused on the US and Europe, with Japan only recently allowing foreign incomers (such as Britain's Cable & Wireless).

In this third industrial revolution, there is enormous jock-

Big deals

Bidder	Country	British target	Deal value, $bn
TRW Inc	US	LucasVarity	6.5
AXA-UAP	France	Guardian Royal Exchange	5.6
Huntsman	US	ICI chemicals	2.7
Edison Int	US	Powergen stations	2.0
Gannett	US	Newsquest	1.6
Ford	US	Kwikfit	1.6
Hicks, Muse, Tate	US	Hillsdown Holdings	1.3
Imetal	France	English China Clays	1.2
PPG Industries US	US	PRC de Soto	1.1
Global Telesystems	US	Esprit Telecom	1.1

Source: KPMG, Acquisitions by non-British of British companies. First half 1999

---

eying for position. British companies have gained the upper hand in cellular phone distribution through the $69.3bn merger of Vodafone with Airtouch Communications of the US. But as a deal this was relatively simple compared with the activities of Bill Gates of Microsoft, who is using the high value attached to his company's shares to gain a foothold in almost every technology. He finds himself as kingmaker in the battle for control of Cable & Wireless Communications by holding large stakes in both would-be buyers, Telewest (which is quoted on the London stock market) and NTL which is on the Nasdaq high-tech market in New York.

Mergers in oil and chemi- cals have been driven by the fall in the price of oil. When it fell to just above $10 a barrel, the oil majors saw themselves staring at losses. The urge to merge was fired by the need to cut costs. In pharmaceuticals mergers have been driven by the soaring cost of research and development. Britain's Zeneca merged with Sweden's Astra in an effort to share the R&D effort at time when ever more needs to be put into it. The creation of Euroland around the single currency has encouraged both national and cross-border financial services deals.

Is agglomeration beneficial? Promises made at the time of takeover, in terms of synergies and cost savings, are rarely fulfiled. When, after a merger, the owners are foreign, the final arbiters on investment and jobs are even further removed from the cutting edge. That can work two ways. BMW's decision to concentrate production in Britain is almost certainly beneficial; it will build quality into British-produced cars. But Zeneca has moved its R&D headquarters to Stockholm, which may weaken the R&D base in pharmaceuticals — one of the few areas where Britain possesses a genuinely world-class industry. It's worth noting that as companies get bigger and focus closely on the core, they may spin off parts of the business: these are sometimes sold to their managements and become a source of new enterprise and entrepreneurship. Vodafone, for those who have forgotten, only really got started as the world's top cellular phone group when it was spun off from an old-line defence electronics conglomerate Racal. Size is not necessarily a barrier to new enterprise.

Alex Brummer is the Guardian's financial editor. Find links to today's Analysis on the Guardian network at www.newsunlimited.co.uk/ analysis

---

Figure 3.4 *Source: The Guardian, 20 July 1999*

others have been much more open. In the world of increasingly free trade, global markets and electronic communication and commerce, it has become more difficult for countries to resist the mobility of capital and the influence of foreign-owned MNCs (see **Figures 3.4** and **3.5**).

In recent years in the UK we have seen governments encourage foreign-owned MNCs to set up a production or service facility in this country and certainly the Conservative governments of the early 1990s were proud of their record at attracting FDI into the UK (see above). It is possible to identify a number of common reasons why such investment may be welcomed. It is usually anticipated that the investment will:

- create jobs and improve the working conditions, living standards and prospects of those in the local labour market, there is an assumption that the generally higher wages paid by inward investors will have a beneficial impact upon wages in the local labour market
- assist with the necessary process of industrialization in undeveloped countries
- assist the host country's development through the process of technology and knowledge transfer and thereby boost the productivity of local manufacturers or suppliers
- generate tax revenues and foreign exchange receipts for the host country government.

There is a tendency to assume that any such investment will have a positive effect upon employment levels and other terms and conditions of employment in the host or receiving country, however it is important to be careful in assessing this impact. In assessing the impact upon jobs what matters are the net employment effects and these are determined through the combined effect of several factors:

- direct job creation, dependent upon the scale of the investment and its nature in terms of the capital–labour mix in the production process
- indirect job creation, dependent upon factors such as whether the company buys supplies and services from the host country market or whether it imports them
- the Trojan horse, or displacement effect of the investment: does this investment displace other local producers and suppliers. If the new investment simply displaces existing investment, then the net effect upon jobs may be nothing like what one might initially expect, this is equally applicable to the impact of FDI that is no more than a change in the ownership of existing assets.

FDI that takes the form of a merger with or acquisition of a going concern may have no beneficial impact upon employment at all and indeed it may in the long term lead to employment decline as activities and structures are rationalized and reorganized on a European or wider international basis.

C&W breaches Japan's defences

David Teather and **Megan Rowling** in Tokyo

The ultra-conservative and arcane world of corporate Japan was given a rude awakening yesterday by the British telecommunications firm, Cable & Wireless, when it became the first foreign company to win a hostile takeover there.

The sums involved — 69bn yen, or £353m — would barely raise an eyebrow in the City, but the nature of the bid for telephone company IDC has had a profound impact on a culture in which open confrontation in business is frowned upon.

C&W, which owned the old Mercury business in the UK, wrenched IDC from an agreed takeover by Nippon Telegraph & Telephone, the Japanese equivalent of BT and the world's biggest telephone company.

Economists predicted that the deal would be followed by a wave of foreign investment. Japan has come under increasing international pressure to open up its markets, but in the midst of an entrenched recession it has become a matter of expediency for many Japanese companies to seek outside help.

Earlier this year French car manufacturer Renault bought 37% of Japan's second-largest car manufacturer, Nissan, for more than £3bn.

The two-month battle for control of IDC had threatened to escalate into a full-blown trade war, with the trade and industry secretary, Stephen Byers, warning the Japanese government — which owns a 59% stake in NTT — not to intervene. The issue will be revisited during a forthcoming trip by Mr Byers to Japan.

"Traditionally Japan has been very hard to break into," said Professor Ray Barrell, a senior researcher at the National Institute for Economic and Social Research. "The government has never encouraged investment and the economy is controlled by very large trading corporations.

"But Japan now finds itself in a most unusual position.

"A lot of the restrictions on foreign ownership have been removed, its stock market is half what it was seven years ago and companies are looking cheap," he said.

Japan's telecoms market is the second largest in the world after the United States, and worth some £62bn a year. It is especially important to groups such as C&W because of the number of high-spending multinationals based there.

IDC, Japan's second-largest operator, carries around 20% of international call traffic in Japan and employs 600 people. Last year the company made profits of £31m.

C&W's hubris in tackling local custom head-on was in marked contrast to BT, which recently acquired a stake in Japan Telecom. That deal was carefully structured to avoid any possible offence by leaving a local company with the largest shareholding.

Negotiating deals in Japan is notoriously difficult, with a raft of unspoken rules. One ex-

---

'The Japanese stock market is half what it was seven years ago and companies are looking cheap'

---

ecutive recalls a week spent in Tokyo where he repeatedly took business cards, placed them in his wallet and slipped that into his back pocket — only to learn later that he had committed grave insults. Business cards are traditionally put in the left inside jacket pocket in Japan to show that they are close to the heart.

The value of foreign investment in Japan is equivalent to only 0.7% of national output, compared to 8.3% in the US and 20.5% in Britain.

Japanese firms have invested particularly heavily in Britain. Car and technology companies have poured money into manufacturing in Britain to avoid export tariffs, and Japanese investment bank Nomura is Britain's biggest pub landlord. It also owns rental group Thorn and caused a storm when it bought some ministry of defence homes.

Conglomerate Sankyo Seiko acquired Daks Simpson in 1991 and Japanese companies have also snapped up prime property including County Hall, the home of old Greater London Council.

C&W won 53% of IDC when two leading shareholders sold out yesterday — the Toyota motor group and Itochu, a Japanese trading group. A C&W spokesman said the company appreciated "the transparent and timely decision" of the shareholders. "We are looking forward to working with the directors and employees of IDC," he added.

C&W was also one of the founding members of the company and held 17.7% while the American mobile telephone company, AirTouch, has 10%. The offer is open until Tuesday next week, and other shareholders are now expected to accept the bid.

Both sides had increased their bids for IDC, but NTT said it would not match C&W's latest offer late on Tuesday.

NTT was bidding for IDC as a way to extend its reach overseas following the end of the government's ban on the company running international services. It has already bought stakes in a number of neighbouring Asian telecoms companies and has a joint venture with America's AT&T to cater for corporate clients.

During the contest, concerns had been raised among the IDC's directors that a western company would compromise job security, and they held a meeting with main shareholders urging them to accept the NTT offer.

One banker said, however, that the sustained fall in the Japanese stock market has put greater emphasis on the need to boost share prices.

Figure 3.5 *Source: The Guardian,* 10 June 1999

Similarly, attracting investment into the UK may in the first instance create jobs, but even where this investment has been attracted by substantial amounts of government aid there is no guarantee that the jobs will be recession proof.

The arguments in favour of governments encouraging inward FDI to boost wages and productivity in the local labour market have also been questioned. Wakelin *et al.* (1999) found that during the period 1991–1996 foreign-owned firms operating in the UK did tend to have a positive productivity gap over home-country firms and that they tended to pay higher wages. However, they also found no evidence that the arrival of foreign firms had a generally beneficial impact upon productivity levels and growth and upon wage levels in local firms in the same sectors.

Over the years there has been much criticism of the activities of MNCs and they have often been accused of exploiting and damaging the countries in which they have invested by:

- causing massive environmental damage through their extraction and exploitation of raw materials and their cynical attitudes towards the land and agriculture
- distorting and destroying traditional cultures
- cynically exploiting host-country labour.

Examples of the latter might be taking advantage of low employment levels in a region to force down the price of labour and the value of other terms and conditions of employment and to impose the MNC's own values and employment practices upon local labour and their organizations. Labour is forced to make concessions in order that the investment is attracted. Once established, the company is often able to continue with such practices by threatening to leave or shift production to other sites where labour is more compliant, examples of the 'exit options' referred to earlier. Again, different labour groups are forced into making concessions in order to keep work.

A practice which achieved a degree of notoriety in the UK in the 1980s, probably not warranted by the frequency of the practice, was to force a number of trade unions effectively to bid against each other for recognition rights in greenfield investment sites. The practice of promoting competition for members among two or three trade unions had some severe repercussions within the trade union movement and the Electricians Union (EEPTU) was expelled from the TUC as a consequence of the internal conflict that was caused by a few companies pursuing policies of such a nature.

The benefits of such investment may be positive for employment levels and for terms and conditions of employment in the host country but they may be negative if the MNC has a strong enough bargaining position and if they choose to use that power to force concessions from the labour force.

One of the criticisms commonly made of the massive increase of FDI in recent years has been that though it may be good for the recipient countries, developed countries may lose out. Where the FDI represents a relocation of investment, assets and activities from a high-cost or developed country to a developing one, the downside in the developed economy is that there is a loss of employment.

Look at Figure 3.3 and identify the examples given there of how outward FDI may result in employment growth in the home market.

Try to answer briefly the following questions without re-reading the text.

1 What distinguishes a MNC from companies that simply trade internationally?
2 What do you understand by the term 'the exit option' and why is it important?
3 Define globalization.

MNC – Approaches to the management of employee relations

One of the issues confronting an MNC is how it should try to manage employee relations in its various subsidiaries and throughout the company as a whole. There have been various views expressed which can very simplistically be separated into:

● those that see the MNC as a force for convergence of regulatory regimes, employee relations systems and structures, that the power of the MNC will be used to force deregulation and a reliance upon market forces and that this will be the base upon which convergence occurs
● those that suggest that tradition and national cultures, encompassing the values that influence attitudes to work and authority etc., and therefore the task of managing people, are so diverse that convergence is unlikely even within a MNC.

Perlmutter (1969) devised a typology of MNCs and their approach to the management of their overseas operations and this typology can be usefully applied to the management of employee relations. Each approach can be seen to be linked to particular beliefs about how operations and relationships should be conducted and what matters in life. He describes four major approaches to the management of overseas subsidiaries: ethnocentric, polycentric, regiocentric and geocentric.

Ethnocentric

This is an approach rooted in a belief by the parent company that the way things are done at home is the best or possibly even the only way of doing them and consequently very little authority is given to locals in the host country. Management of the subsidiary is likely to be a home-country expatriate and the parent company is likely to try to introduce the same policies and procedures wherever the subsidiary is located. Companies managed in this manner are likely to exhibit a common culture wherever located, all subsidiaries are likely to appear the same. Many American and Japanese companies have been criticized for seeking to operate in this way. This approach commonly characterizes the first stage in the development of the MNC and only after time has elapsed will management at the centre be prepared to adopt one or more of the following approaches.

The danger of this approach for companies is that they will take insufficient notice of the traditions and practices that contribute to the host-country regime, that the employees in the subsidiary will not share the same values and beliefs and so they will not conform to the home-country stereotype.

Home-country attitudes and practices may just not work very well elsewhere. An obvious example of the kinds of issues that can arise would be an American company, typically anti-trade union, setting up a subsidiary in Sweden and trying to avoid the recognition of trade unions and joint decision making that are typical of the Swedish employee relations regime.

Polycentric

Here much more notice is taken of local conditions, values and systems. The subsidiary is likely to be managed by a host-country national and regarded as an autonomous business unit. Key decisions, financial investment and overall strategic goals are still determined at HQ but this approach demonstrates an awareness that countries vary considerably and therefore local managers are most likely to have an understanding of the requirements of the local regulatory regime. This approach is much more likely to facilitate the maintenance of policies and practices in the field of employee relations that are consistent with the culture and regulatory regime of the host country.

However, we do also need to bear in mind that adopting a polycentric approach to the management of employee relations can pose problems for the MNC in terms of internal consistency in the way that employees in different countries are treated, their terms and conditions of employment and general management of the employment relationship, and also in terms of consistency between the policies and strategies determined and pursued at the centre and what may be going on at the local level. An example of the latter may be an overseas subsidiary which signs an agreement with a trade union about job security for its members that may then prove an embarrassment to the corporate HQ which is planning a downsizing or cost-cutting exercise.

Regiocentric and geocentric

Here subsidiaries and functions may be organized on a regional or some other geographic basis that is not constrained by national boundaries of either the home country or of the particular country in which activities are being conducted. Control of both staff and decisions are carried out on a regional or other geographical basis, and there will be a tendency for managers to be appointed either from within the particular region or, in the case of geocentric, with no specific country or even region-of-origin dimension to the appointment at all: the best person available is appointed wherever they may be from.

It is companies that conform to one of these latter structures that are perhaps more truly international or global and one would expect the approach to employee relations to be less likely to be conditioned by any particular national culture or regulatory regime. In such companies one might expect the development of region- or worldwide approaches to employee relations policies and practices. It is also companies of this form that are perhaps most likely to pose the threat to national systems that some commentators see as the consequence of globalization.

Schulten (1996) has discussed the development of Eurocentric approaches by companies, the development of structures and the organization of value-adding activities in and on Europe as a region. However, in the area of employee relations there can only be a partial Eurocentric approach given that we cannot yet talk about a single European labour market, that variations in regulatory regimes persist, and some effort has to be put in to complying with the requirements of particular national labour markets. However, if progressive deregulation occurs we might expect the steady development of company-wide Eurocentric approaches to an expanding number of working practices and terms and conditions of employment.

Both Hendry (1994) and Edwards *et al.* (1996) caution against too rigid or exclusive an interpretation of models such as Perlmutter's and make the point that it is quite possible to come across companies that present a combination of these approaches, a hybrid, for example a regiocentric approach to the organization and control of some areas of activity combined with polycentric or ethnocentric approaches in other areas.

As far as employee relations are concerned it does seem that there is greater importance attached to the pursuit of essentially polycentric approaches, certainly a number of researchers have, over the years, pointed up the value of a polycentric approach to the management of employee relations within MNCs. These include Schregle (1981) who asserted that 'industrial relations phenomena are a very faithful expression of the society in which they operate' and Prahalad and Doz (1987) who asserted that 'The lack of familiarity of MNC managers with local industrial and political conditions has sometimes needlessly worsened conflict that a local firm would have been likely to resolve'. Dowling and Schuler (1990) also emphasized the point that employee relations (ER) are so diverse across national borders that it is imperative that MNCs employ a polycentric approach when appointing ER managers.

Such a polycentric approach to the management of ER is also consistent with 'societal effect theory' (Maurice *et al.*, 1980). This implies that specific national cultures and national social systems impact upon and condition the organizational practices of foreign-owned subsidiaries, thereby explaining both the absence of a universal convergence of organization structures and a continuing existence of national diversity. However, some research conducted in the 1980s suggested that the utilization of a predominantly polycentric approach to employee relations was not universal, there was evidence of MNCs adopting partially ethnocentric approaches with an influence of country of origin in some of the employee relations and practices pursued. However, it was also established that country-of-origin approaches were sometimes triggered by other contingencies.

Hamill conducted a number of studies in the 1980s (1983, 1984a and b) and found some evidence that foreign-owned MNCs had an approach to and conducted employee relations differently from native UK-owned companies in the same industry. He found (1983) that:

- USA-owned MNCs were less likely to recognize trade unions and join employers associations
- they were more likely to employ specialist ER personnel at plant level
- they were more likely to have higher wages and better employee benefits than UK companies, but
- they were also more likely to centralize labour relations decision making.

He further found greater similarities between UK- and European-owned firms than between UK- and USA-owned companies. This would appear to be consistent with Bean (1985) who found that European MNCs had tended to deal with labour unions at industry level (frequently through employer associations) rather than at company level. However, as noted above, there is also some evidence that whether a foreign MNC adopts a partially polycentric or ethnocentric approach is contingent upon factors other than country of origin, for example:

- poor performance owing to labour relations problems. The MNC tended to attempt to introduce parent-country labour relations practices aimed at reducing industrial unrest or increasing productivity (Hamill, 1984b)
- the extent to which the subsidiary relied upon the parent company for operating or investment funds. If reliance was great the corporate

involvement in employee relations in the subsidiary was likely to be greater (Hamill, 1984b)

- the relative size of home and foreign markets were identified by Bean (1985) as a factor. Where the home market is relatively large there was a greater tendency for the centre to treat the subsidiary as an extension of domestic operations and therefore one would expect a greater tendency towards central control and ethnocentricity. Lack of a large home market is a strong incentive to adapt to host-country institutions and norms – polycentricity.

Hamill (1984a) also found that UK-based subsidiaries of MNCs experienced larger and longer strikes than did UK-owned companies and suggests that this difference may be attributed to the fact that MNCs had greater resources which enabled them to hold out against a striking workforce and were more able to switch production to another country, thereby avoiding the impact of the strike.

Nevertheless, it does seem that polycentricity in the management of employee relations has been the favoured approach of MNCs that ER in foreign-owned subsidiaries shows few, if any, significant differences from that practised in locally owned companies. In reporting their research, Edwards *et al.* (1996) distinguish simply between nationally and globally oriented approaches. They investigated 101 MNCs, 58 of which were UK-owned, and their findings led them to conclude that while there is evidence of globalism or geocentrism it seems that this tends to be more evident in respect of particular aspects of the firms' organization and activity, which do not generally include employee relations. For example:

- the global movement of managers
- handing profits over to global headquarters
- computerized communications
- giving board members global responsibility for a particular function.

It is much more likely that a national or polycentric approach is taken on employee relations through which the company is able to deal flexibly and responsively with local circumstance, traditions and culture.

As more organizations become genuinely multinational in terms of their ownership (see for example **Figure 3.6**) as well as on the basis of where they conduct their value-adding activities, and as they adopt different regiocentric or geocentric, regional (such as European) or global, structures, we would expect a decline in attempts to implement ethnocentricism since it becomes more and more difficult to establish a country and culture of origin. Indeed, as we have noted above, it may be that companies developing in this way will also pay less attention to polycentricity as their economic power enables them and others to secure a degree of convergence of national systems based in deregulation and the free operation of market forces. This effectively enables them to adopt much the same approach to the management of ER across the range of their activities and across national boundaries.

This is one of the reasons why people are so interested in regulatory developments within the EU and also in the issue of whether there is a convergence in the cultures of countries as they become wealthier (Ronen and Shenkar, 1985). As information and communications technologies, such as satellite communications, appear to make the world smaller, it becomes much more difficult for governments to censor information and control its availability. The pressures for convergence that may be emanating from the multinational capital side of the equation may be either furthered or hindered by the direction of these cultural and EU variables.

It is arguably easier for a MNC to pursue ethnocentric approaches and to seek to develop and maintain a strong and unified corporate culture if their overseas activities are the product of greenfield investment rather than the result of acquisition of or merger with existing operations. In this latter situation the acquiring company is likely to have different corporate as well as national cultures to deal with. Awareness of the issues associated with managing culturally diverse operations and workforces should help and, again, until we have a greater degree of convergence of national cultures and national regulatory regimes, it is likely that the solution will require management teams that are able to think and plan globally with respect to issues such as the production chain or obtaining and utilizing finance but which, at the same time, utilize polycentric approaches to the management of employee relations.

In this section we have been concerned with the issue of whether the MNC does or does not, should or should not, adapt their approach, policies and practices on employee relations to national differences, in a sense the impact that the national regime has upon the incoming MNC. MNCs have a range of options and we have noted that the research evidence in the UK and Europe would tend to support the view that, so far, many such companies appear to take the pragmatic view and adopt a primarily polycentric approach, even if they are pursuing regiocentric or geocentric approaches and ambitions in other areas and functions.

MNCs and national systems

However, there is another dimension to the interaction between MNCs and national systems of employee relations and this concerns the impact that MNCs themselves might have upon and within national systems: the inward influence. We have already noted that MNCs may well have an inward influence through their use of bargaining power, for example to force concessions out of government, employees and trade unions.

A MNC can also have a particular and wider innovatory effect upon the employee relations system within a country by demonstrating the effective-

Sun Life could sell off GRE insurance business

Jill Treanor

The former life insurance business of Guardian Royal Exchange could be sold by its new owner, Sun Life & Provincial Holdings, which is due to publish the outcome of a review into the operation this week.

The City is expecting Sun Life, which bought GRE for £3.4bn earlier this year, to announce with its interim results on Thursday that it does not intend to keep the life business which has £10bn of assets and a million policyholders. It is not clear whether there are any implications for jobs in the life operation.

Sun Life is majority owned by French insurance group Axa. While it might be possible for Sun Life to decide to run down the life business, industry experts believe Sun Life has been looking for a purchaser for the business.

Speculation surrounds Aegon of the Netherlands which has been mooted as potential buyer for the business valued at up to £700m.

The life business has been the subject of a strategic review by investment banking firm Donaldson, Lufkin & Jenrette, also run by Axa, ever since Axa-controlled Sun Life clinched an agreement to buy GRE earlier this year.

The completion of the review marks the end of the overhaul of the troubled GRE business. When it purchased GRE after a bidding war, Sun Life already had an agreement

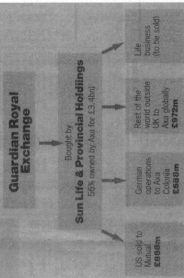

to sell off parts of the business. It sold the US operations to Liberty Mutual and, through its Axa connections, was able to rid itself of the businesses in Germany and other parts of the world outside the UK and Ireland to other Axa entities.

The review of the UK and Irish parts of the business has already concluded that Sun Life should keep the PPP healthcare business, at least for the time being, and the bulk of the Irish business. It is not clear what will happen to Irish life business and the outcome of that review may not be known until next month.

When Sun Life first announced its intention to buy GRE, industry experts had not expected the life business to fit well with with its existing life operation Equity and Life.

"Putting GRE into that wouldn't make sense," one source said yesterday. However, he was sceptical whether Aegon would prove to be the buyer for the business as it might not lie tidily beside its Scottish Equitable business in the UK.

Figure 3.6 *Source: The Guardian*, 10 August 1999

ness of the way in which it organizes work and manages employee relations. Other employers try to copy or mimic the policies and practices: the MNC's essentially ethnocentric approach acts as a model for others. Such effects may well be the product of the adoption of an ethnocentric rather than a polycentric approach, the organization seeks not to adapt to local circumstances etc. but seeks to manage employee relations in the same manner as at home.

One of the major phenomena of the last two decades has been the influence within Europe, and perhaps particularly in the UK, of Japanese systems, attitudes and values relating to the design and nature of work and the attitudes and behaviour expected of employees at work. While not exclusively the outcome of the activities of Japanese MNCs investing in the UK, nevertheless, having reasonably close-at-hand examples of how work is designed and employee relations managed undoubtedly helped the spread and take-up of the phenomenon known as Japanization.

American and other European MNCs can also be seen to have had an impact in the UK. For example, organizations such as Phillips, Volvo, MacDonalds, Disney and IBM have all, at various times, been influential as models of excellence encompassing the management and conduct of employee relations.

We examined some of the popular component practices associated with Japanization in Chapter 2. In particular we looked at techniques and arrangements such as:

- the quality circle and other problem-solving groups
- cellular and team-based methods of working and organizing work
- TQM processes, encompassing an emphasis upon labour, service and product quality that pervades all aspects of the organizations' activity, recognizes their interdependence and is to be achieved through a continuous search for improvement: Kaizan
- JIT and lean production policies and systems
- a system of apparently consensual decision making
- an emphasis upon employee involvement and commitment.

Many UK organizations witnessed the success of the Japanese economy in the 1980s and into the early 1990s and saw these practices and attitudes as sources of competitive advantage which they wanted to achieve themselves and so they sought to borrow from the Japanese model. The implementation of elements of this model has implications for the nature of work and the employment relationship, terms and conditions of employment and the traditions and practice of employee relations in the UK.

The above describes the way in which an ethnocentric approach by the management of a MNC may result in particular attitudes and practices being adopted more widely in the host country. There are ways also in which the same effect may occur as the result of regiocentric or geocentric approaches. Where, for example, a MNC has organized and structured its activities on, say, a European basis (see reference to Eurocentrism above) it may be that internally the company achieves a European approach to at least some dimensions of employee relations, to those elements that are not subject to national regulation, for example the nature of the payment system, the way in which work is organized and the working practices used. As these become increasingly common within the company and across national boundaries, and if they are associated with success, it is quite possible that other employers will borrow them and thereby there is an impact upon national systems.

Activity 3

Read the figure 'It's slash and burn at Nissan' (Figure 3.7). It demonstrates a number of the issues so far discussed in this chapter and in earlier ones. Identify as many as you can.

MNCs and the trade unions

As we shall see in later chapters, trades unions in the UK are still a potent national and organizational influence upon the employment relationship. Where they have been less influential is in the international environment and at a cross-national level. Trade unions in the UK are relatively coherent as a movement and as a voice, but this is not the case in a number of other European countries where traditions have been of competition for members and influence and of conflict rather than cooperation between rival federations. At an international level the trade union confederations have not shown themselves adept at cooperating with each other across national boundaries.

There have been attempts by some of the trade union federations that are organized at international sectoral (industry) level to engage in meaningful dialogue and, in some cases, collective bargaining with individual MNCs as well as with the appropriate employers' federation. The agreements on encouraging social dialogue (dialogue between the social partners – see Chapter 4) within the EU made reference to the sector as well as to what has become known as the interprofessional level (at the level of the EU as a whole) but, in the main, and so far, trade unions have not demonstrated an ability effectively to combat the bargaining power of the MNC. There is little if any evidence that employers want to engage in meaningful discussions with trade unions at the international level, whether it be within a particular MNC or at some other level such as the sector. We do also need to bear in mind that, throughout the developed world, the last fifteen

It's slash and burn at Nissan

**Mark Milner
and Nicholas Bannister**

The scope of the revival plan of Carlos Ghosn, the Renault executive seconded to Nissan as chief operating officer, makes BMW's approach to its loss-making Rover subsidiary look timid and piecemeal.

Rover has been patched up and trimmed by BMW and its predecessors but still appears lacking the vision which Mr Ghosn is bringing to Nissan. Parachuted into Nissan by Renault, Mr Ghosn has been able to slash and burn with a ruthlessness which had escaped the company's Japanese managers in the past.

He is not laden with sentimental baggage. Out go Japanese-style promotions based on seniority. In future promotions will be based on merit. In come share options and other incentives to boost executive performance. Indeed, Mr Ghosn has taken back to Japan the lessons that European and US car makers were forced to learn when Japanese imports flooded their domestic markets.

European car makers had to merge, cut costs, improve quality and use fewer platforms to survive. They have had to accept rapid change and new customer expectations as a way of life.

Nissan's problems illustrate the pressures facing the car industry on a global basis. Customers want more new models more often with more "extras" fitted as standard. Despite the expense of developing new models, competition is helping to push events the customers' way. Although car makers are often dismissive of arguments about too much capacity and the need for industrial restructuring —

not least because taking out capacity can be politically problematical and anyway they may be part of the capacity being rationalised — it is still a factor. Like it or not, manufacturers are having to become leaner and meaner.

Production methods are becoming increasingly flexible to allow shorter production runs. The days of long runs of the same model are over. Customers will no longer tolerate an attitude which says they can have any colour they want, provided it is black. Manufacturing methods have had to turn to greater automation, fewer workers and more flexible shift systems. Productivity — as much if not more a function of investment as working practices — is the key to success.

Twenty years ago just-in-time manufacturing was seen as a Japanese invention which gave the country's car companies a competitive edge. Now supplier parks — where components makers are grouped around car plans — are commonplace.

Hand in hand with a greater choice of models manufacturers are looking for greater standardisation. Though they want to offer greater choice to their customers, the car makers want to do so on the basis of fewer platforms, as car underbodies are known. They also want to use more of the same components on different models.

That is making life tough for the suppliers, too. Though it is difficult to get any European car maker, for example, to admit that there are too many manufacturers in Europe, despite the fact that there are six volume producers — General Motors, Ford, Fiat, Volkswagen, Renault and Peugeot — they are less sentimental when it comes to talk of cutting the number of components suppliers. Forget variety; car

makers are prepared to work with fewer suppliers provided the parts groups are prepared to cut their margins.

The pressures within the industry are affecting its structure. Daimler-Benz's merger with Chrysler and Renault's acquisition of the 37% stake in Nissan are the highest profile moves but are hardly the only harbingers of greater integration. Take Volvo — the Swedish group has pulled out of cars in order to become a bigger player in the truck market. It was not short of buyers. The car division went to Ford but not before it had emerged that Fiat had been keen to buy both the car and truck operations. In Britain BMW and VW got into a kicking match over who would buy Rolls-Royce.

Eventually they settled on dividing the spoils — with BMW getting the Rolls-Royce marque in a couple of years' time and VW retaining Bentley — a purchase which gives it a presence right across the model range, from small cars to the luxury end of the market.

Will there be more to come? There has been speculation that DaimlerChrysler might seek to link up with either Fiat or Peugeot, though any such links are more likely to involve cooperation over DaimlerChrysler's urban Smart car rather than a corporate relationship.

The key targets of new alliances has either to be aggressive, giving access to new markets or defensive, allowing the partners to cut production costs without sacrificing brand loyalty or trimming model choice. Or even, as yesterday's announcement from Nissan shows, both.

Figure 3.7 *Source: The Guardian*, 19 October 1999

years have been a period of almost universal trade union membership decline.

There are a number of relatively common ways in which the MNC can, if it wishes, frustrate or thwart the interests of trade unions organized on a predominantly national basis. Kennedy (1980) identified a number of these and we have referred earlier to the concept of the exit option. An example of the latter would include the ability to shift the value-adding activity elsewhere (as, for instance, in the case of Renault, see **Figure 3.8**, even though this was not a move prompted primarily by a desire to avoid or frustrate trade unions). The ability to do this will to some extent be influenced by the nature and degree to which production chains are integrated across national borders within the MNC and also, of course, by whether there are taxation, volume or other restrictions and barriers to the mobility of goods and services between the countries.

Other ways in which the interests of the trade unions may be thwarted by the MNC include:

- stage an 'investment strike', in which the MNC refuses to invest any additional funds in a plant, as a threat or bargaining counter to obtain concessions from the labour force – a threat to the jobs and livelihood of those currently employed
- the pressure it and perhaps other MNCs may be able to exert upon governments at the national level to either deregulate the labour market/employment relationship or indeed to regulate in favour of the

---

Probably the most famous example of spontaneous and *ad hoc* international trade union solidarity and activity concerned the trade union reaction in a number of European countries (Belgium, France, Germany, Italy, Spain, the UK, the Netherlands, Portugal, Greece and Austria) to the decision by Renault in 1997 to close its factories in Belgium and transfer the production to French plants. This was made worse by the revelation at the time that the company was seeking grants and other forms of assistance from both the Spanish government and the European Commission to build a new plant in Spain. The demonstrations and coordinated protests were to no avail, the company proceeded with the plans that had been announced. Renault demonstrated the power of the MNC to exercise its autonomy and ignore the views of the international trade union movement and also to ignore the requirements of the EU Directive that provides employee representatives with rights to prior consultation in the event of collective redundancies.

Figure 3.8 Closure of Renault factory in Belgium

MNC rather than its employees. The pressure may be based on either a threat to leave the country or not to invest in the country.

- hiding from the unions by having a remote locus of authority (the corporate HQ management of a MNC) which is quite likely to be in a different part of the world and relatively anonymous
- if in dispute with a national-level trade union using what might be formidable financial resources to withstand industrial action in any one subsidiary.

We noted above that Hamill found subsidiaries of US MNCs were neither as likely to recognize trade unions nor to join employers' associations and more recently, many MNCs investing into Ireland have been fiercely anti-trade union. The research conducted by Edwards *et al.* (1996) concluded that as MNCs become more global in their structures and orientation the prospects for trade union recognition for bargaining purposes tend to decline. We should not really be surprised at this since for activities that are organized at a multinational level, whether this be regional or global, there are no trade unions organized at this same level. So that even if a MNC wanted to recognize and bargain it would in the main find it difficult to find an organization that it could meaningfully bargain with at the corporate level. Nevertheless, Edwards *et al.* also conclude that even though many of the companies would choose to avoid trade unions, trade union recognition was not of sufficient importance to most of them that they would base location decisions on this factor.

So far we have concentrated upon the ways in which MNCs may be able to exert influence, but the trade unions do have some means through which they might respond or seek to attain their own objectives.

The trade unions do not have exit options but they also can exert pressure upon national governments to regulate in favour of the unions and their members. They often represent very significant proportions of the national electorate and, within Europe, it is common that the trade unions have formal political affiliations. In some instances, as with the Labour party in the UK, it was the trade union movement that inspired and fostered the development of the political party. We note in Chapter 5 that in the UK in both 1974 and 1979 the activities of the trade unions were instrumental in bringing about the election of a new government. The power certainly has been real, though in the UK there are concerns that this is no longer the case and indeed that the competitive and wealth-creating imperative is for government to pursue MNC friendly rather than trade union friendly policies, in this case labour market deregulation rather than regulation.

Ietto-Gillies (1997) has argued that MNCs can wield considerable power against uni-nationals, governments, labour organizations and consumers and that there is a need to try to reverse this trend and give countervailing power to these other players. It is also important to bear in mind that when dealing with MNCs, unions may have conflicting national interests: national-level trade union officials may have as much, if not more, interest in attracting MNC investment as does the government, it is after all their members who will lose or benefit in terms of whether they have a job or not. Consequently it is not unknown for trade union movements in different countries competing for MNC investment to actually compete with each other in making the regime, business climate and their own attitudes seem as attractive as possible. Organizing cross-border cooperation effectively to combat the power of the MNC is in these circumstances difficult.

The ability of trades unions to influence the policies and activities of MNCs will also to some extent depend upon the structure of the MNC and, as we noted above, the extent and manner of integration of the production chain. For example, we can look back to the example of Ford and Bridgend referred to above, where the engine production for Ford Europe is designed in a manner that results in one type of engine being made in one country and not replicated elsewhere. This provides the unions with a relatively strong base in the short term since industrial action would have significant implications for the production of a particular model and, of course, for the other elements of the supply and production chain which may be spread around Europe. If the Bridgend plant is the only one making the Jaguar engine then in the short term it can bring the production and assembly of Jaguars to a halt. However, the impact in the short term upon sales would also be dependent upon levels of stocks and demand. In the longer term it is possible for Ford to shift the production of the Jaguar engine elsewhere within the European operation and it is at this point that cross-national cooperation rather than competition between different national trade union movements becomes important. If, as in the case of Hoover closing down its operations in France and shifting them to Scotland a few years ago, the unions in the recipient country accept the new production arrangements there is very little that the unions in the country in which operations are closed can do. So, for example, if Ford decided to respond to the industrial action by announcing that it was to shift production of this particular engine to Valencia then unless the Spanish and UK trade unions were able to cooperate with each other it is unlikely that the UK Ford workers would be able to resist. In reality the implicit threat of such 'exit option' action by Ford would be sufficient to ensure that the industrial action either did not take place or was limited. If, continuing with this hypothetical example, the Bridgend plant was not the only one making the Jaguar engine then the threat and impact of industrial action at Bridgend would be even less significant to the company since production and assembly of the car would continue and they would be able to countenance the closure of the Bridgend plant even more speedily. In both instances effective action on the part of the labour force to combat the power of the MNC and its ability in the long term to switch production into another country depends in part upon cross-national cooperation among the trade union movements. In this case the trade union position would be strengthened if the whole car was being made and assembled at, and only at, Bridgend. Then the employees would be able to halt the production of the whole car and the company would have no alternative source of supply. In this case cross-national cooperation between unions would not be relevant. In the very long term the company would be able to shift production but the time and cost would be significant. Where the MNC supply and production chains are organized in this latter manner the exit option is a much less potent weapon or threat.

There have been instances over the years of spontaneous and *ad hoc* international trade union solidarity and activity against particular multinationals as in the Renault case referred to earlier and briefly described in **Figure 3.8**. However, such examples are very rare.

Activity 4

One form of MNC activity and organization is sometimes referred to as the multidomestic. This is characterized by the subsidiary in each country being pretty much a replica of the home country operation and therefore similar to it. Usually this would mean that the whole product or service is supplied, manufactured and assembled within the country in which it is sold. The MNC is made up of a number of reasonably self-contained subsidiaries, each supplying a particular national market, with little or no internal transfer of knowledge, expertise, service or product between them. Think through and outline the strengths and weaknesses of this form of organization with respect to the bargaining power of the trade unions taking action in one of the subsidiaries.

International trade union organization

Trade unions have sought to establish international structures at a number of different levels: sectoral (industry); regional, for example Europe; and global.

Global organizations

On a global level, international trade union organizations have tended to be aligned with political and ideological interests. That is to say, in the West, the International Confederation of Free Trade Unions (ICFTU) emerged, with its counterpart in the then-Communist bloc being the World Federation of Trade Unions (WFTU). Not surprisingly, the ICFTU has been the more influential in the developed world and this has been perpetuated by the impact upon the WFTU of the break-up of the Soviet bloc and the demise of Communism as a significant political/ideological influence. The

ICFTU has an affiliated membership of approximately 120 million with affiliates from more than 130 different countries.

There is a sectoral level of federations in major industries affiliated to the ICFTU. The demise of Communism has left the ICFTU unthreatened by competition but, according to Gallin (1994), it might also be responsible for the organization now having little if any direction.

Neither of these world confederations succeeded in developing a collective bargaining role and their activities have tended to be dominated by political interests and action and, in the case of the ICFTU, the encouragement of trade unionism and representation in developing countries.

In order for international trade union federations to act effectively they have to be given the opportunity and authority by their member federations. This effectively requires national-level federations to be willing to cede some of their autonomy to the international level; there has been and still is considerable reluctance to do this.

Sectoral federations

There is a long tradition of international organization and federation at the sector level. The confederations organized at this level have tended to be called International Trade Secretariats (ITS). It is at this level that the trade unions have tried to devise strategies for combating the power of the MNC. If the MNC's activities are limited to one industry, for example food, engineering, transport or construction, then one can envisage a relatively simple structure in which the industry confederation seeks to deal with the MNC at a company/corporate level. However, the more complex the MNC's sectoral mix of activities (where it controls value-adding activities in a number of different industries the less simple is such an approach) the greater is the likelihood that two or more international sectoral confederations of trade unions will be seeking to deal with the MNC and the greater is the scope for different agendas to be pursued and also for the MNC to take advantage of the complexity if it so wishes.

With the exception of a few French-owned MNCs in the food industry there have been very few successful attempts by the union federations at sector level to persuade the MNC into collective bargaining. However, where it has happened, the content of the agreement has perhaps inevitably been limited to the agreement of broad principles and minimum provisions and rights, agreements of a kind that are often described as 'framework' agreements.

The prospects for significant inroads to be made into the autonomy of MNC managements at this level through the use of persuasion and a reliance upon voluntary mechanisms does seem to be very much dependent upon the wishes of the MNC management and the ability of the ITS to present itself as a coherent entity able to speak clearly and with authority on behalf of its members. With some exceptions this has not as yet often happened, as federation affiliates all ultimately have national constituencies that have to be satisfied.

The European Trade Union Confederation (ETUC)

Founded in 1973, the most influential international trade union organization within Europe is undoubtedly the ETUC with affiliates from twenty-eight countries and an affiliated membership in excess of fifty million employees. However, this influence does not stem so much from successes with individual MNCs, or indeed from success at countering the influence of multinational capitalism, as it does from the formal role afforded the organization in the determination of social policy at the level of the EU. The agreement to create the Single Market in 1986 also contained the seeds of an enhanced social dialogue at the level of the EU. This latter was confirmed at the EU summit in Maastricht in 1991 and we discuss this and the role afforded the ETUC later in this chapter.

Membership is not confined to federations from member states of the EU, over twenty countries within Europe have federations and unions in membership. The vast majority of national-level federations within Europe are members, including now most of the ex-Communist ones; also affiliated are a number of European-level sectoral federations (European Industry Federations, EIF). Estimates are that in excess of 95 per cent of organized workers in Europe are in organizations affiliated to the ETUC.

The ETUC has long been accustomed to lobbying on a wide variety of issues within the EU. Issues include gender equality, protection over closure, health and safety and also broader issues such as social policy and macro-economic policy. However, the ETUC is a diverse organization and it would be wrong to give the impression that there is much cohesion within the movement. The size, nature, traditions and interests of the many union confederations and unions in membership vary considerably, as also does their autonomy and authority in respect of their own membership. Visser and Ebbinghaus (1992) described the ETUC as 'united but fragmented and with little internal cohesion' and, more recently, Dolvik (1997) has emphasized again the point that, like other similar organizations, there are tensions and conflicts between the secretariat of the ETUC and the national confederations that are the bulk of the members. Tensions exist because the secretariat is keen to extend its autonomy and authority to act and take initiatives at the level of the EU, to play a full role in the social dialogue at the level of the EU and as a social partner in the formulation of EU social policy, and because the national federations are in the main unwilling to cede such authority to them. Mirroring these tensions and conflicts are also tensions between the sectoral and intersectoral priorities and agendas.

International regulation and control of MNC activities

As you may have already realized, there are doubts that it is now possible effectively to regulate the activities of MNCs; in a sense effective regulation would in any event require a U-turn on the part of the regulatory authorities such as the World Trade Organization (WTO) that have promoted deregulation and liberalization of world trade. MNCs can exert pressure upon national governments to dismantle consumer protection laws and regulations and the only significant gains made from free trade have arguably been by the MNCs and not the poor countries of the world, the poor people or the consumers.

Towards the end of 1999 the WTO met in Seattle, USA, to agree upon the next round of trade liberalization. The meeting was accompanied by rioting in the streets by environmental, consumer group and trade union protestors concerned that the WTO and the interests of multinational capital and the developing countries were being allowed to destroy the environment and exploit both consumers and labour. Interestingly the USA government was among the main protagonists of the introduction into trade liberalization agreements of a set of core labour standards which would serve to protect the interests of labour in developing countries. Cynics and developing country governments argued that this was simply an attempt at protectionism on the part of developed countries concerned that about losing jobs to the cheaper developing economies (labour standards would effectively push up labour costs in the developing countries) and others saw the position of the US government as a response to the need for trade union support in the USA, given the forthcoming presidential elections in 2000.

There are a number of other international authorities and organizations interested in the various issues and that have in the past tried to secure a consensus among the various parties.

Organization for Economic Cooperation and Development (OECD)

The OECD produced as early as 1975 a Code of Practice containing Guidelines on a range of topics, one of which was Employment and Industrial Relations. This was followed in 1976 by a Declaration on Investment and Multinational Enterprises, which states that companies should not threaten to transfer all or part of their operations from one country to another in order to influence negotiations (including disputes). In other words they should not make use of their exit options referred to earlier.

The OECD Code is a series of non-obligatory recommendations. There is a committee on International Investment and Multinational Enterprises (IME), which consists of representatives of the governments of the OECD member countries, and which hears complaints about non-compliance of the guidelines. Trade unions cannot refer a complaint to the committee directly, they must go through representatives of their country serving on the committee and the opinion emanating from the committee has no legal force.

The International Labour Organization (ILO)

The ILO, established in 1919, has been influential in setting world standards in health and safety and in industrial relations. However, once again, enforcement is difficult (see Chapter 18 of Hollinshead and Leat, 1995, for a detailed account of the origin, development and initiatives of the ILO). The organization has a tripartite membership, with each country delegation comprised of representatives from employers associations, trade unions and governments. The organization sets standards of minimum provision and rights that should be complied with by the various parties in membership. However, governments affiliated to the ILO have the choice as to whether they sign up to particular policy statements, called conventions, and there is very little that the ILO can do to force a government to sign up to any given convention. Examples of the areas in which conventions have been adopted include the right to join a trade union, the right to engage in collective bargaining, health and safety and minimum terms and conditions of employment. However, there is relatively little that the ILO can do to compel governments or individual companies to comply with these standards and conventions if they are determined not to. The Conservative government in the UK in the early 1980s removed from staff at GCHQ the right to join and be represented by an independent trade union, a move that was inconsistent with the ILO convention 87 on freedom of association. But they did it and, whilst roundly condemned in many quarters, their membership of the ILO did not stop them and no action was taken against them. This same Conservative government took a number of other actions during their period of office that was inconsistent with ILO conventions.

The ILO has also produced a code of guidelines concerned with the social policy of MNCs and which sought to deal with matters such as:

- employment
- training
- working conditions
- living conditions
- professional relations.

but ultimately, as with member governments, compliance cannot be enforced, persuasive pressures may be brought to bear but at the end of the day there is little that even these international organizations can do to make a MNC do what it does not intend to.

Activity 5

Try to answer the following questions without consulting the text.

1 MNCs have choices in their approach to the management of employee relations in their foreign subsidiaries. What is the essence of the difference between a polycentric approach and an ethnocentric approach?
2 List three strategies which a MNC may use to frustrate the interests of employees organized on a national basis.

Summary

In this chapter we have noted that the increasing liberalization of international trade has been accompanied by a significant expansion of the activities and complexity of MNCs which now combine a complexity of multinational ownership with control over multinational value-adding activities.

We have noted that MNCs have a range of options when it comes to deciding how to manage employees and employee relations in foreign-based subsidiaries. Traditionally MNCs appear to have adopted either an ethnocentric or polycentric approach to the management of employee relations in their various subsidiaries; in countries where there is significant regulation of the labour market and the employment relationship it is difficult for the MNC to pursue anything other than a partially polycentric approach. However, as liberalization and deregulation continue, in combination threatening the exclusivity of national systems, there will be greater scope for the MNC to develop its own Eurocentric or geocentric approach which is company specific and crosses national borders. Whether this approach or elements of it will then impact upon national systems and possibly encourage a convergence of national systems will to some extent depend upon whether the practices are perceived by other companies to be successful or not.

The trade unions and other regulatory authorities have not so far demonstrated effectiveness at countering or influencing the activities of MNCs and there is no good reason to imagine at this stage that this will change in the foreseeable future. MNCs are able to organize their activities in such a way as to render effective opposition by unions at a national level difficult and cross-national cooperation between trade unions has not been common. There are a number of ways in which the MNC can thwart or frustrate the activities and objectives of the trade unions. The liberalization of trade across national borders and within free trade areas has enhanced the ability of the MNC to frustrate the interests of its employees if that is what it wants to do.

Activity 1

Outward FDI may lead to change in the composition of products being sold in the foreign market and can result in an increase in exports from the home country and thereby an increase in employment at home.

The FDI may lead to economic growth in the host economy which, over a period of time, may lead to increased levels of exports from the home country and thereby increased employment at home.

The FDI may be directed at marketing or sales of goods produced in the home country.

The FDI may be directed at the production at lower cost of intermediate goods which are then returned to the home country for final assembly. This may be the only way that final assembly can be retained in the home country and, therefore, while employment at home may not be increased it may be protected through FDI.

Activity 2

1 The ownership of value-adding assets, production or service activities in more than one country.
2 The term refers to the ability of the MNC to uproot or close down activities in one country and relocate them in another. This ability can be used to threaten governments, employees and their representative organizations in order to obtain concessions or guarantees.
3 Ohmae (1990) said it referred to the emergence of a borderless world or interlinked economy encompassing globalized production chains, product markets, corporate structures and financial flows. An international restructuring of product markets, production and financial markets.

Activity 3

The article demonstrates how the nature and traditions of the employment relationship in a country, which are reflective of work-related values and thereby national culture, can come under threat from merger/acquisition with or by a company from a different culture and also, of course, from the forces of international competition and globalization. Lifetime employment and promotions based on seniority are culturally significant employment traditions in Japan and this article demonstrates that they are now under threat at Nissan in Japan. It will be interesting to watch whether the introduction of merit-based promotion and financial incentives for executives work in Japan, given that they are both inconsistent with the traditions of Japanese culture and are far more consistent with certain Western cultures. This raises the issue of whether national cultures are converging, if these new practices are successful it may be indicative that work-related values in Japan have already become more Western. Alternatively, it may be argued that the introduction of these new arrangements is encouraging a convergence.

The article demonstrates the extent to which global car production has witnessed the phenomenon of merger and acquisition and confirms many of the points made in the earlier chapter on changes to the nature of work. There are references to:

- the importance of standardization of components
- flexible specialization
- the earlier impact in Europe and the West generally of practices and emphases that were in some sense borrowed from Japan as a reflection of the earlier success of Japanese manufacturers, such as the emphasis upon quality, JIT and lean manufacturing.

Activity 4

Here the trade union would be in a relatively strong position if it can halt production, since the subsidiary is the MNC's only source of supply to that national market. However, this strong position will be weakened if the MNC has the financial resources to withstand the strike for longer than the employees can afford to stay out on strike. The MNC position will also be strengthened if it can begin to supply this national market from subsidiaries in other countries. Whether this is possible will depend upon circumstances such as:

- if it has excess capacity elsewhere and the product specifications are similar
- if there is an absence of trade barriers between the two countries
- the nature of the product and the ease and cost with which it can be transported
- if the trade unions in the two countries do not cooperate with each other.

Activity 5

1 A polycentric approach is where the MNC adapts its policies, practices, preferences and procedures to the traditions, values, attitudes and regulatory regime of the host country. An ethnocentric approach is where no such adaptation is made and is where the MNC tries to manage employee relations in the host country in the same way and based upon the same assumptions as at home.

2 They can:
- shift the value-adding activity elsewhere
- stage an 'investment strike'
- exert pressure upon governments to either deregulate the labour market/employment relationship or indeed to regulate in favour of the MNC rather than its employees
- hide from the unions by having a remote locus of authority
- use their formidable financial resources to withstand industrial action.

References

Bartlett, C.A. and Ghoshal, S., 1989. *Managing Across Borders: The Transnational Solution*. Harvard Business School Press. Cambridge, Massachusetts.

Bean, R., 1985. *Comparative Industrial Relations: an Introduction to Cross-National Perspectives*. Croom Helm, London.

Dolvik, J.E., 1997, *Redrawing Boundaries of Solidarity? ETUC, Social Dialogue and the Europeanisation of Trade Unions in the 1990s*. Arena and FAFO, Oslo.

Dowling, P. and Schuler, R., 1990. *International Dimensions of Human Resource Management*. PWS, Kent

Edwards, P., *et al.*, 1996. Towards the transnational company? The global structure and organization of multinational firms. In Crompton, R., Gallie, D. and Purcell, K. (eds), *Changing Forms of Employment*. Routledge, London.

European Commission, 1998. *Employment in Europe 1997*. Luxembourg.

European Commission, 1999. *Employment in Europe 1998*. Luxembourg.

Gallin, D., 1994. *Drawing the Battle Lines Inside the New World Order*. International Union of Food and Allied Workers, Geneva.

Hamill, J., 1983. The labour relations practices of foreign owned and indigenous firms. *Employee Relations* 5(1): 14–16.

Hamill, J., 1984a. Multinational corporations and industrial relations in the UK. *Employee Relations* 6(3): 12–16.

Hamill, J., 1984b. Labour relations decision making within multinational corporations. *Industrial Relations Journal* 15(2): 30–34.

Hendry, C., 1994. *Human Resource Strategies for International Growth*. Routledge, London.

Hollinshead, G. and Leat, M., 1995. *Human Resource Management: An International and Comparative Perspective on the Employment Relationship*. Pitman, London.

Hyman, R., 1999. National industrial relations systems and transitional challenges: an essay in review. *European Journal of Industrial Relations* 5(1): 90–110.

Ietto-Gillies, G., 1997. Working with the big guys: hostility to transnationals must be replaced by co-operation. *New Economy* 4(1) pp. 12–16.

Kennedy, T., 1980. *European Labour Relations*. Lexington Books. Lexington, Massachusetts.

Leat, M., 1999. Multi-nationals and employee relations. In Hollinshead, G., Nicholls, P. and Tailby, S. (eds), *Employee Relations*. Financial Times Pitman Publishing, London.

Maurice, M., Silvestre, J.-J. and Sellier, F., 1980. Societal differences in organizing manufacturing units: a comparison of France, West Germany and Great Britain. *Organizational Studies* 1: 59–86.

Ohmae, K., 1990. *The Borderless World: Power and Strategy in the Interlinked Economy*. Harper, New York.

Perlmutter, H., 1969. The tortuous evolution of the multi-national corporation. *Columbus Journal of World Business* 4(1): 9–18.

Prahalad, C.K. and Doz, Y.L., 1987. *The Multinational Mission*. Free Press, New York.

Ronen, S. and Shenkar, O., 1985. Clustering countries on attitudinal dimensions: a review and synthesis. *Academy of Management Journal*, September, pp. 435–454.

Schregle, J., 1981. Comparative industrial relations: pitfalls and potential. *International Labour Review* 120(1) pp. 15–30.

Schulten, T., 1996. European Works Councils: prospects of a new system of European industrial relations. *European Journal of Industrial Relations* 2(3): 303–324.

UNCTAD, 1999. UNCTAD Report on World Investment 1998. Geneva.

Visser, J. and Ebbinghaus, B., 1992. Making the most of diversity? European integration and transnational organisation of labour. Greenwood, J., Grote, J.R. and Ronit, K. (eds.), *Organised Interests and the European Community*. pp. 206–237.

Wakelin, K., Girma, S. and Greenaway, D., 1999. *Wages, Productivity and Foreign Ownership in UK Manufacturing*. Centre for Research on Globalization and Labour Markets. University of Nottingham.

Additional reading

Barrell, R. and Pain, N., 1997. EU: an attractive investment. Being part of the EU is good for FDI and being out of EMU may be bad. *New Economy* 4(1) pp. 50–54.

Boyer, R., 1993. *The Convergence Hypothesis Revisited: Globalization but till the Century of Nations?* Couvertures Oranges de CEPREMAP, No. 9403, Paris.

Hodgetts, R. M. and Luthans, F. 1997. *International Management, 3rd Edition*. McGraw-Hill.

Marginson, P. and Sisson, K., 1994. The structure of transnational capital in Europe: the emerging Euro-company and its implications for industrial relations. In Hyman, R. and Ferner, A., (eds), *New Frontiers in European Industrial Relations.* Blackwell, Oxford.

Marginson, P. and Sisson, K., 1996. Multi-national companies and the future of collective bargaining: a review of the research issues. *European Journal of Industrial Relations* 2(2): 173–197.

Mueller, F. and Purcell, J., 1992. The Europeanisation of manufacturing and the decentralisation of bargaining: multinational management strategies in the European automobile industry. *International Journal of Human Resource Management* 3(1) pp. 15–34.

Chapter 4

The European Union

Chapter Outline

- Introduction
- History and membership of the EU
- Institutions and decision making processes
  Membership of the institutions
  Other institutions
- Legislative forms and decision making processes
  Legislative forms
  Decision making processes
- The social dimension
- Main initiatives
- Chapter summary

Introduction

In the previous chapters we have already referred occasionally to the EU and in this section we examine the European Union in terms of how the social dimension has and may impact upon employee relations in the UK. At the time of writing and for the foreseeable future the EU is a strange mix of a largely deregulated single market in terms of the mobility of capital, goods and services and labour, but in which there are also strong traditions of social protectionism at a national level that have not been replicated at the level of the Union (**Figure 4.1**).

There are different trajectories or paths available for the future development of the Union, the deregulated approach already present in the single market may be extended further into labour markets to cover the employment relationship. Alternatively, there may be an extension of social regu-

The Roman-German system. Here the state plays a crucial role in industrial relations. There are a core of fundamental rights and freedoms guaranteed by the Constitution and it is these that constitute the base of national industrial relations. It is common in such systems for there to be quite extensive legal regulation of areas such as working hours, the rights of employees to be represented and the mechanisms of that representation. Germany, France, the Netherlands, Belgium and Italy are quoted as being in this category / tradition.

The Anglo-Irish system. Here the role of the state is more limited and there is a much less extensive set of legislatively created and supported basic rights and protections. Governments in these countries have traditionally left more to the parties themselves and stepped in to regulate and protect only when necessary to safeguard either the national interest and / or the interests of certain vulnerable minorities, such as children. These systems are often referred to as 'voluntarist' and in this category are both the UK and Ireland. In the UK it is arguable that this tradition began to be eroded from the 1960s onwards.

The Nordic system. Prior to the enlargement of the Union in 1995 only Denmark fell into this category; however, Sweden and Finland also share this tradition. The difference between this system and that in the Anglo-Irish group is in the degree of emphasis and reliance placed on and in the Collective Agreement. It is suggested that in these countries more emphasis is placed upon the basic agreement freely entered into, usually at national or sectoral level, by both employer and trade union and it is this which provides the central element of the industrial relations system. The state has intervened to regulate only at the request of the parties.

Figure 4.1 Stereotypes of regulatory systems in the European Union. Adapted from Leat (1999)

lation at the level of the Union that results in a more extensive common floor of employee rights, protections and constraints upon the autonomy of managements. Either is possible and both could result in a greater degree of convergence in the employee relations systems and practices within the member states and across national borders: the one base of convergence being deregulation and the other a greater measure of social protectionism than currently exists within the Union as a whole. Currently one would probably expect the former rather than the latter, given the apparent relative power of the social partners and the recent trends towards deregulation in some of the more traditionally protectionist member states. Whichever direction is taken or emerges as dominant there is considerable scope for the employee relations system and practices of the UK to be impacted.

In this section we describe the history and development of the Union, the motives for its formation and the major decision making institutions and processes and we then examine some of the initiatives already taken that can be seen to have impacted upon employee relations in the UK. Inevitably we have to be selective of the initiatives examined in depth.

One point that you need to understand before going any further is that in the Union the term 'social' encompasses employment, so that terms such as 'social policy', 'social dimension' and 'social partners' all encompass the employment dimension and, for example, trade unions and employers' associations.

Objectives

After studying this chapter you will be able to:

- Understand the structure and role of the main EU institutions, including the social partners
- Distinguish between the various decision making processes
- Explain the motivations behind, and the arguments for and against, the need for a social dimension
- Discuss the main initiatives, the arguments for and against, and analyse their impact upon employee relations in the UK.

History and membership of the EU

The Union started life as the European Economic Community (EEC) in 1957 with six members (see **Figure 4.2**), later became the European Community and, in 1993, became the European Union after the ratification of the Treaty changes agreed at Maastricht in 1991. Currently there are fifteen members and a long list of aspiring member states in eastern and southern Europe (see **Figures 4.2** and **4.3**).

The aspirant members can be seen in **Figure 4.3** and these are divided into two groups, those likely to be in the first wave of enlargement and others who are anxious to join but not so far advanced in terms of being able to satisfy the criteria for membership.

Aspirant members have to satisfy a mix of economic, social and industrial and political standards, as indicated in **Figure 4.4**.

In a document entitled *Agenda 2000*, issued by the Commission in 1997, various reasons were given for the judgements on readiness that they had made. Among these were the following:

- Slovakia was singled out as having satisfied the economic criteria but not those relating to democracy, human rights and political stability
- Bulgaria, Romania, Latvia and Lithuania were considered to pass the tests of democracy and human rights but were advised that they have much to do in terms of economic and legal reform
- Turkey was criticized for its (lack of) performance on human rights, for democratic deficiencies and lack of achievement of economic stability.

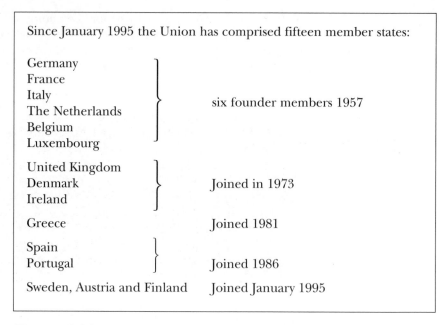

Figure 4.2 Member states of the European Union

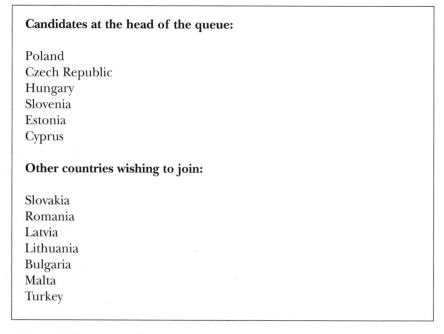

Figure 4.3 Aspirant members

Political – institutional stability to guarantee principles of:

liberty, democracy, the rule of law and respect for human rights, fundamental freedoms and protection for minorities and political union

Economic and financial – commitment to:

- monetary union
- a market economy
- the ability to handle the competition and market forces.

Full membership requires the adoption of the *acquis communitaire* – the body of laws, rights and obligations already adopted by the EU

'all that has been achieved so far, lock, stock and barrel'

Figure 4.4 Criteria for membership

The criteria for membership are not universally popular and are criticized for being too biased in favour of the requirements of business and capital rather than those of the Union's citizens. One of the critical suggestions concerns the perceived need for a Charter of core or fundamental rights, duties and obligations, acceptance of which would form the base for membership as well as forming the base upon which the EU might become a citizens' Europe, a Europe consistent with the principles and traditions of social democracy and not dominated by the single market.

Despite the fact that it was always the intention to create a free trade area and eventually aspire to the creation of a single market there were also other powerful motivations for the formation of the Union back in the 1950s. Among these was the desire to prevent further war within Europe and also to halt the spread of Communism. It was felt that nations bound together in economic and trading terms would be less likely to go to war with each other and, in particular, this was the concern of Germany and France who have a long history of conflict between them. On these grounds judgement of the experiment must be that it has been a success.

Whether in the future citizens of the member states will consider these sufficient benefits will be influenced no doubt by their perception of whether the Union results in greater wealth for all and whether they feel they are being exploited by big business, politicians and officials who may be perceived to be looking after their own interests rather than those of their constituents and citizens.

Institutions and decision-making processes

There are four main Union institutions: the **European Commission,** hereafter referred to as the Commission, the **Council of the European Union** (often also known as the **Council of Ministers**), the **European Parliament** (EP) and the **Court of Justice of the European Communities** (ECJ). The main roles of each of these institutions and the relationship between them are indicated in **Figure 4.5**. The important points to note from this figure are:

- the Council has the decision-making role in respect of treaty revisions, policy determination and the adoption of legislation
- the Commission has the formal role of initiating discussions on policy and legislation and producing the initial proposals (the right of initiative) as well as being responsible for the administration and implementation of the decisions taken; this includes the administration and expenditure of the EU budget
- the Parliament has, until recently, acted as a source of comment upon Commission and Council proposals and positions, but without any decision-making role in respect of legislation and policy. More recently, veto and delaying powers have been obtained through treaty amendments and this is referred to later in respect of the co-decision procedure. The Parliament also has the right to approve the appointment and membership of the Commission and Union budget
- the ECJ has the role of adjudicating on and interpreting the law within the Union, it is the senior court within the judicial system in the EU, the court of last resort.

Membership of the institutions

The Council of the European Union (the Council of Ministers and the European Council)

The Council is an intergovernmental body. Whenever it sits the membership is made up of representatives of the national governments of all the member states. The meetings of the Council tend to be subject-based and the national government representatives are normally the members of those governments with specific responsibilities for the subject matter under discussion, so that as an example when the Council meets as a Social Affairs Council it will be comprised of the representatives of the member state governments with those particular responsibilities. The Council, therefore, is not a directly elected body and the members are not accountable to any particular constituency of electors, they are accountable to their own member state governments.

When issues can be decided by a **qualified majority** each member state is afforded a number of votes linked indirectly to population (see later for the

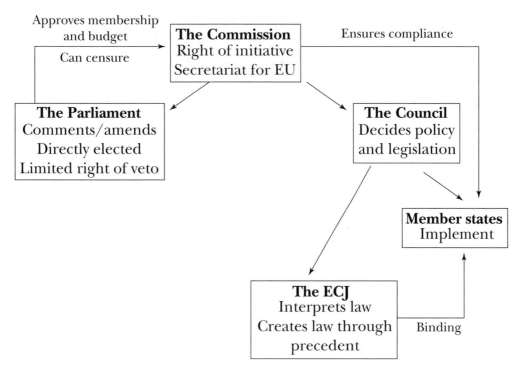

Figure 4.5 The role and relationships of the major institutions

areas of subject matter to which this applies and for details of votes per country). Twice a year the Heads of Member State Governments meet as the **European Council** and it is in these meetings that Treaty revisions and issues such as the enlargement of the Union are determined.

European Commission

Formally the Commission is comprised of a specific number of Commissioners (currently twenty) and it is this group which agrees policy proposals and other initiatives before they go outside for consultation and discussion. The Commissioners are nominated by individual member state governments and, as noted in **Figure 4.5**, their collective appointment is subject to the approval of the European Parliament. The 'big five' member states, Germany, France, Italy, the UK and Spain, all have the right to nominate two Commissioners each and the other ten states each nominate one. Once appointed as a Commissioner they are supposed to work for and represent the Commission and the Union as a whole and not their home member states. The Commission provides the secretariat for the Union and the twenty Commissioners are supported by a civil service. Each Commissioner is allocated responsibility for a particular area of subject matter and he/she is supported by a staff organized in departments called Directorates General (D-G) – a fairly traditional and simple functional structure.

The D-G that deals with the subject matter of employment and other areas of social policy is DG V (five) and is titled 'Employment, Industrial Relations and Social Affairs'.

The European Parliament

As noted above, the Parliament has a history of little power and influence despite the fact that it is the only directly elected institution within the EU. Each of the member states has the right to elect directly a particular number of Members of the European Parliament (MEPs), this allocation is intended to be roughly proportional on population grounds. The numbers of MEPs for each country are shown in **Figure 4.6**. Currently the total is 626, though this may well increase, as the Union is enlarged. Existing members set 700 as the maximum.

Though elected by electors in and on behalf of a particular member state, the MEPs tend to ally themselves in multinational political groupings. They are not sent to the Parliament with a brief to look after the interests of the particular member state from which they come.

As noted in **Figure 4.5** the EP also approves the EU budget and has powers of approval over the membership of the Commission. The Parliament can in certain circumstances adopt a censure motion on the Commission and force its resignation.

The co-decision procedure provides the Parliament with a more influential role in the decision-making process and as the applicability of the co-decision procedure is extended so will the importance of the Parliament's role. (See later in this chapter.)

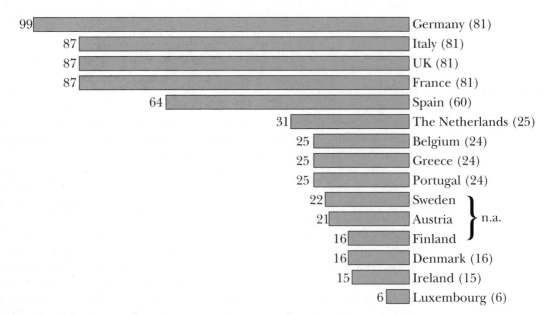

Figure 4.6 Number of MEPs for each member state of the EU in 1995 (figure for 1989 in parentheses)

The Court of Justice of the European Communities

The ECJ is made up of fifteen judges, one from each member state, and nine Advocates-General (A-Gs) who are drawn from the ranks of academics, judges and lawyers in the member states. Cases that reach the ECJ are given to an A-G. He/she conducts a preliminary investigation and comes to a preliminary opinion on the merits of the complaint or application before it is heard by the Court itself. Very rarely are the opinions of A-Gs not followed by the Court.

Other institutions

In addition to the four main EU institutions above there are a number of others that are relevant to the subject matter of employee relations. In particular there are the organizations known as the 'social partners'. We have already discussed one of these in the previous chapter concerned with the regulation of MNCs and their activities in the ETUC.

The social partners

At EU level the **social partners** participate in a process known as the social dialogue. This process occurs most publicly at the level of the Union itself and is between the **European Trade Union Confederation** (ETUC), which is the single representative of the labour movement at EU level, and the employers' associations: the **Union of Industrial and Employers Confederations of Europe** (UNICE), which represents primarily private-sector employers, and the **European Centre of Public Enterprises** (CEEP), representing primarily public-sector employer interests.

The European Trade Union Confederation (ETUC)

It has long been the view of the Commission that the internal market and the deregulation implied by and in its creation would only be possible with the support/acquiescence of European labour. It is therefore necessary that the labour movement within the EU has a voice and it is in this context that the Commission has been supportive of the ETUC, both politically and financially. However, as was intimated above, the organization is not coherent in the priority afforded particular agenda items and there has been conflict both between national and sectoral affiliates and between them and those who give priority to the agenda to be pursued at EU level in determining the EU's social policy.

Employers' organizations

UNICE was formed in the late 1950s and, like the ETUC, represents employers from a much wider constituency than the EU. Unlike the ETUC, the organization has not been keen to become involved with the Commission and ETUC in policy making as a social partner, it has done so but with reluctance and really only because it was concerned that refusal to participate would be counterproductive; at least by participating they would be able to influence the outcomes and hopefully mitigate what they perceive as the worst excesses of labour market regulation, employment and social protectionism.

CEEP. The membership tends to be comprised of individual employers rather than federations and the geographic spread of the members of this organization is much smaller than that of either of the above. As with UNICE, the preference of the membership would be not to participate in the process of social dialogue and social policy formulation in a direct way.

Within the UK at a national level the social partners are the Trades Union Congress (TUC) and the Confederation of British Industry (CBI), though they have not traditionally been referred to in these terms, and they are both affiliates of the appropriate social partners at the level of the EU (see Chapters 7 and 8). Both of these national federations are supporters of the EU concept, though for different reasons.

Legislative forms and decision-making processes

Legislation adopted at EU level takes precedence over national legislation and in the case of conflict or inconsistency between them it is the EU legislation that takes precedence. EU legislation cannot be countermanded at the level of the individual member state. As noted above, new entrants to the Union have to accept the *acquis communitaire* – the existing body of laws and regulations.

Legislative forms

Legislation within the Union can be adopted using a range of different mechanisms and instruments.

Regulations

These are relatively rare but, once adopted, they are applicable directly and generally throughout the EU, they are immediately binding on member states and individuals and do not require any action at member state level to render them effective. The Council can empower the Commission to make regulations.

Directives

Most of the legislation so far adopted in the field of employee relations has been adopted using this form of instrument. A directive is not immediately applicable, and requires some action at member state level for it to be given effect, though this action need not be legislative (implementation can, for example, be through agreement by the social partners).

Normally a directive specifies the objective to be achieved and the date by which it should be achieved, usually referred to as the implementation date, but leaves the precise means of achieving the objective to the individual member states. However, states cannot avoid implementing unwelcome directives because, once the implementation date is reached and irrespective of the progress made at national level towards implementation, the directive becomes the law within the Union. There are further rules with respect to organizations in the public sector or which are 'Emanations of the State', since directives generally become applicable to and in such organizations upon adoption rather than at the specified implementation date.

Decisions

These can be made by the Council and, in some instances, by the Commission and once made they are binding on the parties that sought the decision in the first place. They do not automatically have general effect.

There are also a range of non-legally binding instruments that can be used such as **Recommendations**, **Communications**, **Codes of Conduct or Practice** and **Opinions**. These are often used when one or more of the main institutions wants to exert influence but either knows that they will not gain sufficient support for the proposal to be adopted as legislation or that they don't really have the competence to act. Competence in this sense is provided by the Treaty of Rome, subsequently amended, and if the Treaty does not provide for the Union institutions to act in a certain field of activity then it and they can't lawfully do so. The Treaty provides the EU with its constitution.

Activity 1

Try to answer the following short answer questions without re-reading the text.

1 Which of the central institutions has the right of initiative?
2 Which of the central institutions has the role of adopting legislation?
3 What is the difference between a directive and a regulation?
4 How does the ECJ create the law?
5 What is the *acquis communitaire*?
6 What are the roles of the European Parliament?
7 Who are the social partners?

Decision-making processes

In much the same way as there are different legislative forms and instruments there are also a number of processes through which legislation can be adopted. Initially all legislation had to be adopted unanimously via a procedure known as the **consultation procedure**. Each member state, even the smallest, had the ability to veto legislative proposals that it did not like or want. However, the gradual enlargement of the EU (see **Figure 4.3**), allied to the decision taken in 1986 to create the single market (given that this would require an enormous amount of relevant legislation, much of it deregulatory, to be adopted and implemented in a relatively short time), enhanced the requirement for the decision-making process to be speeded up and encouraged the member states to agree to a new procedure for some areas of subject matter, including many though not all of those that would be necessary prior to the creation of the single market. This new procedure provided for legislation on a certain limited number of subject areas to be adopted by a majority vote ('Qualified Majority Vote' is the term actually used) and the name given to this procedure is the **cooperation procedure**. **Figure 4.7** shows diagrammatically how both of these procedures work, to all intents and purposes the difference between them is:

● that the cooperation procedure provides for a second stage or reading by the Parliament, arguably a greater opportunity for the Parliament to influence the legislative process
● for the legislation to be adopted by a majority rather than requiring unanimity.

We mentioned above that each of the member states has a number of votes that it can cast in the cooperation procedure; legislation adopted through this process must acquire a support level of approximately 70 per cent of the votes available, at the moment this works out at 62 of a total available 87 votes. Looked at from the opposite direction it requires 26 votes to block a proposal – this is sometimes referred to as the blocking minority.

Note that where on second reading the Parliament has rejected the common position adopted by the Council at the end of the first round of consultations, the Council can only overturn that rejection or proceed in accordance with its original common position on the basis of unanimity. If the council is happy to accept the amendments made by the Parliament on second reading then it can proceed on the basis of a qualified majority. However, in both of these processes the final decision rests with the Council and, if the member states who provide the members of the Council have a mind to they can reject the amendments and/or do nothing.

The Single European Act (SEA) did not extend the cooperation procedure to legislative interventions concerning the free movement of people and, most importantly from the viewpoint of employee relations, to the rights and interests of employees; it was only for health and safety at work issues that matters of direct concern in the workplace would be governed by this new procedure and the opportunity for legislative proposals to be adopted by majority vote.

For many within the Union this was an inadequate outcome and there

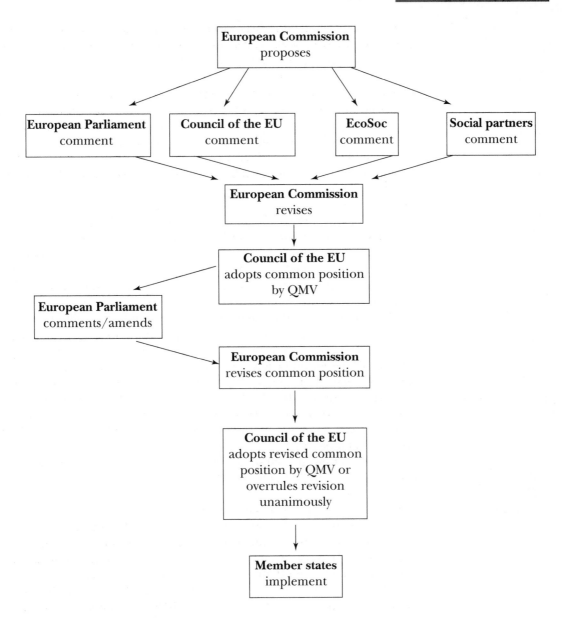

Figure 4.7 The cooperation procedure

have been several arguments since involving member states and the Commission as to whether a particular proposal fell inside the appropriate definitions and interpretations of health and safety. The most infamous of these concerned the UK and the directive adopted in 1994 that sought to protect employees from being forced to work long hours. The ECJ was required to adjudicate on this issue (see below).

Towards the end of the 1980s there were interests within the Commission and a number of member states that wanted to achieve two objectives with respect to the decision-making procedures:

- to enhance the role of the social dialogue in the decision-making process, to provide the social partners with a more influential role in determining social policy and the legislative framework within which employee relations within the Union were to be conducted,
- to extend the range of subject matter in the social and employment field upon which decisions on policy and legislation could be adopted via a majority vote.

The conflict over these issues came to a head at the Heads of Government summit meeting at Maastricht at the end of 1991. The summit was to agree on amendments to the original Treaty of Rome and amongst the proposals for consideration were proposals on each of these procedural issues. The main opponent to both proposals was the UK government and, since changes to the Treaty require unanimity, the UK was able to block the proposals. However, the other member states and the Commission were keen to make progress and were extremely fed up with the attitude of the UK government. Eventually, they and the UK agreed a mechanism whereby the other countries would be able to proceed but without the new procedures applying to the UK. Finally, in 1997, the new Labour government agreed at Amsterdam (another Heads of Government summit to discuss and agree Treaty changes) that the procedures adopted by the other member states at Maastricht should be brought fully into the Treaty and apply to the UK as well as to the other fourteen members.

What then were the substance of these changes? In effect we are confronted with two new but related procedures.

The protocol procedure – social dialogue procedure

The main elements of this procedure are shown in **Figure 4.8**.

The essence of these arrangements is that the Commission can, on its own initiative or at the request of the social partners, invite the social partners at the level of the Union to try to come to an agreement on social policy issues. This can then be used as a draft directive which the Commission can issue and take through the consultation or cooperation procedures, whichever are appropriate given the particular subject matter. Where the social partners do reach an agreement there are two possible options with respect to its implementation:

1 The first is to leave it to the parties at national level, presumably through some form of implementation arrangements agreed between the partners and possibly with government at national level giving legal effect to the arrangements agreed by the national-level partners. Some member states have a tradition of dealing with employee relations matters this way.

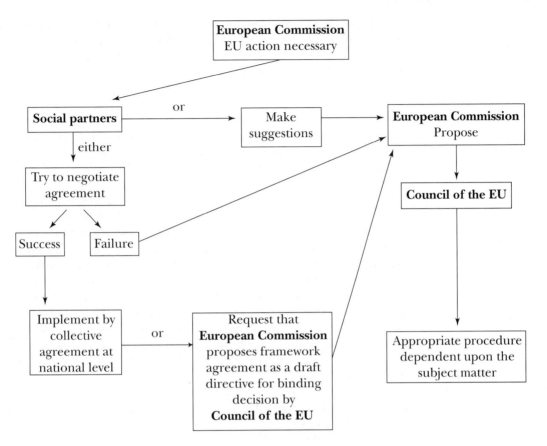

Figure 4.8 The protocol procedure

2 The second provides for the partners to jointly request that the Commission makes a proposal to the Council upon which the Council then makes a decision, the latter being legally binding. This is the procedure that has so far been used on the occasions that the social partners have reached agreement. In each case they have asked the Commission to propose a draft directive to the Council.

Examples of agreements that have been achieved using this procedure and that were then used as the basis for the adoption of directives are those on:

● rights of parents to unpaid leave to look after children and other dependents
● rights of part-time workers in respect to those of full-time workers
● guaranteeing non-discrimination between workers with fixed-term contracts and those with open-ended contracts and regulating the use of fixed-term contracts.

These are Directive numbers 96/34 and 97/81 and 99/70, respectively.

The intention is that any such agreements reached between the social partners should take the form of frameworks or agreements on principle, the details to be worked out at individual member state level.

The co-decision procedure

One of the main purposes of the introduction of this procedure was to give the Parliament a greater role in the decision-making process. This new procedure allows the Parliament to effectively veto proposals and positions adopted by the Council if it disagrees with them. Where the Parliament feels that the Council has taken too little attention/rejects amendments supported by the Parliament or where the Parliament has decided to reject a position adopted by the Council the new procedure provides for conciliation between Council and Parliament. However, if this conciliation fails the Parliament can prevent the proposal/position being adopted. It is relevant to employee relations because, since the ratification and implementation from 1 May 1999 of the Treaty agreements and amendments at Amsterdam in 1997, this procedure replaces the co-operation procedure as the one to be used when the subject matter is such that decisions can be adopted via a majority vote.

As noted above the range of subject matter to which this procedure will apply was extended at Amsterdam to include, in addition to health and safety in the workplace:

- improvement in particular of the working environment to protect workers' health and safety
- working conditions
- the information and consultation of workers
- the integration of persons excluded from the labour market
- equality between men and women with regard to labour market opportunities and treatment at work
- ensuring application of the principle of equal opportunities and treatment between the sexes including the principle of equal pay for equal work or work of equal value.

It is important to realize that with the specific exception of these areas of subject matter and on condition that the Treaty actually gives the Union the competence to take action in a particular area, unanimity is still required. For example, if the Union decided, after the insertion of an appropriate enabling provision in the Treaty agreed at Amsterdam, that it wanted to extend the rights of equality of pay and treatment adopted in respect of men and women to also encompass people of different races, such a proposal would still need to be adopted unanimously; that means that each and every member state no matter how big or small would have to agree and each would therefore have a right to veto the proposals. Such a directive was being discussed at the time of writing.

Activity 2

Outline the main differences between the consultation, co-operation and protocol procedures concentrating upon the roles of the social partners and the EP.

The social dimension

Having briefly introduced the main institutions and decision-making procedures, and particularly the role of the social partners in those procedures, it is now time to identify and briefly discuss the nature and content of the initiatives that have been taken within the Union that can be seen to impact reasonably directly on employee relations in the UK.

First you must realize that the legislative regulation of the employment relationship, employee rights and protections and the conflicts that occur between the parties to that relationship and their representatives, is much more part of the mainland European tradition than it is in the UK (see **Figure 4.1** on different regulatory systems and traditions). We discuss the relevance of ideology to the role that government plays and indeed to the expectations of the other parties in employee relations in Chapter 5. In the main the other member states have traditions of social protectionism and corporatism and variations on those themes. In the UK we have traditions of liberal collectivism and an emphasis upon voluntary collective bargaining and non-intervention by government. The Nordic states have also had a traditional reliance upon collective bargaining but in those states the collective agreement is much more likely to be given legal effect by government.

However, as is discussed in Chapter 5, the period since the late 1970s in the UK has been one in which governments have placed much greater reliance in:

- the process of individual exchange, initiative and enterprise
- the operation of market forces, deregulation of the labour market and the employment relationship including the removal of employee protection
- this has been accompanied by a very determined effort to reduce the power and influence of the trade unions.

It ought not therefore to be surprising that the UK governments of the period 1979–1997 were at odds with the wishes and intentions of most of the other member states and with the Commission.

Before we go any further, though, it is important to understand the main motivation for the creation of a social dimension to the Union and in particular to the single market and therefore the motivation behind the initiatives that have been taken.

Once it was decided to create the single market, thereby removing the barriers to the free movement of capital, goods, services and labour, it was feared that without legislative regulation, support for and protection of employees and other minorities, the forces of multinational capital free of restriction upon movement, acquisition and the location of investment would seek to maximize profit and locate and relocate to those areas of the Union in which costs and restrictions were least (they would engage in 'regime shopping').

Capital is very much more mobile than labour and capital would be relocated within the market to those areas, regions and countries, where the costs of production were the cheapest, a major cost often being that of labour. This would result in jobs being created in one area such as Spain or Portugal at the expense of employment levels in places such as Germany and France. The UK, with a government that was keen to create flexible and deregulated labour markets and which saw lower labour costs as a source of competitive advantage, was seen as a potential beneficiary.

Overall this phenomenon is frequently referred to as 'social dumping'. Concern about social dumping tended to be greatest in those countries with the most developed labour standards and correspondingly highest labour costs. This in turn could lead to significant disruptive effects upon:

- existing patterns of employment and terms and conditions of employment
- the distribution of income and wealth, poverty and social cohesion, both within individual countries and the Union as a whole
- equality of opportunities and pay between the sexes, and indeed the relative wealth and well-being of each of the member states.

In the main the debate has been between:

- those who considered that intervention and regulation would be necessary in order to cushion these effects and to promote the restructuring and more efficient use of labour that was both necessary and an inevitable consequence of the further economic integration envisaged in the creation of the single market
- those who take the view that while integration might have these effects the solution was to leave the market to cope and that to intervene would simply prevent the adjustment mechanisms of the market working effectively.

Union-wide commonality in the regulation of labour markets, the employment relationship, employee protections, etc. (often referred to as the creation of a level playing field within the Union) was perceived to be the way in which the worst excesses of liberalism of capital mobility and free trade would be checked. It was thought that the danger of MNCs shopping between different regulatory regimes and locating activities in those which are the most favourable (cheapest and least regulated) would be mini-mized.

The best indicator of the areas in which the Commission felt action should be taken and rights and protections provided is the **Social Charter** (see **Figure 4.9**).

The Social Charter was proposed at the Heads of Government summit at Strasbourg in 1989 but was effectively vetoed by the UK. As a consequence the Charter has no legal status. However, action has been taken to implement rights and protections in some of the areas specified. Where the Commission thought that agreement including the UK could be reached these were processed using the normal consultation or cooperation procedures, where they thought this unlikely and where possible they proceeded via what, at the time, were referred to as the protocol or social dialogue procedures (see above). Measures adopted within the protocol procedures did not apply to the UK though again, as noted above, the new Labour government agreed at Amsterdam in 1997 that these procedures should be incorporated into the Treaty and it was agreed that measures that had been adopted during the period of the UK's so-called opt-out should be retrospectively implemented in the UK.

The treaty amendments agreed at Amsterdam have given the Charter a kind of quasi legal status since the preamble of the new Social Chapter of the Treaty does refer to the Charter and specifies the intention to give effect to its contents.

However, there does appear to have been a loss of the momentum that was built up in the early 1990s and one explanation for this would be that the determination to provide a social dimension to the Union has in a sense been hijacked by the deregulatory band-wagon that is seen by many as essential to achieving and maintaining international competitiveness and as the solution to or prescription for Europe's unemployment. Interestingly the OECD, in a report in the summer of 1999, cast some doubt upon the assumed relationship between deregulated labour markets, labour flexibilities and employment. In this report the OECD suggests that a flexible labour market, in the sense that there are few employment protections and few restrictions upon management's ability to hire and fire, may benefit those unemployed in that when demand rises they are likely to be able to find work more quickly since for the employer the costs of and restrictions upon hiring are not great. The downside is that when demand falls it is likely that unemployment will rise more quickly and further. In general, regulation benefits insiders at the expense of outsiders and outsiders, once unemployed, are likely to be unemployed longer in a regulated labour market. Employment protection and labour market regulation is therefore likely to slow down the rate at which employment adjustments are made as demand changes (see also Chapter 5 on government as economic manager).

The rights proposed and incorporated in the Charter fell into twelve main sections:

1 Freedom of movement of labour, including the removal of obstacles arising from the non-recognition of diplomas and equivalent occupational qualifications
2 Employment and remuneration, including the rights to fair and equitable wages thereby enabling a decent standard of living
3 Improvement of living and working conditions, specific reference was made to working hours, weekly rest periods and annual leave, temporary, fixed-term and part-time contracts
4 Social protection, here the terms used are adequate and sufficient
5 Freedom of association and collective bargaining. Both workers and employers should have a right to form and join, or not, associations for the defence of their economic and social interests. The associations should have the right to negotiate and conclude collective agreements and the right to take collective action including strike action. Conciliation, arbitration and mediation should be encouraged. This section also refers to improvement of the dialogue between the social partners at European level
6 Vocational training, all workers should have the right of access to such training and retraining throughout their working life
7 Equal treatment for men and women should be assured and equal opportunities should be developed. Particular mention is made of equality of access to employment, remuneration, working conditions, social protection, education, vocational training and career development. Mention was also made of measures to facilitate both men and women reconciling their work and family lives/obligations
8 Information, consultation and participation of workers, with particular reference to organizations with establishments or companies in two or more member states. In particular these rights should apply in cases of technological change having major implications for the workforce in terms of working conditions and/or work organization, where restructuring or mergers also have an impact upon the employment of workers and in cases of collective redundancy procedures
9 Health, protection and safety at the workplace. Specific mention is also made of training, information and consultation
10 Protection of children and adolescents, they should receive equitable remuneration, be protected from working below a certain age and their development, vocational training and access to employment needs should be met. There should also be limits on the duration of such work and on working at night. There should also be an entitlement to initial vocational training upon leaving full-time education
11 Elderly persons upon retirement should have an entitlement to a decent standard of living
12 Disabled persons should be entitled to measures aimed at improving their social and professional integration and in particular to vocational training, ergonomics, accessibility and mobility.

Figure 4.9 The Social Charter. Adapted from Leat (1999)

Explain the relationship between regime shopping and social dumping and why people were worried about the latter.

Main initiatives

So far the main initiatives taken have been concerned to:

- achieve equality between the sexes in terms of pay, access to and treatment at work
- provide employees and their representatives with rights to information and consultation in certain specific circumstances and also in community-scale undertakings – see European Works Council (EWC) Directive 94/95
- achieve an improvement in the working conditions and other measures taken to ensure the health and safety of employees at work
- provide employees with some limited protection from coercion and exploitation
- encourage the social dialogue at EU and sectoral level.

So far there has been relatively little intervention in or interference with the established procedures and processes of collective interaction and conflict resolution in individual member states. It has been suggested, however, that the EWC Directive does signal a change of direction in this respect, since it does specify the procedures and content of information and consultation as well as providing a means to limit the ability of the MNC – Community-scale undertaking – to take decisions in one country that affect employees in another without their knowledge, to play employees in one country off against those in another. However, at the time of writing and for the foreseeable future there are no proposals for the Union to regulate:

- minimum levels of pay
- the right of freedom of association (this includes the right to join a trade union or employers' association)
- the right to strike or impose a lock-out
- the process and status of collective bargaining and/or determination.

Activity 4

Why do you think the social protocol or dialogue procedure was so abhorrent to the 1991 government in the UK that they vetoed its inclusion in the Treaty agreed at Maastricht?

Equality

One of the apparent inconsistencies in the Union's competence has been in the area of equality. Since the original Treaty of Rome in 1957 the Union has had the competence to act in the area of equal pay between the sexes and subsequently it was decided that the Union also had an implied competence in the area of equality of treatment between the sexes on the grounds that this constituted a fundamental human right. The same competence has not applied to other areas of equality: race, ethnicity, age, disability, colour, religion, etc. One of the potentially most significant agreements at Amsterdam applies in this area. We now have a new Article 4 which provides the Council acting **unanimously** with the power to take

Quote

> appropriate action to combat discrimination based on sex, racial or ethnic origin, religion or belief, disability, age or sexual orientation.

Within months of this agreement the new Labour government in the UK was expressing its determination to secure EU-wide legislation outlawing discrimination on the grounds of race and ethnic origin, though it has to be admitted that some other member states will have much greater difficulty with this proposal.

Despite the competence of the Union to act in support of equality between the sexes and the measures that have been taken there are still at the turn of the millennium considerable degrees of inequality and discrimination. There are inequalities of pay, access and opportunity to work and thereby participation rates, to benefits and treatment at work and consequently also in career progression and achievement. The Commission's (1997) *Annual Report on Equal Opportunities for 1996* suggests that the scale of the earnings gap between the genders has changed little over the years despite the existence of the legislation. They conclude that women on average earn some 20 per cent less than their male counterparts. Among manual workers women seem to earn between 65 and 90 per cent of male earnings, variations within this range being apparent between countries, and they suggest that while there is relatively little data it seems that the gender pay gap in the non-manual sector is actually wider still, commonly somewhere between 30 and 40 per cent. Additionally they point out that the gender wage gap tends to be smaller for single women and at younger ages and larger for those with children. It also seems to be the case that the presence of minimum wage arrangements beneficially affect the gender pay gap. The gender pay gap seems to be previously a product of: men and women doing different types of jobs; working women on average being younger than working men; and educational levels and types for women being different to those for men.

As with participation rates (see Figure 4.10) the gender pay gap appears narrowest in the northern member states, Sweden, Finland and Denmark, and widest in Austria, Ireland and the UK.

Activity rates	Total 1997	Men 1997	Women 1975/1997
EU	67.8	77.8	45.6/57.7
Belgium	63.1	72.7	38.7/53.3
Denmark	82.4	87.9	63.4/76.8
Germany	68.7	77.1	49.1/60.2
Greece	62.8	79.8	33.8/47.1
Spain	61.3	75.6	30.0/47.3
France	68.5	75.7	54.0/61.5
Ireland	64.3	78.0	36.1/50.4*
Italy	58.4	73.1	33.2/43.9
The Netherlands	70.4	81.3	35.3/59.2
Luxembourg	62.8	77.7	39.9/48.9
Austria	73.0	83.3	50.8/62.8
Portugal	72.5	82.1	52.0/63.6
Finland	74.0	76.8	67.3/71.2
Sweden	77.4	79.6	70.8/75.0
United Kingdom	76.2	84.4	54.0/68.0

*First time ever above 50 per cent

Figure 4.10 Labour force activity rates in EU by gender. *Source: Employment in Europe 1998*

It is more difficult to obtain statistical evidence on inequalities of treatment but the values in **Figure 4.10** show the inequalities between men and women in terms of their active participation in the labour force. There are both considerable inequalities between the male and female participation rates in the Union as a whole and in the majority of countries, but the figure also demonstrates that there are big differences between countries in the female rate of participation, with the highest rates being in the northern member states. At the same time, the values demonstrate that over the last twenty years or so there has been an increase in the female rate in all countries within the Union.

The Commission has produced evidence of a positive relationship between educational attainment levels and the ability to find and remain in employment. They have come to a number of conclusions concerning this and the issue of gender equality:

- for women, a good level of education seems to be even more important in finding a job than for men
- many women with low educational attainment do not enter the labour market at all
- women tend to be more qualified than men for the jobs they do
- the less well educated men and women are more likely to be unemployed and the relationship between level of educational attainment and propensity to be unemployed is more marked for women.

The persistence of gender inequalities raises a number of issues and questions, the most fundamental of which must relate to the causes of the inequalities and to the adequacy both of the measures taken and their implementation. These issues and the measures taken are discussed in some detail in Leat (1998). We have hinted at some of the potential causes and below we outline the main measures taken. We also later examine the issue of inequality in the context of devising an equal opportunities policy and appropriate procedures (Chapter 11) and we also examine the issue of female participation in the labour force in the section on labour markets in Chapter 6.

Pay

As noted above, the issue of equality of pay between the sexes was addressed directly in the original Treaty of Rome. Currently men and women should receive equal pay for work of equal value, though it is only since the Treaty amendments agreed in Amsterdam in 1997 that **equal value** is actually referred to in the Treaty. The definition of pay is quite wide and includes 'the ordinary basic or minimum wage or salary and any other consideration, whether in cash or in kind, which the worker receives, directly or indirectly, in respect of his employment from his employer'.

While this seems to be a reasonably comprehensive definition or indication of what constitutes pay there have over the years been a number of cases taken to the ECJ in order to clarify particular doubts, for example:

- retirement pensions and redundancy payments (Barber *v.* Guardian Royal Exchange Assurance Group)
- other *ex gratia* payments made after the contract has ended (Garland *v.* British Rail Engineering).

This Article was given specific effect in the UK via the Equal Pay Act of 1970, before the UK's membership of the EU but undoubtedly influenced by the prospect of joining. In addition to doubts and queries about the precise meaning of **equal pay** and what might be included as pay, there have also been considerable concerns as to what exactly is meant by **equal work** and also **equal value**. A directive (75/117) was adopted in 1975 in order to clarify these latter points (The Equal Value Regulations of 1984 constitute the relevant UK legislation) but problems persist, as can be seen from the fact that as recently as 1996 the Commission felt it advisable to issue a Code of Practice on the subject – The Code of Practice on The Implementation of Equal Pay for Work of Equal Value for Women and Men (COM (96) 336).

This Code really seeks to address issues of indirect as opposed to direct discrimination in that it is concerned to advise management and trade union negotiators to be careful when designing job evaluation or payment systems so that systems are not designed that indirectly discriminate against one of the sexes. Examples of system characteristics that may be discriminatory could include: arrangements that attach pay to the possession of longevity of continuous service, the completion of specified training and an ability to work flexible hours. Interestingly the Code states quite clearly that the prime responsibility for the avoidance of discrimination rests with the employers.

There are a number of other difficulties associated with the concept of value, one of which relates to the criteria used for calculating value. For example, should the criteria be:

- the effort, skill and responsibility put into the work, or
- the content of the work, or
- a measure of the value of the output.

Again, over the years there have been a number of landmark ECJ decisions on the issues referred to here but the bottom line is that inequality remains and is significant.

Treatment

The directive on Equal Pay was followed by the Equal Treatment Directive in 1976 (76/207) which sought to ban discrimination on the grounds of sex in all aspects of employment. The UK implementing legislation was the 1976 Sex Discrimination Act and, more recently, the Employment Act of 1989.

The ECJ has also had a role to play in this area of equal treatment, interpreting the legislation and its meaning. In recent times much of this judicial activity has been in connection with issues relating to part-time workers and their rights in comparison with those of full-time workers and, as we have already noted above, there has recently been a directive adopted on this topic pursuant to the agreement reached by the social partners in the social protocol–social dialogue procedures. This initiative had been given considerable impetus by various court decisions since early 1994, which have ruled that it was sex discrimination of an indirect nature to discriminate between part-time and full-time employees in terms of rights to redundancy payments, rights to join an occupational pension scheme and rights to claim unfair dismissal. It was indirect discrimination because the majority of part-time workers and fixed-term employees were female and to discriminate against these categories of contract was to discriminate against women.

It will also be easier to adopt legislation in this area in the future given that equality in respect of treatment and opportunities at work are now among the subjects upon which legislation can be adopted via a majority vote whereas, until the agreement in Amsterdam, unanimity was required. Other legislative interventions in this area include:

- The Directive on Parental Leave (96/34)
- The Directive on the Protection of Pregnant Workers (92/85), even though this was adopted as a health and safety issue.

In addition, there are some non-binding instruments relevant to issues of equality between the sexes at work and in connection with employment, these are:

- Council Recommendation 92/241 concerned with childcare which, amongst other things, encourages the promotion of flexible working as well as a sharing of parental responsibilities
- Council Resolution on Balanced Participation of Men and Women in Decision-making 95/C168/02
- there is also a Commission document and Code of Practice on the Dignity of Women and Men at Work, each of which seek to address the issue of sexual harassment at work and provide policy guidance to practitioners as well as to member state governments and the social partners as formal participants (see also Chapter 11).

One of the issues relating to equality of opportunity and treatment that has caused most consternation within the Union and particularly the Commission concerns the distinction between positive action and positive discrimination. When does action taken to assist the disadvantaged group, for example the organization and funding of training programmes for women who want to return to work after having children to update them with new technologies and skills so that they have greater opportunity, become unlawful discrimination against men?

This particular issue achieved an unwelcome notoriety as a result of an ECJ decision in 1995 in the Kalanke case. One of the regional governments in Germany was pursuing a recruitment, selection and promotion policy that gave automatic priority to women who, it was felt, were under-represented. Automatic preference was given to women as long as they had the same qualifications as any men that may also be competing for the job. The ECJ found the practice to be in contravention of Directive 76/207/EEC (the directive on Equal Treatment) and found that rules and procedures which give one sex **absolute** and **unconditional** priority goes beyond promoting equal treatment or opportunities and oversteps the lawful provisions for positive action. The ECJ found that to **guarantee** women priority went too far.

It seems therefore that positive action giving one sex **absolute** and **uncon-**

ditional priority is unlawful but, as long as the positive action consists of measures such as targets in terms of quotas and time limits, which express a preference but which also allow for exception, then it should remain lawful.

We have not in this section considered to any extent the causes of inequality between the sexes though we have hinted at some, these are addressed in Chapter 11. We list below a range of more commonly propounded explanations and, as we pointed out earlier, if the measures taken by the EU and national governments are to be effective they should seek to address those attitudes and/or phenomena that are considered to provide realistic explanations. Examples of factors that have been suggested as 'causes' or as explanatory variables include:

- birth rates where the relationship tends to be inverse
- the existence of supporting legislation and the presence of an enforcing agency
- the size of the service sector in which employment is in the region of 80 per cent female
- problems associated with gender stereotyping and dominant social attitudes
- the availability of education and training for women
- the availability of part-time and temporarily flexible work
- whether or not maternity leave and/or pay is provided
- the age of the youngest child
- the availability of childcare facilities and their cost
- the availability of parental leave.

One of the apparent paradoxes of this issue is that the measures taken to enhance equality, whether it be in respect of pay or treatment may effectively increase the relative cost of that labour. Examples might include extending to part-time workers the same employment rights and benefits as full-time workers receive on a pro rata basis, or enhanced provisions with respect to maternity leave or maternity pay. If the demand for female labour relative to male labour is price-sensitive, then the impact of measures to enhance equality may have unwanted and unintended effects.

Activity 5

Try to think through the difference between positive action and positive discrimination and write it down in your own words.

Employee participation

Most member state governments within the Union, and certainly the Employment and Social Affairs Directorate within the Commission, have shown themselves over the years to be sympathetic to the notion of employees and their representatives having a role in decision making within employing organizations and also within the economy as a whole. This is demonstrated in the Commission's 1997 consultative Green Paper *Partnership for a New Organization of Work*, which is concerned with issues of employee participation and involvement. The authors of this document argue the desirability of 'A new balance of regulatory powers between the State and the social partners, in particular in the areas connected with the internal management of firms.' and 'the need to review and strengthen the existing arrangements for workers' involvement in their companies' and their intention to launch 'consultations with the social partners on the advisability and direction of Community action in the field of information and consultation of employees at national level'.

Within the Union (see **Figure 4.1** on the different regulatory systems) there are considerable variations in the:

- mechanisms used
- the levels at which it occurs
- the range of subject matter
- the extent to which the practice is legally regulated.

In recent years also the Commission and some of the member states have become more supportive of schemes designed to give employees a financial stake in the ownership and/or performance of their employing organization. In Chapter 5 we examine different ideologies and their relevance for the role that government should perform and the arguments for and against employee participation. We also examine some mechanisms of participation in Chapter 9. Here we must content ourselves with the motives of the Union and the measures that have been taken at this level.

There is a history stretching back to the 1970s of EU initiatives of various kinds designed to provide legislatively supportable rights for employees and their representatives. In the main, these initiatives have been concerned to promote participation of a representative and downward communication/consultative nature, though some of the earlier initiatives were more ambitious, for example the Draft Vredeling Directive. Draft Directive on Procedures for Informing and Consulting Employees in Undertakings with Complex Structures (COM (80) 423, revised by COM (83) 292) and the Draft Directive Accompanying/Complementing the European Company Statute on the Involvement of Employees in the European Company (COM (89) 168, revised by COM (91) 174).

Some initiatives have sought to encourage participation across a range of strategic and financial/business issues, whereas others have been targeted at particular issues and events.

The Commission has been generally supportive of employee rights in this area and has shown itself willing to impose both rights and mechanisms. As Leat (1999) points out, Commission initiatives can be seen as:

- an expression of the desire for and belief in a community founded on consensus and harmony underpinned by a belief in equity and democracy, participation rights providing a counter to the otherwise unfettered rights of capital
- an expression of the belief that providing employees with the right to participate will, through the utilization of their knowledge, skill, problem solving capacity and innovation, provide organizations and economies with the competitive advantage necessary
- a means by which the increasing autonomy and influence of multinational companies might be countered or at the least mitigated.

So there are moral, political, social, economic and rational justifications for the initiatives taken and the policies proposed.

In the remainder of this section we concentrate upon three particular initiatives, two of these have had a chequered history in the UK in that the precise manner of their implementation has been contentious and the third because it is relatively new and potentially significant for the traditions of employee relations in the UK. The three are information and consultation rights in respect of collective redundancies, transfers of undertakings and within Community-scale undertakings.

The Directive on Collective Redundancies (75/129 extended by 92/56 and amended by 98/59)

Here the motivations for the measure can be seen to have been several. On the one hand, the directive is a reflection of the moral imperative that employees have a right to be informed of and involved in decisions regarding their job security and standard of living; there is also the political dimension in that if the labour movement's support for the concept of a single market was ever to be obtained it was not going to be obtained in a legislative and economic context in which business can arbitrarily decide to close and relocate activities (possibly into another member state) without employees even having the legal right to be informed in advance. It is also a reflection of concerns emerging even at this early stage about the activities of multinationals and their ability to make decisions in one country that threaten the jobs and livelihood of employees in another country without informing and consulting with the employees to be affected and their representatives. By giving employees and their representatives a legal right to be consulted in advance there is also the opportunity for alternatives to be considered and explored and the opportunity for the ingenuity, knowledge and skill of the workforce to be brought to bear on the problem.

The directive specified that employee representatives should be given in writing all relevant information including:

- the reasons for the redundancies
- the numbers to be made redundant
- the numbers usually employed
- the time period over which they are to take effect.

The consultation should take place before the redundancies take effect and should take place at the workplace where the redundancies are to occur even if the decision has been taken elsewhere, including in another member state, and the consultation should involve local management. The object of the consultation should be to **agree** on ways of avoiding or mitigating the number of redundancies and their consequences and companies are required to consult in good time to enable agreement to be reached.

Directive on the Transfer of Undertakings (77/187 amended by 98/50)

Here, the prime object of the directive (which is also known as the Acquired Rights Directive) was to give employees some legal protection of their terms and conditions of employment in the event that the organization for which they work is sold or the ownership is in some other manner transferred to another legal entity. However, as part of the strategy for ensuring that these acquired rights are protected, the directive also provides employees and their representatives with rights to be both informed and consulted and that the consultation should be 'in good time'.

The obligation to consult seems to apply to employers in respect of their own employees so that, for example, it is the person or entity that is doing the selling that has the obligation to consult. The potential acquirer has no obligation to talk to the employees until after the deal is done.

The original directives on Collective Redundancies and Transfers of Undertakings were implemented in the UK by a Labour government that, as we discuss in Chapter 5, was engaged in corporatist arrangements with both trade unions and employers and was keen to help the unions in their battle with staff associations and in increasing their membership. The implementing legislation only made reference to information and consultation for recognized trade unions, not 'employee representatives' as in the directive. The failure of the legislation to refer to employee representatives meant that as trade union membership and recognition declined in the 1980s–1990s, fewer employers had any legal obligation to inform and consult on these issues. As the EU authorities were made more and more aware of the deficiencies of the implementing legislation in the UK pressure grew for the law in the UK to be amended. In June of 1994 the ECJ ruled that the requirements of the directives did apply to non-unionized workplaces, that the UK interpretation was incorrect and that non-unionized employees were being deprived by the UK implementing legislation.

The situation was remedied by the Collective Redundancy and Transfer of Undertakings (Amendment) Regulations 1995 (effective 1 March 1996). The law in the UK now requires that UK employers:

- choose whether to consult with a recognized and independent trade union or with elected representatives of the employees that are affected by the events in question
- give elected employee representatives similar rights and protections as would be enjoyed by the representatives of an independent recognized trade union
- consult 'in good time' and not at 'the earliest opportunity' as was the prior terminology.

However, these new regulations do not define 'elected representative' and do not appear to require employers to inform their employees that they are entitled to elect representatives for the purposes of this consultation.

The European Works Council Directive 94/45/EC

There has been a great deal of debate about the likely consequences of this directive, with concerns being expressed by the various interested parties on a number of different dimensions:

- trade unions feel that they might be damaged by it since there is no requirement that the unions be involved in the Works Council; they might be bypassed by employers encouraging employees to not include the union
- employers have argued that the directive is unnecessary, that it will be expensive to operate, be time consuming, damage efficiency and that, more importantly, there will be threats to their business secrets and thereby their competitiveness
- employees and trade unions have concerns that once again the requirement in the directive is only of an 'inform and consult' form rather than something approaching more genuine joint determination or co-decision (see Chapter 9).

In addition to these concerns, analysts and commentators have debated among themselves what the impact of the directive was likely to be upon employee relations in Europe. For example:

- whether the directive would harm or hinder the Europeanization of employee relations, whether it would encourage the development of European-wide systems, both within each of the companies to which the directive applies and/or on a wider dimension between national systems?
- will the EWC provide the base required for the trade unions to acquire knowledge and expertise from each other that currently does not cross national borders?
- does the concept of the EWC present Europe with a new model for the resolution of conflict and/or the achievement of partnership, will it provide a template for the development of structures at a national level, and/or will companies forced to comply at Euro level then begin to

comply also at national level, is it a form of in-firm corporatism (see Chapter 5)?

- will it just be another means whereby an illusion of participation is created but without the autonomy of management being fundamentally challenged?
- would the directive harm or hinder prospects for Euro-wide collective bargaining?
- will the directive lead to the development of new formal and informal relationships between management and employees and between employee representatives/trade union officials across national borders that will in themselves create a more favourable climate for the management of employee relations and the resolution of conflict?
- and/or stronger cross-national links on the union side thereby enhancing their ability effectively to mobilize their resources to combat the interests of capital?

Undoubtedly this directive is rooted in some of the earlier and unsuccessful initiatives and in the Social Charter. It indicates an awareness on the part of the Commission, many of the member state governments and the labour movement that the unfettered power of the MNC, the autonomy and power of the multinational to take decisions in one member state which affect employees in one or more other member states, must to some extent be mitigated.

The directive is in part a response to the increase in the number and scale of multinational activities and undertakings that accompanied and followed the creation of the single market, their ability to divert capital investment from one member state to another, the process we have earlier referred to as 'social dumping' and the absence of alternative employee representative arrangements and structures. These issues and concerns can only be addressed effectively through action at the level of the EU (national governments being relatively powerless as discussed earlier). Whether the directive represents effective action at this level is another of the issues that has been debated.

As noted above in this chapter, this was the first directive to be adopted utilizing the social protocol/social dialogue procedures, even though the social partners were not able to reach agreement, and as such was not initially applicable to the activities of MNCs in the UK. Implementation was in September 1996.

In the directive the term 'Community-scale undertaking' is used to define those companies to whom the directive applies and such an undertaking is one which employs at least 1000 people in the EU, with at least 150 in each of two member states. The ownership of the enterprise is not a factor, companies of any and every nationality are covered as long as the above qualification requirement is satisfied. However, UK companies were not exempted altogether. If their non-UK EU activities qualify them as community-scale then they would have to comply with the directive in respect of all their employees and activities within the other member states, not just those in which they employ in excess of 150.

The new Labour government has agreed to the retrospective implementation of this directive, along with others adopted using the protocol procedures between 1991 and 1997.

The directive places the onus upon the employer to ensure that it is complied with and the parties within an organization covered by the directive have the option of agreeing their own voluntary arrangements as long as they are consistent with the intention and contents of what is referred to in the directive as the 'Mandatory model' (see **Figure 4.11**), the form of EWC that can be imposed upon organizations.

The parties within organizations have had two options for agreeing voluntarily on satisfactory alternative arrangements to the mandatory model. They were able to agree appropriate voluntary arrangements in the two years between adoption and implementation of the directive (called Article 13 agreements) and after implementation of the directive the parties under Article 6 had the option of commencing negotiations to reach such an agreement on alternative arrangements, this process to be completed by September 1999.

The imposition of the mandatory model form of EWC may be the product of companies and employee representatives trying but failing to agree voluntary arrangements, or as the product of one party refusing to even enter into such negotiations, or not taking the matter seriously.

In the main, given the period of years allowed for these negotiations, no companies were likely to have the mandatory model imposed prior to the year 2000 and it is as yet too early to be able to say how many of the companies covered by the directive were in this situation whether by choice or not. Certainly one must expect some companies to take no action until they are compelled to do so and then to undertake the information and consultation process half-heartedly, or at least without much enthusiasm.

Impact

Nakano (1999) reports that by the end of 1998/early 1999 some 540 EWCs had been established. This represented about one-third of the 1678 companies and groups exceeding the employment thresholds of the directive and included those that were brought into the remit of the directive by the UK government's agreement at Amsterdam in 1997 that the directive should in future be applicable in and to the UK. The majority of the 540 EWCs that had been agreed by the middle of 1999 were Article 13 agreements and only 100 were Article 6 agreements.

Analysing the data by country of ownership shows that Germany topped the list with 395 qualifying companies, followed by the USA with 298, the UK with 218 and France in fourth place with 161. It would seem that in excess of 1000 of the multinationals covered by the directive may be in a position to have the mandatory model imposed upon them.

The main points of the specified/mandatory model of an EWC are:

i)   the EWC must have between three and thirty members
ii)   the EWC should be comprised of employees of the undertaking or group elected or appointed by them and in accordance with the national legislation or practice
iii)   the competence of the EWC should be limited to information and consultation on matters concerning the undertaking or group as a whole or at least establishments or undertakings in two different member states
iv)   the composition of the EWC should include at least one member from each member state in which the undertaking or group has an establishment with the remaining membership determined on proportionate grounds
v)   such an EWC is to be reviewed after four years and the parties may choose to allow it to continue or to negotiate an alternative
vi)   the EWC has the right to an annual meeting with central management to be informed and consulted on the basis of a written report provided by management and concerned with:

the progress of the business of the Community Scale undertaking or ... group of undertakings and its prospects.

The **subject matter** of the meeting is then detailed:

- the structure of the business
- economic and financial situation
- the probable development of the business and of production and sales
- the situation and probable trend of employment
- investments and substantial changes concerning organization
- introduction of new working methods or production processes
- transfers of production
- mergers, cut backs or closures of undertakings, establishments or important parts thereof
- collective redundancies.

Figure 4.11 The mandatory model. Adapted from Directive 94/45

It will be a long time before we are able to assess the impact of the directive on employee relations. However, it is undoubtedly a milestone in the development of the social dimension of the EU; it is a direct attempt to limit the otherwise largely unregulated ability of the MNC to conduct employee relations as it wishes and it is the first significant attempt to impose a common procedural model upon employee relations in the EU.

There are already pressures within the Commission to extend the directive (or at least the model) down to a national level and to cover employers of fifty or more employees but there are doubts among some of the member states, including the UK Labour government, Germany, Spain and Greece, who have indicated that they would be opposed to action at an EU level to regulate national-level arrangements and procedures.

The achievement of the directive is really in the level at which the consultation is to take place and in the 'strategic' nature of the subject matter. There are, however, doubts fuelled by the actions of MNCs like Renault (see **Figure 3.8**) that, whatever the EU directives may say and require, MNCs will comply if it suits them but if it doesn't they will do what they consider necessary to satisfy the other stakeholders in the company and pay the price of non-compliance if that is the outcome.

Financial participation

The Commission and other interests have recently become converts of the value of employees having some form of financial participation in their employing organization, whether this be participation through share ownership or more directly in the financial performance of the company through various forms of bonus or performance-related payment scheme.

The Commission has sought to encourage the development of both profit- and equity-sharing arrangements and in 1992, at the behest of the Commission, the Council adopted a non-binding Recommendation (92/443) on Equity Sharing and Financial Participation that encourages member states to themselves encourage such schemes via the creation of sympathetic legal and fiscal environments and regimes. More recently the Commission has encouraged the social partners to consider attempting to reach an agreement on this issue through the protocol or dialogue procedures. Schemes of this nature are generally introduced because there is an underpinning belief that productivity will improve where employees have a stake in the company and its performance. Certainly, governments in the UK over the last couple of decades of the twentieth century appear to have believed in this relationship and generally tried to encourage the implementation and take-up of such schemes.

Activity 6

1 Earlier we gave the Commission's views on why employee participation was desirable, what were they?
2 What do you think are the main reservations on the part of management?

Working time and holiday entitlement

As is noted elsewhere (see Chapter 5), the regulatory traditions in the UK do not encompass a tradition of the statutory regulation of main terms and conditions of employment including working hours and holiday entitlement. There has been some limited statutory regulation on the grounds of health and safety such as night working by women and in certain industries such as coal mining, also in order to protect particular groups of workers thought to be vulnerable such as children. Even without these voluntarist traditions (see Chapter 5) the liberal individualist ideology of the Conservative governments in the 1980s and early 1990s would not have been consistent with the desire of other member states and the Commission to legally regulate the number of hours that employees can be made to work against their will and to ensure that all employees should be entitled to minimum periods of annual paid holiday.

Given the ideological position of the UK government and these traditions it is not at all surprising that the UK government tried to avoid the Directive on the Adaptation of Working Time 93/104 by alleging that it had been improperly adopted as a health and safety issue, a claim rejected by the ECJ in November of 1996. The ECJ adopted the World Health Organization definition of health as:

> a state of complete physical, mental and social well being that does not consist only in the absence of illness or infirmity

and certainly from a lay viewpoint it does seem reasonable to suggest that there are health and safety risks to working long hours with insufficient rest periods and breaks and that night work is likely to have additional health and safety implications.

The UK government had managed to secure some significant opt-outs from the general provisions of the directive on its way through the legislative process, in particular:

- the exemption from the coverage of the directive of certain occupations such as junior hospital doctors
- that the limits upon working hours could be voluntarily varied given the agreement of the parties, whether this be individuals agreeing to work longer hours or the parties agreeing a variation via a collective agreement.

The New Earnings Survey for 1996 indicated that approximately 12 per cent of employees in the UK work more than 48 hours per week and indeed that these employees average 57 hours per week. Eurostat data show that usual average full-time hours per week, at 43.9 hours, worked in the UK in 1996 exceeded any other member state and compared with an EU average of 40.3 hours per week.

In 1999 a number of different surveys provided further evidence on the scale of long hours working in the UK.

A survey funded by the Rowntree Foundation (1999) and reported in *The Guardian* (**Figure 4.12**; see also Chapter 1) confirmed that there is extensive working of long hours in the UK and that there are health and safety impli-

Ejemhen Esangbedo

Information Update Service

Butterworth-Heinemann

FREEPOST

Oxford

Oxon

OX2 8BR

UK

Keep up-to-date with the latest books in your field.

Visit our website and register now for our FREE e-mail update service, or join our mailing list and enter our monthly prize draw to win £50 worth of books. Just complete the form below and return it to us now! (FREEPOST if you are based in the UK)

www.bh.com

Title of book you have purchased:..

....

Subject area of interest:..

Name:...

Job title:..

Business sector (if relevant):..

Street:..

Town:... County:...

Country:.. Postcode:..

Email:...

Telephone:...

Signature:... Date:...

☐ Please arrange for me to be kept informed of other books and information services on this and related subjects (✔ box if not required). This information is being collected on behalf of Reed Elsevier plc group and may be used to supply information about products by companies within the group.

FOR OFFICE USE ONLY

Butterworth-Heinemann,
a division of Reed Educational
& Professional Publishing Limited.
Registered office: 25 Victoria Street,
London SW1H 0EX.
Registered in England 3099304.
VAT number GB: 663 3472 30.

A member of the Reed Elsevier plc group

Staff overworked as job security fears grow

Larry Elliott
Economics Editor

Pressures to boost performance and cut costs have led to an intensification of work and pushed levels of job insecurity to its highest level since the second world war, according to a survey out today.

Nationwide research for the Joseph Rowntree Foundation revealed that health, family relationships and the long-term future of the economy are all being putting at risk as staff are forced to work harder and fear that they will pay the price of the constant search to improve competitiveness.

The study, conducted by Cambridge university's centre for business research, found that levels of stress and anxiety had risen in both the private and public sectors, with by far the biggest increase in job insecurity occurring among professionals, who went from being the most secure group of workers in 1986 to the least secure in the late 90s.

It concluded that while the drive to slash costs and increase profits may have in-

creased efficiency in the short term, "the forces currently driving British industry have worrying implications not just for individual employees and their families, but also for Britain's future growth rates and the health of its 'social environment'."

Far from finding that job insecurity had fallen as unemployment dropped from 3m to 1.25m, researchers discovered that the workplace was permeated by a lack of trust, a sense of a loss of control over the pace of work, anxieties that promotion prospects were being denied and a sense among workers that they were being made to work too hard.

Only 26% of workers said they believed that management and employees were "on the same side", and when asked whether management could be expected to look after their best interests, 44% said "only a little" or "not at all".

The report stressed that some senior managers had been alarmed by the lack of trust and had introduced job security agreements. However, senior managers questioned

said that the commitments to protect jobs were not binding:

Two-thirds of workers said they always or regularly worked longer than their basic hours; just over 30% of men said they were putting in more than 48 hours a week, and 39% said that the length of the working week had increased over the past five years against 15% reporting that it was now shorter.

More than 60% claimed that the pace of work had increased over the past five years as downsizing had put pressure on the remaining workers to do more. Half said current staffing levels were inadequate or very inadequate.

The survey said there was a link between job insecurity and poor general health, with no evidence that employees adjusted to higher levels of stress. "On the contrary, physical and mental well-being continues to deteriorate the longer employees remain in a state of insecurity."

Figure 4.12 *Source: The Guardian*, 23 August 1999

cations and consequences. This survey concluded that two-thirds of workers regularly work in excess of their basic hours, more than 30 per cent of full-time male employees say that they regularly work in excess of 48 hours per week and 39 per cent that their incidence of long hours working had increased in the last five years.

In another survey for the IPD Guest and Conway (1999) found nearly a quarter of employees work more than 48 hours per week and approximately one-third regularly took work home with them. In yet another survey Kodz *et al.* (1999) found similarly that one-quarter of UK employees work in

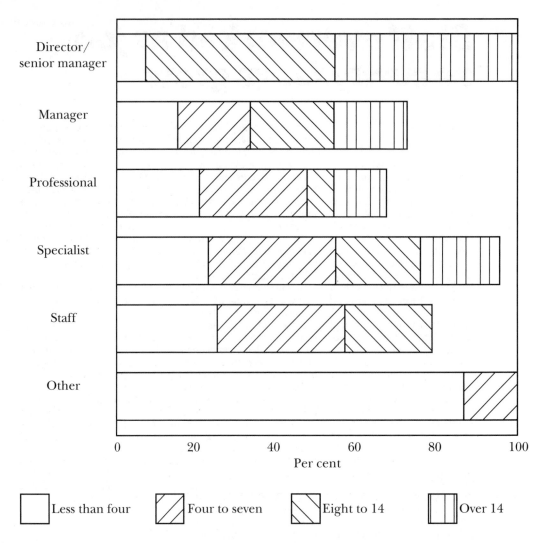

Figure 4.13 Additional hours worked, by occupation. *Source:* Kodz, J., Kersley, B. and Strebler, M., 1999. *Tackling a Long Hours Culture*. Institute for Employment Studies, Sussex University. Cited in Skills and Enterprise Executives Research Review 1/99. Feb 1999. DfEE.

excess of 48 hours per week and that 20 per cent work more than 14 hours a week above their contracted hours. Two out of three people felt that there was a long-hours culture at their workplace and that this was driven by management and reinforced by peer pressure, though it is also pointed out that a similar proportion of those surveyed said that they worked long hours because of a personal commitment to their work. They found sectoral, occupational, age and gender variations and conclude that it is administrative staff and professionals, men with children or dependants, and those over 35 years of age that are most likely to work long hours.

Each of these research reports point out that there are potential disadvantages of these practices, to productivity, health, safety and to social and family life. See **Figure 4.14** for the main elements of the Directive on Working Time.

The directive only became effective in the UK late in 1998 (October) and, at the time of writing, it is far too early to be able to assess the impact upon working customs and lives. However, sceptics have tended to the view that the maximum hours provisions of the directive will have little effect since in the UK they seem likely to only become relevant in circumstances where an employer is seeking to pressure an employee into working in excess of the stipulated maxima against their will and there is the threat of penalty if the worker refuses. It is of note that other members of the EU have not utilized the opportunity for this voluntary opt-out in their implementation of the directive.

The greatest benefit to employees may come from the provisions dealing

---

- Working hours should be limited to an average of 48 per week over a four-month reference period, though this can be extended to 12 months either by member states or by the parties via collective agreement
- Workers should have or receive:
- A minimum of 11 hours consecutive rest in 24 hours, implying a maximum working day of 13 hours
  - A minimum of 35 hours consecutive rest per week in principle to include Sunday
- Each of these latter two can be averaged over a two-week period.
  - A rest break after 6 hours consecutive work
  - Four weeks paid annual leave (three weeks for the first three years of employment) and no payment in lieu, in other words the intention is that the leave should be taken
- The extra provisions covering night workers seek to limit the average length of a night shift to 8 hours in 24, and propose that night workers should have free and regular medical check-ups and the right to transfer to day work on medical grounds.

The parties can voluntarily by collective agreement introduce greater flexibility in implementing the directive as long as adequate and appropriate compensatory rest is given.

The main exceptions cover particular 'problematic' occupations: road, rail, sea or air transport workers as well as managers and trainee doctors, and industries where continuity of production or service is required such as health, the media, post and telecommunications, emergency and public services, security services and public utilities. Currently it is unlikely that the full benefits of the directive will apply to these occupations until beyond 2010, though there was agreement in the summer of 1999 to phase in reductions.

Figure 4.14 Main elements of the Directive on Working Time

with paid annual leave. It was estimated by the Labour Force Survey in 1996, the year in which the ECJ ruled against the UK appeal, that there were as many as 2.7 million full-time workers with less than four weeks holiday entitlement per year and 1.8 million entitled to less than three weeks. Even in 1999 government in the UK was intent on watering down the requirements of the directive in the UK and in July of 1999 they proposed that some of the administrative burdens upon employers (keeping records of how long certain employees work – especially those who have 'volunteered' to opt out of the protection) be eased.

Explain the relevance of whether the directive was properly a health and safety issue.

In this chapter we have briefly examined the main institutions and decision-making processes of the European Union, but the emphasis has been upon the social dimension of the Union, the measures taken and means through which events and legislative interventions in particular impact upon employee relations in the UK.

The emphasis in the Union so far has been upon economic and monetary integration, the creation of single markets in capital, goods, services and labour, and the creation of a single currency. The social dimension of the Union is relatively underdeveloped in comparison.

The institutions of the Union and the member states are increasingly seeking to take decisions utilizing processes that provide the opportunity for majority, as opposed to unanimous, decisions and involve the social partners in the process. The co-decision procedure at last provides a limited degree of additional influence for the EP.

So far the influence of the EU in the social and employment field has been relatively limited, even in the areas of equality between the sexes and health and safety at work where there has been the greatest amount of activity. There have been a few initiatives adopted in other areas, some providing rights to information and consultation on particular issues. The EWC Directive seeks to constrain the ability of MNCs to go regime shopping without their employees knowing about it until it's too late to influence the decision and which addresses the issue of employee consultation at a Euro-corporate level on subject matter that is of a strategic nature. There has also been some limited intervention in the area of working time and holiday entitlement.

There are clearly interests within the EU that seek further convergence of the social (including employee relations) systems within the Union and there are also a number of different views on both the desirability and prospects of and for further convergence and upon the direction that it might take.

Activity Answers

Activity 1

1 The European Commission.
2 The Council.
3 A regulation has direct effect whereas a directive specifies an objective to be achieved by a given date and it is up to the national member state governments how the objective is achieved and the directive given effect.
4 The ECJ arguably creates the law through its interpretation of measures adopted, allied to the principle of binding precedent, and given that decisions of the ECJ take precedence over any and all national legislation.
5 The whole body of laws, rights and obligations adopted by the EU and which must be accepted in their entirety by aspirant members as a condition of their membership.
6 The main roles of the EP are to approve the appointment of the Commission, to approve the budget to be administered by the Commission and to comment upon, amend and sometimes delay or veto legislative positions adopted by the Council.
7 The social partners are the trade unions and employers' associations, which at the level of the EU are the ETUC, UNICE and the CEEP.

Activity 2

In both the consultation and cooperation procedures the social partners and the EP have only consultative roles in that proposals from the Commission go to them for comment. In the cooperation procedure the EP has second opportunity to comment and amend the common position adopted by the Council but these amendments can be overturned by the Council acting unanimously. The protocol procedure does nothing for the role of the EP but it does give the social partners the opportunity to play a much more influential role in that they can reach an agreement on a set of proposals which they can then ask the Commission to issue to the Council as a draft directive.

Activity 3

Regime shopping is the term used to describe the process through which MNCs are able to examine and compare the regulatory regimes in a number of different countries and effectively to shop between them. They choose to locate and invest in the one(s) that are most beneficial in terms of a range of matters such as taxation rates and provisions, planning regulations, rates of pay and labour costs generally, and the degree to which management's autonomy might be limited by a set of legislative provisions creating and giving rights to employees and thereby imposing constraints upon management's ability to act freely.

The concept of social dumping refers to one of the possible outcomes of this shopping process, to the location of investment into the cheaper and less regulated areas of the Union and thereby the potential creation of dislocation and unemployment in areas of the Union that are among the more regulated and expensive – where living standards are higher. Some have suggested that if social dumping was allowed to proceed unchecked the outcome in the long term would be a downward spiral of living standards within the Union.

Activity 4

The protocol/dialogue procedures provide a role and degree of influence for the social partners (the trade unions and employers' associations) in decision-making as a precursor to legislation that is inconsistent with the traditions of the UK, with the ideology of the Conservative government of the time and with the history of that government which had spent the previous twelve years determinedly reducing the power and influence of the trade unions.

Activity 5

The essence of the distinction would seem to be that the positive action should be directed at benefiting the under-represented or disadvantaged sex but it must not preclude the possibility of a member of the other sex benefiting if their circumstances are the same. In the case of recruitment, selection, promotion, etc., quotas are acceptable as long as the appointment of a member of the other sex is not precluded. Exceptions from the intended outcome must not be prevented.

1 The Commission believes in the political/democratic and moral imperatives which see employee participation as a dimension of democracy and equity. It wants a Union where the decision making is by consensus and characterized by harmony. It also has concerns about the ability of the MNCs to go regime shopping and engage in social dumping. There is also concern that the MNC is in a position to exploit labour, taking decisions in one country that affect the livelihoods of employees in another and which may have undesirable consequences in terms of social dislocation and exclusion. Even if the information and consultation rights so far given to employees and their representatives cannot prevent management acting autonomously they should at least give employees early warning. The Commission also believes that there are positive elements to such participation and that providing employees with the right to participate will, through the utilization of their knowledge, skills, problem solving capacity and innovation provide organizations and economies with the competitive advantage necessary.

2 The main management criticisms of the proposals and arrangements tend to include:

- it makes decision-making a longer process and thereby reduces the flexibility of the organization, both of which are anti-competitive in the global economy
- the process is expensive to implement and administer
- there are dangers of confidential information being leaked to competitors
- it impacts upon their right to manage and therefore their ability to do their job properly and exercise their expertise
- business is not a democracy and this should be recognized.

Activity 7
Had the directive not been introduced as a health and safety issue it could only have been adopted through the achievement of unanimous support in the Council and the UK government of the day would have been able to, and would have, vetoed the proposal. As a health and safety issue it could be adopted via a qualified majority vote.

References

European Commission, 1997. *Annual Report on Equal Opportunities for 1996.* Brussels.

Guest, D.E. and Conway, N., 1999. *Fairness at Work and the Psychological Contract.* IPD, London.

Kodz, J., Kersley, B. and Strebler, M., 1999. *Tackling a Long Hours Culture.* Institute for Employment Studies. Sussex University. Citied in Skills and Enterprise Executive Research Review 1/99. DfEE, Sheffield.

Leat, M., 1998. *Human Resource Issues of the European Union.* Financial Times Pitman Publishing, London.

Leat, M., 1999. The European Union. In Hollinshead, G., Nicholls, P. and Tailby, S. (eds), *Employee Relations.* Financial Times Pitman Publishing, London.

Nakano, S., 1999. Management views of European works councils: a preliminary survey of Japanese multinationals. *European Journal of Industrial Relations* 5(3) November. pp. 307–326.

OECD, 1999. *Annual Employment Outlook 1999.* Geneva.

Additional reading

Carley, M., 1993. Social dialogue. In Gold, M. (ed.), *The Social Dimension – Employment Policy in the European Community*. Macmillan, Basingstoke.

Due, J., Madsen, J.S. and Jensen, C.S. 1991. The social dimension: convergence or diversification of industrial relations in the Single European Market. *Industrial Relations Journal* 22(2): 85–102.

Gold, M., 1993. Overview of the social dimension. In Gold, M. (ed.), *The Social Dimension – Employment Policy in the European Community*. Macmillan, Basingstoke.

Hall, M., 1994. Industrial relations and the social dimension. In Hyman, R. and Ferner, A. (eds), *New Frontiers in European Industrial Relations*. Blackwell, Oxford.

Lecher, W.E. and Platzer, H.-W. (eds), 1996 *European Union – European Industrial Relations? Global Challenges, National Developments and Transnational Dynamics*. Routledge, London.

Lecher, W.E. and Rub, S., 1999. The constitution of EWCs: from information forum to social actor? *European Journal of Industrial Relations* 5(1) pp. 7–25.

Rivest, C., 1996. Voluntary European Works Councils. *European Journal of Industrial Relations* 2(2): 235–253.

Schulten, T., 1996. European Works Councils: prospects of a new system of European industrial relations. *European Journal of Industrial Relations* 2(3): 303–324.

Turner, L., 1996. The Europeanization of labour: structure before action. *European Journal of Industrial Relations* 2(3): 325–344.

Visser, J. and Ebbinghaus, B., 1992. Making the most of diversity? European integration and transnational organization of labour. In Greenwood, J., Grote J.R. and Ronit, K. (eds.), *Organized Interests and the European Community*. Sage, London. pp. 206–237.

Part Three
The National Context

Chapter 5

Government, ideology, the political and legal contexts

Introduction

As was noted in the first chapter of this book the activities of government form part of the backdrop to, or national context of, the employment relationship and thereby employee relations. We also pointed up the relevance of ideology or belief to the process through which governments determine the kind of society that they perceive to be desirable, this encompasses their views as to:

- the appropriate locus and distribution of power within society and between different interest groups and sectors of society
- their economic, social, industrial and environmental objectives
- their willingness to intervene
- their willingness to enter into a political exchange with the other actors,
- the policies that they pursue in these areas.

As Blyton and Turnbull (1998) assert 'the influence of the modern state permeates every aspect of people's working and non-working lives'.

Government is of course only one element of the state and the latter concept would normally also be accepted as encompassing the armed forces, the police, the civil service, other administrative mechanisms and institutions and the judiciary. In this chapter we are primarily concerned with the roles and influence of government rather than the state, though we do also include the Advisory, Conciliation and Arbitration Service (ACAS) in this chapter and this organization might properly be perceived as an organ of the state.

Kochan *et al.* (1986) suggest government values and choices, with respect to macroeconomic and social policy, influence both the processes and outcomes of employee relations. Generally there is a measure of consensus among observers that government may perform four main roles through which the context, interrelationships, processes and outcomes of employee relations may be influenced. These four roles are as:

- legislator
- manager of the economy and influence upon labour markets
- employer
- conciliator or arbitrator.

These four roles provide the structure to this chapter, except that in the first section we examine briefly the notion of ideology and the main stereotypes. Some would argue that the government no longer performs a role as economic manager, that a *laisser faire* ideology precludes this role or that the room for national governments to take meaningful action or initiatives is now severely limited by factors such as the globalization of markets and the UK's membership of the EU (see Chapter 4).

Others would also argue that government in the UK for many years now has not actively intervened as a conciliator or arbitrator but government does still promote and support the Advisory, Conciliation and Arbitration

Service (ACAS) as an independent tripartite agency offering these services at public expense and so we include the role here in this chapter. Even though this section is primarily concerned with the role and work of ACAS, it does constitute part of the national context.

Government is both a major contextual feature and influence at the national level and an actor within the employee relations system (see Chapter 1 and the discussion there of Dunlop's (1958) concept of an industrial relations system) and as Crouch (1982: 146) points out, government is the only one of the main actors able unilaterally to change the rules.

Traditionally it was rare for UK governments to pursue particular employee relations objectives and strategies for their own sake, their interventions into these areas were much more likely to be contingent upon the pursuit of particular political, economic and social objectives, such as achieving low inflation or full employment or the redistribution of income or wealth in a more equitable manner. However, arguably the Conservative government, elected in 1979, departed from this tradition and did pursue certain employee relations objectives directly and vigorously, for example the reduction of trade union power and the 'democratization' of the trade union movement (see Chapter 7 on trade unions) though even here one can detect other economic, political and social agendas.

Objectives

After studying this chapter you will be able to:

- Understand and explain the main constituents of liberalism and corporatism and their relevance for the policies pursued by government.
- Explain the roles through which government impacts upon employee relations in the UK.
- Outline the legal context of the employment relationship and employee relations.
- Understand the changes that have been introduced into the public sector and their impact upon employee relations.
- Understand and explain the different implications of Keynesian, Monetarist and neo-classical prescriptions for the conduct of economic and labour market policy.
- Explain the differences between conciliation and arbitration and the role of ACAS.

Ideologies and political approaches

Liberal individualism and liberal collectivism

In the first chapter you were introduced to the concepts of **liberal individualism** and **liberal collectivism**, each of which for the purposes of this book are to be treated as related but separate ideologies, sets of values and beliefs.

Go back to Chapter 1 and read that section again and the answer to Activity 5 of that chapter.

The point was made there that from the late 1940s until 1979 and the election of a Conservative government, the ideology that dominated in the UK was the liberal collectivist. The election of 1979 returned a government of a more liberal individualist persuasion.

Liberal collectivism had underpinned the post-war consensus that had facilitated the emergence and development of a system of industrial relations at the core of which was free collective bargaining and which was known as **voluntarism**. This voluntarism has also been characterized as a system based in mutual autonomy, a system of industrial self-government. Flanders (1974) had identified the key features of voluntarism as encompassing a general desire that wages and other terms and conditions of employment be determined by the parties through the process of free or voluntary collective bargaining rather than by state regulation and that the agreements arrived at should not be legally binding except in as much as they constituted terms in the individual employment contract (see later section in this chapter on the contract of employment). Among developed economies the UK is unusual in this respect, that collective agreements freely entered into are not legally binding, whereas similar agreements entered into by individuals are commonly legally enforceable as contracts (see also Chapter 9 in which we examine collective bargaining).

These two different sets of values and beliefs, liberal collectivism and individualism, also each have implications for attitudes towards the desirability, efficiency and efficacy of public ownership and the public sector.

Simply, the liberal individualist approach in its purest form sees no role for the public sector, the market mechanism is perceived to be the most efficient means of allocating resources between different uses and market forces should be allowed to operate unencumbered by the imperfections introduced by public ownership, especially where that ownership constituted a monopoly influence. The same reasoning has also been applied to the role of trade unions which, in this context, are perceived as monopoly suppliers of labour, and are therefore sources of imperfection in the labour market. Individual enterprise and decision making are at the heart of the liberal individualist position.

The liberal collectivist also believes in the essential efficiency of the market and private ownership but also takes on board the reality that there is not an equality of bargaining power between individuals within society and that some sectors of the population and industry need to be protected and regulated in the national interest so that all may benefit, even though there is no equality in terms of ability to pay. Traditional examples of justified public ownership and provision would include the utilities, for example water and power, and of course health care and education.

Corporatism

So far we have given the impression that the only two sets of values and beliefs influencing governments since the late 1940s were those of liberal individualism and collectivism. However, it can also be argued that in both the 1960s and 1970s we had governments that sought to determine economic, social and industrial policies in a manner that was consistent with **corporatism**, rather than liberal collectivism. You will find some differences of view amongst analysts and commentators as to the extent that liberal collectivism dominated the post-war period, some take the view that the dominant ideology or political approach prior to 1979 was liberal collectivism with one or two short-lived corporatist experiments in the 1960s and 1970s, while others argue that the 1960s and 1970s were dominated by corporatism (Salamon, 1999: 181).

Corporatism as an approach to government, policy making and administration is reflective of the belief that liberal systems, based as they are in decentralized decision-making through the process of competition and the associated application of power by the various parties, are inevitably inefficient, disruptive and, perhaps most concerning for government, unpredictable and uncontrollable. Additionally these liberal decision-making processes are quite capable of resulting in inequalities and unfairness. Consequently there may be a shift in the direction of a preference for:

- mechanisms which serve to integrate the interests of capital, labour and government, usually through some process of exchange or bargaining,
- political institutions which facilitate tripartite discussion and decision-making, particularly with respect to economic, industrial and social policies, such as the pursuit of economic growth, full employment and price stability.

Government then seeks to play an active role mediating the interests of capital and labour and in partnership with these competing interest groups, directing the activities of the still privately owned enterprises.

It is an approach which emphasizes the interdependence of the various interest groups and the notion of partnership, rather than encouraging competition between them, and which of course provides government with a greater capacity to influence and control compared with a decentralized market mechanism.

In some countries such as Germany, the Netherlands and Sweden, with lengthy corporatist traditions, it has been quite common for the partnership to be emphasized by the use of the term 'social partners' when referring to the representatives of capital and labour and, indeed, this is the term used within the European Union (see Chapter 4). Commonly, representatives of capital and labour participate with government representatives in a tripartite administration of the mechanisms established to achieve the agreed policy objectives. However, it is also the case that in the last decades of the twentieth century some of these countries have begun to witness a shift in the dominant political value system away from that which underpins corporatism towards liberalism and in particular its implications for regulation of the labour market and the role and scale of the public sector.

Typically corporatism in developed and democratic societies is of a voluntary and bargained nature where the various parties willingly participate in the process and where the outcomes are the product of bargaining between them. Examples might be a temporary agreement whereby the non-governmental interest groups agree to moderate their demands for wage or price increases in return for concessions from the other parties which might take the form of increased social security benefits, enhanced co-determination rights for employees or renewed commitments by both government and employers to full employment. For employers, the concessions might involve investment allowances, tax allowances or reductions in company taxation. There are a massive range of social, economic and industrial objectives that can be pursued through such arrangements and, as noted above, one of the most common is wage restraint.

An example of bargained corporatism was the Social Contract agreed in 1974 by the incoming Labour government with both the CBI, representing the employers (see Chapter 8) and with the TUC, representing the trade unions (see Chapter 7). In this tripartite agreement the unions agreed with the others that they would exercise wage restraint in return for the employers exercising restraint on price increases and the government giving them a more active and influential role in economic and industrial policy making and in the regulatory institutions. The unions also sought a code of individual and protective employment rights, positive rights, as well as an extension of trade union immunities – see below. The unions obtained a measure of success in this respect and during the first two years of this government and its corporatist experiment the degree of legal regulation of the employment relationship was significantly enhanced through the enactment of three major pieces of trade union and employee friendly legislation (the Trade Unions and Labour Relations Act of 1974 (TULRA), the Health and Safety at Work Act 1974 (HASAW), and the Employment Protection Act of 1975 (EPA)).

ACAS was also created in this period with a governing council that was made up in equal shares of trade union representatives, employer representatives and independent experts. Perhaps unfortunately the experiment didn't last as each of the parties began to perceive that the others were not delivering their part of the deal. This is consistent with the comments of Keller (1991) who pointed out that the participants are likely to continue as such only as long as they are satisfied with the outcomes and it is quite common for such arrangements to break up or fall into disrepair.

A corporatist approach to government and to policy making then provides for a more interventionist role for the government in terms and conditions of employment and for legal regulation of the employment relationship in general. Certainly it implied the cessation of free collective bargaining as evidenced by various attempts in these years to apply both bargained and coercive incomes policies.

Think about the three ideological stereotypes detailed here and in Chapter 1 and think through the implications of each for the role of government in employee relations.

Government as legislator and the legal context

Underlying principles and developments since 1960

Before we look at traditions and developments in the role of government as legislator and an outline of the current legal context for the employment relationship, it is important to realize that different authors have over the years devised different typologies of the category or type of legislation. Among the most common is to distinguish simply between legislation directed at the individual compared with that directed at collectives and collective interactions, they have distinguished on the grounds of the prime object of the intervention.

Others (Hollinshead and Leat, 1995) have argued the case for distinguishing between legislation aimed at protecting the interests and rights or freedoms of the parties compared with legislation primarily concerned with regulating the relationships between them, providing a legal framework within which the parties interact and pursue the resolution of the conflicts between them.

Yet another is that of Dickens and Hall (1995) who have sought to distinguish between legislation concerned to regulate:

● employer–worker relations
● employer–union relations
● union–member relations.

The latter seeks to take account of developments since the early 1980s whereby governments in the UK have shown a greater willingness to intervene to grant protective rights for employees as members of a trade union, and in a sense against their union, so that, for example, today members of a union have a right not to be unfairly disciplined and/or expelled from membership. Before these latter interventions the relationship between a trade union and its members was subject to and governed by common law and the law of contract, with the union's own rules constituting the main terms of the contract.

The dividing line between the various categories is often blurred and there is no one right typology; it is largely your prerogative to use the one that seems to you to be the most useful or the one you feel the most comfortable with.

As noted above, prior to 1979 the dominant, but not exclusive, approach had been underpinned by all the main actors sharing the belief that the two main participants to the employment relationship and their respective representative institutions should be allowed jointly and voluntarily to regulate the relationships between them and to resolve the conflicts that inevitably arose – voluntarism. The implications of such a voluntarist approach are that government should remain on the sidelines, intervening only when absolutely necessary to protect minority groups who might otherwise be exploited and to protect the national and public interest, a tradition of non-intervention by government and an absence of legislation.

Prior to the 1960s, governments had acted in a manner consistent with this principle of voluntarism. There was very little legislative intervention, some to protect women and children, some to establish minimum standards with respect to health and safety (a series of Factories Acts), and some to protect employees in industries where it was difficult, often for logistical reasons, for trade unions to recruit and represent and where employees might otherwise be exploited. In some of these sectors National Joint Councils (NJC), created as a result of the report of the Whitley Committee in 1919 and resurrected in the Second World War, were in many cases converted into Wages Councils. These latter bodies, being tripartite in nature, set minimum main terms and conditions of employment which were legally enforceable. The intention was that Wages Council activity would encourage the formation of voluntary collective bargaining.

The voluntary nature of the system applied both to collective relationships and to individual employment matters. As we have already pointed out, the parties had a freedom to enter into collective bargaining, there were no means by which they could be compelled to do so and the outcomes were not intended to be legally binding, to have legal force though again, as noted earlier, the contents of the agreements made commonly achieved some legal force as they become terms implied into the individual contract of employment.

The legal framework tended to rely upon the law of contract and the principles of common law (see **Figure 5.2**) and to emphasize freedoms, immunities and negative rights rather than positive rights, for example:

- the freedom to join a trade union rather than a positive right to do so
- the freedom to enter into collective bargaining
- trade unions immunities from civil action being taken against them by a third party to recoup losses resulting from industrial action, rather than a positive right to take that action.

In this latter regard individuals taking strike action are in breach of their contract of employment: they do not have a positive legal right to take such action.

Even much of the protective legislation of the last thirty years has been negative in character and emphasis, e.g. rights not to be unfairly dismissed rather than a right to be employed, not to be discriminated against rather than a right to be treated equally, etc.

However, in the 1960s the dominance of the voluntarist approach began to be eroded. There were numerous pressures working upon government to adopt a more interventionist role and even before the election of a Labour government in 1964 (perhaps by inclination more interventionist and potentially corporatist in orientation), government had begun to intervene to protect and further the interests of employees and this continued throughout the decade. The Contracts of Employment Act 1963, the Industrial Training Act 1964, the Redundancy Payments Act 1965, the Trades Disputes Act 1965, the Race Relations Act 1968 and Equal Pay Act 1970 collectively constituted a significant departure from the voluntarist tradition.

Among the pressures for greater intervention, employers and government were becoming concerned at the increasing evidence of unofficial strikes, trade unions were concerned at some judicial decisions affecting their traditional immunities, and government was also becoming increasingly concerned with issues concerning the performance of the economy and the need to control inflation.

In 1965 the government established the Royal Commission on Trades Unions and Employers Associations (Donovan) to investigate the problem posed by increasing unofficial industrial action and increasing inflationary pressures. The recommendations of the Donovan Commission were essentially procedural and structural and did not recommend further statutory intervention; in other words they did not in the main see the need to break significantly from the voluntarist tradition. It was the Labour government's only partial acceptance of the Commission's recommendations and its subsequent proposals in 1969 for legislative reform and in particular for legislative sanctions on unofficial industrial action which signalled the end of its period in office.

In the period from 1970 to 1974 there was a Conservative government in office that signalled a radical departure from the voluntarist tradition. It rejected Donovan and the liberal collectivist proposals for change and proceeded in the belief that trade unions had become too powerful, and that statutory intervention was necessary to curb it. The Industrial Relations Act 1971, in addition to creating specific rights and protections for employees for the first time in certain 'unfair' dismissal situations, also banned pre-entry closed shops, and created a Trades Union Registrar with powers to vet trade unions' rules to assess their independence and suitability for collective bargaining and with whom trade unions were required to register if they were to retain legal protections, rights and immunities. The Act effectively nullified post-entry closed shops by giving employees the right to belong or not belong to a trade union. It also sought to make collective agreements legally binding, created new provisions to assist trade unions gain recognition from relevant employers and gave the Secretary of State for Employment powers to apply to the newly created National Industrial Relations Court (NIRC) to delay strike action for sixty days and order a compulsory ballot of members to assess support for the action. We also witnessed workers' leaders being sent to gaol for refusing to call off strike action. The Act was complex, to some extent contradictory and was widely avoided, employers and trade unions often colluding together to nullify some of its provisions, in particular the provision that collective agreements were to be legally binding unless both parties specified in writing at the end of the agreement that this was indeed not their intention – most did so.

Not only was the Act a failure but it undoubtedly contributed to the defeat of the government in 1974 and, as we have already noted above, to the return of a new Labour administration with corporatist intentions that encompassed a commitment to a return to free collective bargaining, though its attempts at statutory incomes policies a year or two later soon put that commitment into a different perspective.

In the first couple of years of office the Conservative government adopted a range of employee and trade union friendly legislation which included repeal of the Industrial Relations Act 1971 and adoption of the Trade Unions and Labour Relations Act 1974, and The Employment Protection Act 1975. All of which served to restore trade union rights, freedoms and immunities pretty much to the pre-1971 position, as well as creating new statutory rights for employees in areas such as maternity leave, lay-off pay and paid leave in redundancy situations. Shop stewards were given rights to paid time off for training and other legitimate activities, a procedure was created for assisting trade union recognition, employers were legally required to give unions information for bargaining purposes and were required to engage in compulsory consultation prior to collective redundancies.

In addition, in 1974, the Health and Safety at Work Act was enacted giving employees and trade unions new rights and further individual rights were created in the Sex Discrimination Act of 1975.

The corporatist nature of this period of government is further demonstrated by the creation of a number of new tripartite institutions to administer and enforce these rights. In addition to ACAS, the period between 1974 and 1979 witnessed the creation of:

- the Equal Opportunities Commission
- the Commission for Racial Equality
- the Health and Safety Commission
- the Health and Safety Executive.

It was also decided that industrial tribunals, initially created by the Industrial Training Act 1964, were to be used to hear applications from individuals who felt that one or more of these statutory rights had been infringed, particularly those relating to dismissal and sexual or racial discrimination.

In many respects the period 1974–1979 represents the high point of trade union influence in the UK, certainly membership peaked in 1979.

The collapse of these corporatist experiments, the militancy of the trade unions and the anguish experienced by the general public through the winter of 1978/9, the so-called winter of discontent, during which government and the trade union movement were seemingly at war with each other and through which the general public suffered considerable deprivation and discomfort, provided fertile ammunition for the Conservative party in the 1979 general election. They campaigned on the grounds that the unions were too powerful and they clearly paraded before the electorate their liberal individualist, *laisser faire* beliefs and economic, industrial and industrial relations policy proposals. Consequently, when elected they proceeded with a series of legislative interventions which, piece by piece, served effectively to limit the power and influence of the unions, dissolved many of the tripartite institutions, diminished the rights and protections of employees at work and from the arbitrary actions of their employers, and increased the rights of trade union members in their relationships with the union in the name of enhancing trade union democracy.

Unlike 1971, the Conservative government elected in 1979 approached the task of tackling trade union and employee power gradually. The rights, protections and immunities afforded to these groups were perceived as sources of imperfection in labour markets and were therefore to be reformed, if not removed altogether. The new government believed and argued that these rights and protections enabled employees to insist upon restrictive practices which significantly hampered management's abilities to introduce the new technology, production and working methods, numerical and temporal flexibilities (see Chapter 2) essential to restoring national competitiveness.

The extent and nature of the subsequent legislative interventions can be seen from **Figure 5.1** in which we list the major Acts of Parliament concerning the employment relationship and the parties to it that have been adopted since 1979 and in which we briefly outline the major initiatives taken by each.

The Employment Act 1980
- repealed the statutory procedure through which unions could obtain recognition
- restrictions on the closed shop, people were to be given the right not to join on grounds of deeply held personal convictions, and any new closed shop was required to demonstrate an 80 per cent support level (or 85 per cent of those voting)
- repealed procedures whereby the Central Arbitration Committee could extend collective agreements within industries to companies and groups of workers not currently covered
- secondary picketing outlawed, new legal requirements for picketing to be lawful
- gave employers legal remedies against secondary action and picketing
- public funds were made available to unions to encourage them to hold postal ballots for electing officers and before important policy decisions
- employees' unfair dismissal rights were significantly reduced, as were rights to maternity leave and reinstatement, the relevant qualifying periods were increased from six months to twelve months

The Employment Act 1982
- continued the fight against the closed shop by requiring periodic ballots on all existing arrangements
- tightened the definition of a trade dispute, reduced the scope of issues upon which trade unions could lawfully take industrial action and thereby retain their immunities from being sued in respect of loss suffered by others as a result. Excluded from the scope of lawful action were secondary and political actions
- became lawful selectively to dismiss strikers after a specified period of strike activity.

The Trades Union Act 1984
- pre-strike ballots became a legal pre-requisite for strike action to be lawful
- union executive committee members (voting) to submit themselves to periodic re-election (at least every five years)
- unions wishing to have a political fund should have this approved by the membership in a secret ballot at least every ten years.

Figure 5.1 Main Acts of Parliament, and major initiatives of each, concerning the employment relationship adopted since 1979

The Wages Act 1986
- removed young persons (those under 21 years of age and arguably those in greatest need) from the protection of the Wages Councils and also reduced the scope of the Councils' activities.

The Sex Discrimination Act 1986
- restrictions on (protection of) women's working hours removed.

The Employment Act 1988
- gave trade union members the right not to be disciplined for not taking part in lawful industrial action and the right to take legal action against the union if that industrial action was taken without the appropriate secret ballot
- established a new role of Commissioner for the Rights of Trade Union Members (CROTUM)
- all senior union officials (all NEC members irrespective of whether right to vote or not) were to be chosen by secret ballot
- the post-entry closed shop finally rendered unenforceable.

The Employment Act 1989
- repealed laws protecting young people through the regulation of the hours they could work and their working conditions
- limited trade union officers' rights to time off for trade union activities
- exempted small firms from the requirement that they should have written disciplinary procedures.

The Employment Act 1990
- effectively made the closed shop inoperative, action in support cannot now be lawful and refusal of employment on grounds related to union membership (pre-entry) is also not lawful
- employers were given greater freedom to dismiss employees taking unofficial industrial action
- rendered unlawful industrial action taken in support of employees dismissed for taking unofficial action
- balloting provisions were tightened up and pretty well all secondary action now falls into the unlawful category.

The Trades Union Reform and Employment Rights (TURER) Act 1993
- wages councils were finally abolished
- employees were given a right to belong to any union of their choice, thereby undermining long-standing jurisdictional and no-poaching agreements within the TUC-affiliated union movement
- employers were given the responsibility of ensuring that individuals authorize deduction of union dues from their pay (check-off agreements) at least once every three years, thereby posing a threat to union finances
- role of ACAS was diminished by removing from it the responsibility to encourage the extension of collective bargaining
- The Transfer of Undertakings Regulations (1981) which protect employees' job rights and terms and conditions in such circumstances were amended (in accordance again with EU requirements) to include public-sector transfers

Figure 5.1 (*continued*)

- employees were given further protections from being penalized for undertaking legitimate health and safety activities
- employees through their representatives were given information and consultation rights in the event of collective redundancy
- subject to the receipt of qualified legal advice, employees given right to conclude agreements with their employers by which they opt out of their statutory rights regarding termination of employment and sexual and racial discrimination
- lawful for employers to offer inducements to employees to switch to individual contracts including inducements to opt out of collective bargaining and/or leave a trade union, arguably for the first time it became lawful to pay non-union members more than union members
- the traditional tripartite nature of industrial tribunals potentially weakened by allowing certain cases to be heard by the Chair alone with just one lay member
- unions required to give the employer at least seven days' notice of their intention to hold the necessary ballot and/or take industrial action
- citizens are given the right to take legal action in cases of unlawful industrial action affecting the supply of goods and services
- various provisions concerning trade union amalgamation ballots, political funds and other union financial matters
- employees now to be given a more detailed written statement of main particulars/terms of their contract of employment.

Employment Rights Act 1996
- in the main a consolidation of existing rights.

The Employment Relations Act 1999
- employees and their trade unions to be given limited rights to force an employer to recognize the union for the purposes of collective bargaining given evidence of majority membership or adequate support levels in some form of ballot
- disputes on these provisions to go to the Central Arbitration Committee
- some amendments to the procedural rules on trade union ballots in respect of taking industrial action
- requirement for employers to consult recognized trade unions on training plans and policies
- dismissal of strikers will be unlawful for the first eight weeks of lawful action
- employee to have right to be represented by a trade union in disciplinary and grievance hearings irrespective of whether the union is recognized
- employees to obtain the right not to be unfairly dismissed after the completion of one year of continuous employment (two years before) and limit for maximum award raised
- waiver of unfair dismissal rights prohibited in fixed-term contracts
- maternity leave rights extended to eighteen weeks (forty weeks after one year of continuous service)
- effect to be given to the European directive on parental leave but the rights to be to unpaid leave
- the European directive on equality for part-time workers to be given effect.

Figure 5.1 (*continued*)

Figure 5.1 demonstrates clearly that since 1979 there has been a great deal of statutory intervention and regulation of the employment relationship:

- at the level of the individual contract of employment (mostly in terms of altered rights and protections)
- concerning the framework for collective relationships and interactions
- concerning the relationship of the individual trade union member with his trade union.

Without going back to the text, try to remember what is meant when we say that the UK legal framework has tended to emphasize freedoms, immunities and negative rights rather than positive rights and give some examples of each.

Look back over the preceding pages concerning the legal context and in particular **Figure 5.1**, and work out for yourself the *major* elements of the legal framework in the UK regarding:

- the framework for collective relationships and interactions
- the relationship of the individual trade union member with his trade union.

Don't concern yourself with the individual contract of employment, that is the subject of the next section.

There has been a perceptible shift by government in favour of market or liberal individualism and deregulation and much of the statutory intervention since 1979 has been motivated by a belief in the efficiency of the market and the 'need' to remove regulations, rights and protections that were perceived to constitute barriers to efficiency and competitiveness, what we later refer to as institutional reform (see section on labour market reform later in this chapter).

The initiatives that have been undertaken exemplify a conviction that trade unions and employees were too powerful within the employment relationship. Through these changes government has returned to management and employers greater freedom to employ on their own terms. Lawful industrial action has been made more difficult and narrowed in scope and it must be remembered that this is in a context whereby employees in the UK do not have a constitutional or statutorily backed right to strike and such action has always effectively rendered the employee in breach of his/her contract of employment.

The individual employment relationship and the law – the contract

There are many common misunderstandings and questions about the contract of employment. For example:

- does the contract have to be in writing?
- what constitutes the contract?
- where do the terms of the contract emanate from and do they all have to be expressed clearly and agreed between the parties?
- do the rights granted to individual employees by statute form part of the contract and, if so, how?
- we have already intimated that terms of the contract can be derived from collective agreements between employers and trade unions and, if this is so, what other sources might there be?
- is the answer to these questions clearly spelled out somewhere in the law?

Some of these questions can be answered quite easily and clearly, however some of them are also difficult to answer clearly.

Contracts do not have to be in writing, they do not have to be expressly agreed by the parties in their entirety though some of the terms may be, the employer is legally obliged in most cases to give the employee a written statement detailing some of the main particulars of the contract (these are spelt out in Section 1 of the Employment Rights Act 1996, see below) but this document rarely is sufficiently comprehensive for it to constitute the contract. Yes, many of the statutory rights do constitute part of the contract and in the main these will be assumed to be incorporated into the contract even though they may not be the subject of discussion or agreement between the parties, in fact the parties may not even know of them. Other sources of terms implied and incorporated into the contract may be custom and practice, collective agreements, common law rights and duties, staff handbooks and various other documentary sources.

In many organizations the Section 1 written statement is erroneously referred to as the contract when it is only likely at best to refer to some of the more important terms of the contract. Many people, unfortunately in the author's experience including many personnel practitioners, are of the view that the contract does have to be in writing and that if there isn't a document purporting to be a contract duly signed by both parties or their agents then there isn't a contract. The contract exists whether written or not!

The Section 1 (Employment Rights Act 1996) statement

The requirement for employers to give their employees written details of some of the main particulars of the terms of their employment contract dates from the Contracts of Employment Act 1963, revised subsequently and, as noted above, the current state of the law in this area is contained in the 1996 Act.

The Section 1 statement should give employees written details of the following:

- Names of employer and employee
- Date of commencement of continuous employment
- Rate of pay and frequency of payment
- Hours of work
- Holidays and holiday pay
- Matters concerning sickness and sick pay
- Pension rights and arrangements
- Indication of job title
- Notice to be given and received
- Details of grievance and disciplinary procedures and arrangements
- Place of work
- Details of collective agreements that directly affect the contract and the names of the parties that made them

In some instances the requirement to provide these details can be satisfied by a reference in the statement to other documents where the details may be found, e.g. in relation to the details of sickness and pension rights and grievance and disciplinary procedures.

This legislative requirement only applies to those employed for eight hours a week or more and the requirement is that this statement be given to the employee within the first two months of their employment. The written statement is not the contract and has no direct legal force at all, though employees can make a complaint to an Employment Tribunal (the new name for Industrial Tribunal) if they are not provided with these details. We noted above that the terms of a contract may be expressed or implied and, where expressed, this may be done in writing or orally. The Section 1 statement is usually the best evidence of the express terms of the contract.

Implied terms

The implied terms of a contract are in the main implied either from statute or from the decisions of the courts over the years as what is known as the common law duties and obligations of the parties were developed. Terms implied from these sources apply in general to all contracts of employment but, again, these are not the only sources of implied terms. Terms may be implied from custom and practice in a particular organization or they may be implied from the conduct of the parties – in these latter cases the implied terms are likely to be more specific to the contracts of a particular group of employees or indeed to a particular individual contract.

There are now, after the developments of the last thirty years, a whole range of statutory rights and obligations which, to all intents and proposes, constitute implied terms of the contract, they exist as terms of the contract of employment without their being expressed in the contract or indeed in the statement given to employees. Examples would be in the following areas:

- written statement
- maternity pay and leave
- minimum notice periods
- redundancy pay
- not to be unfairly dismissed
- time off for public activities and duties
- health and safety responsibilities
- equal pay
- not to be discriminated against
- data protection.

Very rarely would these rights be written into even the most comprehensive of Section 1 statements or a document purporting to be the contract, but they are nevertheless there as rights and obligations of the parties to the employment relationship.

The other major source of implied terms is from **common law** (**Figure 5.2**). This represents the decisions of the judiciary over the centuries and, to some extent what they have decided to be both custom and practice and fair and reasonable. Specifically we can say that from this source the employee and employer each have a number of obligations and rights.

We noted earlier that terms could be implied from **custom and practice**. Here, the test to be satisfied is whether the custom or practice is 'reasonable, certain and notorious', in other words, do the courts consider it reasonable:

- in the context of what might be normal in that industry
- is it capable of relatively precise definition?
- did the parties know about it?

Where the courts conclude that the answers to these questions are positive then it is likely that they will take the view that the custom or practice does constitute a term of the contract.

As we see there is a complex legal context to the employment relationship and to the behaviour of the parties and their representatives or agents. This context derives from a number of different sources only some of which can be said to be outcomes of direct government intervention. Nevertheless there is sufficient evidence in this section to demonstrate the influence

Employees have a duty to:

- provide faithful service which would include a duty not to commit theft or fraud
- be willing and available to work
- exercise reasonable care in the performance of that work
- not wilfully to disrupt the employers undertaking
- obey reasonable orders
- work for the employer in the employer's time
- respect trade secrets and not to disclose sensitive and confidential information.

Employers have a duty to:

- treat the employee with mutual trust, confidence and respect
- pay the agreed wages
- provide the opportunity for the wages to be earned. It is a moot point as to whether there is an obligation to provide work, but failure to satisfy this requirement is likely to require some payment in lieu of the opportunity to work and thereby earn the agreed wages
- take reasonable care to ensure their employees' safety and to indemnify them for injury or loss, or expense, incurred.

Figure 5.2 Principles of common law

which government can bring to bear upon this legal context and the relevance of their political ideology to the nature, extent and content of that intervention.

The election of a Labour government in 1997 does not appear to herald a return to the legal situation as it was prior to 1979. The new government has made it quite clear that the trade union movement is not to be treated any more favourably than are the interests of business. There were a number of commitments made, for example:

- to reintroduce a statutory means by which trade unions could obtain recognition for collective bargaining from employers given evidence of adequate support levels
- to introduce a minimum wage
- to sign up to the social chapter of the EU Treaty as amended at the Amsterdam summit in the summer of 1997 (see Chapter 4)
- to end the requirement for a three-yearly renewal of check-off arrangements
- for some protection for lawful strikers against unfair dismissal.

However, there was no general commitment to repeal the legislation of the preceding eighteen years or radically to alter the balance of the legal context surrounding the employment relationship.

Explain the meaning of the term 'Implied' with regard to the terms of a contract of employment and identify the main sources of such implied terms.

Government as employer and the public sector

The size and nature of the public sector is inevitably linked to the dominant notions that government has about the kind of society that they consider desirable which, as discussed earlier, is at least in part a product of ideology, their economic and social objectives and their beliefs and judgements about how these may be best achieved. As we have detailed in the section of this chapter looking at the legislative role of government the election of a Conservative government in 1979 constituted something of a watershed and this is also the case with regard to the role and scale of the public sector and to the management of employee relations within the sector.

Most analysts appear to agree that, prior to 1979 and perhaps with the exception of rates of pay, the public sector set an example to the private sector with respect to the employment and management of human resources and industrial relations, the example set being consistent with both liberal collectivist and pluralist notions and perspectives. Trade union membership and recognition were encouraged and terms and conditions of employment were determined jointly through collective bargaining at national level. The systems of industrial relations were formal, constitutional with an emphasis upon agreed procedures and centralized.

At local level the role of personnel management, and to some extent also union representatives, was essentially that of administering and interpreting the national agreements, some of which were both enormous and enormously complex. Black and Upchurch (1999) quote the example of the Civil Service Pay and Conditions of Service Code as containing 11,500 paragraphs of regulations from major pay scales down to 'daily pedal cycle allowances'.

In most instances also there were procedural agreements in place in respect of grievances and appeals against decisions made locally which ensured that final decisions were taken at the centre, in many ways resembling judicial processes that provide for appeal to the highest court in the land. Decisions made at the centre in this way also tended to constitute binding precedent for the practitioners at local level and were often promulgated as such in newsletters and other communications by both sets of parties to these central institutions.

Terms and conditions of employment, with the exception of pay, were generally better than those in the private sector, especially in areas such as job security, pension rights, entitlements to sickness leave and pay, holiday entitlements, working hours and the limitations upon management prerogative imposed through the emphasis upon joint decision making and consultation. In the main, pay was determined through collective bargaining but the scope available to the bargainers was limited. The base for pay determination tended to be derived from comparisons made with the rates being paid in the private sector for similar skills or jobs. It was always a catching-up process in that the rates agreed for the forthcoming year tended to reflect the rates already being paid in the private sector. This didn't pose too much of a problem whilst inflation was low but as inflation increased in the 1970s (in 1974/5 it reached 24 per cent) the issue of public-sector pay became a major one, not helped by successive governments seeking to exert a moderating influence upon rates of pay in the private sector by restraining pay in the public sector. Employees and their union representatives began to feel that they were the subject of what these days might be referred to as 'double whammy'. As has been mentioned above, the culmination of these policies and dissatisfactions with pay policy in the public sector was the 'winter of discontent' of 1978–9 and the subsequent election of a Conservative government. During this pre-1979 period the emphasis in the public sector was upon service provision.

1979 represents the high point of the size of the public sector, at least as measured by the numbers employed. Figures for employment in the public sector since 1979 are shown in **Figure 5.3**. In 1979 some 7.4 million people were employed and this constituted almost 30 per cent of the total working population; by 1997 this had declined to just over 5 million and 20 per cent of the working population. There are still some 600,000 civil servants employed directly by the Crown; other sizeable sectors are the NHS, which employs in excess of 1 million, and local government, which in total employs some 2.5 million including in education, the police, the fire service and social services as well as those employed within local authorities. Central government constitutes the employer of all these people in a direct or indirect manner. Central government is certainly the paymaster and, through funding allocations, is able to influence rates of pay and other terms and conditions of employment.

Much of this reduction in the numbers employed in the public sector has been achieved as a result of a radical programme of denationalization or privatization, allied to policies of severe financial stringency in those sectors remaining where managers have been required to achieve successive cost efficiencies and savings year on year with government using a policy of **cash limits** and its ability to control public-sector borrowing as levers to achieve these objectives. At the same time government has tried to convince itself and the public at large that the quality of service provision has not suffered as a result.

The train crash at Paddington in the autumn of 1999 raised again the issue of the potential for conflict between the need for organizations in the private sector to make profit and the need to invest in order to maintain adequate levels of safety for the consumers of the service. This tragic event

	1961	*1979*	*1989*	*1996*	*1998*
1. Public corporations	2.2	2.06	0.84	1.51[a]	n.a.
2. Central government[b]	1.79	2.39	2.3	0.99[a]	n.a.
3. Local government	1.87	3.0	2.9	2.65	n.a.
Total 2 + 3	3.66	5.39	5.2	3.64	3.47
Total 1 + 2 + 3	5.86	7.45	6.04	5.15	n.a

n.a. not available.

[a]Reflects the creation of NHS Trusts, which are classified as public corporations, along with organizations such as Royal Mail and the Bank of England. Previously employees in the NHS were counted as part of central government.

[b]Includes members of the armed forces.

Figure 5.3 Employment in the public sector 1961–1998 (in millions)
Source: Labour Market Trends (various issues) and *DTI Statistical Bulletin*, August 1999

prompted debate about the effect of privatization upon safety levels and standards and whether it was necessary to take the railways back into public ownership in order to ensure that a safety culture is maintained. The inquiry into these issues will undoubtedly also address the question of whether investment levels in the industry were sufficient prior to privatization, given the policies of cash limits and cost reduction pursued by governments as indicated above.

Employee relations since 1979

The Conservative government elected in 1979 was firmly of the view that the trade union movement was too powerful and a source of imperfection, regulation and rigidity in the labour market. Additionally the public sector was too big, it took too large a share of the nation's resources, it was inefficient, insufficiently responsive to the needs of society – not market responsive, employees were far too protected and too comfortable and management was weak.

The incoming government therefore began a programme of initiatives geared towards achieving the objectives of reducing the size of the public sector and the burden of public expenditure, making the public sector more market responsive and efficient and reducing the power of the unions, the unions in the public sector being singled out as of particular concern given their size and their ability to resist government policy initiatives. It was public-sector unions, in particular in the coal mining industry, that had been at the root of the defeat of the previous Conservative government in 1974 and it was the public-sector unions, particularly in local government, that had been in the forefront of resistance to the Labour governments' incomes policies in the late 1970s and the ensuing troubles in the winter of 1978–9.

We have noted above the legal initiatives that the Conservative governments of the period 1979–97 took and we will not repeat that discussion here, as indeed we will not discuss the economic policy initiatives taken since, again, they are dealt with elsewhere in this chapter. Here we are concerned with the measures taken in the public sector.

We have already noted above that the size of the public sector has been reduced through the process of denationalization and privatization. Through the period 1979–97 in excess of forty companies were privatized, including the utilities, telecoms, rail, British Airways, Jaguar cars, various ports and airports, etc. See **Figure 5.4**.

A policy that we have not yet mentioned is Compulsory Competitive Tendering (CCT), a mechanism that often had the effect of achieving the private-sector provision of previously publically provided services. Underpinning this policy initiative was the realization that the purchasing and provision of public-sector services could be separated. The public-sector tradition had been to combine determination of need (where this happened at all) and the acquisition of the services thereby required with

Company	*Year*
National Freight Company	1982
Britoil	1982
Associated British Ports (formerly British Transport Docks Board)	1983
Enterprise Oil (separated from British Gas Corporation)	1984
British Telecom	1984
British Shipbuilders: various dates from	1984
British Gas Corporation	1986
National Bus Co. Subsidiaries	1986–88
British Airways	1987
British Airports Authority	1987
British Steel	1988
Regional Water Authorities & Water Authorities Association	1989
Area Electricity Boards and National Grid Company	1990
National Power and Powergen	1991
Scottish Power	1991
British Coal Mines	1994
British Rail	1995
British Energy	1996

Figure 5.4 The more important privatizations, 1982–97.
Adapted from Kessler and Bayliss, (1998:148), Macmillan, Basingstoke

their provision, within the same organization. So that, as an example, the need (demand) for health services and their provision (supply) were determined and provided within the same organization and, similarly, the demand for and supply of refuse collection was determined within the same local authority. CCT was a mechanism that sought to address these issues through making local authorities and others put the provision of the service out for competitive tender to organizations in the private sector, the contract for the provision of the specified service in terms of quantity, frequency and quality would then be awarded to the cheapest tender, or bid.

In the health service we saw a separation between purchasing and providing achieved through giving health authorities the purchasing role and forcing the providers, the hospitals, doctors etc., into separate organizations: health service trusts (which have remained part of the public sector) which were able to compete with one another for contracts to provide services. Again the opportunity was also given for private-sector organizations to enter into this competitive process.

Running through and underpinning these initiatives is the belief in the efficiency of the market mechanism and the value of introducing market forces and competition into these sectors, the benefits to be achieved were variously greater efficiency, cost reduction, enhanced responsiveness to the customer and better quality service provision. In addition to these initiatives management were also exhorted by government to stand up to their employees and in particular their unions, to re-exert their authority and prerogative, and government often refused to allow disputes to go to arbitration (see later section on ACAS). Government has used its ultimate control over funding to encourage public-sector managements to introduce changes to work practices and payment schemes, the most common example in recent years probably being some element of individual performance-related pay. They have also used their control of funding indirectly to influence and contain rates of wage increase, making use of the cash limits mechanism to encourage the directly involved parties to confront a trade-off between employment, efficiency and wage rates.

The emphasis placed upon performance-related pay is reflective of initiatives whereby managements were also encouraged to introduce into the public sector a greater emphasis upon performance and performance measurement. Business units and cost centres were created with the emphasis being upon cost reduction and measures of output per unit of financial input, rather than the tradition of service and effectiveness.

Initiatives were also deliberately taken to bring into the public sector managers from the private sector in the belief that they would be more in tune with and more adept at achieving what the government wanted.

Where organizations were created anew, even though they remained in the public sector, for example the NHS Trusts, they were required by government to develop their own terms, conditions and contracts of employment and employee relations policies and procedures. One of the government's intentions in doing this was to fragment employee relations in the public sector, to force a decentralization of employee relations, break up the centralized determination of terms and conditions and the highly structured and bureaucratic procedures referred to earlier which, it was felt (by government), contributed significantly to the power of the public-sector unions. It was also firmly part of the government agenda to force pay determination down to a local level because it was thought that the national determination of pay inevitably led to rates that were far higher than would otherwise have been necessary to attract labour in many local labour markets, this in turn forcing up rates for other labour in those same local labour markets as other employers competed for that labour (see **Figure 5.5** in which attitudes towards local pay determination for nurses are reflected and in which also it is clear that central government retains control over pay determination in the NHS despite the creation of NHS Trusts etc. and the presence of a supposedly independent pay review board).

By and large, public-sector employees have the same or equivalent employment rights and protections as those in the private sector, although some groups have had their freedom to join a trade union and rights to be represented arbitrarily removed. This happened in 1984 to GCHQ employees, GCHQ being a highly sensitive national security establishment, and teachers had their collective bargaining rights removed from them by the Remuneration of Teachers Act 1987. Perhaps more important still was the belief/determination of the government to argue that the Transfers of Undertakings Regulations 1981 did not apply to the public sector. This is legislation introduced as a requirement of the UK's membership of the EU (the directive on the Transfer of Undertakings 77/187, also known as the Acquired Rights Directive) which sought to protect employees, their employment and their terms and conditions of employment in circumstances where employing organizations were bought and sold, where ownership changed hands, was transferred.

Throughout the 1980s and into the 1990s the government refused to acknowledge the relevance of the directive to those in the public sector, to operations that it itself controlled. It is difficult to escape the conclusion that the reason for this was because it saw the requirements of the directive as undermining its desire to reduce costs in the public sector by forcing service provision into the private sector where employees could be paid less and where they would have worse terms and conditions of employment. This was a particular issue where local authorities were being forced to put service provision out to tender and where contracts were being won on the basis that the service would be provided more cheaply. Government was finally forced to accept that it had not implemented the directive appropriately and non-commercial organizations were brought into the scope of the regulations in the Trades Union Reform and Employment Rights (TURER) Act 1993.

From the perspective of the employees and their representatives all of these initiatives had a number of significant implications. Employees were in many instances confronted fairly suddenly with significant cultural

Staged award angers profession while NHS leaders claim lack of funds will mean cuts to services

David Brindle, Social Services Correspondent

NURSES' anger at the staging yesterday of their 3.3 per cent pay award was partly blunted by what they saw as a precious victory over local pay determination.

Although ministers and health managers insisted local pay remained on the agenda, and the 1997 national rise would represent a "breathing space", nursing unions declared the issue dead.

Christine Hancock, general secretary of the Royal College of Nursing, said: "The pay review body has looked at what has happened, listened to what people like us have said and signalled an end to the local pay experiment. It has failed."

Malcolm Wing, deputy head of health at Unison, the biggest health union, said: "The review body's decision to make a national award is a huge snub to the Government, which has been trying to force local pay on the NHS."

Nurses, together with health visitors, midwives and therapists, will receive 2 per cent of their increase on April 1 and the remainder on December 1. The staging means the rise is worth 2.4 per cent in 1997/98, barely level with the current rate of inflation.

Stephen Dorrell, Health Secretary, said the extra, unbudgeted cost of full payment of 3.3 per cent from April 1, as recommended by the review body, would have undermined improvements in patient services.

However, NHS leaders warned that the cost of even the staged increase would hit services. Phil Hunt, director of the National Association of Health Authorities and Trusts, said: "A lot of trusts are telling us they can't afford even 2 per cent."

Karen Caines, director of the Institute of Health Services Management, said: "The money to meet these awards, even though they may be staggered, is just not available within existing trust budgets."

The review body report says that while nurses' motivation and commitment remain high, morale is often low. Heavy workloads, staff shortages and lack of promotion opportunities are combining to depress many.

"We were also struck by the number of complaints from staff at the increasing amount of paperwork they were required to complete, resulting in part from poor information systems," the report says.

The review body criticises trusts for failing to take the initiative on local pay. Results of the two-year local pay experiment have been limited, with only just over half all trusts having reached agreement on a local top-up for last year's national 2 per cent rise.

Figure 5.5 *Source: The Guardian*, 7 February 1997

change and with insecurity; many were actually made redundant either prior to privatization or subsequent to it. Many public-sector employees were quite suddenly confronted by a management with a different agenda; service provision was no longer as important as cost reduction, performance measurement and efficiency. Employees were also confronted with new ways of working and with initiatives such as performance appraisal. Whereas in the past employees and their representatives had recourse to appeal, grievance and dispute (see Chapter 10 for the difference between these latter two) procedures outside the organization they found these avenues cut off and they were confronted with a more assertive and influential local management, even though that local management was often quite inexperienced in employee relations matters.

These changes also confronted the unions with resourcing issues since, as employment declined so did union membership, and as this declined so did their income. However, at the same time as income was declining the unions were in many cases being forced to deal with a much larger number of organizations at a local level rather than with the one body at national level. Not surprisingly, the unions fought hard to resist the government's wish to decentralize and localize employee relations in the public sector, with some eventual success, for example within the health service and education.

The public sector has seen pro-rata more overt industrial conflict over the last two decades than has been the case in the private sector and this would appear, in part at least, to be a response to the changes that government have sought to introduce and to the government's determination to succeed and if this meant standing up to the unions and resisting strike action then so be it. The most infamous instance of this determination was the strike in the coal industry in 1984–5, but there have been many other instances of attempted resistance in the civil service, the health service, by teachers in schools and further education, in local authorities, on the railways and even by ambulance workers.

In the face of such a concerted and significant series of initiatives to change employee relations in the public sector it is perhaps surprising that trade union membership is still considerably higher than in the private sector (see Chapter 7 on trade unions) and the unions have managed to resist the drive for localization of bargaining and the determination of terms and conditions to a much greater extent than one might have expected, with main terms and conditions still determined at national level in sectors such as the NHS and education (see also **Figure 5.5**).

Picking up on the discussion in the first chapter of this book regarding the difference between employee relations and industrial relations, Black and Upchurch (1999) suggest that the framework in much of the public sector is still, as we come to the end of the century, indicative of industrial relations rather than employee relations.

The election of a Labour government in 1997 doesn't seem to herald much change in government attitudes towards the public sector and particularly to the issue of pay within it. Government determined early on that it would adhere to the outgoing government's spending plans and this inevitably meant that restrictions upon public-sector pay would remain. It seems as convinced as earlier governments that there is something to be said for linking pay to some measure of performance, even in the face of significant union opposition. This has already been quite apparent with the government's determination to introduce a performance-related pay system for teachers, an initiative which the government in 1999 was keen to dress up as a means of enabling significant pay increases for teachers.

There is some evidence that the government is not intent upon pursuing the decentralization of the determination of basic pay and other terms and conditions of employment and the fragmentation of collective bargaining, and the commitment to providing legislative support for trade union recognition would appear to indicate that maybe the worst is behind the public-sector trade unions, a feeling perhaps strengthened by the decision to restore the right to join a trade union to staff at GCHQ – see earlier.

However, set against this is an apparent association with local management's autonomy to vary unilaterally terms and conditions of employment in the fire service in the pursuit of efficiencies and flexibilities. Also, comments earlier in the summer of 1999 about the unwillingness of public-sector workers to accept change. Privatizations are still on the agenda, for example air traffic control (though there is a possibility that this proposal may be negatively impacted by the concerns raised by the Paddington rail disaster) and pressures upon the size of the public sector are likely to remain as are the pressures to continually force economies out of the system. There is still a belief that the public sector is full of inefficiency, that considerable cost savings are waiting to be achieved and that businessmen from the private sector are more likely to achieve these efficiencies than are those in the public sector (see **Figure 5.6**). This figure also indicates that the new government appeared to believe that there were considerable gains to be obtained in terms of public-sector productivity and performance and refers to the earlier statement by the Prime Minister that he bore the scars on his back from trying to obtain change within the public sector.

For further information and views on the transformation of employee relations in the public sector see Ferner and Colling (1995), Beaumont (1992), Winchester and Bach (1995).

Activity 6

Read again this section on the industrial/employee relations systems in the public sector before and after 1979, pick out the main elements and contrast them.

Economic manager – labour market policies and unemployment

Prior to the mid-1970s there had been a long-standing consensus at the political level that governments had a responsibility to try to ensure full

Business 'hit squad' to cut public waste

Panel aims to improve taxpayers' value for money

Mark Atkinson
Economics Correspondent

The government is drafting in a hit squad of seven business leaders to clamp down on waste and inefficiency in the public sector, the treasury chief secretary Alan Milburn announced yesterday.

In a move which threatens to reignite internal Labour rows over the public sector, Mr Milburn said the team would help identify root and branch changes needed to ratchet up public sector productivity and performance.

"Delivering tangible change for the better in Britain's key public services is the priority for the remainder of this parliament," Mr Milburn said. "The government is committed to delivering modern first class services which make the best use of the extra cash the government is providing. We are determined that £40bn worth of extra investment in health and education brings £40bn worth of improvement."

The public services productivity panel, set up after last summer's comprehensive spending review, which set in train a rolling three-year programme of public spending, will be chaired by Mr Milburn.

It will include Andrew Foster, controller of the audit commission; John Makinson, group finance director of the media group Pearson; Dame Sheila Masters of accountants KPMG; John Mayo, finance director of GEC; Clare Spottiswoode, of management consultants PA Consulting; John Dowdy, of McKinsey's; and Byron Grote, executive vice president of BP Amoco.

Reporting to a cabinet committee chaired by the chancellor, Gordon Brown, the panel's members have each been given specific areas of government to investigate, with the ultimate goal of helping to achieve efficiency savings of £8bn a year by 2001-02.

They will be allowed to carry out spot checks on front-line public services and pose as "mystery shoppers".

While the recruitment of a further body of expertise from the private sector into government will boost Labour's pro-business credentials, it risks increasing resentment among civil servants, still smarting over the prime minister's declaration last month that he bore scars on his back from wrestling with the public sector.

The deputy prime minister, John Prescott, hit back by saying that Britain should be proud of its public sector, which had delivered benefits to the public where the private sector had failed.

Other moves by the government to reduce waste have included the announcement of a review by Mr Milburn last week into the spiralling costs of ill-health retirement and a clampdown on sickness absence.

Figure 5.6 *Source: The Guardian*, 9 August 1999

employment and there was consensus that this could best be achieved through the expansionary management of aggregate demand within the economy in accordance with the prescriptions of Keynes. Also in line with the Keynesian approach, there was a commitment to social protection. A range of mechanisms were available for use to stimulate demand including fiscal and monetary instruments, i.e. taxation and government borrowing provided the resources for public expenditure and interest rates and the exchange rate could also be used to manage the level of demand.

Demand-management policies and instruments can, of course, also be used to achieve the objective of low inflation or price stability. The instruments are used to damp down or choke off demand on the assumption that this would reduce inflationary pressures in the economy, beneficially influence a nation's international competitiveness and thereby achieve growth via exports. Demand management, then, was variously used to expand demand in times of economic slump or recession and to damp down demand and thereby combat inflationary pressures.

Throughout the 1950s and 1960s unemployment and inflation were both relatively low, as producers in the UK were confronted with friendly market conditions around the world. However, and after the inflationary impact of the oil price rises of 1973–4, by the mid-1970s not only had inflation risen to all-time post-war highs (in excess of 20 per cent per annum) but unemployment was also rising, a combination referred to as 'stagflation'. Government's attempts to control inflation through corporatism and prices and incomes policies failed and eventually they had to approach the International Monetary Fund (IMF) for a loan to cover an expanding balance of payments deficit and public-sector borrowing requirement (PSBR), this latter in part the product of higher social security bills as unemployment rose and partly the product of high pay increases in the public sector as the unions fought to keep up with inflation.

The IMF insisted that the UK government change tack as far as economic policy was concerned and they insisted that what was needed was the implementation of monetarist policies giving priority to the control of inflation, public expenditure (including public-sector wages) and the PSBR, and thereby the country's international competitiveness. The instruments of the new way were to use the government's ability to control the supply of money into the economy and public expenditure and, if necessary, short-term unemployment was to be allowed to rise as the trade-off for low inflation. These essentially supply-side policies had a demand effect which is deflationary rather than expansionist.

The Conservative government elected in 1979 was firmly committed to implementing policies similar to those required by the IMF and to do so vigorously; priority was to be given to the control of inflation. The underpinning ideology was liberalist and essentially individual. The market was to be allowed to reign, including in the labour market where there was also a conviction that institutional deregulation (see below for some examples), also often referred to in terms of institutional or regulatory flexibility, was essential in order to encourage enterprise and employment. Social protection was to be reduced (thereby also reducing public expenditure) as an incentive for the unemployed and disadvantaged to accept responsibility for their own fate and wherever possible obtain work; enterprise was to be encouraged and industries and companies that could not compete were to be allowed to founder. So the government operated a mix of:

1 *laisser-faire* policies towards markets

2 controls on money supply and public expenditure, supply-side initiatives which also had an indirect and deflationary impact upon demand

3 policies geared towards reforming labour market institutions and regulations and through which they:

- limited the bargaining power of the trades unions
- eliminated the remnants of minimum wage protection through the wages councils
- made it more difficult for employees to gain entitlement to legislative protection and/or compensation from arbitrary action by the employer, for example through unfair dismissal proceedings and redundancy pay
- made it easier and cheaper for employers to hire and fire
- amended restrictions upon hours of work, the use of certain atypical contracts
- removed some of the restrictions upon the employment of cheap labour such as immigrants and children.

These policies had an immediate impact in the labour market and over a relatively short period, 1979–81, unemployment doubled from 1.14 million (4.7 per cent) to 2.3 million (9.4 per cent) and by 1986 it had reached over 3 million (11.4 per cent), most of this in manufacturing industries. Employment in manufacturing industries declined by over 2 million between 1979 and 1987.

In the early 1990s the UK again experienced a massive recession during which unemployment rose again close to the three million mark and there was another substantial erosion of employment in manufacturing. However, at the end of the millennium unemployment and inflation were both at relatively low levels in the UK, but so also were rates of economic growth.

See Chapter 6 on the labour market (see **Figure 6.2**) for statistics on unemployment in the UK over the last quarter of the twentieth century, the gender composition and the rates of both youth and long-term unemployment. Unemployment characteristics of ethnic minorities are also referred to in this section of Chapter 6.

There has been much debate in the 1990s, particularly within the EU, about the causes of and solutions to the problem of unemployment (Leat, 1998) and a new orthodoxy appears to have developed which supports the policies pursued by governments in the UK over the last twenty years. This orthodoxy tends to diagnose the illness as not so much one of quantity as quality of labour supply, including skill level and type. In particular it is the mismatch between the skills, or lack of them, of the unemployed and those required in the expanding sectors of the economy and by those employers that are creating jobs and recruiting.

The solution is perceived to be available through a mix of supply-side initiatives and active policies (see **Figure 5.7**) geared towards:

The terms 'active' and 'passive' are used to describe and differentiate forms of labour market initiative.

Passive
Objectives:

- the protection of those out of work
- make unemployment more bearable.

In this respect, some argue that passive policies actually encourage unemployment.
Policies and interventions include:

- improved unemployment benefits/social security payments
- redundancy schemes and pay
- early retirements not linked to health.

Active
Objectives:

- the provision of additional employment opportunities
- the protection of existing employment
- making it easier for those out of work to find another job.

Initiatives might include:

- to create jobs, either directly or through some form of employer subsidy or business start-up scheme
- to provide additional training opportunities
- the improvement of the public job search and matching arrangements.

Figure 5.7 Passive–active labour market policies/initiatives

- the improvement of the quality of the labour force
- ensuring that the skills which people have are the skills which are needed in the economy
- improving the services which are concerned with job search and skills matching.

These supply-side measures are to be combined with a deregulated or lightly regulated labour market (see above), coupled with the diminution of social protection and benefits. Together the mix is perceived to facilitate the achievement of international competitiveness as well as being the solution to unemployment.

The Labour government elected in 1997 seem determined to continue these trends, intervening in an active fashion on the supply side of the labour market through schemes such as **The New Deal** (see **Figure 5.8**), expanding the number of student places in further and higher education and making it more and more difficult for people to be both economically inactive and in receipt of some form of social security or unemployment benefit. There seems no let-up in the pursuit of active as opposed to passive labour market policies.

Figure 5.9 gives comparative information on the proportions of GDP spent through the public sector on both active and passive policies and initiatives and how the distribution of this expenditure between active and passive has changed through the 1990s.

It is difficult to evaluate how successful schemes of this kind are and, as pointed out by Smith in **Figure 5.10**, in order to establish the success of the scheme one almost needs to be able to establish what would have happened to the individuals concerned if the scheme had not been in existence or if the individuals concerned had not started on the scheme. The article in **Figure 5.10** is also of value because it points up some of the difficulties of conducting research when the subject of the research is people and their behaviour.

Certainly schemes of this kind are not cheap to run, as indicated by the figures mentioned in the article.

The Labour government's New Deal scheme seeks to address the issue of unemployment, initially among the young and those unemployed for more than six months, though latterly it has been extended to the long-term unemployed. The government announced in November 1999 that the scheme was to be extended also to those over fifty years of age and out of work. It seeks to do this through a mix of supply-side and active initiatives which are geared towards improving the employability of the unemployed.

The unemployed are effectively presented with four options all of which involve training:

- a job with an employer
- work with a voluntary organization
- work on the environment task force
- full-time education or training.

There is to be no fifth option: in other words, staying at home on full benefit is not intended to be an option for the young able-bodied. The offer of employment with training renders the employer to a financial subsidy for a period of six months. The employment element of the scheme is only temporary in that employers are not required to provide permanent employment opportunities.

In addition there are to be improved job search assistance and matching services.

Figure 5.8 The New Deal

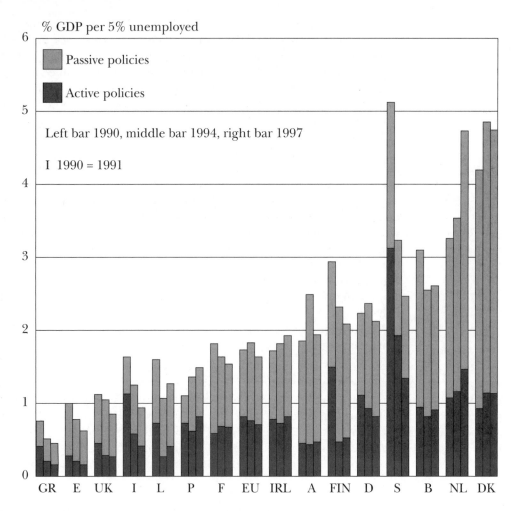

Figure 5.9 Public expenditure on active and passive labour market policies in member states, 1990, 1994 and 1997. *Source:* Employment in Europe 1998: 130

One of the problems with schemes of this kind is that there is always the danger that the employment opportunities offered to scheme members are offered for the wrong reasons, to get the subsidy on offer, and that the employment will simply be a replacement for someone who has been sacked in order to provide it: it is not in any sense a net addition to the total of employment opportunities.

The other main danger is that employers will make the promise of providing training and developmental work experience but that they will renege on the deal and take the money but not provide the benefits to the individual. The behaviour of both the scheme member and the employer needs to be monitored in order to ensure that the scheme is delivering what

Debate Jeffrey Smith

New Deal needs some figuring out

Do active labour market policies like the New Deal actually increase people's chance of getting a good job once they leave the programme? The government, which has invested more than $3bn in the New Deal, must think so but evidence from new research in the US casts doubt on that.

The New Deal, like the workforce investment act in the US, provides job search assistance, job matching services and skills training to people looking for work. The trick in evaluating these policies is figuring out what would have happened to participants had they not taken part in the programme.

A natural starting point assumes that without the assistance provided by the programme individuals would remain unemployed. Backers of active labour market policies like this assumption because it makes the effect of the programme as large as possible. If we assume that without the

New Deal none of its participants would have found work, then all of the jobs which participants find must result from the programme.

James Heckman from the University of Chicago and I have examined what would have happened to participants in an American employment and training programme had they not taken part. We have unique experimental data from recent evaluation of the job training partnership act (JTPA) programme in the US.

In the JTPA experiment, people who applied to and were eligible for the programme were assigned completely at random to one of two groups. The first (the treatment group) was given access to the programme's services. The second (the control group) was excluded from the programme for 18 months.

We found that members of the control group became employed almost as often (for male youth, more often) than those who had access to programme services. For most demographic groups, the data suggest that the programme increases employment rates by only a few percentage points.

While a small positive impact may suffice to pass a cost-benefit test (as the JTPA programme appears to do for most adults) it presents a very different picture of programme performance than the assumption that no one would have found employment without the programme.

We also examined what happened to participants' earnings after they went through the programme. While most

Data suggest employment programmes have a small positive impact

evaluations compare the earnings and employment of participants before and after the programme, once again we were able to compare their experience with the control groups. We find that people often choose to participate during a period of unusually low earnings. This makes sense: someone with a stable job will not seek out these programmes even if eligible.

Because participants tend to experience temporary labour market troubles just before participation, before-after comparisons attribute to the programme the rebound that would occur even without it.

In addition to their scientific contribution, our findings have important implications for evaluation policy. When the JTPA experiment found no effect of the programme on the employment and earnings of youth, Congress cut the budget for the youth component of the programme by more than 80%.

Obviously, we cannot say whether or not the New Deal programmes recently introduced in the UK will be effective. What we can say are some things about how to find out.

First, evaluation is not easy. It means allocating enough money to involve top scholars. It also means spending enough on data collection (and possibly experimentation) to produce an evaluation that will meet the standards of academic research.

Second, social experiments should play an important role within an overall regime of programme evaluation. While not perfect, experiments often

Just because a venture is popular does not mean that it works

provide clear evidence of programme success or failure.

Third, data collected as part of the official evaluation must be made available for use in further research. Government officials often resist this because initially positive results may be overturned by further analysis. A government seriously interested in evaluation, as the Labour government claims to be, must bear this risk.

Fourth, the government must take the results of its own evaluations seriously. Just because a programme is popular or has entrenched constituencies in favour of it does not mean that it works. If compelling evidence exists that a programme does not work, then the probability of its demise must increase. Otherwise, money spent on evaluation would be better returned to the long-suffering taxpayer.

Jeffrey Smith is associate professor of economics at the University of Western Ontario in London, Canada

Figure 5.10 *Source: The Guardian, 2 August 1999; 28 July 1999 and 13 August 1999*

Employers renege on New Deal training

Research shows abuse of subsidy system is widespread

Charlotte Denny

Employment minister Andrew Smith yesterday defended the success of Labour's flagship New Deal programme as research showed employers are undermining the scheme. Companies are said to be reneging on their obligation to provide training for young people in exchange for a government wage subsidy.

Mr Smith has threatened to withdraw the £60-a-week subsidy from employers who fail to provide one day a week's training for New Deal recruits. But one in three employers told researchers from the Employment Policy Institute that they were not providing any training for New Deal employees and one in five said they had no plans to do so.

"In a sample like this it's slightly worrying that a third of employers say they aren't providing any training," said John Philpott, the EPI's director. "The Department for education and employment ought to be doing some kind of audit to establish how much training is being undertaken."

Mr Smith said the training provided by employers was constantly monitored. "I strongly urge any person on the New Deal who is not receiving this training to contact their personal adviser immediately."

More than 54,000 employers have agreed to provide subsided places since the New Deal began nationwide last April. The programme is expected to cost the government nearly £2bn over the next three years. Labour has promoted it as a radical break from the deadend work schemes provided for young people by the previous government.

The research, jointly conducted with the Prince's Trust and the Institute for Personnel and Development, shows a big gap between the expectations of young recruits, who hope they will gain the skills to get a better job, and employers' anticipation that young people will arrive from the employment service ready trained.

"There is a fundamental expectations gap among both groups with employers feeling let down by the calibre of recruits and young people feeling disappointed that they are not given greater opportunities to improve their skills and employability," the report says.

Mr Philpott said the credibility of the New Deal in the eyes of young people was at risk if employers reneged on their side of the deal.

Figure 5.10 (continued)

35% of New Dealers leave for 'unknown destination'

Trainees lured from scheme by short-term jobs

Phillip Inman

The majority of young people who "disappear" from the government's New Deal employment training scheme find employment, but most of them are taking short-term jobs and are unemployed again after only a few months, according to a study by the National Centre for Social Research.

Figures for June show that 35% of the 140,000 18- to 24-year-olds who have participated in New Deal training are still classified as having an "unknown destination", which means the employment service has lost track of them after they left the scheme.

The high level of "missing" New Dealers has concerned ministers since the scheme was begun early last year. Ministers feared large numbers of the participants were rejecting the New Deal and living in poverty without a job or access to benefits.

In response the employment service, which is managing the New Deal for the government, commissioned the NCSR to contact a sample of young people who joined the scheme in the first wave to assess their employment records.

The research showed that 57% of people who left the scheme without notifying the employment service took up a job offer but only 29% were in paid work when contacted six to eight months later.

Ministers will take comfort from data showing a majority of those leaving the scheme are offered jobs, but critics argue the evidence suggests that most of them have "ended up in poor-quality, unsustained employment".

Paul Convery, a director of the Unemployment Unit & Youthaid, said the employment service needed to put more effort into tracking people who leave the scheme and finding them long-term employment,

especially as most of those who quit were from the most disadvantaged groups.

Some 10% of the missing New Dealers had never worked in paid employment, 18% were from ethnic minority backgrounds – against 13% for the whole New Deal population. Thirty-nine per cent had been sentenced to a fine, probation or community service or been given a police warning, 8% had been in prison or a young offenders' institution and 8% in the care of social services. The majority go back to claiming jobseekers allowance.

A spokesman for the department of employment, transport, education and the regions, said the NCSR's figures were very positive.

In May, the latest period for which figures are available, 114,370 people had gained a job through the New Deal, with 84,450 of them employed for more than 13 weeks and 69,200 being unsubsidised.

Figure 5.10 (*continued*)

it is supposed to and that the participants are acting with good faith.

These points are made in the second article of **Figure 5.10**, which reports the results of some early research into the scheme, how it is working and whether it is being effective. The articles also make clear that there is another problem area and that relates to the differing expectations of the employers and the employees.

Another criticism of schemes of this kind is that they often do not result in long-term quality employment opportunities for those graduating from the scheme. This is as much a more general criticism of the pursuit of supply-side and active policies in that you can, through training and work experience, remedy some of the reasons for an individual being unemployed, giving enhanced individual employability, but if the jobs aren't there at the end of the day you can do more harm than good because you encourage the development of expectations which then are not fulfilled.

As is said in the last article in **Figure 5.10** which reports on some other early research on the impact of the scheme and which suggests that this early research indicated that most of those leaving the scheme had 'ended up in poor quality, unsustained employment'. This latter article also provides some insight into the scale of the scheme and the numbers of young unemployed people that were involved in the early stages.

Activity 7

1 Read the article by Smith in **Figure 5.10** and note down the main research issues and difficulties that occur to you.
2 Read again the three articles in **Figure 5.10** and the text of this section. The New Deal is an example of a supply-side and active initiative initially aimed at the problem of youth unemployment. Identify and list the main advantages and disadvantages of this kind of policy.

Let us now return to the debate about the validity of the recent orthodoxy that deregulation and flexibility are the route through which unemployment can best be resolved and which, as we noted earlier, have been at the root of government policies and initiatives in the UK over the last quarter of the twentieth century and which have also made significant inroads into the thinking of other governments and institutions in the EU.

It is important to be aware that there are different views on this and there are others who argue that with inflation having been effectively forced out of the global economy by competition, the recipe for reducing unemployment should now emphasize faster rates of economic growth and that this can be influenced by governments through policies encouraging an expansion of demand rather than through supply-side measures or institutional deregulation.

In the summer of 1999 the OECD added some credibility to this alternative view in its annual Employment Outlook (1999), in which it asserted that it could find no direct link between either tough regulations giving employees job security or levels of trade union membership and strength, and the overall incidence of high unemployment. It acknowledged that regulatory flexibility may assist the speed with which labour markets respond to changing patterns of demand and that inflexibility and trade union strength may protect insiders at the expense of outsiders, making it more difficult for those not in employment to break into employment. This may mean that once in work it is likely that an individual is relatively protected, but once out of work, once they become an outsider, the period of unemployment is likely to be longer. This report points out that without an adequate level of demand within the economy there is nothing for the flexible labour market to respond to. So economic growth and demand for labour are the drivers of employment expansion, a deregulated and institutionally flexible labour market will facilitate the speed and ease with which the labour market responds; supply-side policies may enhance employability but don't create jobs.

No doubt this debate will run and run but inevitably research findings of this kind will give succour to those who argue for governments to take initiatives that expand demand and create jobs – a kind of reconstructed or neo-Keynesian approach implying an element of demand management. Examples of the kind of expansionary demand side initiatives that might be acceptable are:

1 increased public expenditure on infrastructure schemes which stimulate demand for labour
2 other schemes directed at job creation in the public sector and geared towards the employment of the young or long-term unemployed, as in the creation of community work and welfare programmes, or
3 schemes that encourage employers to employ more labour by making the employment of labour cheaper, for example by government reducing the non-wage cost of employment such as employers' national insurance and social security contributions.

Again, it is likely that policies of such a kind would need to be targeted at the groups suffering the most, the young and long-term unemployed, and they would need to have the requisite skills, etc.

ACAS – Advisory, Conciliation and Arbitration Service

In addition to the roles already described in this chapter, government has traditionally provided a range of third-party services to the parties to the employment relationship that may assist in the resolution of conflict between them, and also some advisory and research services. Since 1974 the ACAS has been the main source of these services.

ACAS was created in 1974 by the incoming Labour government. This government replaced the Conservative one that had passed the Industrial Relations Act and it was this incoming government that had the agreement with the unions and employers that we have referred to earlier as the Social Contract. At the level of the governing council ACAS was an example of the tripartite approach that we have associated with a corporatist ideology, however it was given a formal role emphasizing the improvement of industrial relations through the extension of collective bargaining and through encouraging the voluntary development and reform of collective bargaining machinery. In this context the organization can be seen to be reflective of the traditional liberal collectivist perspectives and preferences of the parties and also in many ways consistent with the diagnosis and recommendations of the Donovan Commission (see above) emphasizing a voluntarist approach and the need for procedural reform. In many ways the creation of ACAS and the role afforded it can be seen to mark a transition from liberal collectivism to corporatism, the emphasis upon the resolution of conflict through voluntary collective bargaining, but also signalled is a greater willingness to support this with a legislative framework and a preference for tripartite administration.

Given the inclinations of the Conservative governments from 1979 onwards it is surprising that the formal requirement to encourage collective bargaining was not actually removed until 1993 in the TURER Act.

Until very recently all of ACAS's services were provided free of charge to the consumer but ACAS can now charge for some of its advisory services.

What services does ACAS provide?

For once the name of the organization is an accurate indicator of the roles provided: **advice**, **conciliation** and **arbitration**. The organization offers a range of advisory mechanisms including advice and information given to telephone callers (in excess of 500,000 in 1998, many of these calls are for information concerning an individual's legal rights and the interpretation of the law), in various publications and through a mechanism which ACAS itself calls **Advisory Mediation**, which it describes as 'a cooperative and joint problem solving approach to resolving issues faced by employers, employees and their representatives ... it represents a practical expression of partnership at the workplace' ACAS (1998: 43).

ACAS suggests that this can help prevent disputes, tackle underlying problems, develop better solutions, encourage the acceptance of change and result in more constructive working relationships. They tend to use two main mechanisms for this, the Joint Working Party and the Joint Workshop. Both of these are non-negotiating bodies but the intention is that they should produce agreed outcomes, in the former instance the hope is that the agreed outcomes will include a solution to the problem and agreement to implement, whereas in the latter case the hopes are perhaps a little more limited. Sometimes an ACAS official will act as the chair of the joint body or forum.

This is a process consistent with the change of emphasis in ACAS's role that has occurred over the years and which was finally signalled by the removal of the responsibility to encourage collective bargaining. The emphasis is upon working together, cooperation and problem solving rather than upon encouraging the resolution of conflict through power-based bargaining (see Chapter 9 for more information on the nature of collective bargaining).

People often have difficulty with the distinction between the two other main services offered, arbitration and conciliation:

- **arbitration** is where the parties involved ask a third party to **decide**, much like a judge, an issue or dispute between them which they cannot themselves resolve
- **conciliation** is where in the event of a dispute between the parties they both ask a third party to **help** them come to an agreement. These disputes may concern an individual employee or a group.

With arbitration there is at least a moral obligation on the parties to accept the arbitrator's decision, with conciliation the parties can accept or reject the suggestions of the conciliator. It is relatively common for the process of conciliation to result in the formation of a Joint Working Party as part of the settlement and as a way of progressing matters, in other words advisory mediation is often an outcome of the conciliation service offered. An example is given in **Figure 5.11**.

Workload

Individual conciliation

The main activity of ACAS (at least as measured by the number of cases dealt with) is the provision of conciliation services in the event of an individual's application that one or more of their statutory rights has been infringed. ACAS has a statutory duty to promote a settlement in a wide range of employment rights complaints, which either have or could be made to an employment tribunal.

As noted in **Figure 5.12** the caseload in this area of work totalled in excess of 113,500 cases, a continuation of the rising trend which passed the 100,000 mark for the first time in 1996. Approximately 35 per cent (40,000+) of this total concerned complaints and disputes relating to unfair dismissal, followed in terms of the number of cases by those concerning the protection of wages (25,000) and breach of contract (23,500). Other major

There are two principal methods for delivering ACAS advisory mediation assistance:

- *joint workshops* which provide a non-negotiating forum for parties to explore problems and identify appropriate courses of corrective action, including an agreed agenda for taking matters forward

- *joint working parties* (JWPs) which are non-negotiating bodies, typically chaired by ACAS staff, through which employer and employee representatives work together, adopting a structured problem-solving approach – problems are defined, information is gathered and considered, options are evaluated, and solutions are agreed and implemented.

Advisory mediation is not only a tool for preventing disputes, it may also be used to help parties resolve an existing dispute. An example of this occurred in 1998 during a dispute at *The Guardian* newspaper. In mid-July ACAS was jointly requested by *The Guardian* and the National Union of journalists (NUJ), to conciliate on the 1998 pay award, in accordance with the parties' procedure agreement. Although conciliation helped to progress some of the issues, such as the use of casual workers, it was not possible to reach agreement over the newspaper's proposal for sub-editors to change from a four-day week to a nine-day fortnight. At a chapel meeting in September it had been anticipated that there would be a call for an industrial action ballot; but instead the chapel accepted a management offer of a working party, and a joint request was made to ACAS to chair it.

The joint working party met over four consecutive days in early October, and a possible solution began to emerge. Following the final meeting of the working party a joint presentation of the proposals to the sub-editors, chaired by ACAS, took place. It became apparent that the proposals were broadly acceptable and ACAS was requested to organize a ballot for the forty-six affected to determine whether they would agree to work the extra shifts that they had provisionally been designated. The ballot was run using a combination (predominantly by e-mail) with only two sub-editors declining to accept the proposals. Following this result, there was a chapel meeting at which the proposals on pay, casual workers and new rotas were unanimously accepted.

Figure 5.11 *Source:* ACAS (1999) *Annual Report for 1998:* 53–54

areas of complaint relate to the infringement of rights under one or more of the Acts concerned with equality and discrimination.

These figures do appear to indicate an enormous number of individuals alleging that an employer or some other party, another employee or a trade union, had infringed one or more of their legal rights with regard to work. It seems reasonable to assume that the increase over the years in the numbers of these cases is a response to the increased number of statutory rights acquired by employees in recent years, but it is also possible that it is a reflection of people both becoming more aware of their rights and being increasingly willing to exercise them.

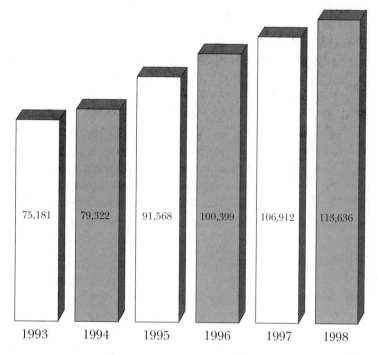

Figure 5.12 Individual conciliation cases. *Source:* ACAS (1999) *Annual Report for 1998:* 72

Other workload areas

The demand for collective conciliation to help parties resolve disputes appears to have been relatively stable in recent years, in each of the last five years the number hovering just above or below 1300. In 1998 the number of advisory mediation projects completed was 530 and the number of arbitrations arranged was only 51. This latter figure represents arbitrations under ACAS's auspices, not conducted by an ACAS officer but arranged by them, ACAS keeps a register or list of people prepared to conduct arbitrations.

Activity 8

Explain the difference between arbitration and conciliation.

Activity 9

One or other of the parties are often reluctant to allow a dispute to go to arbitration and the incidence of arbitration is less than the incidence of conciliation. Why do you think this is?

Summary

In this chapter we have examined the various roles or ways in which government at a national level forms part of the context in which employee relations are conducted. In the main we have concentrated upon the four functions or roles, of legislator, employer in the public sector, as economic manager and labour market influencer, and as the paymaster for the services provided by ACAS.

In all of these areas attention has been paid to demonstrate the relevance of ideology, values and beliefs, to the objectives determined and the policies and strategies pursued.

In the context of the influence of government upon employee relations in the UK it seems clear that 1979 and the election of a Conservative government constitute watersheds. Analysts may argue as to whether economic policy or the new legislative framework were the more influential but there is little disagreement that profound change was signalled by this event, economic policy was driven by a conviction that competitiveness on the world stage was linked to the achievement of control over inflation and that unemployment was a price worth paying, trade union power had to be diminished, management had to reclaim its authority and the regulations and institutions of the labour market and social protection had to be reformed.

In the public sector it signalled the end of a dominant concern with service provision and equity, social welfarism and the beginnings of a period of management by confrontation, deteriorating employee terms and conditions of employment and greater insecurity and a determined drive to decentralize and localize the determination of terms and conditions of employment and the conduct of employee relations. This was to be accompanied by a drive for efficiencies and economies with the emphasis upon performance and output productivity per unit of input.

At the turn of the millennium there was little if any evidence that the election of a Labour government in 1997 would have anything like the same degree of impact, since they seem to have many of the same values and beliefs as underpinned the Conservative government's programme of reform.

In the final section of the chapter we examined the roles of ACAS and the trends in and distribution of its workload.

Activity 2

Liberal individualism: here the government will have a minimal role in regulating the interactions and processes of employee relations. There will be a reliance upon individual exchange in the market place and individual contract. Government may intervene to enhance the freedom of the parties to employee relations, hence there may be emphasis upon deregulation of the labour market and to eliminate or reduce monopoly and other sources of imperfection in the market such as the formation of collectives and the utilization of collective power in the reconciliation of the conflict between buyers and sellers. Both trade unions and collective bargaining are frowned upon.

Liberal collectivism/voluntarism: recognizes that individual sellers of labour do not have an equality of power with the buyers of labour, it is an illusion that facilitates paternalism and exploitation. In this context collectives (for example trade unions) provide a legitimate source of countervailing power and, while they might not be encouraged by government, it is unlikely that a government of this persuasion would take steps to discourage them or reduce their ability to act on behalf of and pursue their members' interests. It is an ideology that countenances:

- a preference for the parties voluntarily to resolve their differences usually reflected in an emphasis upon collective bargaining though there may be some limited regulation of the interaction of the parties
- some limits on individual freedom
- government intervention to protect the national interest and vulnerable groups or individuals such as in an insistence that the legal system provides employees with minimum rights and protections and where necessary a social safety net.

Corporatism: here there is an implication that order and equity are best achieved centrally, hence government will seek to mediate between the interests of labour and capital and integrate the competing interests into some form of centralized decision-making process which is likely to be tripartite and the main protagonists are encouraged to see themselves and to act as social partners. The emphasis is likely to be on interdependence and consensus rather than competition. The integration of the various interests may be achieved on a voluntary basis with the decision-making achieved through the process of bargaining or it may be the product of coercion.

Activity 3

The emphasis upon freedoms, immunities and negative rights is consistent with the liberalist traditions and is usually contrasted with the systems of positive rights typical in most developed economies and in countries that have formal and written constitutions. Examples might be:

- the freedom to join a trade union or enter into collective bargaining rather than a positive right to do so
- trade union immunities from civil action being taken against them by a third party to recoup losses resulting from industrial action, rather than a positive right to take that action
- the right not to be unfairly dismissed or unfairly selected for redundancy or not to be discriminated against on the grounds of sex, marital status or race rather than the positive right to be employed or treated equally.

Activity 4
- The framework for collective relationships and interactions.

The individual employee now has a right to join or not join the trade union of his or her choice and there is no longer any protection for closed shop arrangements.

The Employment Rights Act 1999 provides trade unions with a positive right to recognition from employers for the purposes of collective bargaining providing that certain threshold levels of support for the union are met from among the workforce. There is no legal requirement that employers actually share the decision-making in respect of organizational and employment issues and, even where collective bargaining is entered into and an agreement is made, the agreement is not intended to be legally binding or to have contractual force.

There are some legislative requirements for employers to inform and consult with employee representatives on a range of specified issues such as health and safety matters, the transfer of undertakings, the protection of employee rights, terms and conditions of employment and prior to the introduction of collective redundancies.

There are a range of conditions that have to be met by the union, both relating to the subject matter of the action and the procedures to be followed, if industrial action by the union is to be lawful. Secondary and unofficial action is likely to be unlawful.

- The relationship of the individual trade union member with his trade union.

There are legal provisions regarding and covering a member's contributions to a union political fund, the deduction at source of a member's subscriptions, or dues as they are traditionally called, the disciplinary action that the union can take and the circumstances in which it can be taken lawfully and fairly. In this latter connection the Employment Act 1988 gave trade union members the right not to be disciplined for not taking part in lawful industrial action and the right to take legal action against the union if that industrial action was taken without the appropriate secret ballot. The election of members of the National Executive Committee (NEC) of the union is also regulated by the law.

The trade union member has a right to ask the Commissioner for the Rights of Trade Union Members (CROTUM) to investigate allegations that he or she has been unfairly treated by the union or that one or more of their statutory rights *vis-à-vis* the union and membership has been infringed.

Activity 5

'Implied' in this context really means exactly what it says, terms are implied or incorporated into the contract and do not need to be expressed either orally or in writing by the parties or their representatives. They form part of the contract without the parties necessarily agreeing that they should be or, indeed in many instances, even being aware that they form part of the contract.

The main sources of such terms are statute or the decisions of the courts over the years as common law duties and obligations of the parties were developed. Terms implied from these sources apply in general to all contracts of employment.

Terms may also be implied from custom and practice. Here the test that has to be satisfied is whether the custom or practice is 'reasonable, certain and notorious' or they may be implied from the conduct of the parties.

Activity 6
Before 1979:

- trade unionism/recognition both encouraged
- collective bargaining at national level/centralized and joint determination of terms and conditions of employment
- locally the role of employee relations activity was to interpret and implement national agreements
- main terms and conditions were determined using the principle of comparability
- there were sophisticated, jointly agreed and formal procedural arrangements for dealing with matters of interpretation and individual grievances.

1979 onwards:

- a determination to reduce the size of the public sector and the numbers employed through policies such as privatization and competitive tendering and where possible a worsening of the terms and conditions of employment as a means of achieving cost reductions
- the introduction of performance-related pay and the performance ethic
- a preference for individual contracts and a desire to decrease the power of the trade unions and if necessary to take them on and beat them
- a move to decentralize and devolve both operational and collective bargaining structures including the base for the determination of pay and other main terms and conditions of employment
- a rejection of the principle of comparability
- a determination to resist unions/insist on managerial prerogative

the introduction of market forces, such as by the separation of the roles of purchaser and provider, as further incentive to eliminate waste.

Activity 7

1 As Smith says, the assumption that usually seems to underpin evaluation of initiatives of this kind is that without the policy initiative all the participants would have remained unemployed and this assumption enables the best picture possible to be presented of the success of the initiative.

An accurate evaluation of such initiatives must reject such an assumption and really needs to be based on an assessment of what would have happened if the policy had not been implemented. Through knowing what would have happened without the initiative and what did happen with the initiative it becomes possible to evaluate the impact of the scheme more accurately.

Smith suggests that one way of doing this is to use two groups, one of which is the control group that does not take part in the scheme, while the other does. The two groups should be as alike as possible other than for their differential participation in the scheme. In the experiment described by Smith this was achieved through the completely random allocation of individuals eligible for the scheme to one of the two groups.

2 Advantages.

- The main advantage of schemes of this kind is that they should result in a reduction of the levels of unemployment and this is achieved through an enhancement of the quality and employability of unemployed labour. The employability of unemployed labour is enhanced through the acquisition of knowledge and skills that are in short supply and for which there is demand. The training and employment opportunities offered through the scheme therefore must be focused or targeted.
- The policy should also highlight and improve the efficiency and effectiveness of the searching and matching processes and service institutions.
- Where the initiative incorporates a reduction of employment protection and the creation of subsidies to employers it is possible that the scheme will create employment opportunities in the private sector as well as in socially or environmentally friendly activities.

3 Disadvantages and dangers.

- There is always the danger that the employment opportunities offered to scheme members are offered for the wrong reasons, for example in order to get the monetary subsidy on offer to employers, and that the employment opportunity will simply be a replacement for someone else who has been sacked in order to provide it and therefore not a net addition to the total of employment opportunities.

- The other main danger is that employers will make the promise of providing training and developmental work experience but that they will renege on the deal and take the money but not provide the benefits to the individual. Employers may perceive the scheme as a source of cheap labour with little or no employment protection.
- The articles also make clear that there is another problem area and that relates to the differing expectations of the employers and the employees.
- Another criticism of schemes of this kind is that they often do not result in long-term quality employment opportunities for those graduating from the scheme.
- You can, through training and work experience, remedy some of the reasons for an individual being unemployed, you may have enhanced individual employability, but if the jobs aren't there at the end of the day you can do more harm than good because you encourage the development of expectations which then are not fulfilled.
- The end result may be that scheme members end up in poor quality, unsustained employment.

Activity 8

Arbitration is where the parties ask a third party to decide an issue or dispute between them which they cannot themselves resolve; conciliation is where in the event of a dispute between the parties they both ask a third party to help them come to an agreement. With arbitration there is at least a moral obligation on the parties to accept the arbitrator's decision, with conciliation the parties can accept or reject the suggestions of the conciliator.

Activity 9

One of the main reasons is that in agreeing to go to arbitration the parties almost always have to agree to accept the decision of the arbitrator whatever it may be, the parties therefore are agreeing to give up control and management in particular is often (wisely) reluctant to do this. If management allow an issue to go to arbitration they are immediately giving up their ability to control a particular situation or determine terms and conditions of employment. However, it is relatively common that the parties are willing to agree to arbitration on some types of issue and not on others, for example as a manager you might be prepared to allow arbitration on an individual grievance or collective dispute that is about the interpretation or implementation of an existing set of rules yet refuse to allow it when the dispute is about the negotiation of new substantive terms and conditions of employment such as rates of pay or hours of work.

References

ACAS, 1998. Annual Report for 1997.

ACAS, 1999. Annual Report for 1998.

Beaumont, P., 1992. *Public Sector Industrial Relations.* Routledge, London.

Black, J. and Upchurch, M., 1999. Public sector employment. In Hollinshead, G., Nicholls, P. and Tailby, S. (eds), *Employee Relations.* Financial Times Pitman Publishing, London.

Blyton, P. and Turnbull, P., 1998. *The Dynamics of Employee Relations.* 2nd Edn. Macmillan, Basingstoke.

Colling, T. and Ferner, A., 1995. Privatisation and marketisation. In Edwards, P. (ed.), *Industrial Relations Theory and Practice in Britain.* Blackwell, Oxford, pp. 491–514.

Crouch, C., 1982. *The Politics of Industrial Relations.* 2nd Edn. Fontana, London.

Dickens, L. and Hall, M., 1995. The state: labour law and industrial relations. In Edwards, P., (ed.), 1995. *Industrial Relations Theory and Practice in Britain.* Blackwell, Oxford.

Dunlop, J.T., 1958. *The Industrial Relations System.* Holt, New York.

Edwards, P., (ed.), 1995. *Industrial Relations Theory and Practice in Britain.* Blackwell, Oxford.

Flanders, A., 1974. The tradition of voluntarism. *British Journal of Industrial Relations* 12(3) pp. 352–70.

Hollinshead, G. and Leat, M., 1995. *Human Resource Management: An International and Comparative Perspective on the Employment Relationship.* Financial Times Pitman, London.

Keller, B.K., 1991. The role of the state as corporate actor in industrial relations systems. In Adams, R.J. (ed.), *Comparative Industrial Relations, Contemporary Research and Theory.* Harper Collins, London, p. 83.

Kessler, S. and Bayliss, F., 1998. 3rd edition. *Contemporary British Industrial Relations.* Macmillan, Basingstoke.

Kochan, T.A., Katz, H.C. and McKersie, R.B., 1986. *The Transformation of American Industrial Relations.* Basic Books, New York.

Leat, M., 1998. *Human Resource Issues of the European Union.* Financial Times Pitman, London.

OECD, 1999. *Annual Employment Outlook 1999.*

Salamon, M., 1999. The state in employee relations. In Hollinshead, G., Nicholls, P. and Tailby, S. (eds), *Employee Relations.* Financial Times Pitman Publishing, London.

Winchester, D. and Bach, S., 1995. The state: the public sector. In Edwards, P. (ed.), *Industrial Relations Theory and Practice in Britain.* Blackwell, Oxford, pp. 304–334.

Additional reading

Crouch, C., 1993. *Industrial Relations and European State Traditions.* Clarendon, Oxford.

McCarthy, W.E.J. (ed.), 1992. *Legal Intervention in Industrial Relations.* Blackwell, Oxford.

Edwards, P., *et al.*, 1992. Great Britain, still muddling through. In Ferner, A. and Hyman, R. (eds), *Industrial Relations in the New Europe.* Blackwell, Oxford.

Farnham, D. and Horton, S. (eds), 1993. *Managing the New Public Services.* Macmillan, Basingstoke.

Goldthorpe, J.H. (ed.), 1984. *Order and Conflict in Contemporary Capitalism.* Clarendon, Oxford.

Gospel, H.F., 1992. *Markets, Firms and the Management of Labour in Modern Britain.* Cambridge University Press, Cambridge.

Hyman, R., 1995. The Historical Evolution of British Industrial Relations. In Edwards, P. (ed.), 1995. *Industrial Relations: Theory and Practice in Britain.* Blackwell, Oxford.

Appendix: Acts of Parliament

The Contracts of Employment Act 1963
The Industrial Training Act 1964
The Redundancy Payments Act 1965
The Trades Disputes Act 1965
The Race Relations Act 1968
The Equal Pay Act 1970
The Industrial Relations Act 1971
The Trade Unions and Labour Relations Act 1974
The Health and Safety at Work Act 1974
The Sex Discrimination Act 1975
The Employment Protection Act 1975
The Employment Protection (Consolidation) Act 1978
The Employment Act 1980
The Transfers of Undertakings Regulations 1981
The Employment Act 1982
The Trades Union Act 1984
The Wages Act 1986
The Sex Discrimination Act 1986
The Remuneration of Teachers Act 1987
The Employment Act 1988
The Employment Act 1989

The Employment Act 1990
The Trades Union Reform and Employment Rights (TURER) Act 1993
The Employment Rights Act 1996
The Employment Relations Act 1999

Chapter 6

Demography, labour force and market characteristics and trends

Chapter Outline

Introduction

- Demography

- Composition of the labour force
  Distribution by gender
  Sector and region

- Unemployment
  Youth and long-term unemployment

- Participation in education and training and employment

- Chapter summary

Introduction

As has been indicated in the section on the international environment (see Chapters 2, 3 and 4) the UK is inevitably affected by many of the developments identified; the labour force and market in the UK do not exist in isolation from these events and influences. In this chapter we concentrate upon characteristics, developments and trends at the UK national level but you should bear in mind that many other countries are experiencing similar events and pressures and, of course, that as a member of the EU, the UK labour force and market are in some sense each part of a larger European whole. That is not to say that there is yet a single EU labour market but there are definite trends and intentions in that direction. In this chapter reference is made on a number of occasions to trends and characteristics of labour markets and forces in the EU, this will enable you to view the labour market in the UK in its immediate wider context and also fulfils the purpose of facilitating comparative analysis.

The main demographic influences that we discuss relate to the ageing of the UK population, which is a product of two main influences: declining birth and mortality rates. Labour force characteristics and trends covered include the sectoral shifts in employment, the gender and ethnic constitution of the labour force and the trends in the education and training participation rates.

On the labour market front we discuss employment and unemployment levels, employment creation and trends in part-time and full-time working, the relationship between educational attainment levels and employment and some regional, ethnic and gender dimensions of the UK labour market. We have already referred to and provided some evidence of the long-hours culture that appears to pervade UK employment in comparison with the EU in the earlier section on the Working Time Directive (see Chapter 4).

In this chapter we concentrate upon the labour force, its composition and identifiable trends, rather than upon policy initiatives. Some policy initiatives were examined and discussed earlier in Chapter 5 and, if you have not read that yet or not for some while, it is advisable that you do so before continuing.

Objectives

After studying this chapter you will be able to:

- Identify and explain the main demographic trends and in particular the phenomenon of an ageing population and workforce
- Understand the dynamics of the UK labour force including regional and sectoral trends in employment, the gender and ethnic constitution of the labour force and the trends in the education and training participation rates
- Discuss trends in employment creation and in the employment of part-time and full-time workers
- Identify the unemployment blackspots and discuss the relationship between educational attainment levels and employment.

Demography

As noted in the introduction the two main demographic trends impacting upon the labour market and the constitution of the labour force are:

- a declining birth rate
- declining mortality rates.

Birth or fertility rates tend to be measured in terms of births per woman in the population and in the UK this figure in the mid-1990s was slightly less than 1.8 per woman. Within the EU this is a relatively high figure and the only countries with a higher average are the Scandinavian countries, Sweden, Denmark and Finland. Over the last fifty years there have been a number of different trends in the UK. In the post-war period there was an initial boom in births and then, through to about 1964–5, there was a steady rise in this fertility rate from around 2 in the late 1940s to a high point of 2.9 in 1964. Between 1964 and 1977 there was a rapid decline to an average of about 1.7, since when there has been relatively stability. Currently there are slightly less than 12 million children in the under-16 age group (the under-16 age group being significant because this roughly equates to a section of the population that is not economically active) but this is projected to fall quite rapidly through to 2007–8, when it is projected that the figure will be between 11.3 and 11.4 million, and then more gradually down to slightly below 11 million by the year 2020 (Office of National Statistics, 1999). One of the effects of this decline between the mid-1990s and around 2005 is that there will be a significant impact upon the age distribution of the population of working age with the numbers entering the active population (the 20–29 age group) declining by between 18 and 20 per cent (European Commission, 1996). Over the same period there will be a slight increase in the population aged between 20 and 60 years, with the 50–60 age group showing the biggest percentage increase of approximately 21 per cent. In short, projections suggest that over the period 1995–2005 the age structure of the population of working age will change quite markedly with a decrease in the initial age range of 20–29-year-olds and an increase in the 50–60 years group. Beyond that we expect that the fertility rate trends will lead to a continuing but gradual decline in the number of children below 16 years and therefore to the numbers in the working population initial 20–29 age range.

At the other end of the spectrum, mortality rates are declining and therefore life expectancy and average age are increasing. This will contribute to some extent to the increased numbers in the older age groups among the population of working age but will have the greatest significance upon the proportion of the population that are of pensionable age. Above we have been discussing the decline in the number of children below the age of 16 years and we mentioned that in the year 2007–8 the number will be between 11.3 and 4 million. This is a significant year in that it is the year in which projections indicate that the number of people of pensionable age will for the first time exceed the number of children (see **Figure 6.1**). In 1996 the number of people of pensionable age was 10.7 million, this will increase to 11.5 million in 2007 and then on to 12 million in 2020. The figures in the period 2010–2020 are to some extent temporarily depressed given that over this decade the pensionable age of women is set to rise from 60 to 65 years in the UK. After this the numbers in the pensioner group will continue rising.

Average age in the UK is projected to rise from 38.4 years in 1996 to 41.9 years in 2021. Life expectancy for women is between five and six years more than for men and in the UK in the mid-1990s these figures were approximately 79 years and 74 years, respectively. The expectation is that life expectancy will continue to increase, so that for example it is projected that over the next twenty years the life expectancy of each sex will increase again by between three and four years.

This sex differential in life expectancy also applies at younger ages so that men in the 50–64 age group have mortality rates >60 per cent greater than they are for women in the same age range. Partly as a consequence of this the sex profile of the economically active population in this age range is changing quite markedly and it is projected that by about 2010 there will be roughly equal numbers of economically active men and women in this age group(ONS, 1999).

The different employment experiences of the sexes in the over-50 age group have been quite marked in recent years:

- in 1979, 84 per cent of men in the 50–64 age group had paid employment, by 1998 this figure had declined to 69 per cent, and perhaps as

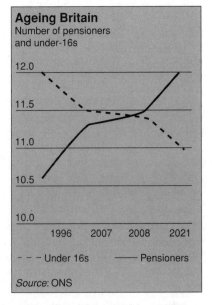

Figure 6.1 *Source: The Guardian*, 29 May 1999

important was the fact that of the 31 per cent not working 27 per cent were economically inactive

- the proportion of women in the 50–59 age group with paid employment in 1998 was 62 per cent and this had increased from 55 per cent in 1986.

These trends are illustrated by the figures for changes in economic activity for the year to May 1999 which showed that of the overall increase in economic activity of 291,000, there were rises in the 35–49 (>192,000) and the over 50 (>190,000) age groups and in the age groups below 35 there was an overall decline (Labour Force Survey, cited in Labour Market Quarterly Report, 1999).

These developments and trends have a number of implications for employee relations, perhaps particularly in the area of equal opportunities and the avoidance of discrimination on grounds of both sex and age (see Chapter 11). However, there are also implications for policies towards temporal and numerical flexibility, designing and arranging work, employment contracts and terms and conditions of employment including superannuation or pension provision and policies on retirement and retirement age, so that they are all more compatible with the age and sex structure of the labour force available. The trade unions also need to be aware of these trends if, as we discuss later (Chapter 7), they are keen to increase their membership.

There are also of course implications for recruitment and selection, training and development policies and practices.

Composition of the labour force

Apart from the changes already referred to above concerning the trends in the age composition of the labour force, we need to identify a number of the other main trends and developments of recent years, in particular the trends in the sex composition and in the sectoral distribution.

However, before proceeding to these topics it is worth pointing out that the Labour Force Survey data (Department for Education and Employment Skills and Enterprise Network (DfEE), 1999) indicate that in the quarter ending May 1999:

- total employment in the UK was 27.4 million
- of this 6.8 million people were working part-time, 24.8 per cent
- 3.2 million (12 per cent) were self employed
- 1.8 million were unemployed according to the LFS/ILO definition, 6.2 per cent (seasonally adjusted).

Distribution by gender

Of the total in employment in May 1999 (DfEE, 1999) 15.1 million were men and 12.3 million were women, women therefore made up 44.8 per cent of the total in employment. Over the year to May 1999 the number of men in employment increased by 132,000 and the number of women by 186,000.

Of the 3.2 million self-employed only 820,000 (26 per cent) were women, whereas of the part-time workers 5.4 million (79.4 per cent) were women.

Activity 1

From the information presented above, Labour Force Survey data relating to May 1999, you can work out the proportion of men and women employed part-time in the UK in 1999.

Activity 2

Look at **Figure 6.2**. The figure gives a whole range of statistics for 1997, the latest year for which the complete set was available at the time of writing.

Identify and comment upon:

• the trends that can be identified concerning the proportions of each sex working part-time
• trends in the employment rates for each sex
• how these combine to provide FTE employment rates.

Example: we can calculate that in 1975 women constituted 38 per cent of the total in employment and this percentage has consistently risen over the intervening years to 41.6 per cent in 1985, 44.6 per cent in 1995 and to 44.8 per cent in 1997.

Figure 6.2 also enables us to identify that the unemployment rate for women is consistently below that for men and, perhaps particularly of relevance to some of the discussion later in the chapter, men appear to suffer more from long-term unemployment than do women.

Other findings not specifically concerned with the gender distribution and composition of the labour force include:

• the proportion of those in employment that are self-employed has also risen but not as consistently, from 8.1 per cent in 1975 to 12.6 per cent in 1997 (and to 11.7 per cent in 1999)
• the proportion of those in employment who are working part-time has risen from 21.2 per cent in 1985 to 24.9 per cent in 1997 (see Figure 6.2) (24.85 per cent in 1999).

So we have already identified some elements of the sex composition of the labour force and we know that in the year to May 1999 more women entered the labour force than men so that the female proportion of those in employment must have risen compared with men. This represents a continuation of a trend that has been ongoing for several decades and is shown in **Figure 6.2.** From the figure it is possible to calculate the proportion of women in the

Total	1975	1985	1990	1991	1994	1995	1996	1997
Total population	56226	56685	57561	57808	58895	58606	58802	59000
Population of working age (15–64) (000)	34767	36706	37018	37033	37286	37411	37511	37571
Total employment (000)	24667	24282	26783	26207	25657	25936	26177	26612
Annual change in employment	–	–0.2	2.0	–2.2	–0.7	1.1	0.9	1.7
Employment rate (% working-age population)	71.0	66.2	72.4	70.8	68.8	69.3	69.8	70.8
FTE employment rate (% working-age population)	n.a.	57.6	62.7	61.1	58.8	59.1	59.3	60.2
Self-employed (% total employment)	8.1	11.4	13.4	13.1	12.9	13.0	12.6	12,6
Employed part-time (% total employment)	n.a.	21.2	21.7	22.2	23.8	24.1	24.6	24.9
Employed on fixed-term contracts	n.a.	7.0	5.2	5.3	6.5	7.0	7.1	7.4
Share of employment in agriculture (%)	2.8	2.4	2.2	2.3	2.1	2.1	2.0	1.9
Share of employment in industry	40.4	34.7	32.3	31.2	27.8	27.4	27.4	26.9
Share of employment in services	56.8	63.0	65.5	66.5	70.1	70.5	70.6	71.2
Activity rate (% working-age population)	73.3	74.7	77.8	77.6	76.2	76,0	76.0	76.2
Total unemployed (000)	817.3	3141.3	2022.4	2528.4	2744.0	2496.8	2339.8	2022.9
Unemployment rate (%)	3.2	11.5	7.0	8.8	9.6	8.7	8.2	7.0
Youth unemployed (% labour force 15–24)	n.a.	18.5	10.8	14.3	17.0	15.9	15.5	14.2
Long-term unemployment (% unemployed)	n.a.	48.1	35.5	29.6	45.4	43.6	39.8	38.6
15–19-year-olds in education/training (%)	n.a.	n.a.	n.a.	n.a.	71.2	71.7	70.9	70.6
20–24-year-olds in education/training (%)	n.a.	n.a.	n.a.	n.a.	23.6	23.2	23.8	24.3
Men								
Total population (000)	27361	27611	28118	28246	28592	28728	28840	28967
Population of working age (15–64) (000)	17337	18333	18529	18536	18740	18812	18886	18897
Total employment (000)	15252	14172	15207	14753	14153	14357	14423	14685
Annual change in employment		–0.7	1.4	–3.0	14	1.4	0.5	1.8
Employment rate (% working-age population)	88.0	77.3	82.1	79.6	75.5	76.3	76.4	77.7
FTE employment rate (% working-age population)	n.a.	75.1	79.0	76.6	72.1	72.5	72.4	73.4
Self-employed (% total employment)	10.6	14.7	18.0	17.7	17.6	17.8	17.1	16.9
Employed part-time (% total employment)	n.a.	4.4	5.3	5.5	7.1	7.7	8.1	8.8
Employed on fixed-term contracts (%)	n.a.	5.7	3.7	3.9	5.5	6.2	6.0	6.5
Share of employment in agriculture (%)	3.6	3.1	3.0	3.2	2.9	2.7	2.6	2.5
Share of employment in industry (%)	49.8	45.5	43.7	42.5	38.8	38.3	38.5	38.0
Share of employment in services (%)	46.5	51.4	53.3	54.3	58.3	59.0	58.9	59.5
Activity rate (% working-age population)	91.5	87.6	88.6	88.3	85.2	85.0	84.4	84.4
Total unemployed (000)	605.0	1886.6	1206.4	1615.6	1813.3	1623.5	1524.3	1259.8
Unemployment rate (%)	3.8	11.8	7.4	9.9	11.3	10.1	9.5	7.8
Youth unemployed (% labour force 15–24)	n.a.	19.7	11.9	16.6	19.7	18.0	18.0	15.9
Long-term unemployment (% unemployed)	n.a.	55.2	43.9	34.2	51.2	49.6	45.9	44.8
15–19-year-olds in education/training (%)	n.a.	n.a.	n.a.	n.a.	72.6	73.4	71.9	70.5
20–24-year-olds in education/training (%)	n.a.	n.a.	n.a.	n.a.	24.9	24.5	24.7	25.0
Women								
Total population (000)	28865	29074	29443	29562	29803	29878	29962	30033
Population of working-age (15–64) (000)	17430	18372	18489	18498	18547	18598	18625	18672
Total employment (000)	9415	10110	11576	11454	11504	11579	11754	11927
Annual change in employment (%)		0.7	27	–1.1	0.1	0.7	1.5	1.5

Figure 6.2 Key employment indicators in the UK. *Source:* European Commission, 1999. *Employment in Europe 1998*. p.164. Luxembourg

Total	1975	1985	1990	1991	1994	1995	1996	1997
Women (continued)								
Employment rate (% working-age population)	54.0	55.0	62.6	61.9	62.0	62.3	63.1	63.9
FTE employment rate (% working age population)	n.a.	41.0	47.4	46.5	46.3	46.6	47.0	47.7
Self-employed (% total employment)	4.1	6.9	7.5	7.2	7.2	7.0	7.0	7.2
Employed part-time (% total employment)	n.a.	44.8	43.2	43.7	44.4	44.3	44.8	44.9
Employed on fixed-term contracts (%)	n.a.	8.8	7.0	7.0	7.5	7.8	8.2	8.4
Share of employment in agriculture (%)	1.5	1.3	1.1	1.1	1.2	1.2	1.2	1.0
Share of employment in industry (%)	25.5	19.5	17.3	16.7	14.2	14.0	13.9	13.2
Share of employment in services (%)	73.1	79.2	81.5	82.2	84.6	84.8	85.0	85.7
Activity rate (% working-age population)	55.2	61.9	67.0	66.9	67.0	66.9	67.5	68.0
Total unemployed (000)	212.3	1254.7	816.0	912.8	930.7	873.3	815.5	763.1
Unemployment rate (%)	2.2	11.0	6.6	7.4	7.5	7.0	6.5	6.0
Youth unemployed (% labour force 16–24)	n.a.	17.0	9.6	11.6	13.7	13.3	12.5	12.2
Long-term unemployment (% unemployed)	n.a.	36.0	23.1	21.8	33.9	32.3	28.1	27.8
15–19-year-olds in education/training (%)	n.a.	n.a.	n.a.	n.a.	69.8	69.9	9.8	70.7
20–24-year olds in education/training (%)	n.a.	n.a.	n.a.	n.a.	22.2	21.8	22.8	23.6

Source: Total employment is an average of quarterly Labour Force Survey data; working-age population and other employment details are from the Community Labour Force Survey (LFS).

Total unemployed and youth unemployed are harmonized Eurostat figures; long-term unemployment is from the LFS. See notes to the table for the European Union.

Figure 6.2 (*continued*)

total number in employment in a range of years and over time.

It has been commonplace to assert that increases in employment in the UK in recent years have been dominated by part-time opportunities and that almost all the increase has been among women. This would appear to be true of the 1990–94 period but not so for the period 1994–97.

Data from European Commission (1998) show that in the earlier period, full-time employment of men declined by more than 1 per cent per year and that while there was an increase in male part-time employment it was significantly outweighed by the decrease in full-time employment. In the same period for women the trends were similar but of a different order, with the decline in full-time employment being very much smaller and averaging approx. 0.4 per cent and only just outweighing the increase in part-time employment.

In the latter period there has been an increase in both the full- and part-time employment of both men and women but the increase in full-time employment exceeded the increase in part-time employment.

Sector and region

Also apparent from **Figure 6.2** are the variations over the same period in the **sectoral distribution of those in employment**. The values clearly show that the shift from agriculture and industry continues, as does the increase in

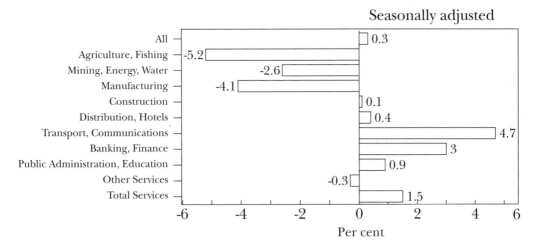

Figure 6.3 Changes in workforce by industry (March 1998 to March 1999). *Source:* Labour Market Quarterly (August, 1999)

the total and proportionate employment in the services sector. In 1975 these figures were 2.8 per cent, 40.4 per cent and 56.8 per cent, respectively; by 1997 they were 1.9 per cent, 26.9 per cent and 71.2 per cent, nearly three-quarters of those in employment are employed in services. Inevitably these figures reflect the changes that have occurred over the period in the structure of industry and economic activity. **Figure 6.3** shows the increases and decreases in main employment sectors in the year to May 1999 and these are consistent with the trends mentioned above.

Figure 6.2 shows how a much higher proportion of women than men are in employment in the service sector, the figures for 1997 being 85.7 per cent of women and 59.5 per cent of men.

Allied to the sectoral shift in employment there have also been regional changes with employment opportunities in the north of England declining with the decline in manufacturing and the extractive industries (mining, energy and water) and employment in the south increasing with the increase in employment opportunities in the services sector. It is anticipated that these trends will continue and that the increase of employment opportunities in the south will be accompanied by population drift from north to south. This will be accompanied by a continuation of the redistribution of income and wealth from north to south.

Unemployment

We have already examined employment rates and in your perusal of **Figure 6.2** you may have noticed that there is a reference to both employment rates and activity rates, both as a proportion of the working-age population.

Activity rates are generally higher reflecting the fact that there are people who are economically active but not in employment.

In this section we are concerned with the issue of unemployment and it is important to realize that there are different definitions of unemployment and that there are two main and different time-series of statistics used in the UK.

The first is the series that governments have until recently preferred to use as the official indicator, the claimant count series. The other is based upon the data collected by the Labour Force Survey (LFS)and is not limited to those actually registered as and claiming unemployment and related benefits. The LFS series is much closer to the base used by the ILO for the purpose of international comparison, to the base used within the EU for the official statistics and is the base upon which the unemployment values in **Figure 6.2** are calculated.

In essence both seek to ascertain by means of survey the numbers of people:

a) without work, by which is meant both paid employment and self-employment
b) who are available for/to work
c) who are actively seeking work, specific evidence of which may be required.

These are then expressed as a percentage of total labour force including members of the armed forces.

The LFS treats as unemployed, those people without a job who were available to start work in the two weeks following the survey interview and who had either looked for work in the four weeks prior to the interview or were waiting to start a job that they had already obtained.

Inevitably the LFS definition will include more people than are entitled to claim unemployment benefits and therefore the LFS/ILO figures are higher than are those based on the claimant count. However, there are also problems with the LFS data since they tend to ignore those who are homeless: it is a household survey!

An indication of the degree of difference between the two series can be seen from the figures from both in May of 1999. The LFS/ILO series produced a total of 1.8 million (6.2 per cent), the claimant count series 1.285 million (4.4 per cent).

If you examine **Figure 6.2** again you can see how unemployment has varied within the UK over the period since 1975. The more recent figure of 6.2 per cent in the summer of 1999 indicates a continuation of the decline begun between 1991 and 1994.

The cost of unemployment tends to be measured in terms of production foregone or lost and the costs of maintaining people in the state of unemployment. However, we need also to keep in mind that there are emotional, personal and social costs that are much more difficult to quantify. There are other definitions of unemployment. These are listed in **Figure 6.4**.

There are other definitions of unemployment as well as those used by the LFS and the claimant count:

1 the relatively simple measure of the difference between the supply of and demand for labour in a price adjusting market, with the excess supply comprising active searchers and the excess demand represented by unfilled vacancies

2 a measure of immediately available workers willing to accept market clearing wages

3 the difference between employment levels at a market clearing equilibrium wage and employment at the prevailing market wage where the latter is greater.

Figure 6.4 Definitions of unemployment

We noted earlier that **Figure 6.2** shows that the unemployment rate for women in the UK is consistently lower than it is for men. This is a trend that is also seen from the claimant count figures which, in June 1999, gave a male unemployment rate of 6.2 per cent compared with the figure for female unemployment on this base of 2.3 per cent. There are also regional variations and using the claimant figures the region with the highest rate in June 1999 was the northeast at 7.4 per cent followed by Northern Ireland and then Scotland. The regions with the lowest rates are the southeast, east of England and the southwest, which respectively had rates of 2.5 per cent, 3.1 per cent and 3.3 per cent.

Among the more intractable unemployment problems in the UK, as in most of Europe, are the problems of youth and long-term unemployment. Youth in this context applies to people under the age of 25 years and long-term is defined for these purposes as continuous unemployment exceeding one year in duration. Governments have devised a whole host of schemes and policies over the years (in Chapter 5 on the role of government we discussed the Labour government's scheme called the New Deal) to try to tackle the problem of youth unemployment but have generally paid less attention to the issue of long-term unemployment.

This latter is perhaps the more intractable given that many of the people in this category are over the age of 50 years and/or are unemployed as a consequence of structural changes which have involved the decline and in many cases the disappearance of the industries in which they worked and the skills which they once had. Employers' generally negative attitudes to employing the older worker obviously don't help with the resolution of this dilemma. It is also the case that the longer a person is unemployed the more difficult it becomes for them to obtain employment. Their skills and experience have a declining value the longer they are out of work, their employability declines.

Activity 3

We mentioned in the section on Demography that the gender distribution of the active population over the age of 50 years is changing quite quickly and gave one explanation. Now that you have read the next section are there additional explanations, and what are they?

Youth and long-term unemployment

We have already noted that youth and long-term unemployment (defined as the proportion of the unemployed that have been so for periods in excess of one year) are particular problems and in our earlier discussion of governments' role in economic management we discussed some of the various initiatives that have been taken to try to address this. The New Deal scheme was initially directed at the youth unemployment problem but has subsequently been extended to the over-50 age group early in 2000.

There is a difference between the two groups and the nature of their problems and needs. The young unemployed tend to have little or no skills of a vocational kind and little or no relevant work experience, the long-term unemployed may well have skills and experience but they are often those that in some sense belong to a bygone age. Additionally, the long-term unemployed have the problem of having been insiders who are now outsiders; many of the young have never been insiders. Many of the long-term unemployed are also over the age of 50 and they additionally have to overcome discriminatory attitudes related to their age.

Activity 4

Look again at the data in **Figure 6.2** and identify the main characteristics of and trends in youth and long-term unemployment in the UK since 1985.

In comparison with the rest of the EU the scale of the problem of both groups in the UK is not so severe. However, there are particular discrepancies between the unemployment experience of women in the EU and in the UK. In the EU the unemployment rates for women exceed those for men, the rates of youth unemployment are higher for women than for men and the long-term unemployment rates for women are higher than for men and have been close to 50 per cent throughout the whole of the period since 1985.

The problems of youth and long-term unemployment are exacerbated by membership of an ethnic minority and by disability. Not only are unemployment rates greater amongst these groups but membership of one of these groups also tends to mean that once unemployed the individual will remain unemployed longer than able-bodied and 'white' claimants. In the research review published by the DfEE Skills and Enterprise Network (1999: 6–7) the following results are asserted from research conducted among the claimant unemployed.

Members of ethnic minorities:

- stay jobless for twice the length of time of other claimants
- are likely to find it more difficult to obtain jobs than white claimants despite holding more academic qualifications
- are also likely to stay in a job for less time
- have a lower proportion of claimants in work immediately prior to claiming
- are much more likely to have moved directly from being in full-time education into joblessness
- who were in work prior to becoming claimants received lower wages than other claimants.

Disabled people are also likely to spend twice as long in unemployment once they make a claim, they are also less likely to have adequate qualifications and work experience.

Participation in education and training and employment

There has been an increased degree of research activity into the relationship between educational attainment levels and employment in recent years prompted in part, no doubt, by the debates in the UK in the latter part of the 1990s about the merits, demerits and impact of changes introduced by government to the funding of higher and further education. However, other motives for this interest and concern include:

- the perceived need for a more highly educated and skilled labour force to facilitate adaptation to and assimilation of technological change and changes in working practices
- to enhance UK competitiveness
- concerns about the role of education and training in achieving greater equality of opportunities
- decline in the demand for unskilled labour.

Again if we revisit **Figure 6.2** we can see the proportions of UK 15–19-year-olds and 20–24-year-olds in education and training. The data are also provided separately for men and women. The series only goes back to 1994 but we can detect some slight signs of trend movement. With only four years of data available in this figure it would be unwise to draw firm conclusions concerning trends and probable future developments but there does appear to have been an increase in the proportion in the 20–24 age group; a greater proportion of men in the 20–24 age group are in education and training than women but the gap has narrowed in favour of women. In the younger age group there would also appear to have been a shift in favour of women. The UK rates are the lowest of all the countries in the EU (see **Figure 6.5**).

Age group	EU			UK		
	All	M	F	All	M	F
15–19	83.2	82.5	83.8	70.6	70.5	70.7
20–24	38.0	36.4	39.6	24.3	25.0	23.6

Figure 6.5 EU and UK rates of participation in education and training in 1997

Relating educational attainment levels to employment experience has so far resulted in findings indicating that:

- there is a generally positive relationship between educational attainment levels and the ability to find and remain in employment
- this applies in all age groups and tends to become more marked as age increases
- for women a good level of education seems to be even more important in finding a job than it is for men
- many women with low educational attainment do not enter the labour market at all
- women tend to be more qualified than men for the jobs they do
- the less well-educated men and women are more likely to be unemployed
- the relationship between level of educational attainment and propensity to be unemployed is more marked for women
- long-term unemployment is also more likely the lower the level of educational attainment.

Activity 5

Without going back to the text try to remember the main differences between the people included in each of (1) the claimant unemployment count and (2) the LFS unemployment data. What are the strengths and weaknesses of each series?

Summary

In this chapter we have examined statistical evidence of various features of and trends in the UK population and in the composition and structure of the labour force and the labour market.

There are two main demographic trends, a declining birth rate and declining mortality rate. These both have and are going to have a significant impact upon the age distribution of the population, the population of working age and on the age distribution of the active population; in all cases the shift will be in the direction of the older age groups. Average age and life expectancy are increasing. Women will continue to have an advantage over men in terms of life expectancy.

The female proportion of the working population is increasing and women tend to dominate the service sector and part-time working. It has been commonplace to assert that increases in employment in the UK in recent years have been dominated by part-time opportunities and that almost all the increase has been among women. This would appear to be true of the 1990–94 period but not so for the period 1994–97. Full-time employment for men has been in decline but the employment resurgence of the late 1990s appears to have provided at least a temporary halt to this trend.

The shift from employment in agriculture and industry continues as does the increase in the total and proportionate employment in the services sector; the regional drift of employment from the north to the south also appears set to continue.

The unemployment rate for women in the UK is consistently lower than it is for men. Unemployment in the north is higher than in the south and there are particular problems with both youth unemployment and long-term unemployment. There is evidence that those in ethnic minority groups and the disabled experience greater and longer unemployment than do others.

Participation rates in education and training are relatively low in the UK and there is evidence that there is a positive relationship between educational attainment and employment prospects. However, it also seems that education is more important for women in this context than for men and indeed that women need better qualifications than men to obtain an equivalent job.

Activity Answers

Activity 1
Men: 1.4 million working part-time (6.8 minus 5.4) as percentage of 15.1 total in employment, equals 9.3 per cent.
Women: 5.4 million as percentage of 12.3 equals 43.9 per cent.

Activity 2
- The proportion of men in employment who work part-time has increased from: 4.4 per cent in 1985 to 8.8 per cent in 1997 and (see above) to 9.3 per cent in 1999
- the proportion of women in employment who work part-time has remained relatively stable between 43 per cent and 45 per cent over the period 1985–1997 and also in 1999: 43.9 per cent (see above)
- employment rates between the sexes have also changed significantly over the period, the employment rate for men having declined from 88 per cent in 1975 to just under 78 per cent in 1997, whereas the figures for women show an increase from 54 per cent in 1975 to 64 per cent in 1997
- the different gender experiences in terms of the proportions that work part-time lead to significantly different full-time equivalent employment rates. The difference between the employment rate for men and the FTE rate is relatively small – 4.3 per cent in 1997 being the largest since 1975. On the other hand the difference for women is 16.2 per cent in 1997 reflecting the much greater proportion of women who work part-time. The gap between the two figures has widened gradually since 1985 and this presumably is a reflection of the gradual increase in the proportion of women working part-time, particularly since the early 1990s.

Activity 3
Other explanations might include:

- decline in manufacturing and increase in service sector, women tend to dominate employment in the services sector as men dominate manufacturing
- the increased incidence of early retirements for men and the reluctance of employers to take people on at this age.

Activity 4
Trends:

- in all cases, in the combined figures and in those treating men and women separately, the youth and long-term rates exceed the aggregate rate
- the long-term rates exceed the rates of youth unemployment
- the youth and long-term rates for men are greater in all cases than for women

- over the majority of the period the long-term rate for men has been in excess of 40 per cent.

Activity 5

The claimant count series includes as unemployed only those who are not working, who are registered as such with the appropriate authority and who qualify for unemployment or some other unemployment related social security benefit. The main weakness of this series is that it will exclude people who are not working, for example because they have taken early retirement, and who are not entitled to receive any state benefits but who would like to work if they could obtain employment. It also excludes many women who are married, not working, would like to but do not register as unemployed and are not entitled to receipt of benefit.

The LFS data are based on a survey of households, are therefore sample-based data, and include as unemployed those:

a) without work, by which is meant both paid employment and self-employment
b) who are available for/to work, by which is meant that they were available to start work in the two weeks following the survey interview
c) who are actively seeking work, which means that they had either looked for work in the four weeks prior to the interview or were waiting to start a job that they had already obtained.

The major weakness in the LFS series is that it excludes people who are not members of households and therefore the majority of those who are homeless are likely not to be included in the figures.

References

Office of National Statistics, 1999. *Social Focus on Older People*. Stationery Office, London.

Department for Education and Employment, Skills and Enterprise Network, 1999. *Labour Market Quarterly Report*. August. Crown, Sheffield.

Department for Education and Employment, Skills and Enterprise Network, 1999. *Research Review*. May. Crown, Sheffield.

European Commission, 1996. *The Demographic Situation in the European Union, 1995*.

European Commission, 1999. *Employment in Europe, 1998*. p. 164. Luxembourg.

Chapter 7

Trade unions

Chapter Outline

- Introduction
- Definitions
- Staff associations
- The objectives of trade unions
- The TUC
- Why do people join trade unions?
- Trade union membership
- Internal government, organization and democracy
- Trade union recognition
- Survival strategies
  Social partnerships
  Partnership agreements
  Servicing or organizing approaches
- Chapter summary

Introduction

In the context of the Dunlop model referred to in Chapter 1, trade unions are one of the major actors in the system. They exist in order to both protect and further the interests of their members but, like other interest groups and institutions in society, the trade unions have to operate within contexts that constrain their freedom and their power and ability to pursue their interests selfishly and, of course, they have to interact with other interest groups and achieve an accommodation, commonly requiring compromise.

Some would argue that this was not always so and that towards the end of the 1970s it was felt by many politicians, employers, managers, commentators and indeed by many of the general public that the trade unions in the UK were so powerful that they were not effectively constrained by these environments and interactions. It was arguable that the trade unions had, in effect, gained control of sufficient of these environments to enable them to pursue the interests of their members and their leaders selfishly and at the expense of others in society and indeed at the expense of society itself. Through their links with and influence within the Labour Party (the government of the day) they were able to play a major part in the determination of the government's social, industrial and economic policies and were able to ensure a legal environment that was beneficial to them and their interests. This ability to influence the environment within which they operated gave them a degree of bargaining power that enabled them to ignore or overcome any opposition.

It is doubtful that the trade union movement was in fact as influential as the above would suggest and indeed the general election in 1979 was at least in part occasioned by the determination of the government of the day to pursue economic and industrial policies that were perceived to be in the national interest and not in accord with the wishes of the union movement. However, it is certainly the case that the Conservative Party were victorious in that election and that an important element of their campaign was the promise that they would take steps to reduce the influence of the trade union movement. Much of what has happened since can be viewed as the fulfilment of that promise and the state of decline in which the trade unions find themselves at the end of the millennium is perceived by many to be the outcome of that surfeit of power and influence and the cynical use of it to pursue their own selfish interests. It is a moot point whether the interests that were pursued were those of the trade union members or those of the leaders.

We return to some of these arguments and events later in this chapter but for the moment it is necessary that we deal with some elementary issues, the first of which are to decide upon an appropriate definition of what a trade union is and what distinguishes them from other organizations.

In the remainder of the chapter, and against a background of pressures for change and debates about the nature and direction of the trade union response, we examine the objectives of trade unions, the reasons why people join them including the evidence of trade union wage gaps, the levels, structure and trends of trade union membership and numbers in the UK, the nature and role of the Trades Union Congress, the stereotypical democratic form of trade union organization and internal government, the issue of trade union recognition and the strategies that may ensure the survival of the trade unions into the new millennium.

After studying this chapter you will be able to:

- Distinguish various definitions of trade unions on the grounds of purpose, membership and means
- Understand what distinguishes trade unions from other employee representative organizations and arrangements
- Identify and analyse the objectives of trade unions in the context of a distinction between business and welfare movements
- Critically examine and discuss the reasons why people join trade unions and the interrelationship with trade union objectives
- Explain why trade union membership has been in decline
- Explain the role of the TUC
- Explain how and why unions are regarded as democratic in terms of their internal organization and government
- Identify and discuss various criteria by which the degree of democracy may be determined
- Identify trends in trade union recognition and discuss the proposals to give trade unions legal means of enforcing recognition upon hostile and reluctant employers
- Assess some of the debates about what the unions should do now to ensure their survival in the twenty-first century.

Definitions

Over the years there have been many different definitions of trade unions and in some respects they can each be seen as reflective of the time at which they were devised. The earliest of the well-known definitions is that of Webb and Webb (1894):

a continuous association of wage earners for the purpose of maintaining or improving the conditions of their working lives.

The legal definition in the UK dates from the Trade Union and Labour Relations Act 1974 and states that a trade union is:

an organization, whether permanent or temporary, which consists wholly or mainly of workers of one or more descriptions and is an organization whose principal purposes include the regulation of relations between workers of that description and employers or employers' associations.

Yet another is that devised by Hirsch-Weber (1970) who suggested that trade unions are:

associations of workers who by means of collective bargaining endeavour to improve their working conditions, and economic and social position.

Yet another and the last that we are to include here is that devised by Salamon (1992) who suggests that a trade union is:

any organization, whose membership consists of employees, which seeks to organize and represent their interests both in the workplace and society and, in particular, seeks to regulate their employment relationship through the direct process of collective bargaining with management.

Look at the four definitions of trade unions above and distinguish between them on the grounds of membership, purpose and means.

A point made earlier was that to some extent, definitions of trade unions can be seen to be reflective of the era in which they were devised and you might consider whether definitions of the late 1990s would give the same importance to achieving objectives through the process of collective bargaining given the decline in its use and in the extent of its coverage throughout the 1980s and early 1990s – see the statistics in the later section of this chapter on recognition and in Figure 7.5.

It is also important to realize that not all trade unions are the same and one way that has been devised to distinguish between them is known as the notion or concept of **Unionateness**. This concept was devised by Blackburn (1967) who was concerned to address the issue of the extent to which a particular trade union was in his terms 'a whole-hearted trade union, identifying with the labour movement and willing to use all the power of the movement'.

Today the concept is useful as a means of indicating some of the dimensions upon which trade unions can and do vary.

Blackburn identified seven different criteria of unionateness:

- whether the organization regards collective bargaining and the protection of its members' interests as employees as a major function
- whether it is independent of employer influence for the purposes of collective bargaining
- whether it is prepared to be militant and use all forms of industrial action that may be effective
- whether it declares itself to be a trade union
- whether it is affiliated to the Labour Party
- whether it is affiliated to the Trades Union Congress (TUC) – the central, national or peak association of trade unions in the UK (we look at this in more detail later in this chapter)

● whether it was registered as a trade union, a legal status that provided advantages at the time relating to the handling of the union's financial affairs.

Not surprisingly, some commentators have sought to use this concept for the purpose of devising definitions of trade unions in addition to those already referred to above. One such example is Farnham and Pimlott (1995) who suggest that a trade union may be conceptually defined as:

> any organization of employees which, first, has as one of its main objectives negotiating with employers in order to regulate the pay and conditions of its members and, second, is independent of the employers with which it negotiates or seeks to negotiate.

You might want to think again about the appropriateness of this definition in the context of those above and the significance of changed environments and circumstances. It is the first of those that we have looked at that incorporates the notion of independence as a criteria to be satisfied for an organization to be considered as a trade union and the adoption of such a definition has implications for the position of staff associations.

The independence of a trade union from the influence and control of an employer has long been an issue and, in the UK, the legal rights and immunities which trade unions enjoy are linked to their obtaining from the Certification Officer confirmation that they are indeed independent in this respect. The Certification Officer was given this role by the Employment Protection Act 1976. The linking of rights and immunities to independence encouraged many employee organizations which had previously been regarded as either staff or professional associations, and indeed in many instances had proudly proclaimed that they were not a trade union, to seek a certificate of independence as a trade union. Others entered into merger or other amalgamation arrangements with organizations already confirmed as independent trade unions.

Staff associations

Staff associations often act like trade unions in that they seek to determine with the employer the terms and conditions of employment of their members but they are often not independent of the employer, variously relying upon him/her for facilities and/or finance. Membership of a staff association is usually limited to the employees of one organization and in this respect they may appear to resemble the enterprise unions that are characteristic of Japan. In many instances they have been established with the considerable help and encouragement of the employer, sometimes in the hope that the staff association will prevent the spread of trade unionism within the company and that they will be easier to deal with than would a trade union.

Almost always the membership of staff associations has been dominated by white-collar as opposed to manual or blue-collar workers. Over the years there have been many examples of conflict between staff associations and trade unions. The banking, insurance and finance sector appears to have been particularly prone to the establishment of staff associations though, as noted above, over the years many of the associations formed have subsequently become trade unions in their own right or have been merged into other trade unions. The major trade union in this sector, the Banking, Insurance and Finance Union (BIFU) is itself an example of this process.

Nevertheless there are still a number of staff associations and in some organizations in recent years managements have demonstrated a resurgence of interest in the establishment of a staff association as a preferable alternative to an independent trade union. This has sometimes occurred in conjunction with management derecognition of an independent trade union and the creation of alternative consultation arrangements with white-collar staff, such as a company council. Some of the privatized utilities sought to take advantage of their newfound independence from the public sector (where the employee relations traditions were consistent with a pluralist perspective and the joint resolution of conflict and determination of substantive and procedural outcomes) to create new arrangements of this kind, South West Water being an example. From the employee viewpoint however, staff associations, house unions and company councils all appear to suffer the same potential disadvantages associated with being reliant upon the employer for funds and facilities, not being able to derive support, strength, expertise and resources from a wider membership base or from membership of the wider trade union movement and being inherently vulnerable to pressure from the employer to not damage the organization's competitive position, to not rock the boat.

The activists in these associations and arrangements are potentially vulnerable to pressure from the employer, given that they rely upon the employer for their security of employment and career progression and they have no external support. Trade unions are also likely to argue that the staff association member suffers in comparison because the activists are not likely to have had the training or developed the expertise in protecting and progressing the interests of their members that a trade union representative has.

Managements with a unitarist perspective are likely to see trade unions as unnecessary and an illegitimate intrusion into the workplace, as organizations which lay an unwarranted claim upon the loyalty of employees, a loyalty which should be solely owed to the organization. In such a context it is likely that, given the opportunity, management will opt for a staff association or staff or company council arrangement rather than trade unionism. The former are all in-house arrangements and management are likely to feel that they provide much less opportunity for the conflict of loyalty which management perceives as the inevitable consequence of employee membership of a trade union.

The objectives of trade unions

Trade unions like other organizations have purposes, they exist for a reason and seek to achieve certain objectives. In looking at some of the many definitions of trade unions above we have already seen that the objectives can vary over time, between unions and also that there are different views as to the legitimacy of certain objectives and areas of activity.

There seems little dispute over the legitimacy of trade unions having as objectives the protecting and furthering of the interests of their members in the workplace and in relation to terms and conditions of employment. Even so, though there is scope for disagreement and difference here as, for example, over the issue of industrial democracy or co-determination. Many managers, politicians and indeed some trade union members would argue that, even though it is an objective that is in a sense confined to the workplace, joint management of enterprises is not a legitimate trade union objective. Even if there is a measure of general agreement that it is legitimate for trade unions to pursue objectives in the workplace, though there may be differences over the legitimacy or desirability of certain specific workplace objectives, there are many who would take the view that the pursuit of objectives outside the workplace is not a legitimate arena for trade unions.

The alternative view might be that since terms and conditions of employment, the nature of the employment relationship and the overall well-being and interests of its members are subject to so many external constraints it is incumbent upon the trade union movement to seek to influence, possibly even control, that external environment.

It has been a characteristic of trade unionism in Europe that these wider objectives have been pursued, there is a tradition of trade unions and their federations having a class base, having political affiliations and using these affiliations and their own industrial power to achieve social change. In this context European trade union movements have often been classified as welfare or political movements compared with the more instrumental and workplace-oriented business unionism in the USA or the enterprise unionism of Japan. It isn't possible here to undertake a comparative analysis of trade unionism around the world but if you wish to read more about this aspect of the subject see Hollinshead and Leat (1995: Chapter 5).

As with other movements in Europe, UK trade union history is characterized by this political and social approach and this is perhaps best illustrated by the list of objectives that the TUC devised and presented to the Royal Commission on Trade Unions and Employers Associations (Donovan) in 1965. This listed ten main objectives which are paraphrased here and are not in any priority order:

1 improved terms of employment
2 improved working conditions including the physical environment

3 security of both employment and income
4 industrial democracy
5 full employment
6 fair(er) shares in national income and wealth
7 improved social security
8   the public control and planning of industry
9 a voice in government
10 improved public and social services.

Only the first four of these could be regarded as being concerned with the workplace.

Debates in the 1990s on the subject of trade union objectives, attitudes towards employers and survival strategies are discussed in a later section.

The TUC

The trade union movement in the UK has been relatively unusual in that it has developed without the plethora of national-level federations that characterize many European movements. The Trade Union Congress, formed in 1868, is the single peak association for the trade union movement as a whole in the UK.

The number of trade unions in the UK reached a peak of 1384 in 1920, of which 213 were affiliated to the TUC. By the late 1990s the number of unions affiliated to the TUC had declined to around 60 out of a total of about 230. Despite the fact that the TUC-affiliated unions constitute only a minority of the total they have in membership just over 80 per cent of the total of trade union members and include the larger trade unions. Certainly, in recent decades this decline in the number of trade unions has been largely the product of rationalization through the mechanisms of amalgamation and merger, whereby two or more unions agree to join together to form one. Mergers and amalgamations occur for many reasons and in recent years many have occurred in response to the problems, both financial and organizational, caused by declining membership, rapid industrial restructuring and the decline of many of the traditional industries and skills that provided the core of trade union membership, and the need to gain both organizational and financial economies of scale to be financially viable.

Initially the formation and existence of the TUC was to provide the labour movement with a political voice and this still remains a main function. These days this political voice is arguably listened to more within the context of policy and decision making in the European Union than within the UK. There still are close links between the Labour Party and the TUC but they are weaker than they were and the decline of the TUC's influence within the Labour Party looks set to continue under New Labour even though the union movement is still a major funder of the political party.

The TUC has other important roles.

1 It is concerned with the prevention and, if necessary, resolution of inter-union conflicts. In the main these disputes tend to occur either over jurisdictional issues, who represents who, or over demarcation matters, who has a 'right' to particular work.

For many years through to the 1970s inter-union disputes were perceived, along with unofficial industrial action, as peculiarly British problems and the result of multi-unionism whereby there were far too many trade unions competing both for members and for the right to undertake particular categories of work. The incidence of such disputes has diminished in recent years as the trade union movement has rationalized itself and as the structure of the industrial landscape has changed. Additionally, employers have taken the opportunity provided by increasing globalization of product markets and competition to negotiate flexibility from employees. The ability of the TUC to police and encourage the development of harmonious inter-union relations was harmed by the Trade Union and Employment Rights Act 1993 which, among other things, made it more difficult for trade unions to exclude or expel individuals from membership and this makes it more difficult for unions to ensure that poaching of members doesn't occur. Prior to the legislation it was possible for the TUC in such circumstances to resolve matters by telling the union that was found to be guilty of poaching to return the members concerned to the appropriate union, it is no longer lawful for unions to expel from or refuse membership to an individual for reasons of this kind. Individuals in the main have a right to belong to whichever trade union they wish. Where unions are suffering financially, as many have in recent years as their membership has declined (see below), this legislation may well encourage further competition for members between unions as they try to achieve efficiency through a larger market share in any particular recruitment arena or constituency.

There is some evidence at the end of the twentieth century that the new legislative regulations regarding trade union recognition coming into force in the year 2000 (Employment Relations Act 1999) are creating conditions in which there may be increased dangers of competition between unions as they compete to do deals with employers who are concerned to avoid having a union forced upon them and who are therefore showing a greater willingness to enter into voluntary arrangements with the 'right' union, as the employer perceives it. In response to this the TUC issued a consultative document to its members in the spring of 1999 entitled 'British Trade Unionism – the Millennial Challenge' in which it seeks to address the issues of both avoiding and dealing with disputes that do arise.

2 Substantial educational, advisory and informational roles are also performed and provided for affiliates.

3 The TUC is the public voice of the union movement both at home in the

UK and abroad through its membership of various international trade union organizations.

4 The TUC has also been at the forefront of debates and initiatives concerned with rationalizing the structure of the movement and the formulation and implementation of survival strategies as the movement heads into the twenty-first century. We look at some of the options and debates in the last section of this chapter.

The TUC is one of the relatively few national organizations specifically to reserve seats on the executive committee, called the General Council, for representatives from ethnic minority groupings and women.

Why do people join trade unions?

There are inevitably a number of reasons why people both form and join trade unions. No one reason will apply to all individuals and again the sections above do already give us some clues to the answer to this question. It has traditionally been argued and accepted that trade unions were initially formed and that people joined them as a response to the market weakness of the individual and in the belief that market strength can be achieved through collective organization and collective action. The motives in this context, then, are primarily economic and are a response to the exploitation of labour in a capitalist market-based system. The primarily economic definition of trade unions adopted by Webb and Webb (1894) can be seen in this context as an attempt at market regulation. Put very simply, it is the belief in and reality of strength in numbers, that employees joined together in unions and acting together can get a better deal and better combat employer power in the marketplace.

Evidence from the 1980s and 1990s still confirms that there are positive union wage gaps, by which we mean that in otherwise comparable workplaces average wages are higher in those that are unionized. There is some evidence that this gap has been decreasing since the early 1980s. The 1990 WIRS data have been analysed (Stewart, 1994) to show that the gap for skilled workers has declined from around 3.4 per cent in 1984 to 1.5 per cent in 1990, and for semi-skilled workers the gap has similarly declined from 10.0 per cent to 6.3 per cent. Main (1996) suggests, on the basis of earlier data, that trade union membership may create a union/non-union wage gap of some 6–8 per cent for unionized males and 14–19 per cent for unionized females.

Other reasons for joining include a mix of normative and instrumental motives.

1 Some people join because they have values and political beliefs that coincide with those of the union movement. In countries such as France and

Italy there are significant religious dimensions to the trade union movements and people would join the union that represented people sharing their religious beliefs.

2 Prior to the effective outlawing of closed shop arrangements it was argued that many employees joined trade unions not because they wanted to but because they were effectively press-ganged into it through peer pressure and the more instrumental consideration of wanting to obtain or wanting to keep a job. It is unclear the extent to which peer pressure might continue to be a significant influence in encouraging people to join or indeed to not join.

3 Gaining access to and use of the services that the unions normally provide such as:

- individual protection and representation at work. Trade unions are often the first port of call for a member if and when he or she feels that one of their statutory employment rights has been infringed. This may be their right not to be unfairly dismissed or not to be discriminated against on the grounds of sex or race, where the employee has a grievance or indeed in circumstances where management make allegations against the individual that might result in disciplinary proceedings and action against them. It is impossible to know how many members of trade unions each year make use of these representative and/or legal advice services, many of the instances remain unrecorded; they are conducted by the relevant lay officials within organizations and resolved relatively amicably and often quickly. Nevertheless, we should acknowledge that the frequency of such episodes may be very large indeed and more than the number of individual applications to employment tribunals each year which, as we have pointed out earlier in Chapter 5, exceeds 100,000 cases

- a range of financial and other membership services such as are offered by many other voluntary organizations and which may well include discounted rates and prices from various goods and service providers – mortgages, pensions, loans, credit cards, insurance, car rentals, etc. Many commentators and others over recent years have argued that the development of services of this nature should be deliberately undertaken as a means of encouraging people to join, as a recruitment attraction, and a number of trade union leaders have argued that the unions need to change their attitude towards their members so that they regard and treat them as customers rather than as troops that can be marshalled to fight industrial battles. Nevertheless, as Heery (1996) points out, demand for this new type of union service does not seem to be great outside a small number of occupational groupings such as nursing and teaching

- educational and other career development opportunities within the movement. Some of the larger trade unions still operate their own educational services whereas others buy into those provided by the TUC.

Waddington and Whitston (1997) report the results of a survey that covered 11,000 union members in twelve different unions, which took place between 1991 and 1993. They found that the most frequently given reason for joining was related to the need for support at work in the event of a problem, this was followed by a belief that better pay and conditions of employment would be obtained and the third most common reason for joining was related to a belief in and sharing of the values of trade unionism, a normative type of commitment to trade unionism. They found little support for the view that the provision of financial, insurance and similar membership services was a potent weapon in the union armoury in the fight to increase membership. Their research provides little support for those pressing the case of business unionism as the model to ensure the union movement's future in the UK.

In addition to the above it is significant that some of the international and comparative studies that have sought to explain why trade union membership in one country is historically different from another have highlighted the importance of effective local/workplace organization, visibility, availability and apparent achievement as factors influencing the joining decisions of employees. In essence, that people can only join organizations that are available to them and that they are more likely to join if they see that the union is achieving for employees in the workplace; this is discussed further in Hollinshead and Leat (1995: Chapter 5).

Trade union membership

Traditionally, to which union someone belonged, or were able to join, was largely determined by the level and nature of the skill they possessed or by the occupation or industry that they worked in. It was in this context that trade unions in the UK were categorized as being one of three types:

- **craft**, where the possession of a particular skill was the requirement for entry and membership, e.g. ASLEF – the railway engine drivers' union
- **industrial** or **occupational**, the latter being much more common in the UK than the former, e.g. the National Union of Mineworkers or National Union of Teachers
- **general**, where membership was not specifically linked to either of the above and the union was likely to represent large numbers of semi- and unskilled employees in a number of different industries and companies, e.g. the Transport and General Workers Union.

In more recent years this traditional classification has become less and less relevant as industry and the trade union movement restructured. Early in the 1960s, Turner (1962) suggested that it was more sensible to distinguish between those unions that pursued open membership policies and those that pursued closed policies.

Activity 2

Take a moment now to look back at the traditional typology and decide where each of the three might fit into Turner's classification system.

As noted in the Introduction, the period since 1980 has seen a continuing decline in the number of trade union members. As with any comparative analysis of statistics, whether it be across national borders or over time, it is important to try as far as is possible to compare like with like. This is often not as easy as it sounds, for example even time-series of statistical evidence from the same source often encompass changes in and refinement of definition and methods of deriving and obtaining the information. However, in this instance, whichever series of data are examined the trend of membership decline is apparent.

Trade union membership data tend to be presented in two ways: one, the obvious one, is of the total numbers of people in membership, and the second makes use of a concept known as membership density. This latter measure is a percentage actual of potential and therefore a membership density of 50 per cent would indicate that half of those that could be members were in membership. There have been numerous debates over the years as to how one should define potential in this context and some statistical series have taken potential to be all those in employment. Others argue that the registered unemployed should be added to the potential total as well, while yet others argue that the potential measure should also include all those working that aren't either owners or senior managers of organizations.

No one definition or formula is the correct one, what you need to bear in mind is that to some extent people, authors, politicians, trade unions and others choose to use the definition that best suits their purpose. For example, trade union officers and leaders are likely to use the definition that gives the highest density figure, whereas one might expect employers and right-wing politicians believing in the freedom of the individual and the sanctity of individual choice and exchange to choose the one that gives the lower density measure.

An example of the differences that might result are shown in **Figure 7.1**. This particular series of information is gathered from the Labour Force Survey (LFS) which compiles information from a sample of those in employment in a particular reference week. An alternative source of data on trade union membership comes from the Certification Officer who

Year[a]	Number of members (000s)	Percentage change in membership since previous year	Union density of all in employment (per cent)	Union density of employees (per cent)
1989	8964		34.1	39.0
1990	8854	–1.2	33.4	38.1
1991	8633	–2.5	33.3	37.5
1992	7999	–7.3	32.1	35.8
1993	7808	–2.4	31.3	35.1
1994	7553	–3.3	30.0	33.6
1995	7275	–3.7	28.8	32.1
1996	7215	–0.8	28.2	31.3
Change since 1989	–1749	–19.5	–5.9	–7.7

Includes all those in employment, except for the final column which is employees only, excluding members of the armed forces.

Those who did not report their union status, or who were not contactable in the autumn quarter, have been allocated on a pro-rata basis.

a   From 1989–1991 union membership questions were asked in the spring. Since 1992 they have been asked in the autumn quarter.

Figure 7.1 *Source:* Cully and Woodland (1997) Trade Union Membership and Density in UK 1989–96

derives figures from the information presented to him by the trade unions themselves who are required to provide annual returns. Cully and Woodland acknowledge that the Certification Officer series is likely to provide a higher figure of trade union membership, for example their own data are obtained only from those in employment and therefore exclude trade union members who are unemployed or otherwise economically inactive in the week that forms the base of the LFS data.

The peak of trade union membership in this country was in 1979 and it is acknowledged that membership in that year exceeded 13 million. Since then, as noted above, there has been continuous decline so that in 1996 the LFS data show only 7.2 million in membership – but remember here you are not comparing like with like. The 1979 data were compiled from information provided by the unions themselves.

Cully and Woodland confine themselves to a comparison with 1989, the year that the LFS began to collect this information, and this shows that there has in this period been a decline of some 20 per cent, though the rate of decline has fallen or begun to bottom out, a conclusion that would appear to be confirmed by the figures for 1998 – see below.

Other characteristics and trends identified in Cully and Woodland (1997) are that the rate of decline has been particularly marked among:

- male employees
- manual employees
- production industries.

All areas and categories that formed the core of trade union membership (see **Figure 7.2**).

Density has fallen more slowly among:

- female employees
- those working part-time
- non-manual employees.

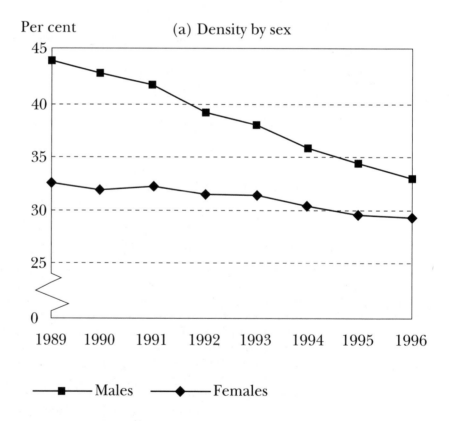

Figure 7.2 Union density by various characteristics, 1989–96. Adapted from Cully and Woodland (1997)

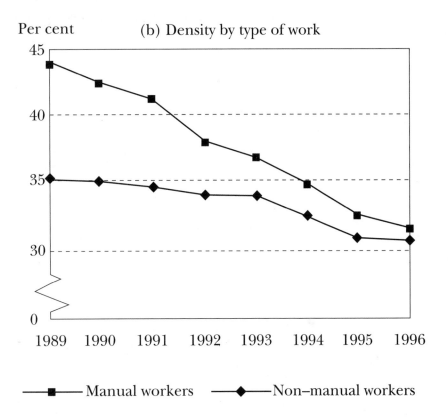

Per cent   (b) Density by type of work

——■—— Manual workers   ——◆—— Non–manual workers

Figure 7.2 (*continued*)

Look at the table in **Figure 7.3** and deduce from it what you can about the characteristics and structure of trade union membership in the UK in the middle of the 1990s. Write down your observations.

   Other characteristics that emerge from this article are that membership density varies with age group and the higher rates are among the over-40 age groups. An interesting variation on the norm is among the under-30 year-olds where density among women exceeds the density among men. A similar higher density figure among women than men is found when you categorize according to ethnic origin, among non-white employees. Another interesting and perhaps surprising conclusion is that there is a positive relationship between level of educational qualification and union membership, those with qualifications above 'A' level being apparently

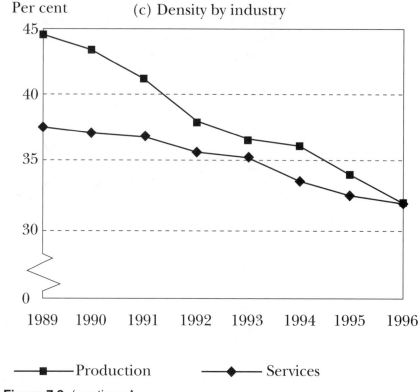

Per cent   (c) Density by industry

──■── Production   ──◆── Services

Figure 7.2 (*continued*)

more likely to be a union member than those with lower level qualifications or none at all.

LFS data collected in the autumn of 1998 gave overall membership of trade unions as 7.1 million, a density of 30 per cent of the employed workforce, a very slight increase of 4000 over the figures for 1997 and the first increase since 1979. Certification Officer figures for 1997 show a total trade union membership of 7.8 million, Annual Report of the Certification Officer 1998, p. 48–9. Crown Copyright 1999, London, compared with 7.1 million in the LFS serie.

The categories in which membership had most increased included women (up 60 000 on the 1997 figures), Pakistani and Bangladeshi workers where the density of membership had increased from 16 per cent to 20 per cent over the year, and part-time workers where density had increased from 21 per cent to 22 per cent. Afro-Caribbean membership density was 36 per cent, the highest rate for any ethnic group, including white. There was a continuation of the decline among male manual workers in the manufacturing and other traditional industries.

The public–private sector split in the 1998 LFS data was recorded as 60 per cent density in the public sector compared with only 19 per cent in the private sector.

1992 SIC^c	Industry	All	Men	Women	Full-time	Part-time	Private sector	Public sector	Non-manual	Manual	Less than 25 employees	25 or more employees
	All employees^b	**31**	**33**	**29**	**35**	**20**	**21**	**61**	**31**	**31**	**16**	**39**
A, B	**Agriculture, forestry and fishing**	8	10	5	9	4	8	*	10	8	8	9
C	**Mining and quarrying**	38	42	*	39	*	39	*	20	51	*	42
D	**Manufacturing**	31	34	22	32	15	31	61	16	41	8	36
15-16	Food, beverages and tobacco	35	37	31	36	30	35	*	14	45	8	39
17-19	Textiles, clothing and footwear	30	30	31	33	18	30	*	13	36	7	36
22	Printing and publishing	27	34	14	29	12	27	*	15	42	17	31
24	Chemicals	26	30	18	27	*	26	*	14	43	*	28
25	Rubber and plastics	19	21	12	20	*	19	*	10	24	0	23
27-28	Basic and fabricated metals	29	32	12	30	*	29	*	14	36	7	37
29	Machinery	31	34	16	31	*	31	*	15	42	5	37
30-33,	Electrical equipment	19	20	17	19	14	19	*	11	28	6	22
34	Motor vehicles	53	55	40	54	*	53	*	27	65	*	56
35	Other transport equipment	54	56	*	55	*	53	*	43	63	*	59
E	**Electricity, gas and water supply**	61	67	42	63	*	61	*	54	75	*	61
40.1	Electricity	68	72	*	69	*	67	*	63	75	*	67
41	Water	51	56	*	53	*	48	*	40	*	*	48
F	**Construction**	25	28	12	27	8	15	74	19	31	12	35
G	**Wholesale and retail trade**	11	10	12	11	10	11	*	10	14	4	17
51	Wholesale trade	8	9	7	8	5	8	*	5	14	3	12
52	Retail trade	13	12	13	15	11	13	*	12	19	5	21
H	**Hotels and restaurants**	7	5	8	8	6	5	39	8	6	5	8
I	**Transport and communication**	47	53	30	50	22	40	79	34	57	23	55
60.1	Rail transport	75	78	*	77	*	74	*	*	84	*	77
64.1	Postal services	64	71	44	71	33	34	80	42	75	32	73
64.2	Telecommunications	50	54	42	52	*	50	*	41	70	*	48
J	**Financial intermediation**	36	32	40	35	40	36	47	37	*	45	33
65.1	Banks and building societies	49	41	56	48	55	49	*	50	*	69	43
66	Insurance	28	35	21	31	*	29	*	28	*	*	28
K	**Real estate and business services**	13	14	12	14	10	8	62	12	15	8	17
L	**Public administration**	61	65	56	64	43	31	60	63	44	52	62
M	**Education**	55	65	51	69	31	28	60	65	29	47	58
80.1-80.2	Schools	59	76	53	77	31	29	63	74	27	50	62
80.3	Higher education	47	52	43	52	33	*	48	47	47	*	49
N	**Health and social work**	47	53	46	54	37	15	64	54	33	30	55
85.11	Hospitals	54	58	53	61	44	17	64	58	41	33	60
O	**Other services**	23	31	16	29	13	12	48	25	21	15	33
90	Sewage and refuse disposal	54	60	*	60	*	34	68	51	56	*	62

*Base too low to provide a reliable estimate.

^aSee technical note for details on classifications.

^bIncludes all employees except those in the armed services.

^cStandard Industrial Classification

Source: Labour Force Survey

Figure 7.3 Union density: detailed selected industries by other characteristics ^a 1996. *Source:* Cully and Woodland (1997)

The first findings from the 1998 Workplace Employee Relations Survey (WERS), Cully, M. *et al.* 1998 which are based on information from employers, indicates that overall trade union density was 36 per cent. The data confirm that there are positive associations between both trade union recognition and membership density and size of workplace. They also confirm that the attitude of management appears influential with regard to both union membership density and recognition; where managers are in favour of union membership the density figure is 62 per cent and the rate of recognition is 94 per cent.

Inevitably, many researchers and commentators have sought to explain the reasons and causes of the long-term decline in both trade union membership and density. What has become clear is that there is no one explanatory variable and that a number of developments can be argued to have contributed. Among these are:

- the macroeconomic climate, macroeconomic policy, recession and unemployment
- the gradual but nevertheless substantial legislative attack upon the trade unions that was mounted by the Conservative Party whilst in government between 1979 and 1997. This encompassed the removal of legal rights to recognition and the encouragement of collective bargaining, limits upon picketing and secondary action, the eventual outlawing of the closed shop, the removal of the ability of trade unions to discipline members for not taking part in lawful industrial action, the development of increasingly strict constraints upon the unions' freedom to take industrial action and the creation of a legal right to not be a member of a trade union
- change in the structure of industry, the decline of manufacturing and extractive industries, the growth of the service sector and the attack mounted against employment and joint regulation in the public sector
- both an ageing population and the increased participation of women in the labour force
- the attitudes of employers, their resistance to sharing employer prerogative and their opportunism in taking advantage of the circumstances created by the above (see the evidence from the 1998 WERS above)
- employer reaction to the need to become more competitive in the global market and perhaps particularly their desire to introduce greater flexibility to working practices and their use of labour
- changes in values and culture in the UK reflected perhaps most obviously in the emphasis given to enterprise and individualism
- the unions themselves, the attitudes and behaviour of both leaders and members, particularly in the early period of Conservative government when, as noted in the introduction to this section, there was a degree of popular support for the policies of reducing trade union power and influence.

Internal government, organization and democracy

Trade unions are voluntary bodies, which in the main people join because they want to. They are also democratic in that the policies of the union are determined through mechanisms and structures that provide members with the opportunity to participate in this decision making, either directly or indirectly through elected representatives. However, before examining the issue of democracy in more depth we need to outline the way in which unions tend to be structured for the purpose of internal government and how the activities of the union are organized. It is only possible in this introductory text to outline a stereotype of typical arrangements and this is indicated in **Figure 7.4**.

The figure demonstrates that policy and decision making begins at the bottom of the organization with the members who elect an individual to represent them in discussions and negotiations with management at the place of work. Normally these 'lay' representatives are called shop stewards and they remain employees of the employing organization and not employees of the union. These shop stewards then represent their members at the lowest level of official organization within the union – the branch. Depending upon the size of the workplace and the concentration of members, the branch may be either geographically or workplace-based. Whichever base is used for determining the branch network, and it is quite

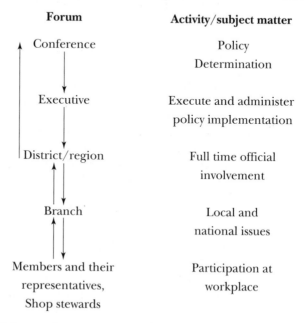

Forum	Activity/subject matter
Conference	Policy Determination
Executive	Execute and administer policy implementation
District/region	Full time official involvement
Branch	Local and national issues
Members and their representatives, Shop stewards	Participation at workplace

Figure 7.4 Internal government of a union

common to have a mix within the same union, decisions of the branch are fed up through the hierarchy of the union organization through trade, district or regional arrangements to the annual or biannual conference of the union as a whole. Commonly the branch members will elect the members of the district or trade committees and these latter in turn elect or nominate representatives to the next level of union management including the delegates to the national conference. It is this national conference that is the policy-making body for the union. Since an annual or biannual conference of delegates from the branches or districts cannot in practice be responsible for the day-to-day operations of the union and for the execution of the policies determined, trade unions tend to devise some form of executive committee arrangements.

Usually the executive committee of the union is comprised of a mix of senior elected representatives and full-time paid officials and, in addition to executing the wishes of the conference, they are likely also in practice to be in a position to amend or determine policy between conferences as events unfold. On really major issues the union may convene a special or extra-ordinary conference to determine a particular policy stance. You will find those who argue that the reality usually is that the executive committee is the real seat of power within a union and that this is the major policy-making forum rather than the formal position which allocates that role to the conference.

Since legislation in the Trade Union Act 1984 the members of the executive committee must be elected via a secret postal ballot of the members at least once every five years. This applies to the principal paid and full-time officials of the union as well as to the other members.

One of the advantages of these arrangements has been that unions have been able to operate relatively cheaply, relying upon the unpaid shop stewards to undertake a great deal of the servicing of members at the level of the workplace. Full-time officers of the union commonly only become involved in servicing members and furthering their interests above the level of the branch. McIlroy (1995: 39) estimated that in the 1960s the ratio of full-time officers to members was somewhere near 1:4000.

Returning to the issue of democracy, there are a number of different definitions, models and perspectives. In many respects the simplest definition is that commonly associated with the American President Abraham Lincoln, who talked of government of the people by the people and for the people. In relatively small organizations or units it is possible to achieve this objective through the direct participation of all the 'people'. However, as the size of the unit to be governed increases it becomes more difficult to achieve efficient and effective government if decisions have to be taken by all the members and so there is a tendency for the organization to develop mechanisms that rely upon the election or appointment of representatives to act on behalf of a number of ordinary members. This latter is often referred to as the representative or parliamentary model of democracy and is contrasted with the direct or participatory model.

Many years ago Michels (1966) developed his 'Iron Law Of Oligarchy', whereby it is argued that increasing size, the need for administrative efficiency and organizational effectiveness would inevitably lead in organizations such as trade unions to a concentration of power into the hands of an elite or oligarchy. This elite were likely to be in position because of their skill, knowledge and expertise, which they were then able to use, if they chose, to pursue their own interests as well as, indeed possibly instead of, the interests of the membership as a whole. The longer this elite is in power the greater is the likelihood that the leadership will become distanced and divorced from the membership. Such a situation has obvious dangers for the maintenance of democracy within the union.

As noted in the introduction to this chapter the Conservative government elected in 1979 were of the view that the union movement as a whole had too much power and, as a corollary to this, there was a feeling that the unions were being led by militant unrepresentative minorities who took advantage of the absence of democratic accountability within the unions to pursue their own, often political, ends at the expense of the interests of the members. Whether this was the case or not, the new government determined, in their terms, to return the unions to their members, to bring democracy back to the union movement.

To this latter end the government adopted a number of measures to encourage membership participation in the election of senior union officials and members of the executive committee and in decisions concerning the taking of industrial action, primarily through the enforcement of a requirement for secret postal ballots and direct democracy, but at a distance. This approach suggests that the government adhered to the parliamentary model of democracy. They also took a number of measures aimed at diminishing the power of the union in regard to the rights of members, for example the restrictions upon the right of the union to discipline and expel members referred to earlier and additional rights for members to examine the financial affairs of the union.

Critics of these legislative measures have pointed out that they reflected a concern with only one or two of the dimensions of democracy and that there are others which were not addressed. Examples of other criteria of democracy might variously include:

- the existence of opposition factions within the union and whether they are provided with equal facilities to get their message across to the members, especially prior to elections for membership of the various layers of the internal structure referred to earlier
- the degree of debate and discussion within the union and the presence of mechanisms facilitating this
- the closeness of election results, the assumption being that landslide victories might be indicative of an absence of democracy
- the decentralization of decision making within the union; the assumption again being that the closer to the membership decisions are taken

the greater will be the transparency of the decision making process, the greater will be the visibility of the union and the greater will be the members' interest and participation. Also it may be suggested that the greater the decentralization of decision making the greater are the checks upon the union leadership and the less opportunity they have actually to give effect to Michels' fears

- the participation and representation of particular factions or groups in the activities of the union and in the decision making process, examples usually quoted are the participation of ethnic minority groups and women in the affairs of the union, the extent to which the structure of the membership is reflected in the decision making processes.

Activity 4

Read the material on democracy again and

1 identify the two main models of democracy and briefly distinguish between them
2 devise a list of the factors that would appear in the light of the above discussion to both encourage and/or frustrate democracy within the union movement.

Trade union recognition

It was noted in an earlier section that one of the legislative changes (The Employment Act 1980) introduced by the Conservative governments of the 1980s constituted a removal of the rights and mechanisms that the trade unions had available throughout the 1970s to enforce recognition upon employers for the purposes of collective bargaining, even in the face of employer opposition.

The significant decline in both trade union membership and in the number of trade unions, referred to above, has also been accompanied by a significant decline in their influence as measured by the incidence of trade union recognition and collective bargaining. The scale of this decline was indicated in the results of the 1990 Workplace Industrial Relations Survey (WIRS; Millward *et al.*, 1992), which showed a decline in the percentage of workplaces in which a trade union was recognized for collective bargaining purposes. The decline was apparent in both private and public sectors, though the evidence confirmed that recognition was still more common in respect of manual workers, manufacturing and the public sector.

More recently the Labour Force Survey, which has been collecting infor-

Table 6 Union recognition and collective bargaining in Great Britain,[a] 1993–1996

Year	Number of employees in workplaces with recognition[b] (000s)	Percentage change in number since previous year	Percentage of employees in workplaces with recognition	Number of employees covered by collective bargaining (000s)	Percentage of employees covered by collective bargaining
1993	10 420		48.9		
1994	10 374	−0.4	48.2		
1995	10 226	−1.4	46.8		
1996	10 141	−0.8	45.8	8091	36.5
Change since 1993	−279	−2.7	−3.1		

[a] Includes all employees, except for members of the armed forces.

[b] Those who did not report their union recognition status, or who were not contactable in the autumn quarter, have been allocated on a pro-rata basis.

Source: Labour Force Survey

Figure 7.5 Union recognition and collective bargaining in Great Britain, 1993–96 Cully, M. and Woodland, S. 1997.

mation on these matters since 1993, has confirmed a continuance of the decline in recognition. The results for 1996 (see **Figure 7.5**) show that the percentage of employees in workplaces where trade unions are recognized for the purpose of collectively negotiating the pay and conditions of employees was down to 45.8 per cent (estimated to represent 10.1 million employees). However, not all employees in such workplaces are themselves covered by collective bargaining and it was estimated that only some 8.1 million (36.5 per cent) of employees had their pay and conditions determined through this mechanism. The LFS data collected in the autumn of 1998 confirmed a continuation of the decline with only 44 per cent of employees working in places where unions are recognized.

The 1998 WERS data also indicates a continuing decline in the proportion of workplaces where there is recognition for collective bargaining purposes and this was the case in only 45 per cent of all workplaces, this compares with figures of 66 per cent in 1984 and 53 per cent in 1990.

Earlier, Metcalf (1993) pointed out that in private-sector workplaces that were less than ten years old unions were much less likely to be recognized than was the case in workplaces that were more than ten years old. This may indicate that recognition was easier to obtain in the 1970s and before, and that once obtained it was easier to retain.

It would be easy to assume that the decline in trade union recognition was the result of planned and deliberate derecognition by employers, taking the opportunity afforded by the new economic, political and legislative climate of the 1980s to rid themselves of an unwelcome representative of their employees and challenge to their authority and autonomy. While this has undoubtedly happened in some cases, and perhaps particularly in industries such as newspapers and the media, it would seem from the research that the incidence of such positive derecognition strategies has not in fact been that great.

Claydon (1996) concludes from his review of incidents of derecognition over a decade or more that it is possible to identify two general approaches to derecognition:

- **reactive** – representing a management response to a weakening of trade union power within the organization usually owing to one or more changes in the organization's industrial relations environment rather than it being the result of purposive action by management
- **purposive** – reflective of long-term effort by management to eliminate unionized industrial relations from the organization.

There have been debates about the nature of the relationship between declining trade union membership density and derecognition with two views expressed, one being that weaker unions reduce the perceived need and incentive for management to derecognize, the other, which appears to be borne out more by the evidence, is that there is a positive relationship between the two, that is that as unions become weaker they become less able to fight derecognition and in such circumstances managements are more likely to take their opportunity and derecognize. Claydon tends to favour this latter view and further suggests that unions should be wary of entering into what are referred to as cooperative relationships with employers since there is little or no evidence to suggest that such an approach dissuades managements from pursuing policies aimed at derecognition.

There are potentially important implications here for the new 'partnership' approach being advocated by the TUC – see the later section on trade union survival strategies.

Looked at from the viewpoint of the unions and their members, trade union recognition is a crucial step in the achievement of their objectives. Indeed, in the context of the current UK legal system, recognition is essential for access to the protections, rights and immunities that are afforded the unions by the law. If in this context management are free to refuse to talk to and bargain with trade unions, to recognize them, even where significant proportions of their labour force clearly want to be represented by the union, there really are potentially terminal implications for trade unionism in the UK. It is therefore not surprising that union leaders have argued that it is crucial for the effectiveness and survival of the movement that they be granted a legal right to recognition from hostile and reluctant employers and appropriate mechanisms of enforcement. It is equally understandable that employers and their organizations and representatives should in many cases resist the introduction of such a right.

The new Labour government elected in 1997 indicated that they intended to introduce such a right in certain prescribed circumstances and where certain conditions are met. They tried to get the two parties, represented by the TUC and the CBI, to reach an agreement on the details of the conditions and circumstances that would have to be met for recognition to be enforced against a reluctant employer, but this was only partially successful. Among the main sticking points to a comprehensive agreement were concerns and differences of view and perceived interest on exemptions for small firms, the proportion of a workforce or bargaining unit that would need to vote in favour for the right to be triggered, the notion of an automatic right to recognition where a majority of a workforce are already union members, and who it was that would have the right to determine the bargaining unit: the electorate or constituency in electoral terms. See **Figure 7.6** for a summary of the respective positions of the two sides, as represented by the TUC and the CBI, as they stood just before the publication of the government's proposals.

Eventually, in May 1998, the government issued its legislative proposals in a White Paper entitled 'Fairness at Work' and this became the base for the 1999 Employment Relations Act (see **Figure 5.1**). In essence, if a majority of a bargaining unit is in membership of the union, recognition will be automatic. Otherwise a majority must vote in favour and this majority must constitute at least 40% of those eligible to vote in the ballot.

At the time of writing, towards the end of 1999, the Act's regulations regarding trade union recognition and individual representation via a right to 'accompaniment' in disciplinary and grievance procedures seem set to come into force in the summer of 2000. ACAS (see Chapter 5) has been given the task of producing codes of practice and guidance in these areas.

Survival strategies

We mentioned at the outset of this chapter in looking at definitions of trade unions the significance of time and changing circumstances. Over the last twenty years in particular the union movement in the UK has been confronted by a hostile environment and a number of major challenges, among which are:

- a hostile government determined to reduce the unions' power and influence and which pursued a radical legislative programme geared towards the achievement of this objective
- economic recessions encompassing the highest rates of unemployment since the early 1930s
- increasing internationalization of business and the concentration of economic power in fewer and stronger hands
- technological development and change on a scale and at a rate not pre-

What the CBI is insisting on	What the TUC is insisting on
1 Unions must prove that 30 per cent of employees support bid for recognition before there is any final ballot.	1 There should be a single test: either a ballot, or a fast-track route with a union proving it has 50 per cent membership.
2 Firms with fewer than 50 employees should be exempt from a right to union recognition law.	2 No one should be denied access to a union just because they work for a small company.
3 Employers should have the right to decide which group of workers should be balloted on whether they want union representation.	3 Where the two sides disagree about the bargaining unit, an outside agency should arbitrate, otherwise wily bosses will simply alter their business structures.
4 Union recognition should be granted only if a majority of all eligible employees back it – not just a majority of those voting.	4 Insisting on a majority of all eligible workers could lead to unfairness. For instance, an 80 per cent yes on a 60 per cent turnout would be deemed a vote against union recognition.
5 Employees should be free to opt out of union collective representation, even if half the workforce has voted for recognition.	5 Modern unions are used to negotiating reward packages with individual variation.
6 Training should be excluded from collective bargaining as it relates to individual needs and business practice.	6 Involving unions in training is one of the best ways to gain the commitment of a workforce to raise skill levels.
7 Strikes should be banned in disputes about union recognition.	7 It would be unfair to further limit union rights, especially as the TUC isn't proposing an equivalent range of civil law sanctions on employers.

Figure 7.6 *Source: The Guardian*, 17 March 1998

viously encountered, which had major implications for the demand for traditional skills and products

- a degree of industrial restructuring not previously encountered in peace-time
- cultural change in which traditional values of collectivism and solidarity

have been threatened by a government- and employer-inspired emphasis upon individualism and enterprise

- new management initiatives emphasizing managerial control and employee involvement as individuals and on management's terms
- significant membership decline with consequent major effects for the financial strength of the movement and for the services that can be provided for members.

The above list is not exhaustive and not intended to be in any order of importance and it is also important to appreciate that there interrelationships between many of these developments and forces for change.

Not surprisingly, and after an initial period in the 1980s when it is alleged that union leaders were unable to appreciate the scale and permanence of what was happening around them, these developments have forced the unions to debate what they could and should now do and it is these major debates that we concentrate upon for the rest of this section. In the main the debates have centred around:

- the objectives that the unions should pursue and the priorities attached to them
- how to stop the membership and financial haemorrhage
- how to secure the return of a friendlier government
- the (new) strategies, towards employers and government, that might provide hope of improved relationships.

In the context of these debates we have seen the emergence of the New Realists, who have been characterized as in opposition to the Traditionalists. This has been characterized as a debate between those, on the one hand, who believe the time has come to adopt different objectives, to emphasize activity and achievement in the workplace and more cooperative approaches such as are embodied in the notion of partnership agreements, and the Traditionalists on the other, who retain a belief in the essentially conflictual nature of the employment relationship, the original objectives of the movement and who are willing, where necessary, to utilize adversarial means. For the moment at least it would seem that the New Realists have won the day.

Indeed it is arguable that relatively few of the objectives considered central to trade unionism in the UK in the 1960s (see earlier section of this chapter on 'The objectives of trade unions') would be considered central today.

In 1994 The TUC re-launched itself and in so doing addressed the issue of trade union objectives in a changed environment. The relaunch confirmed a new and different focus, which it has been argued is so fundamental that the movement in the UK no longer sits within the social or political movement category referred to earlier, that this re-launch of the TUC was proof of a shift in the direction of business unionism and workplace-based objectives.

However, the movement has not completely forsaken the pursuit of objectives outside the workplace gates. In the TUC General Council Report for 1995 and in discussion of the re-launch emphasis is given to:

● 'priorities rooted firmly in the world of work'

though reference is also made to

● 'Full employment remains our central objective'
● the union movement seeking to influence all the main political parties.

The TUC also refers to initiatives and objectives in areas not specifically mentioned in the earlier evidence to the Donovan Commission, in particular in the areas of:

● corporate governance
● top peoples' pay
● in the area of equality.

The trade unions argue that they are being realistic in amending their objectives and perhaps particularly their priorities, that they are responding to the new economic, legal, political, social and cultural reality of 1990s Britain and that they are doing so against a background of considerable decline. It is in this context that the terms New Realism and New Unionism were devised and applied.

The minority Traditional wing, in addition to considering that the original objectives should be pursued, also argue that in responding to the New Reality by becoming more workplace-oriented and less concerned to achieve a transformation of and a more egalitarian society, the movement is in fact demeaning its history and itself as well as contributing to its long-term marginalization.

Social partnership

Even more recently the TUC has decided to emphasize what it perceives to be a social partnership approach and this implies further adaptation of objectives as well as implying the utilization of different means for their achievement. This development has been associated with the New Unionism and, for the unions, this model of partnership seems to imply 'working together', with management at the level of the firm or workplace to achieve what are referred to as common objectives such as fairness and competitiveness and, at a national level, talking with government and employers' associations to achieve objectives such as attracting inward investment and promoting training and equal opportunities. The overarching objective of the new TUC and its members in the last few years of the

1990s would seem to be the achievement of full and fair employment and to do so where possible through partnership with both employers and government.

Partnership agreements

Inevitably this term will encompass types of agreements with different content. Among the best known partnership agreements are those at Tesco, Littlewoods, Legal and General and Barclays and the participants to these agreements assert that they are central elements in the companies' efforts to transform the nature of employee relations. Other similarly styled agreements will be little more than expressions of intent and, at their worst, cynical attempts on the part of the employer to draw the sting of trade unionism by involving the union in a single union, no strike, compulsory arbitration deal with vague promises of involvement and cooperation. The Amalgamated Engineering and Electrical Union (AEEU) has signed a number of agreements that may fall into this latter category. There was a partnership agreement at Rover also, though the notion of partnership did not seem to extend to the owners BMW keeping the unions informed of their plans to sell or close the operation early in 2000.

The Tesco agreement provides for a company-wide system of staff forums comprised of union and non-union representatives who meet with management to discuss and where possible agree upon a wide range of issues including matters of pay. This is combined with a payment scheme that provides for workers to receive shares in the company and overall the forums appear to adopt a joint problem-solving approach to the resolution of issues raised. It is also the case that since the agreement was reached there has been a significant increase in trade union membership within the company, a reflection of workers seeing management and the union actively cooperating to resolve problems. Cynics, however, wonder whether the agreement will stand the test of recession and redundancy.

While the current emphasis may be upon cooperation, many of the trade unions seem ready to retain the ability and willingness to be militant if partnership doesn't work and this puts into a less favourable perspective the willingness of some unions to sign away their rights to take militant action in return for compulsory arbitration.

The TUC would appear to see the content of a model partnership agreement containing enhanced flexibility and commitment to the success of the organization from the employees and union in return for trade union recognition, guarantees on job security and an enhanced focus upon the quality of working life from management. It will be difficult for trade unions to resist this style of agreement even if they want to if, as in the case of Tesco, it seems that they assist the union in the task of recruiting new members.

Servicing or organizing approaches?

As noted above, the debates over survival strategies have not only been concerned with the matter of objective and their relative priority, there has also been considerable attention paid both to the question of how to halt the loss of membership and how to recruit more members. Depending upon their membership base and policies, trade unions have been confronted often with quite different membership environments over the last two decades, those with an open membership approach have tended to fair better than those that restricted their membership to people in a particular trade, occupation or industry. These latter are more vulnerable when the trade, industry or occupation is in decline. It is also the case that labour market and industrial trends which have seen a greater proportion of women working, a greater proportion of the labour force working part-time and flexibly (see Chapter 6) and a continuing enhancement of the service and small-firm sectors have also posed particular problems for the union movement in the UK, which has not traditionally shown itself to be adept at recruiting and retaining members in these and other groups and sectors. The dominant membership of the union movement in the UK has been white males in manufacturing and extractive industry.

A friendlier government was always perceived as a potential, if partial, solution to this problem and, with the election of New Labour in May 1997, it would seem that to some extent this has now been achieved. We have referred earlier to the legislative proposals on trade union recognition for collective bargaining purposes and it is anticipated by many that it will become easier for unions to recruit members against the background of this legislative right.

The TUC General Secretary, John Monks, told the 1999 TUC annual conference that membership should rise by 1 million members over the following five years as a result of the new friendlier legislative climate. The GMB union reported to the conference that it had concluded more than 100 new recognition agreements in the preceding twelve months as the impending legislative changes, allied with the unions' greater willingness to contemplate and enter into partnership agreements, seemed to be creating a more union-friendly climate amongst employers.

However, despite the different circumstances and environments confronting individual unions there has also been a more general discussion within the movement on the respective efficacy of the organizing and servicing approaches to enhancing union membership, each of which implies a different perspective of why people join unions and what they want from their union membership.

The servicing model of union membership is also associated often with the New Realism referred to above. It is a model that perceives union members as individuals who will be attracted into membership by the range and value of the services which the union offers to them. It is a model that has been equated with private-sector organizations such as the RAC and insurance companies. In the light of this approach we have seen many trade unions expanding the range of membership services to include credit cards, discounts agreed with providers of various services, insurance and mortgage facilities. Bassett and Cave (1993) have argued this role model, others have argued that this is a model that overestimates the extent to which workers in the UK of today have bought into the new individualist and enterprise culture and they cite research which demonstrates that protection and representation at work are still the dominant reasons why people join trade unions (Whitston and Waddington, 1994, 1995; Waddington and Whitston, 1997).

As noted above, the alternative approach to the servicing model is referred to as the organizing model and this approach is more consistent with the traditional notions of collectivism, self-help and democratic organization. Recruitment and membership enhancement in this model are bottom-up activities. Blyton and Turnbull (1998) characterize this difference as the difference between the union member who asks what the union will do for him (servicing) and another who asks what we can achieve with the union (organizing).

Figure 7.7 shows in tabular form the main features of each of the two models.

In the mid-1990s it appeared that the New Realists and the servicing model may have been in the ascendant, but there is also evidence of significant minority support for the alternative viewpoints and model and it seems unlikely that these debates have been concluded. In 1997/8 the TUC gave additional impetus to the organizing model with the creation of its 'organizing academy' geared towards the training of new organizers. The emphasis is upon recruitment of new members and upon organization rather than upon servicing existing members.

Activity 5

Examine the two articles from *The Times* (**Figure 7.8**) in which Bill Morris and Ruth Lea present their views on the issue of whether trade unions need and should be given statutory rights to recognition for collective bargaining purposes and summarize in writing the main elements of the respective arguments.

Having done that, identify which of the main perspectives referred to in Chapter 1 is being demonstrated by each, think about which of the two positions reported in the figure seem to you to be the most reasonable and decide whether in principle you are in favour of the Morris or Lea position and explain your reasons.

You might also reflect what these respective positions tell you about the debates concerning the nature of the employment relationship and the inevitability and subject matter of conflict referred to in an earlier chapter.

Servicing model
- Union is seen as external – a third party
- Union official tells members how 'the union' will solve their problems
- Union relies on employer to provide lists of workers' names to union official
- Union relies on employer for workplace access
- Hard selling of union membership
- Union sold on basis of services and insurance protection
- Reliance on full-time officials to recruit and to solve problems
- Aim is to recruit only – to sign on the dotted line – not to organize
- Workers blame 'the union' when it can't get results
- Officers resent members for not coming to meetings or participating in activities. Members complain they pay fees and the union does nothing
- Management acts – union reacts – always on the defensive

Organizing model
- Members own the campaign to unionize their workplace
- Members generate own issues and organize to solve them together
- Names and information are provided by workers to union themselves
- Initial organizing can be done outside work – in coffee bars, pubs or at members' homes
- First recruiting steps are to establish contacts, find natural leaders, uncover issues
- Workers empowered to find solutions themselves through education and mutual support
- Workers encouraged to build the union through one-to-one organizing and to solve problems themselves
- Recruitment and organizing are integrated
- Members share decisions and solve problems together with union leaders – share responsibility
- Members identify with the union and contribute. An attack on the union is seen as an attack on themselves
- Union has its own agenda, is pro-active, keeps management off balance; members are involved

Figure 7.7 Two models of trade unionism.
Source: IDS Focus, No. 91, Autumn 1999, p. 10

A defining moment for our 'one nation'

Often one moment, seen in hindsight, can be said to have defined the future of a government. Norman Lamont emerging on to the steps of the Treasury to announce Britain's withdrawal from the ERM was a defining moment for the last Government, from which it never recovered.

As one who still shares in all the hopes aroused in the country on May 1 last year, I am anxious to see that the Government gets it right in the forthcoming *Fairness at Work* White Paper, since it could well be Labour's defining issue.

I say that, not as the representative of a sectional interest out to gain private advantage, but as one who believes that resolving the issue of rights at work is, firstly, vital to the interests of millions of people, and, secondly, a clear indication as to whether the Government will stick with its vision of an inclusive society. It is therefore central to the future relationship between trade unionists and the Government.

How we arrived at this crossroads is well known by now, but a brief recapitulation of the main points at issue may be helpful. Certainly, Labour's election manifesto pledged that trade union recognition should be granted where a majority of employees demonstrated, through a ballot, that they wanted it.

We are fortunate to live in a country with a long democratic tradition, where ballots are not unfamiliar creatures. It is widely — indeed, were it not for the CBI, I would say universally — understood that in a ballot the side claiming the support of a majority of those who took part should prevail. In attempting to undermine this simple and clear understanding of democracy, the CBI has started many hares running — perhaps this just reflects the absence of democracy as we know it in the conduct of business and the boardroom.

The CBI's plans would give greater weight to those who abstain than to those who vote. If there is a problem here, I say let it be taken to an acceptable adjudicator, or the representation agency proposed by the TUC, rather than re-write the rules of democracy.

Worst of all, the CBI has argued that "small firms", employing fewer than 50, should be entirely exempt from the legislation, an exception so vast (and one not even hinted at in Labour's manifesto) that the word "loophole" does not do it justice.

About seven million people work in such firms, and often it is they who endure the lowest pay and worst employment practices. Certainly, when my own union ran a low-pay hotline and when the TUC ran a more recent "bad bosses" hotline, many of the calls we took were from people employed in smaller firms and keen for some form of union support. Were these millions sold a pup when they voted for Labour in the expectation of union rights?

Alas, this approach to union recognition is consistent with the CBI's principled opposition to so many of the changes the country needs. It has opposed a minimum wage, consultation rights for employees and the whole European social chapter.

We can be sure that, had the CBI been around in the last century, it would have produced a pile of learned research on the job-destroying impact of banning the slave trade or stopping sending children up chimneys.

The TUC and the CBI have been engaged in a game of concession-bargaining: the CBI bargains, the TUC is expected to concede. The more the TUC concedes, the more the CBI demands — no sooner had we offered an exemption for firms employing fewer than ten workers, than the CBI urged a level of 50 In the end, the only way to deal with ransom notes from a "concession bargainer" is to just say No.

I am not surprised as at the CBI's position. It represents a particular class and a particu-

> **❛ In concession bargaining, the more the TUC concedes, the more the CBI demands ❜**

lar interest. It is the Government that I want to convince. We are not seeking special privileges for trade unions, simply the "fairness" we have been so long promised. I fear that our case is not being studied on its merits — instead, employee rights are being treated as a sort of political football in a game of pro-business machismo, designed to prove how different this Labour Government is from preceding ones. However, I believe that, in standing up for rights at work, trade unions are actually working to help create the "one nation" society and the social cohesion which the Prime Minister has rightly made his standard. The workplace cannot be excluded from that project, nor can the necessary transformation be left to the benevolent employer alone. And while individual employee rights are, indeed, essential, it is false to pose these against trade union rights, since in so many situations it is only through collective support that individual rights can be successfully asserted.

As the organisations for those who seek a collective voice at work, we cannot and will not support legislation which, at best, could be unworkable and, at worst, actually entrenches the worker's lack of rights and makes the task of union organisation still more of a struggle. We have to draw a line here, or trade unions could inadvertently sacrifice the long-term future of employee rights for short-term expediency.

It is because this issue is of such over-riding importance that the T&G believes that the full TUC Congress should be recalled to consider the White Paper. While I have the highest regard for my colleagues on the General Council, we are not the whole movement, merely a part of it. A recalled Congress does not put political tanks on anyone's lawn — it would simply be an exercise in membership participation on the most important decision involving workers' rights for more than 20 years.

Indeed, why stop there? All Labour Party members were invited to vote on the "road to the manifesto" document. The seven million trade unionists could be invited to vote on the White Paper's proposals — now there would be an exercise in rank-and-file consultation.

The author is General Secretary of the T&GWU.

Figure 7.8 *Source: The Times* 5 May 1998

Activity 6

Have another look at the list of objectives specified by the TUC in their evidence to the Donovan Commission included earlier in this chapter and think which of them might be realistic for the trade union movement to actively pursue today.

Also, and separately, ask yourself two other questions connected with this list: first, which of the ten objectives you consider to be legitimate and second, which other objectives might you include in such a list today?

Let firms stay free to decide on recognition

There is little doubt that the centrepiece of the long-awaited *Fairness at Work* White Paper will be the contentious issue of compulsory recognition of trade unions for collective bargaining. The position of the Institute of Directors (IoD) is quite clear. We oppose compulsory recognition. Moreover, this position has been fully backed by a recent survey of our members.

Let us, however, emphasise what it is that we oppose. We are not opposed to the principle of recognition provided that managers and directors are free to make the decision. Many companies, especially big manufacturers, already recognise unions for collective bargaining purposes on a voluntary basis. If companies believe that recognising unions is preferable to other options, that is their choice. Other companies do not recognise unions because, for example, they take the view that recognition could be damaging and disruptive to the business itself and, ultimately, to the job prospects of all their employees.

They may feel, too, that to recognise unions would be unfair to their non-unionised employees. This right of choice should stay, and any appeal to employees' "democratic rights and fairness" should instantly be dismissed as irrelevant. Businesses are not political entities and they are not representative bodies (as, incidentally, trade unions — and the IoD — are).

To emphasise this last point, it is worth stating quite clearly that companies are not democracies and that their leaders are not "democratically" accountable. No. Directors and managers are appointed to run companies for, and are accountable to, the shareholders; and they have all the responsibilities that this entails. They have moral obligations to the de facto owners of their companies to achieve, as far as they can, the maximum long-term shareholder value of those companies. In trying to achieve that aim, directors have responsibilities to other stakeholders — including employees, suppliers and customers. Of course, they do.

But at the heart of any decision taken by any directors is the knowledge that they are dealing with capital entrusted to them by the shareholders.

If directors have responsibility for running the company for its shareholders and "carrying the can" if things go wrong, they should have the control. And they should not be burdened, distracted and delayed by any manifestations of compulsory "industrial democracy". We know of few people who believe that those who have the responsibility for running events should not have fair control over how they run those events. But there is a strange denial, in some quarters at least, of the validity of this law of natural justice when it comes to the issue of compulsory recognition of unions.

It is quite unfair to expect people to assume responsibility without control. (Many psychological studies confirm that the most stressed people are those with responsibilities who feel they do not have control.) So, directors and managers should clearly be able to choose whether to recognise unions.

We realise, however, that compulsory recognition of unions was a 1997 Labour Party manifesto commitment and accept, with regret, that it will be introduced. The manifesto said: "People should be free to join or not join a union. Where they do decide to join, and where a majority of the relevant workforce vote in a ballot for the union to represent them, the union should be recognised. This promotes stable and orderly industrial relations." Of course, the devil is in the detail and the debates on what is the "relevant workforce" have already been long and heated — and even before we have seen the White Paper.

We in the IoD have followed the discussions between the CBI and the TUC with considerable interest and note their not insubstantial disagreements. Perhaps I could mention two. The first relates to the difficulties of defining the bargaining unit. The CBI has said that it wishes the bargaining unit to be defined as closely as possible to the existing business structures (which we would support), while the TUC wants the bargaining unit to take into account other criteria, such as the wishes of the workforce concerned. Alas, one can already see the scope for discord here, and the idea that compulsory recognition will promote "stable and orderly industrial relations" (to quote the manifesto) seems all too wide of the mark. On the contrary, any discussions on the definitions of specific bargaining units seem to us to be potentially time-consuming, divisive and disruptive.

The second, and the more widely reported, disagreement relates to the precise definition of the relevant workforce in calculating the majority voting for union representation. The CBI wishes for a majority of all the workforce eligible to vote for representation before a union is recognised. The TUC, on the other hand, wishes for a majority of the workforce actually voting for representation to be enough for union recognition. Clearly the CBI's intention (and I trust I am not misrepresenting them) is to dilute the burden on employers of compulsory recognition and we would say "amen" to that. The criticism that "the CBI's proposals are not really democratic and the TUC's are because, in elections, the majority of those voting usually carries the day" cuts little ice with us. As we have pointed out, the whole notion of democracy in companies is so thoroughly flawed that references to what happens in genuinely democratic situations are quite irrelevant.

Speculation about the contents of the *Fairness at Work* White Paper including compulsory recognition remains a hot topic — not least because of the political implications. One of the speculations includes the idea of a requirement for a minimum turnout (with rumours that No 10 may be pushing for a figure as high as 70 per cent) before a recognition vote is valid. We would support this proposal, and, indeed, any other proposal that would lessen the impact of the unfortunate policy of forcing union recognition on unwilling employers.

The author is Head of the Policy Unit of the IoD.

> **❝ If directors carry the can if things go wrong, they should have the control ❞**

Figure 7.8 *(continued)*

Summary

In this chapter you have been introduced to trade unions as one of the major actors in the employee relations system in the UK. You have examined and compared definitions and how they change over time, why they are formed and what their objectives may be and how those may also change over time. You have also examined the main reasons why people join trade unions and recent trends in the size, structure and characteristics of their membership. The TUC, the single peak association in the UK, has been introduced and its main roles described. We also examined the stereotypical model of trade union government and the relevance to it of the notion of democracy. You have also been introduced to the debates surrounding the issue of trade union recognition and whether it should be subject to statutory regulation as proposed in the government's White Paper – 'Fairness at Work' and which formed the base for the Employment

Relations Act 1999. It is apparent from this debate that underlying it are some very fundamental differences of view as to the legitimate nature of business organizations and to whom they are and should be ultimately responsible.

Finally we examined some of the debates that have been ongoing within the movement about how best to secure the survival and future of the movement and it became apparent when examining these debates that central to them are the issues of appropriate and legitimate objectives and perceptions of the reasons why people join.

*Activity
Answers*

Activity 1

The first definition specifies that trade union members should be wage earners and that the purposes of the union activity should be to maintain or improve the conditions of the members' working lives, an implication at least that the union should confine its activities and aspirations to the workplace. This definition does not specify a preferred or essential means for achieving these objectives.

The second, the legal, definition talks in terms of the members being workers and adopts a wider view of purpose, acknowledging as it does that the union may have a number of purposes. In this instance the definition does not specify that the union should seek to maintain or improve, it simply talks in terms of seeking to regulate the relations between the members and employers, the employment relationship. There is an implication of joint regulation with employers but it is not specifically stated as such. Here no specific means is referred to.

The third definition combines elements of the previous two in that, like the second, it is workers that are specified as the members but, as in the first, the purposes include specific reference to seeking to improve rather than just to regulate. However, this definition differs from the previous ones in a number of other important respects, the means of collective bargaining is specifically incorporated and the implication perhaps is that this is the preferred mechanism for seeking to improve their working conditions. This definition is the first of the four to openly acknowledge that the union has legitimate interests and purposes extending beyond the workplace to include their economic and social position. A view that has been the subject of much debate over the years and to which we return later.

The last of the definitions is somewhat of a composite of the earlier ones encompassing as it does wide workplace and social purposes and regulation of the employment relationship through collective bargaining. However, there are also some interesting differences in that this definition does not refer to workers or wage earners but to employees and this is also the first of the definitions to refer to management rather than employers. Both of these last points may be perceived to be a product of and consistent with changing times and changes in the organization of industrial and service activity.

Activity 2
By and large craft and industrial/occupational are likely to be closed whereas general are likely to fit into the open category.

Activity 3
From the table you should have deduced that union membership density is higher (highest) among and in:

- men than women
- full-time compared with part-time workers
- the public sector compared with the private sector
- larger organizations (over twenty-five employees) than in small (under twenty-five employees)
- the utility sector (gas, electricity and water supply), rail transport, postal services and public administration – all of which showed a density figure in excess of 60 per cent.

You should also have noted that the density among manual workers is not higher than among non-manual workers, and you might have noted that in those industrial sectors in which there are both a public- and private-sector trade union, density in the public sector is without fail greater than in the private.

Activity 4

1 The two main models are:

- the representative or parliamentary model
- the direct or participatory model

and the main difference between them is that the former relies on elected representatives to take part in the decision making processes on behalf of those they represent whereas, in the direct model, the members take part themselves.
2 Factors influencing democracy:

- size and the need for administrative efficiency and organizational effectiveness
- the concentration of power in the hands of an elite or oligarchy and their ability to pursue their own interests as well as, indeed possibly instead of, the interests of the membership as a whole
- isolation of a ruling elite from the membership
- ballots (secret and/or postal) of the membership in the election of senior union officials and members of the executive committee and in decisions concerning the taking of industrial action
- restricting the right of the union to discipline and expel members

- rights for members to examine the financial affairs of the union
- the existence of opposition factions within the union and whether they are provided with equal facilities to get their message across to the members
- the degree of debate and discussion within the union and the presence of mechanisms facilitating this
- the closeness of election results
- the decentralization of decision making within the union
- the participation and representation of particular factions or groups in the activities of the union and in the decision making process.

Activity 5

Much of the debate between the two centres on the issue of democracy. Morris argues not only that business should be run in a more democratic fashion with employees having rights to participate in decision making, for example through collective bargaining, but also that the principles of democracy, majority voting determining the outcome, should prevail in the balloting arrangements case. He also makes passing mention of class conflict and of the *raison d'être* of unionism – collective strength. He suggests a willingness to put disputes before some form of arbitrator.

Lea, on the other hand, makes it perfectly clear that in her view democracy has no place in business; companies and businesses are not democracies and the rights of shareholders should always prevail over those of other interests. It is an argument that clearly and unequivocally supports managements' claim for the right to control business organizations and to do so unilaterally. The interests of capital should always predominate and it should be up to the directors of companies to decide whether to engage in union recognition and collective bargaining, irrespective of the wishes of the employees.

Morris presents an essentially pluralist perspective compared with the firmly unitarist views and values of Lea.

Only you know which of the two positions you favour and of course you may adopt a position somewhere between the two.

Activity 6

The original list was:

1 improved terms of employment
2 improved working conditions including the physical environment
3 security of both employment and income
4 industrial democracy
5 full employment
6 fair(er) shares in national income and wealth
7 improved social security
8 the public control and planning of industry
9 a voice in government

10 improved public and social services.

In considering this issue, Farnham (1997) suggests that only the first three of these would be pursued by trade unions in the UK in the late 1990s and each of these are workplace-based, consistent with the model favoured by the New Realists and by the TUC at its relaunch. However, even though the relaunch confirmed a new and different focus indicative of a shift in the direction of business unionism, the movement has not completely forsaken the pursuit of objectives outside the workplace. As noted in the text, the TUC General Council Report for 1995 asserts its continuing concern to achieve full employment and to influence all the main political parties.

The TUC also refers to initiatives and objectives in new areas:

- corporate governance
- top peoples' pay
- in the area of equality.

Even more recently the TUC has decided to emphasize what they perceive to be a social partnership approach and this implies further adaptation of objectives to include:

- working together with management at the level of the firm or workplace to achieve organizational objectives such as enhanced competitiveness, enhanced flexibility and commitment to the success of the organization from the employees and union (compare these to the objectives prescribed by Guest (1989a) in his model of HRM referred to in the next chapter), in return for trade union recognition, guarantees on job security and an enhanced focus upon the quality of working life from management
- talking with government and employers' associations at a national level to achieve objectives such as attracting inward investment and promoting training and equal opportunities.

Traditionalists retain a belief in the original objectives of the movement.

If we try to be objective ourselves it is probably the case that from the original list of objectives numbers 4, 8 and 9 are not realistically achievable, the possibility of achieving the others is perhaps greater. In the author's viewpoint it is legitimate for the union movement to pursue all of the original list of objectives as well as all of those indicated by the TUC more recently.

Hopefully, in thinking about these issues and questions you have a clearer picture of where you lie on the spectrum of viewpoints and you will also have realized the importance again of the issue of perspective.

References

ACAS, 1996. *Annual Report.*

ACAS, 1997. *Annual Report.*

Bassett, P. and Cave, A., 1993. *All for One: the Future of the Unions.* Fabian Society, London.

Blackburn, R., 1967. *Union Character and Social Class.* Batsford, London.

Blyton, P. and Turnbull, P., 1998. *The Dynamics of Employee Relations.* 2nd Edition. Macmillan, Basingstoke.

Certification Office for Trade Unions and Employers Associations 1999. *Annual Report of the Certification Officer 1998.* Crown, London.

Claydon, T., 1996. Union derecognition: a re-examination. In Beardwell, I. (ed.), *Contemporary Industrial Relations: A Critical Analysis.* Oxford University Press, Oxford.

Cully, M. and Woodland, S., 1997. Trade union membership and recognition. *Labour Market Trends,* June.

Cully, M., *et al.,* 1998. *The Workplace Employee Relations Survey: First Findings.* DTI, ACAS, ESRC, PSI. Crown Copyright, London.

Farnham, D., 1997. *Employee Relations in Context.* IPD, London.

Farnham, D. and Pimlott, J., 1995. *Understanding Industrial Relations.* 5th Edition. Cassell, London.

Guest, D., 1989a. Human Resources Management: its implications for industrial relations and trade unions. In Storey, J. (ed.), *New Perspectives on Human Resource Management.* Routledge, London.

Heery, E., 1996. The new New Unionism. In Beardwell, I. (ed.), *Contemporary Industrial Relations: A Critical Analysis.* Oxford University Press, Oxford.

Hirsch-Weber, W., 1970. Quoted in Varde Vall. M. Labor Organisations. Cambridge University Press, p. 53. Cited in Salamon, M., 1992. *Industrial Relations.* 2nd Edition. Prentice Hall, Hemel Hempstead.

Hollinshead, G. and Leat, M., 1995. *Human Resource Management: An International and Comparative Perspective on the Employment Relationship.* Pitman Publishing, London.

Leat, M., 1998. *Human Resource Issues of the European Union.* Financial Times Pitman Publishing, London.

Main, B.G.M., 1996. The union relative wage gap. In Gallie, D., Penn, R. and Rose, M., 1996. *Trade Unionism in Recession.* Oxford University Press, Oxford.

McIlroy, J., 1995. *Trades Unions in Britain Today.* Manchester University Press, Manchester.

Metcalf, D. 1993. *Transformation of British Industrial Relations; Institutions, Conduit and Outcomes 1980–90.* Centre for Economic Performance, Paper No. 151, L.S.E., London.

Michels, R., 1966. *Political Parties.* Free Press, New York.

Millward, N., Stevens, M., Smart, D. and Hawes, W.R., 1992. Workplace

Industrial Relations in Transition. Dartmouth, Aldershot.

Salamon, M., 1992. *Industrial Relations.* 2nd Edition. Prentice Hall, Hemel Hempstead.

Stewart, M., 1994. *Union Wage Differentials in an Era of Declining Unionisation.* University of Warwick, Warwick.

TUC, 1995. *General Council Report for 1995.*

TUC, 1999. *British Trade Unionism – the Millennial Challenge.*

Turner, H.A., 1962. *Trade Union Growth, Structure and Policy.* Allen and Unwin, London.

Waddington, J. and Whitston, C., 1995. Trade unions: growth, structure and policy. In Edwards, P. (ed.), *Industrial Relations Theory and Practice in Britain.* Blackwell, Oxford, pp. 151–202.

Waddington, J. and Whitston, C., 1997. Why do people join trade unions in a period of membership decline? *British Journal of Industrial Relations* December.

Webb, S. and Webb, B., 1894. *The History of Trade Unionism.* Reprinted by Augustus Kelly, New York, 1965.

Whitston, C. and Waddington, J., 1994. Why join a union? *New Statesman and Society* 18 November, pp. 36–38.

Chapter 8

Managing employee relations

Introduction

Historically, the management of employee (industrial) relations has been regarded as a part of the area of expertise, if not the province, of Personnel Management (PM) (see the IPD definition of employee relations included in the first chapter). However, in more recent times and with the emergence of Human Resource Management (HRM) there have been debates about who should be responsible for the management of employee relations in an organization, with the HRM school being associated with the drive to push this responsibility down to line managers. HRM has also been associated with an emphasis upon individualism and has been characterized as anti-trade union and underpinned by a unitarist perspective, whereas personnel management was considered consistent with pluralism, industrial relations and joint decision making. We briefly examine the elements of this debate and some of the models of HRM as part of the context within which changes in objective and management style have occurred.

We identify a number of the objectives that management may have in its conduct of employee relations and we also introduce you to a number of the different styles that management may adopt in its conduct of these matters. Objectives and style are often interrelated and the one may dictate the other; the pursuit of particular objectives may necessitate, or at the least imply, the use of a particular and appropriate style.

There are a number of typologies of style, some of which distinguish between styles on the grounds of the implied attitudes to trade unionism and the sharing of decision making implied by recognition of trade unions. We examine a couple of the more acclaimed typologies and some of the implications of managing employee relations both with and without trade unions.

Employers' organizations have in many ways suffered a similar fate to trade unions in recent years and in the final section of the chapter we briefly examine this decline, the implications for their purpose and the priorities attached to the services they provide for their members. Like trade unions they also have had to address the issue of survival.

Objectives

After studying this chapter you will be able to:

- Explain differences between Personnel and Human Resource Management and the specific implications for the management of employee relations
- Discuss the nature of management objectives in respect of employee relations and explain why the dominant one may be control over the labour process
- Identify and describe the variety of managerial styles and explanatory models

- Explain why the more recent models seek to encompass individualism and collectivism and the dynamic nature of style
- Identify the features of the external environment and the organizational characteristics that act as constraining influences upon the styles adopted by senior management
- Analyse and explain the developments over the last two decades which have presented management with the opportunity to manage without trade unions.

Personnel Management, HRM and the management of employee relations

As noted in the introduction to this chapter there has been considerable debate in recent years concerning the responsibility for, objectives of, direction and changing nature and style of employee relations management in UK organizations. This debate has taken place against a background that has included:

- the decline of the trade union movement
- different government values and objectives demonstrated through an ideological and legislative onslaught on the trade unions and the traditional pluralist institutions, the privatization of much of the public sector and the forced introduction of the private-sector model of employee relations management into what remains of the public sector
- the emergence of Human Resource Management and debates about whether, and if so how, personnel management and HRM are different.

Quite early in this latter debate Guest (1987 and 1989a) concluded that there was an incompatibility between 'the essentially unitarist HRM and pluralist tradition of industrial relations in the UK' and that HRM policies might well pose a threat to the trade unions and to the other main industrial relations institutions.

In the remaining sections of this chapter we look at managerial objectives and styles of managing employee relations including the management of employee relations in a non-union environment. It is possible to argue that the changes in objective, style and practice identified and discussed in these later sections are simply the product of management acting opportunistically, taking advantage of a new environment containing a series of new contingencies. Others argue that these changes are not so much the product of opportunism but the result of the adoption of a different philosophy and approach (HRM?), driven for example by the need to be competitive, and indicative of new and different strategic choices being made.

However, before we go any further it is necessary briefly to examine Personnel Management, its emergence and traditions, and how it relates to the management of industrial/employee relations.

Personnel Management

One thing we can say at the outset is that the management of industrial relations was perceived to be very firmly core to the 'territory' of Personnel Management and, as we noted in Chapter 1, the IPD claims employee relations as part of this territory. Personnel Management emerged towards the end of the nineteenth century out of the concern of some few employers for the welfare of their employees and their appointment of predominantly female welfare officers. As the years went by the scope and range of the activities and responsibilities of Personnel Management expanded but this welfare tradition remained strong if not central. These early welfare workers were given a dual role representing the interests and views of the employer and management to the employees but also representing the views and interests of employees to the other members of management. These appointments and the role afforded them are indicative of a pluralist approach in that different interests are being recognized. However, the motives of Christian charity and paternalism of these early employers were by no means wholly altruistic since there was clearly a recognition on their part that healthy and fit employees would be more productive.

Personnel Management's responsibilities for the management of industrial relations really took hold in the 1950s as the trade union movement increased in size and influence. The post-Second World War boom created enormous demand for UK manufactured goods and the more widespread adoption of mass production techniques to satisfy these new mass markets created circumstances in which there was relatively full employment and it was relatively easy for the trade unions to recruit members and represent them. As labour became a relatively scarce resource its bargaining power increased, along with its determination to achieve a better deal. Companies found themselves in need of skilled and adept negotiators who could form relationships with the trade unions and develop with them the joint mechanisms necessary to ensure efficient and effective resolution of this conflict. The personnel practitioners tended to acquire this role and over a period of time they became the accepted and largely acceptable face of management in this new industrial relations arena. In addition to seeking consensus and acting for management in the negotiations to resolve conflicts the personnel practitioner also became the administrator and in a sense the custodian of the implementation of the agreements that were jointly achieved.

This new role and influence, however, also brought with it a number of ambiguities and dilemmas. As personnel practitioners became responsible for negotiating, administering and implementing agreements on terms and conditions of employment, tensions emerged between them and line management some of whom felt that their own role and influence in the management of employees was being usurped. There were tensions and uncertainties as to who was responsible for what and whether the role of the personnel practitioner was to be an essentially advisory one or indeed whether they were to have executive responsibilities in areas such as the determination of terms and conditions of employment and the handling of discipline and grievances. In a very real sense there was the possibility of a split occurring between the personnel practitioner and other members of management who often regarded the personnel function as not really part of management at all but as some sort of intermediary between management and the employees. Also an intermediary that often seemed to have different values and interests to those of management, a degree of sympathy and empathy with the interests and intrinsic welfare of the employees that, in managements' eyes, somehow set the personnel function and its members apart.

As Torrington (1989) pointed out

… personnel management is directed mainly at the employees of an organization; … personnel managers are never totally identified with management interests, as they become ineffective when not able to understand and articulate the views and values of the employees. To some extent the personnel manager is always a mediator between them and us.

As competition and the economic environment became tougher and government and employers began to look for scapegoats for the UK's economic woe and failures, the trade unions and to some extent the personnel function became demonized. These new pressures heightened the potential for conflict between the competitive organizational need for efficiency in the use of labour and the personnel function's traditional concerns for justice and equity in the treatment of employees.

Personnel practitioners began to look for new roles that would indicate the coincidence of their interests with other members of management and management functions and it was in this context that there was further emphasis placed upon the personnel function's responsibility for manpower planning, organizational design and development. It was also against this background that the concept of HRM emerged from the USA with a different set of underpinning values, priorities and imperatives. To some personnel practitioners this appeared as a source of potential salvation, to others it was a threat to their traditions, values and role.

In sum, Personnel Management emerged out of paternalism and a concern for employees' physical welfare and issues of social justice, more latterly this became a concern for the intrinsic health and welfare of the employee. As the century progressed and the imperatives of the environment changed and developed, it acquired other roles, but it is a function that suffers from tensions and ambiguities both internally and between itself and other management functions.

Human Resource Management

The debates surrounding the nature, objectives and contribution of Personnel Management to organizational success which have been outlined and alluded to above seemingly pall into relative insignificance in comparison with the questions asked of and debates surrounding HRM, for example:

- what is it?
- what are the objectives?
- does it exist in the UK?
- is there a unity of form and style?
- what are the implications of implementation for industrial relations and trade unions?

We cannot in this work look at all of these debates in detail but it is important to realize some of the positions, interpretations and prescriptions, since they have a bearing upon the management of employee relations in the 1990s and into the twenty-first century.

We have already alluded above to some of the distinguishing features of HRM in comparison with Personnel Management.

We referred earlier to Guest's (1987 and 1989a) conclusion that the values underpinning HRM are unitarist and individualist and that the introduction of HRM might well pose a threat to the trade unions, which can be contrasted with the pluralist underpinnings of Personnel Management and the dominant collectivist approach to managing industrial relations through the three decades following the Second World War. Decades during which trade union membership and influence increased significantly.

In 1987 Guest had already suggested that HRM and PM could be distinguished by the form of attachment emphasized and the nature of the employment relationship. In the case of PM it was a relationship where the form of attachment was one of compliance and the psychological contract was one emphasizing a fair day's work for a fair day's pay. Whereas, with HRM, the form of attachment characterizing the employment relationship was a moral or normative commitment with a psychological contract emphasizing reciprocal commitment.

We also noted earlier that Torrington (1989) asserted that Personnel Management is directed mainly at the employees and their needs; in comparing Personnel Management with HRM he suggests that the focus of HRM is primarily on the organizations' needs. He utilizes the distinction between demand and supply and suggests that PM is primarily concerned with the supply of labour, which it tends to see in terms of employees, whereas HRM is primarily concerned with the organization's demand for labour, which can be met through various forms of contracting other than the tradition of employment. Patterns of employment, labour utilization and attachment consistent with the notion of the flexible firm (see Chapter 2) are much more compatible with HRM than PM. He further suggests that HRM seeks to eliminate the mediation role referred to above and tends to emphasize strategy and planning rather than problem solving and mediation.

See **Figure 8.1** for a selective comparison between HRM and PM on a range of different dimensions.

Dimension	PM	HRM
Perspective	Pluralist	Unitarist
Level of trust	Low	High
Attachment	Compliance	Commitment
Terms of contract	Collective agreement	Individual
Psychological contract	Fair day's work for fair day's pay	Reciprocal commitment
Time horizon	Short term	Long term
Approach	Reactive *ad hoc*	Proactive, strategic
Conflict	Institutionalized	De-emphasized/denied
Communication	Restricted/indirect	Individual and direct
Responsibility	Centralized, specialist	Devolved, line manager
Focus on needs of	Employees	Management

Figure 8.1 Selective comparison between PM and HRM. Adapted from Guest (1987) and Storey (1992)

These contributions as reported here would imply that there is a measure of unity among analysts on the meaning and nature of HRM and how it compares with PM, but this is far from the truth and this is reflected in the number of different models of HRM that have been devised over the years to explain and answer the questions posed above.

The notion that HRM represents a strategic approach has been popular, since it tends to support the claim by HRM/PM specialists that the function needs to be integrated fully into the formulation of corporate policy and strategy and that it therefore must be represented fully at the highest decision-making levels of the organization. In other words, it is a definition that adds weight and importance to the function and the contribution that it can make to the success of the organization. Guest (1989a) was critical of this and similar definitions and argued that a strategic approach or focus was insufficient to differentiate HRM from PM, since PM itself had

always espoused the importance of adopting a strategic view. It has been less successful in practice. What is more important is the input to this strategic concern. In other words what is needed is not just the capacity to think strategically but some distinctive view of the strategic direction that should be pursued. It is this direction that constitutes the distinctive feature of HRM. p. 42.

It was at this point that Guest developed a framework or model of HRM in which he asserts/prescribes that the objectives of HRM were/should be:

1 integration of strategy, attitudes and behaviour
2 commitment of employees to the goals and values of the organization (an example of normative or attitudinal commitment)
3 flexibility in terms of organizational and work structures and employees, all of which facilitates innovation
4 quality in terms of the staff employed, the management of them, their performance and in terms of the output of employee activity.

HRM policies	Human resource outcomes	Organizational outcomes
Organization/ job design		**High** Job performance
Management of change	Strategic integration	**High** Problem-solving Change
Recruitment, selection/ socialization	Commitment	Innovation
Appraisal, training development	Flexibility adaptability	**High** Cost-effectiveness
Reward systems		
Communication	Quality	**Low** Turnover Absence Grievances
	Leadership/culture/strategy	

Figure 8.2 A theory of HRM. *Source:* Guest (1989b) p. 49

The achievement of these outcomes is assumed to enhance individual performance and facilitate the achievement of desired organizational outcomes.

The prescriptive emphasis upon specific outcomes of this model sets it apart from those referred to as matching and contingent models where the emphasis is not upon the prescribed outcomes but upon the influences on the determination of its HR strategy (strategic choices made), the interactions between the organization and its environment and the importance of coherence between objective, strategy and practice. Matching and contingent models tend to emphasize strategic process rather than strategic outcomes.

Guest's model has more in common with the model of Beer *et al.* (1984). See **Figure 8.3** which the authors described as a model that is also a map of the territory.

The Beer *et al.* model is more analytical emphasizing the potential for influence of both various stakeholder interests and contextual factors, both internal and external. However, this model also identifies specific HR outcomes:

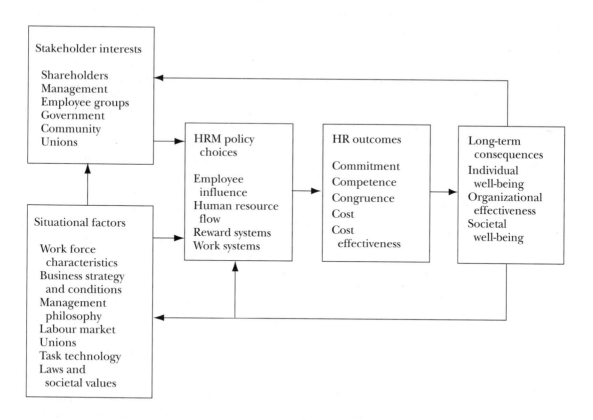

Figure 8.3 Map of the HRM territory. *Source:* Beer *et al.* (1984)

- high commitment of employees to organizational goals
- high individual performance leading to cost effectiveness

which are similar to those identified by Guest but there are also differences in that the Beer *et al.* model recognizes specifically that employees are stakeholders in the organization. Some would argue that the underpinnings contain elements of pluralism in that the model at least recognizes the existence of different interests in the organization. The possibility of conflict between these different stakeholders' interests, particularly between the interests of employees and employers, is recognized and emphasis placed upon the need for these to be resolved to the satisfaction of both (all) parties through processes resulting in trade-offs.

In the context of this model there is no doubt that the management of employee relations are part of the HRM territory.

Both the Beer and Guest models, in identifying the areas in which HRM policy decisions need to be made, do spell out areas of HRM activity (see **Figure 8.4**).

One of the most significant contributions made to these debates concerning HRM and what it is and how it is different was made by Storey (1987, 1989) who suggested that there were different forms of HRM. He distinguished between 'hard' and 'soft' versions or forms of HRM and this leads on to the likelihood of a spectrum, at one end of which is a hard version of HRM driven by the strategic objectives of the organization and where labour is perceived in the same terms as any other resource, something to be acquired, deployed, developed for the achievement of organizational objectives, used and then disposed of. At the other extreme of the spectrum is the approach that sees human resources as potent sources of innovation and competitive advantage, as valued assets rather than as variable costs, where the employees are involved in the organization through various communications mechanisms and the outcome is a labour force highly motivated and committed to the values and goals of the organization. This latter form is distinguished as soft HRM. In each case the underpinning values are unitarist and individualist and the objectives are performance oriented, but the two stereotypes reflect different views of how best to achieve these objectives, different views on the nature of man and what might motivate him. The soft version rests largely upon beliefs consistent with the theories of man and motivation associated with people such as Maslow (1943), McGregor (1960) and Herzberg (1966), beliefs that man can be motivated by recognition, achievement and involvement and that leadership style is an important influence upon motivation and performance.

The two stereotypes are also arguably reflective of different market realities and production strategies. For example, short-term cost reduction may be the competitive imperative and, in such circumstances, it might be inevitable that a hard variant is pursued, whereas in an organization with a

Human resource flows
- Into, through and out of the organization, to include:

  - recruitment and selection
  - appraisal and assessment
  - development
  - promotion
  - termination

Reward systems
- To attract, motivate and retain labour and to include:

  - pay systems
  - motivation
  - other benefits

Employee influence
- Employee participation and employee relations to include:

  - trade unions and collective bargaining
  - the issue of managerial prerogative
  - other participatory mechanisms such as works councils etc.

Work systems
- The organization of work and work practices to include:

  - job design
  - the nature of the technology and issues of workpace and the source of control, the machine, management or the employee
  - the flexibility of labour and technology

Managing change

Communications which should be goal directed

Figure 8.4 The subject matter of HRM. Adapted from Beer *et al.*, 1984 and Guest 1989b

much longer time horizon, and where the source of competitive advantage is knowledge and innovation, it might be realistic to pursue a set of policies and practices more akin to the soft variant.

Critics of HRM have argued that the Storey stereotypes don't so much represent the range of HRM in action as the difference between the rhetoric and the reality (Legge, 1989), with the hard version of HRM representing the reality and the soft version the rhetoric, it sounds good but you can't find it in action.

Activity 1

Take a look back at this material distinguishing soft and hard versions of HRM and try to work out for yourself where the following might fit on the spectrum:

- Personnel Management
- the models of Guest (1989b) and Beer *et al.* (1984).

HRM and developments in employee relations

As we discussed in the first chapter of this book the development and adoption of the term 'employee relations' rather than 'industrial relations' is itself symptomatic of the influence that HRM has had upon the nature and management of the employment relationship. It is difficult to establish causal relationships but we can certainly identify a number of employee relations developments over the last two decades that are consistent with the emergence of HRM.

The soft versions of HRM are consistent, for example, with the introduction of:

- direct employee-oriented communications mechanisms as a means of achieving greater employee involvement, itself perceived as a means of achieving high employee commitment rather than a compliance
- Quality of Work Life changes in the design and organization of work, (referred to in Chapter 2) soft HRM tends to assume that employees will be motivated by schemes such as job enlargement etc.
- the introduction of Japanese methods – QCs, TQM, JIT, etc. are consistent with the drive for quality employees and quality output
- the decline in trade union membership, recognition, participation in decision making and influence – the decline of collectivism
- the emphasis upon the employment relationship as characterized by cooperation rather than conflict and, in particular, partnership approaches
- some of the more paternalist management styles referred to later in this chapter
- an emphasis upon individual contract and labour flexibility as depicted in the model of the flexible firm
- continuing emphasis upon managerial prerogative.

The harder versions are consistent with:

- enforced trade union derecognition and a refusal to grant recognition

for purposes of collective bargaining
- authoritarian and autocratic management styles
- enforced flexibility such as zero hours contracts and/or enforced working of long hours or the deliberate avoidance of employees' statutory rights
- the minimization of costs, low rates of pay and poor working conditions
- a continuation of the process of deskilling and degradation
- management policies that discriminate and exploit.

In both instances, hard and soft, management are unwilling to share or give up control of the labour process.

Activity 2

Commonly, employee development is perceived as an activity central to HRM, as is the achievement of high quality performance and employee commitment. Which of the two stereotypes (hard or soft) does this perception fit?

Management's objectives

Management's employee relations objectives, or at least some of them, have been alluded to in previous chapters. For example, in examining definitions of employee relations and the nature of the employment relationship it became clear that some analysts think that the prime management objective is to buy labour at the lowest price while others see the dominant objective as attaining control over the labour process (remember the views of Ruth Lea as expressed in **Figure 7.8**). However, it isn't always easy to establish employer/management objectives, one reason being that often they aren't written down anywhere. Nevertheless, there are a range of possibilities that are reasonably common, many of which can be seen to be driven by the need to be competitive as well as by considerations that may have more to do with values and beliefs.

Marchington and Wilkinson (1996) identified (parentheses this author's):

- reducing unit labour costs, not just wages
- increasing labour productivity (this has potential for overlap with the above)
- minimizing disruption and the incidence of overt conflict (this term is often used to distinguish conflict that results in action, and which is

therefore visible, from conflict which exists but which, for many reasons, may remain hidden or is latent)

● achieving greater stability by channelling discontent through agreed procedures

● increasing employee cooperation and commitment so as to increase the likely acceptance of change and enhance productive efficiency (this is something we address again in Chapter 9 concerned with those processes referred to as employee involvement).

Marchington and Wilkinson (1996) comment that some analysts would argue that all of these objectives are subservient to the prime objective of control over the labour process.

There are other objectives that are not mentioned above, amongst which might be a determination to reduce the influence of and possibly rid the organization of trade unions and joint or shared decision making, thereby re-asserting managerial prerogative and reinserting management as the single legitimate focus of employee loyalty. It is unclear the extent to which this has been an explicit and actual objective of management in the UK over the last fifteen to twenty years but there is certainly evidence that it has happened.

The 1990 WIRS (Millward *et al.*, 1992) survey material and more recent Labour Force Survey data have provided evidence of the following trends:

● a significant reduction in the number of workplaces in which trade unions were recognized for collective bargaining purposes

● a decline in trade union membership figures

● a decline in the number of workplaces in which wages and other terms and conditions of employment were determined jointly through the collective bargaining process.

The 1998 WERS (Cully, M., *et al.* (1998)) associates trade union density and union recognition in organizations with the attitudes of management in that organization and there are clear relationships, so much so that the analysts assert that 'these figures suggest that anti-union sentiments on the part of employers provide a considerable hurdle to overcome if unions are to win members and recognition'.

The data confirm no causal relationships but, where management are generally favourably disposed towards trade unions, some 94 per cent of the organizations do recognize a trade union. However, where management are not in favour of trade unions only 9 per cent of workplaces recognize a trade union.

Another objective may be to create an employee relations environment in which employees are able to satisfy their needs at work and achieve enhanced fulfilment. We noted in Chapter 2 that it is claimed that this latter has been at the root of many of the experiments in job re-design over the last twenty years or so. Yet other objectives may be specifically oriented towards the achievement of labour flexibility, both functional and temporal.

So there are quite a wide range of outcomes that may constitute the employee relations objectives of management and these may well vary over time and be either helped or hindered by the environment, economic, political and cultural. Which of these are pursued by employers, and with what priority, at any particular moment will be dependent upon a whole range of factors and influences.

Depending upon your perspective you may perceive some or all of these objectives contributing to an improvement in the **quality** of employee relations or indeed to a deterioration of quality (see Chapter 1).

Drawing upon the foregoing and your reading of earlier chapters devise a list of what you think might be the employee relations objectives of employees.

Managerial style(s)

Early models of managerial styles and approaches to the management of the employment relationship and employee relations are reflective of the distinction drawn above between the unitarist and pluralist perspectives. Fox (1974) made the first really significant contribution to this debate by identifying four styles, each of which could be located in terms of these frames of reference or perspective. This contribution by Fox has, in many respects, formed the base for subsequent amendments and contributions, so that the latter work of Purcell and Sisson (1983), Purcell and Gray (1986), Purcell (1987), and Purcell and Ahlstrand (1989, 1994) can all be seen to be derived from and are adaptations of Fox's original model.

Before proceeding to look at some of this latter work it is important that we seek to define our terms. The definition of style or approach that seems to have the greatest degree of credibility currently is that of Purcell (1987). He suggests that by 'style' is implied: 'the existence of a distinctive set of guiding principles, written or otherwise, which set parameters to and signposts for management action in the way employees are treated and particular events are handled'.

As noted in the first chapter, managerial style forms part of the organizational context within which the employment relationship is managed and employee relations occur. It is clear that management has some discretion in the style that it adopts and many have argued the styles adopted to be a consequence of the preferences of and strategic choices made by management, though there are also undoubtedly some environmental and other constraints upon this choice.

Culture and ideology are two such environmental constraints that explain in some measure national differences in dominant style. To this one can also add the institutional arrangements in any particular national system. A couple of simplified examples may demonstrate the importance of these contextual features.

For example, the dominant style of employee relations management in Japan might be classified as paternalist authoritarian, reflecting the dominance of the Confucian culture with its emphasis upon obedience, the ordering of relationships according to status and the importance of family and responsibility. In this context management are afforded the opportunity to exercise their authority in a benevolent fashion, which they do, they certainly do not concede their authority and responsibility to employees or indeed to the trade unions. Employees are both given the opportunity and are obliged by their membership of the organization family to:

● contribute to the family or group well being
● take part in quality circles and contribute to continuous improvement
● take part in other forums which provide ideas and solutions to problems which are then filtered as they rise up through the various layers of the hierarchy.

They are also expected to demonstrate their commitment to the family, put in long hours and form and join trade unions that are contained within the organization.

In contrast, and given that it is difficult to talk as if there is only one culture in the USA, it is common for the dominant characteristics of the American culture to be presented as one that emphasizes competition, individualism and individual achievement and reward and, in this context, there is no substantial tradition in the USA of managements favouring trade union based employee relations systems and styles. Where possible managements have tended to pursue policies of outright opposition or, alternatively, the more sophisticated paternalist approach whereby they seek to create work environments that encourage the employees to believe that they do not need a trade union. Employees do not feel the loyalty to the organization that is characteristic of Japan and they are much less likely to voluntarily participate in processes that are geared to achieving benefits for the organization unless there is also something in it for them.

You should by now have realized that in this context we are not dealing with individuals' preferences and style of managing, it is the approach that has been determined at a corporate level, or which is adopted, demonstrated and encouraged by senior management, that is our concern. However, we do also need to bear in mind that there will be variations within organizations and the model preferred and selected at the level of senior management may well not be the style actually adopted throughout the whole organization. It is quite common to find discrepancy between the policy or strategy espoused at an organizational level and that practised on the shop-floor.

Look now at **Figure 8.5,** which reproduces the amended model of Purcell and Gray (1986) that depicts and describes five ideal or pure types of style used by managements in managing employee relations. In each case the figure also indicates the interrelationship between style and the expected role of central personnel management. It is no accident that each of the styles depicted in this figure are expressive of particular attitudes towards trade unions and the recognition of them for collective bargaining purposes.

Figure 8.5 also indicates that the style adopted is a function of a range of other circumstances and contexts. Make a list of those you can identify as relevant.

It has been noted already above that some features of the external environment (culture and ideology) can be seen to act as constraining influences upon the styles adopted by senior management, though it is difficult to know the extent to which management preferences and the approach adopted are in practice constrained.

In your study of the figure above you have just identified a range of other contextual influences and constraints, most of which can be organized into one or more of the categories identified by Marchington and Wilkinson (1996):

- the product market
- technology
- the labour market
- the social, legal and political environment and institutions.

There are also a series of organizational variables that may well have an impact and we have already mentioned some of these such as size and ownership, others might include organizational structure and the degree of centralization.

You may want to look again at **Figure 1.5**.

Title	Description	Most likely to occur in these circumstances	Expected role of central personnel management
Traditional	Labour is viewed as a factor of production, and employee subordination is assumed to be part of the 'natural order' of the employment relationship. Fear of outside union interference. Unionization opposed or unions kept at arm's length.	Small owner-managed companies (or franchise operations). Product markets often highly competitive with the firm having a low share leading to emphasis on cost-control and low profit margins.	For personnel specialists.
Sophisticated human relations or paternalists	Employees (excluding short-term contract or sub-contract labour) viewed as the company's most valuable resource. Above-average pay. Internal labour-market structures with promotion ladders are common with periodic attitude surveys used to harness employees' views. Emphasis is placed on flexible reward structures. Employee appraisal systems linked to merit awards, internal grievance, disciplinary and consultative procedures, and extensive networks and methods of communication. The aim is to inculcate employee loyalty, commitment and dependency. As a by-product these companies seek to make it unnecessary or unattractive for staff to unionize.	American-owned. single-industry, larger financially successful firms with a high market share in growth industries (electronics/finance sector).	Strong central personnel departments developing policies to be adopted in all areas of the company.
Sophisticated moderns: Consultative	Similar to the sophisticated human resource companies that unions are recognized. The attempt is made to build 'constructive' relationships with the trade unions and incorporate them into the organizational fabric. Broad-ranging discussions are held with extensive information provided to the unions on a whole range of decisions and plans, including aspects of strategic management, but the 'right of last say' rests with management. Emphasis is also placed on techniques designed to enhance individual employee commitment to the firm and the need to change (share option schemes, profit sharing, briefing or cascade information systems, joint working parties, quality or productivity circles/councils).	British/Japanese-owned single-industry companies which are large and economically successful, often with a large market share. Companies with relatively low labour costs (process industries) often adopt this style.	Central personnel departments produce policy guidelines or precepts providing advice and central direction when required.
Constitutional	Somewhat similar to the traditionalists in basic value structures but unions have been recognized for some time and accepted as inevitable. Employee relations policies centre on the need for stability, control and the institutionalization of conflict. Management prerogatives are defended through highly specific collective agreements, and careful attention is paid to the administration of agreements at the point of production. The importance of management control is emphasized, with the aim of minimizing or neutralizing union constraints on both operational (line) and strategic (corporate) management.	Single-industry companies with mass production or large-batch production requiring a large unit of operation. Labour costs form a significant proportion of total costs. Product-market conditions are often highly competitive.	Relatively strong emphasis on the central personnel auditing/control function.
Standard moderns: Opportunistic	The approach to employee relations is pragmatic. Trade unions are recognized in some or all parts of the business, often inherited with company acquisition. Employee relations are viewed as the responsibility of operational management at unit and/or division level. The importance attached to employee-relations policies changes in the light of circumstances. When union power is high and product and labour markets buoyant. or when legislative needs dictate, negotiation and consultation is emphasized. Fashionable employee-relations techniques are adopted over short periods as panaceas. When union power is low, or product markers become unfavourable or major technical change threatens existing practices, unions are 'rolled back', and management seeks to regain its prerogatives. There can be marked differences of approach between establishments or divisions and between various levels in the hierarchy.	Most common in conglomerate multi-product companies which grew by acquisition and diversification, especially in the engineering and heavy manufacturing industries with long traditions of unionization.	Relatively weak central personnel departments with personnel specialists at operating-unit level having a fire-fighting role, reacting to union claims and the impact of labour legislation. The personnel function tends to have a chequered history: sometimes strong, sometimes weak.

Source: J. Purcell and A. Gray (1986) 'Corporate personnel departments and the management of industrial relations: two case studies in ambiguity'. *Journal of Management Studies.* March pp. 214–15.

Figure 8.5 Five styles of industrial relations management. *Source:* Purcell and Gray (1986) Copyright Blackwell Publishers Ltd.

Product market

Marchington and Wilkinson (1996) suggest that there are sub-divisions to this category of external environmental influence: orientation, intensity of competition and the rate of change in the size of the market. By orientation they mean the nature of the customer served by it, such as whether the customer is domestic or business, whether the product is subject to fashion and associated change or whether the product is sold on the basis of its quality or durability.

An example of how the nature of the product market may influence or constrain management style may be derived from comparing a company operating in a fiercely competitive, fashion-based and therefore potentially volatile market, where the competition is on price rather than quality, with one that is dealing with a stable product in a growing and not very competitive market where the competition is on quality rather than price. One would expect these circumstances and constraints to contribute to the two companies adopting quite different styles, notwithstanding the preferences of the senior managers themselves.

Technology

Technology can affect management style also in a number of ways, it in part determines the requirement for labour, the type and quantity, the value added and thereby the price at which it is profitable to hire. It also has a potentially significant impact upon labour productivity and the proportion of total costs attributable to labour. The rate of technical change influences change within the organization, changing job descriptions and the career prospects of individuals and groups.

The labour market

There are some reasonably predictable labour market influences and constraints, such as the level of unemployment, the supply of labour available both in terms of quantity and in many cases more importantly the quality, skill levels and mix. Other labour market factors might include the presence of trade unions and their policies with respect to exerting an influence over the labour supply. Unions have often been criticized for seeking to control the supply of labour and thereby influence the price at which that labour may be hired.

Social, legal and political environment

You may have found this the easiest since we had a particularly visible example in the UK over the last two decades of the twentieth century, in particular linked to the election of a Conservative government in 1979 and subsequently. It is not possible here to do more than touch the surface of the scale and nature of the impact of this change in the political and subsequently also the legal and social environments (but see Chapter 5). Suffice it to say that many analysts have documented the attack upon the trade union movement, the rejection of tripartism and the search for consensus, the increased emphasis upon deregulation and flexibility, the re-assertion in the public sector of management's right to manage and the concentration upon cost efficiency. These and other developments have facilitated approaches and styles that are very different to the bargained constitutional style that dominated the public sector and manufacturing industry prior to this change in political climate.

We have noted in the first section of this chapter that the popularity and adoption of HRM rather than the more traditional PM has itself been encouraged by some of these same environmental and contextual developments.

Criticisms and developments

Criticisms of the Purcell and Gray model (**Figure 8.5**) and other early models devised in the UK included the assertion that the models did not facilitate identification and recognition of the tendency of many managements to distinguish between and treat differently employees as individuals and employees gathered together into collective organizations.

It was suggested that in some organizations management adopted different approaches and styles to each of these two scenarios. Purcell (1987) made the first significant attempt to devise a model that recognized this reality and this has been adapted and developed subsequently, Purcell and Ahlstrand (1989, 1994), though it should be noted that the research upon which this was based is concerned with multi-divisional organizations and we do need to bear in mind that size is a factor that may well explain differences between organizational approach or style.

In this context Purcell defines individualism and collectivism as follows:

- **individualism:** the degree of weight attached to issues such as the welfare of employees and their development
- **collectivism:** the extent to which management provide for and embrace employee collective organization and representation.

Another criticism of the early models, which the Purcell and Ahlstrand model seeks to encompass, is that no recognition was made in these models of managements' style changing over time, the dynamic dimension. The matrix depicted in **Figure 8.6** incorporates the dimensions of individualism and collectivism and provides a base that can be used to plot changes in style as they occur over time. The arrows on the figure indicate a range of

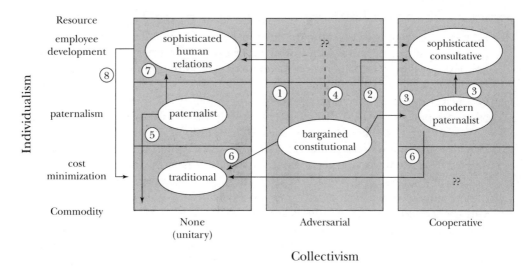

Figure 8.6 Movements in management style in employee relations. *Source:* Purcell and Ahlstrand, 1994 pp. 209–10

movements over time that in some respects can be seen to represent stereo-types of arguably common trends in changing managerial styles in recent years and these are identified in the accompanying notes to the figure.

Look again at the material on HRM and PM and decide which of the styles in this Purcell and Ahlstrand matrix (**Figure 8.6**) seem to be consistent with the concept of HRM and its implications for the management of employee relations.

It is also sometimes possible to use this matrix as a base for distinguishing espoused style from the reality of employee experience so that, for example, many employees in the public sector might well argue that through the late 1980s and early 1990s managements have been espousing a style consistent with high levels of individualism and low collectivism ('Sophisticated human relations' in the matrix). Yet the employees' experience has been closer to a style consistent with low individualism and low collectivism ('Traditional' in the matrix), where the dominant concern appears to have been with cost-cutting and by-passing or derecognizing the trade unions (Baldry, 1995). Some would see this latter

1 Employees encouraged to sign new individual contracts and union recognition for collective bargaining purposes withdrawn. New work practices, recruitment, selection, appraisal, and training initiatives implemented in accordance with 'soft' HRM and employee development policies.

2 Co-operative, consultative relations with trade unions/works councils/company councils developed alongside the introduction of employee development-type politics.

3 Co-operative, consultative relations initiated with unions as a prelude to subsequent initiatives in employee development. The new relationship with unions is often triggered by a crisis in the competitive position of the firm such that choice is forced. Competitive analysis reveals that the strength of the major firms in the market is based in part on employee development policies.

4 Unstable conditions exist as unions are bypassed in the change programme to introduce employee development policies. Subsequently either union membership declines and recognition is withdrawn, or both unions and management 'learn' to modify their behaviour to each other to emphasize partnership, or initiatives fail and the bargained constitutional pattern is reinforced.

5 Growing competition, falling profit margins, and declining market share force a reappraisal of employment policies leading to the introduction of cost minimization, reduction in job security, and reduced employee benefits. Or new entrants to the market base their competitive advantage on cheaper labour.

6 A new tough regime is introduced often triggered by a change in ownership, competitive tendering, subcontracting or acquisition. Union recognition is withdrawn and cost minimization policies reinforced, with employees working under worse conditions.

7 Emphasis placed on employee productivity achieved through employee development policies and technical change, based on realization that it is desirable to encourage employees to use diagnostic skills and their knowledge for the benefit of the business and to satisfy customers. Usually associated with reduction in numbers employed and thus rapid, early rises in productivity. The difficulty is to sustain this.

8 Rapidly falling market share in a depressed or mature market leading to substantial loss of profitability forces a major reappraisal of employment policies. These are often justified on the grounds of temporary expediency but, once implemented, are difficult to escape from. A change in top management is often a precursor to the abandonment of the employee development policies, and substantial cuts in employee investment. Often triggered by the arrival of low-cost entrants to the market and a slow response by the firm, leading to crisis and draconian action.

Figure 8.6 (*continued*)

in terms of a shift towards an approach consistent with the unitary model or paradigm.

The employees in such circumstances are likely to be confused in the first instance by their management appearing to say one thing and do something else but, after a while the impact upon employees is quite likely to involve a loss of trust and development of a degree of cynicism. Employees in this context, as in the one above, are likely to perceive that a different style altogether should be adopted, in this latter case either a return to the bargained constitutionalist style that, prior to the 1980s, was the norm in the public sector in the UK, or movement in the direction of the sophisticated consultative. In both cases employees would be expressing a preference for a style that encompasses employee collective organization.

In this section we have examined some of the several models of managerial style and we have emphasized the impact that external contexts and environments may have upon the style chosen by management and also that which is appropriate. Certainly some of the literature infers that an analysis of context can be used to establish whether the style used is appropriate or whether some other would be more consistent with the contextual circumstances. Nevertheless, it is important to realize that the ultimate discretion is with management and it may well be that for reasons of their own managements choose to operate with an approach to employee relations which is not appropriate in the context of the above analysis.

Activity 6

In the discussion above of the impact that various external contexts and features may have upon management's choice of style in the management of employee relations a number of comparisons were suggested. Consider each of the examples below and indicate in each case which style you think would be appropriate. You can use the Purcell and Ahlstrand model as the base for your answers.

1 Product market: fiercely price competitive and fashion-based. Stable market not very competitive and with competition on quality rather than on price.
2 Technology: long production run, capital intensive, low labour requirement and low labour cost per unit of process technology. Small batch, multi-skilled, flexible specialization, relatively high labour costs.
3 Strong entrenched unions and a shortage of skills. Trade union-free with plentiful supplies of skills.

Managing with or without unions?

Trade unions are the subject matter of the previous chapter, however, before we proceed in a section that concentrates upon managing without unions it is important to at least consider whether there are any advantages for management and the organization in recognizing and working with the trade unions. After all, we can't assume that all employers that have or do manage employee relations with trade unions do so against their will and that they are in a real sense dragged kicking and screaming to the negotiating table.

Freeman and Medoff (1984) highlighted one of the advantages of recognizing and dealing with trade unions and that was that they provide an effective mechanism through which the two groups can communicate with each other. This is often referred to as the 'voice' argument and some organizations that have found themselves in a new position of not dealing with trade unions have discovered after a while that there are problems in communicating with employees, a role that they used to leave to the trade union.

Trade unions are often also useful to management as a mechanism through which employee discipline and fairness and equity of treatment can be achieved. However, perhaps the greatest advantages to management lie in the opportunity unions provide to create and operate effective conflict resolution mechanisms and grievance procedures without having to deal with each employee as an individual. Decisions that are the product of agreement with the trade unions are also invested with a useful degree of legitimacy as far as the workforce is concerned and, where they have been arrived at through processes that have involved the trade union, it is much more difficult for the employees to then not comply with the agreement.

We have noted in the chapter on trade unions that in recent years there has been an increased willingness for employers and unions to agree partnership arrangements. These emphasize the joint interests of the parties in the success of the business and provide a role for the unions in a range of problem-solving activities facilitating the utilization, in the interests of the company, of the knowledge and expertise of the workforce.

There is a degree of coincidence between the objectives of these agreements and the more prescriptive models of HRM referred to earlier. If the active participation of the labour force in the resolution of problems and enhanced employee commitment and flexibility can all be obtained by management in return for recognizing the union then this does make the prospect of managing with trade unions much less threatening, especially if in return also the management achieve a single union, no strike and compulsory arbitration deal and retain their autonomy to decide issues in the event of a failure to reach agreed solutions.

To some extent the models referred to in the previous sub-section do provide information on a range of reasons and circumstances that may explain managements seeking to manage employee relations without trade unions; managements have in many cases taken advantage of opportunities to do so. There are some pretty obvious reasons why managers might prefer to avoid trade unions and paramount among them probably are reasons associated with the issues of autonomy and control, the belief that as management they should have the right and need to be able to manage unilaterally.

As noted earlier there have been a number of environmental developments over the last two decades – political, economic, social and cultural –

that contributed to the creation of circumstances that were much more conducive to managing without unions.

However, there have been similar declines in trade unionism in other countries over the same period (Hollinshead and Leat, 1995: chapter 5) and it may well be that there are common international influences at work that have enhanced the ability of and opportunity for managements to try to downgrade the role of the unions. Examples may well include changes in technology and competitive and production strategies and the encouragement of models of the firm and forms of organization that emphasize flexibility, including both numerical and functional flexibility.

The Purcell and Ahlstrand (1994) matrix (see **Figure 8.6**) is again useful in that the trends identified and represented by the various arrows on the figure do include some examples of firms moving from a position in which they recognized trade unions and engaged in consultation and collective bargaining (see Chapter 7) to a position in which they no longer do so, where they utilize a style that encompasses a very much reduced or non-existent role for the trade unions. Arrows 1 and 6 indicate shifts of this nature over time and it is clear from the commentary on arrow 6 that this particular shift is one that has occurred with some degree of frequency in the public sector as a result of the pressures of cost efficiency and the policies of privatization, competitive tendering and decentralization.

However, it would be a mistake to assume that all the instances of managements moving from a position of managing with unions to one of managing without them was the product of a concerted effort by the managements concerned to achieve this particular objective. There is no doubt that in many instances managements will have willingly reacted to and taken advantage of an opportunity presented by the interaction of some of the external influences mentioned above. In some they will have had little choice as the employees themselves presented management with a *de facto* derecognition situation, while in others managements will have adopted this new style or strategy only with regret since, as noted above, the impact of trade unionism upon the management of human resources and a labour force is by no means always negative from management's viewpoint.

Looking back again at the Purcell and Ahlstrand (1994) matrix (**Figure 8.6**) it is clear that low collectivism or non-unionism takes different forms, occurs for different motives and may have good as well as bad consequences for employees. The emphasis upon the individual, as opposed to the collective, may be:

- primarily developmental, with the employer anxious to invest in the labour resource
- paternalistic and beneficial to labour through the provision of benefits and treatment that is directed at convincing the employees that they can have no need for the union, that the union has no significant role since management is doing for the employees everything and more that the union would normally be expected to do

● upon the treatment of labour just as any other resource, to be acquired, used and disposed of at the least cost, a strictly utilitarian approach.

Organizations in the latter category may be relatively small and pursuing a competitive strategy that incorporates a strong element of price competition, hence the pressure upon costs. Many such organizations are also characterized by a lack of personnel procedures and personnel expertise. From the viewpoint of the employee, attitudes of government and other regulatory agencies and institutions to the responsibilities of small employers towards their employees have not been helpful. Throughout Europe the small employer tends to be protected from regulation on the grounds that to not do so imposes financial and administrative burdens that would be sufficiently significant to damage business prospects and therefore harm the prospects for job creation and employment generally.

Unfortunately it is often the case that it is the employees of small firms that are in most need of protection and least likely to be represented by a trade union. For logistical reasons alone trade unions find it most difficult to organize and effectively represent employees in small firms and locations where few are employed.

The initial findings from the 1998 WERS confirm that the incidence of trade union recognition tends to be positively associated with the number of employees, the percentage of workplaces in which trade unions are recognized increases from 39 per cent in workplaces employing less than 50, to 78 per cent in workplaces employing 500 plus. We have already noted that employer attitude also seems to be influential in whether there is a trade union presence within an organization and this would certainly seem to be supported by the experience at Tesco following the conclusion of a partnership agreement.

In addition to the typologies of style that we have already looked at there have been some attempts to devise models encompassing differences of style in non-union organizations, for example McLoughlin and Gourlay (1994) and Guest and Hoque (1994). We look here at the model devised by Guest and Hoque but, before doing so, try the next activity.

Activity 7

Try to answer briefly the following questions without looking back at the text that you have just read.

1 Identify some of the environmental constraints upon managerial styles.
2 What have been the major criticisms of early style models?
3 Identify some of the environmental developments that have allowed managements to downgrade the role of trade unions.

Guest and Hoque devised a four-fold typology of non-union firms and their policies/strategies/styles towards employee relations. Each of the four tends to represent a stereotype and you should realize that many firms will exhibit a mix of characteristics that don't conform with one particular type, they may partially fit in one category demonstrating some of the characteristics but not all of them. The typology demonstrates the range of characteristics that have been found.

They have used the terms 'the good', 'the bad', 'the ugly' and 'the lucky' to depict the four styles or types of non-union firm. The first of these, the good, would exhibit the following characteristics in their pure form:

- they are often large employers with a clear strategy for managing people and often an emphasis upon staff as their most valuable asset, their source of competitive advantage
- they often operate union substitution policies and provide an attractive alternative, part of which is the motive for being a market leader on pay and benefits
- they are likely to afford a high priority to recruitment, selection and induction as a means of identifying and inducing 'right' attitudes and norms
- they place stress on training and development and upon information sharing through mechanisms such as team briefing
- they will try to demonstrate their commitment to providing secure and satisfying work
- they may well operate single-status policies, ostensibly treating all employees the same with few if any discrimination between categories of staff
- they may well also operate individualized payment schemes often linked to performance appraisal thereby, they argue, rewarding best those who contribute the most.

A number of household name firms fit into this category, or at least they would claim to do so, and these would probably include Marks & Spencer, IBM, Hewlett Packard and J. Sainsbury. You may well know others that fit. Depending partially upon perspective and partially upon experience, organizations of this kind are sometimes criticized for presenting an illusion to their employees and being manipulative.

Very far removed from the good are the bad and the ugly. In both cases we are describing sweat-shop type conditions. The difference between these two is not so much in the actual terms and conditions of employment and the management of employees, these are likely to be very similar, the difference tends to lie in whether or not it is a deliberate policy to deprive employees of their rights and manipulate and exploit them (the ugly) or not (the bad). Guest and Hoque suggest that firms who fall into this category are often suppliers to larger organizations, sometimes locked into contracts that put them under pressure on quality and delivery, which also puts them under extreme pressure to minimize costs and waste. Just-in-Time systems may well generate the conditions in which suppliers are confronted by these pressures.

Characteristics of the 'bad' employer include:

- low pay
- no fringe or welfare benefits
- personalized rather than formal relationships, often a reliance upon personal exhortations and cajoling
- few if any procedures in areas such as discipline or employee grievances, and little if any health and safety protection, monitoring or inspection and quite commonly the working conditions are hazardous
- a harsh disciplinary regime and a hostility towards trade unions
- little dissemination of information.

The last of the four categories is the lucky. Here Guest and Hoque are describing those firms that exhibit little sophistication but which also demonstrate no deliberate attempt to manage by fear and union suppression. The overall impression with these firms is that they are essentially opportunist, pragmatic and reactive. There is little planning, few if any policies or procedures, low pay and poor benefits and, probably more by luck than judgement, no trade union presence. It is a form that can perhaps best be described by the term 'ad-hocery'.

The 1990 WIRS material (Millward *et al.*, 1992) also produced some further information on the employee relations policies and practices in non-union concerns, for example they found that:

- employees in non-union companies received less information about their conditions of work than those in large companies
- management styles in non-union concerns tended to be more authoritarian
- non-union employers were less likely to pursue equal opportunities policies.

Take a look at the cases described briefly in **Figure 8.7** 'Uphill struggle for forgotten strikers' and try to locate them in the various models of style that we have examined briefly in this section.

Uphill struggle for forgotten strikers

THE pickets' encampments around the Magnet Kitchens factory on the outskirts of Darlington — caravan offices, makeshift shelters and Portaloos, placards declaring "scabs will always walk alone" — betray the signs of a marathon industrial siege.

At the end of next week, 300 Magnet workers sacked for striking to win an across-the-board pay rise after a three-year freeze will mark the first anniversary of their dispute with a march and rally at the factory gates.

Picketing of all three gates has continued round the clock for 12 months, punctuated by occasional violent attacks, which the sacked strikers believe are organised by "scab" workers hired to take their jobs.

The 24-hour picketing is underpinned by the now familiar infrastructure of long-term industrial guerrilla warfare: showroom protests, women's support groups, high-profile legal backup, shareholder meeting lobbies, regional support groups and fundraising gigs.

The approach is mirrored in intractable disputes across the country — the product of Britain's unique trade union legislation, which gives no formal right to industrial action and allows employers to sack strikers at will.

In the best-known case, more than 300 Liverpool dockers sacked by the partly government-owned Mersey Docks and Harbour Company for refusing to cross a picket line will next month reach the second anniversary of their dispute. It has attracted strong international support, including action around the world against ships that use the Mersey port.

At Critchley Labels in south Wales, 31 workers have been locked out since February, when they went on strike in protest against the company's decision to "derecognise" the Communication Workers' Union. And for the past eight months, 41 skilled sheet metal workers have been picketing a Coventry car and aircraft panelmaker, Project Aerospace, which sacked them for striking last December.

With the exception of the

Case 1

Magnet Kitchens
Darlington, Co Durham. Involves TGWU, GMB, AEEU, UCATT. After a three-year pay freeze, Magnet workers went on strike in August 1996 in support of an across-the-board pay rise after an offer of 3 per cent for about two-thirds of them. The company, which sacked about 350 strikers with an average 24 years' service on September 3, recruited replacement workers and now says "there is no dispute".

Case 2

Critchley Labels
South Wales. Involves CWU. The company, which makes safety labels and was bought from BT four years ago, derecognised the union in December 1996. When 31 members with 471 years' service between them went on strike in protest in February, they were all sacked. John Monks, TUC general secretary, called Critchley "the worst example of industrial relations in Wales".

Case 3

Project Aerospace
Coventry. Involves MSF. Forty-one skilled sheet metalworkers were locked out on December 10, 1996, as they prepared to stage an indefinite strike. The workers had already taken action over pay, demands for a pension and sick pay scheme and the removal of asbestos from the factory. Negotiations are taking place.

Case 4

Liverpool Docks
Merseyside. Involves TGWU unofficially. About 320 dockers employed by the partly government-owned Mersey Docks and Harbour Company were locked out in September 1995 for striking in support of 80 sacked workers at a satellite firm, Torside, in a casualisation dispute. Strongly supported internationally, the dispute is unofficial. The sacked dockers, who demand reinstatement, have rejected a series of pay-off deals.

Liverpool docks dispute, all were legal, official strikes staged after winning strong majorities for action in postal ballots. But, despite a dramatic victory this year in a lockout and occupation at the Glacier factory in Glasgow, all the strikers know they are engaged in an uphill struggle.

Such drawn-out, localised lockouts — usually involving intense commitment and sacrifice — can have an impact far beyond the numbers taking part. They also highlight the one-sidedness of industrial relations law in a way that the Government may find difficult to ignore.

Labour's response has been sharply divergent in different parts of the country. In south Wales, MPs like Llew Smith and Don Touhig — parliamentary private secretary to the Chancellor, Gordon Brown — and Glenys Kinnock, the MEP, have joined the Critchley picket line. The Welsh Office minister, Peter Hain, has taken up the strikers' cause. But in the case of Magnet, the two MPs with most strikers living in their constituencies — Tony Blair and Alan Milburn, Darlington MP and health minister — have shunned the dispute.

Labour is committed to legislation to outlaw the sacking of those taking part in lawful strikes, but has dropped an earlier commitment to guarantee re-instatement.

In the meantime, employers are happy to take advantage of the licence they are allowed. As Andy Murphy, manufacturing director at Project Aerospace, said: "When the law does change, we might change our ways. In the meantime, good old Maggie".

But Hazel Fisher, a Magnet striker sacked after 20 years, is undaunted: "We're not going to walk away — we've nothing more to lose".

Figure 8.7 *Source: The Guardian, 11 August 1997*

Look back over the foregoing material and devise a profile of the kind of organization that is perhaps the most likely to be non-union.

Employers' associations and the CBI

There is a tendency for students and others to think that the only collective organizations involved as actors or participants in employee relations are the trade unions and this is not so. Employers also form and join collective associations and these form part of the national and international context within which employee relations in an organization are conducted. Outside the UK these two forms of collectives are often referred to as the social partners.

In the UK the fate of employers' associations since 1980 has, in many ways, mirrored that of the trade unions: numbers and membership have declined and they have been forced to appraise the services they offer their members and in a sense their reason for existence. In some respects this has encouraged the development of new and alternative roles, in others there has been a refocusing and prioritizing of their functions.

In this section we examine these developments in the context of the historical emergence of and roles performed by employers' associations, we examine why employers' associations were formed, why employers join, the apparent dichotomy involved in such collaboration by parties that normally compete with one another, the relevance of multi-employer collective bargaining and its decline and what the prospects appear to be for the associations that remain.

However, before going any further, we must point out that in this book we are concerned only with those associations that have an employee relations role; they may also have a trade role but it is the employee relations role that concerns us. There are many trade and other associations of employers, chambers of commerce, rotary clubs, etc., that do not have such a role and these do not constitute employers' associations for the purposes of this book.

Definition

In the UK the definition usually used is the legal one in TULR(C)A 1992, which states that an employers' association 'consists wholly or mainly of employers or individual owners of undertakings of one or more descriptions and whose principal purposes include the regulation of relations between employers of that description ...and workers or trade unions...'.

As already noted above, the fortunes of the employers' association movement seem to coincide with or mirror that of the trade union movement and, as we examine elsewhere, also with the popularity of multi-employer collective bargaining.

The number of employers' organizations in existence and conforming with the definition above is quite difficult to establish. However, if such an association wants to protect its legal status it has to register with the Certification Officer (see previous chapter), and by the early 1990s this source indicated that there were in the region of 250 associations, compared with 340 in 1979. An earlier estimate by the Commission on Industrial Relations (CIR) put the number in the late 1960s/early 1970s at somewhere around 1200 associations concerned with the negotiation of wages and other terms and conditions of employment, of which approximately one-quarter were national in scope with the remainder being local associations (CIR, 1972: 13).

Why employers form associations and their main roles

It might seem strange that employers form and join collective associations and that they act collaboratively within them, given that in a capitalist system employers as producers and sellers of products and services in the same industry or area are commonly in competition with one another. There are a number of explanations for this and a brief consideration of these reasons also illustrates some of the more important roles of such organizations.

The CIR study (1972: 5) states: 'Employers organize for the economic purpose of influencing wage determination to their advantage and combine as a countervailing force to trade union organization and as a defence against such trade union tactics as 'picking off' individual employers'.

Organization in these terms is initially a reactive or defensive measure, the employers form and join in response to the presence and activities of trade unions who will themselves seek to influence wage determination to their own advantage. When confronted with employers in a trade or area that are not organized it is possible for the union to decide which of the employers is in the weakest position and/or can afford to pay employees the most and to seek to negotiate an agreement with this single employer, which they then attempt to extend to the rest.

However, the CIR also points out that employers organize not only to prevent the bidding-up of wages by the unions but also to stop the undercutting of wages by any employer, a prevention of competition. It is the desire to control and stabilize wages that in this instance encourages the formation of associations.

There are other reasons; the desire for stability and order also encouraged these organizations to formulate and agree procedure; and mechanisms external to the employing entity for the resolution of grievances and disputes (see Chapter 10). The externalization of responsibility for the determination of terms and conditions of employment and the regulation of the employment relationship and resolution of grievances, etc., enabled companies to avoid the expense and hassle of employing their own expertise and dealing with their own industrial relations problems.

This externalization was criticized by the Donovan Commission Report in 1968 as being one of the reasons why informal systems of industrial relations had emerged in companies, one of the main 'problems' at the time. Employers were criticized for having abrogated their responsibilities and were encouraged to grasp the nettle and take responsibility for the conduct and management of industrial relations, to bring them back inside the employing organization.

This recommendation is variously credited with a measure of the responsibility for the subsequent decline in multi-employer bargaining and with the decline in the number and influence of employers' organizations. The climate created in 1979 and subsequently by the election of a Conservative government antagonistic to the trade unions and determined to reduce their influence, allied to their determination to pursue different economic priorities, probably assisted in this process. The potency of the threat that the unions posed to an individual employer receded, as did their ability to take effective action.

In addition to these regulatory roles employers' organizations, like trade unions, also provide advisory services to their members and represent their interests to other organizations, interest groups and to the regulators at national level and within the European Union. They act as pressure groups.

It has been suggested that as the regulatory role of employers' organizations has declined the priority attached to these other roles has been enhanced. As companies internalized the regulation of terms and conditions of employment they had a greater need for employee relations advice and, as the significance of the EU has grown, so has the role and influence afforded the social partners.

The retreat from voluntarism on the part of governments since the 1960s has also had an impact. As the volume and frequency of legislative intervention has increased so has the need of employing organizations for advice on their legal rights, responsibilities and obligations. As one might expect it is the smaller employer that has the greatest need for these services, large and multinational employers are usually well able to look after their own interests in these arenas.

Other factors that are held to encourage the formation of employers' organizations relate to the homogeneity of the product and labour markets, the extent to which the employers are producing the same product and require the same labour and the extent to which employers are using the same technologies; in short the degree of common interest. The argument is that the greater the commonality of interest the greater are the chances and prospects of an employers' organization being formed and being effective.

The Confederation of British Industry

This is the main national-level organization to which most of the other organizations, along with many individual companies, belong. It is an association or federation of associations and such associations are sometimes referred to as 'peak' associations. The CBI was the result of a merger between similar associations in 1965.

The CBI is in the main a political lobbying organization and it perceives itself as representing the voice of British business to government, the general public, the regulatory institutions within the EU and on a wider political and world stage. We have noted elsewhere that the CBI was active in its lobbying of New Labour over the impact of proposals for legislation to give trade unions and their members rights to trade union recognition and to individual representation on disciplinary matters and grievances (see **Figure 7.6**).

Unlike 'peak' employers' federations in some other countries, and unlike many individual industry-wide and district employers' organizations in the UK that are its members, the CBI has never participated in collective bargaining. It also is a source of information and advice to members on employment and related matters. The scope of the CBI's activities are not limited to employment and employee relations, it covers the general business, commercial and trade roles too.

Summary

In this chapter we have examined the development and traditions of Personnel Management and the emergence and adoption of Human Resource Management. We have also compared the employee relations implications of both and distinguished between the hard and soft versions of HRM. We have seen that management may have a number of objectives in respect of employee relations, though some would argue that the dominant one may be control over the labour process, and they pursue these objectives utilizing a number of different approaches or styles. There are a number of models and the later ones try to encompass both individualism and collectivism and acknowledge the dynamic nature of style. You have also been made aware that some features of the external environment act as constraining influences upon the styles adopted by senior management.

In the last two decades, notwithstanding the recent attraction of partnership agreements, management has been presented with the opportunity, or has chosen, to manage without trade unions and there are again a number of different non-union scenarios and forms of employee relations management. The future is inevitably going to be influenced by the new legal rights to recognition in certain circumstances and, given certain support thresholds, we should expect a reversal of the trend to less recognition. These rights and arrangements look to be coming into effect from the summer of the year 2000.

Employers, like employees, have formed and join collective associations. The industrial relations and regulatory roles of these organizations have declined in importance in the last thirty years subsequent to the Donovan Commission Report. As these roles have declined in importance so has the membership and number of employers' organizations, but other roles have emerged to at least partially take their place. The CBI is the peak association for employers and its role is primarily that of representing business and its interests to government and to society at large.

Activity Answers

Activity 1
They are all likely to figure towards the softer end of the spectrum.

Activity 2
Employee development can be pursued for both hard and soft motives. In the case of a tight fit matching model employee development might be pursued as a means of squeezing the last drop of potential and performance from employees, whereas in a softer context, as perhaps provided by the Beer *et al.* (1984) model, development may be perceived more in terms of providing employees with the opportunity to grow through work and with empowerment, a mechanism through which commitment to organizational goals may be enhanced, as something which benefits the individual as well as the organization.

Activity 3
There are again a considerable range of possibilities but you should have identified at least some of the following:

- collective strength, usually through trade unionism, as a means of exerting greater pressure to achieve some of the others below
- a higher price for their labour
- control of the labour process, control of the job or at least greater participation in the decision-making processes, preferably through the process known as collective bargaining
- resistance to greater flexibility and more productive use of the labour resource
- the rule of law as embodied in a wide range of agreed procedures and rules and thereby the maintenance of the status quo
- self-fulfilment/actualization.

Activity 4
Among others perhaps your list should include: size, ownership, the nature of and degree of competition in product markets, market share, the nature of the technology in use, proportion of labour to total cost, and whether the organization operates within a single industry or whether it is a conglomerate operating across industrial boundaries.

Activity 5
The first point to make is that there are of course different models and forms of HRM. However, given an appropriate environment it is probably reasonable to assume that managements in organizations seeking to implement HRM will seek to avoid trade union recognition and will have a preference for individualism and individual relations and contract. The choice between the three styles at the individual end of the axis can arguably be seen as reflective of the difference between hard and soft HRM, with the Traditional style being at the hard end of the spectrum referred to earlier and the Sophisticated Human Relations style being at the soft end. Where managements are persuaded of the need or usefulness of involving employees via representative consultation and/or other cooperative mechanisms it may be that the soft HRM approach would be consistent with a Sophisticated Consultative approach.

Activity 6
1 The fiercely price competitive and fashion-based market will encourage employers towards cost minimization and a traditional style, whereas in a stable quality competitive market the style adopted is likely to facilitate the sophisticated human resource or paternalist styles.
2 The former may give scope for a more consultative and sophisticated human relations approach than is possible in the latter, where the emphasis may have to be upon a more traditional and authoritarian approach with greater emphasis upon cost control, even though such an approach may not fit very well with the disposition of the highly and multi-skilled labour force.
3 Employers faced with a market in which the trade unions are strong and entrenched and in which there is a shortage of appropriate skills are likely to be pressured towards a bargained constitutional style whereas in a trade union-free market with a surplus of the required skills available the management would be more able successfully to pursue a style that was either paternalist or traditional.

Activity 7
1 ● Culture and ideology
  ● the product market
  ● technology
  ● the labour market
  ● the social, legal and political environment and institutions.
2 They did not facilitate identification and recognition of the tendency of many managements to distinguish between and adopt different approaches and styles to employees as individuals and employees when gathered together into collective organizations. Another criticism of the early models is that no recognition was made in these models of managements' style changing over time.

3 The changed political environment in the UK since 1979:

- changes in technology
- product market developments leading to sectoral decline
- economic and social influences, such as:

  - the increase in unemployment
  - the deregulation of the labour market
  - the increased feelings of insecurity
  - changes in values and attitudes.

Activity 8

J.J. Fast Food Distribution – very much in the traditional category of the older model of Purcell and Gray and, if you view it as a non-union work-place, it would certainly fit into the bad category and possibly into the ugly.

Magnet Kitchens – are on the move, you could argue that the company exhibits the opportunistic characteristics of the standard modern but with traditional undertones and, if you now regard the company as a non-union one, it will fit into the bad/ugly area.

Critchley Labels – is now a non-union employer having derecognized the union and sacked those employees that were members. It seems likely from the thumb-nail sketch presented that the management style fits between the bad and the ugly. The chances are that, prior to acquisition of the company from BT, there was an employee relations tradition of the bar-gained constitutionalist variety and developments since then could be per-ceived as a move towards the traditionalist style.

Project Aerospace – from the information presented it is still a union-ized company. However, there are clear signs that the management is of the opportunistic standard modern persuasion, taking advantage while they can and probably with underlying traditional values and preferences.

Liverpool Docks – movement from a bargained constitutional style, again traditionally associated with the public sector and this industry, towards the traditional.

Activity 9

Among the characteristics identified you should probably have picked up the following:

- small–medium size
- young
- private services/high tech
- independent
- foreign owned
- employing substantial numbers of white collar/part-time/ethnic minori-ties labour.

References

Baldry, K., 1995. Changes in the management of employee relations in Royal Mail. Unpublished M. Phil. Thesis. University of Plymouth.

Beer, M., Spector, B., Lawrence, P.R., Quinn Mills, D. and Walton. R.E., 1984. *Managing Human Assets.* Free Press, New York.

CIR, 1972. *Study No. 1. Employers Organizations and Industrial Relations.* HMSO, London.

Cully, M., *et al.* 1998. The Workplace Employee Relations Survey: First Findings. DTI, ACAS, ESRC, PSI. Crown, London

Devanna, M.A., Fombrun, C.J. and Tichy, N.M., 1984. A framework for strategic Human Resource Management. In Fombrun, C.J., Tichy, N.M. and Devanna, M.A. (eds), *Strategic Human Resource Management.* Wiley, New York.

Dunlop, J.T., 1958. *Industrial Relations Systems.* Holt, New York.

Donovan Commission Report, 1968. *The Report of the Royal Commission on Trade Unions and Employers Associations.* Command 3623. HMSO, London.

Farnham, D., 1993. *Employee Relations.* IPM, London.

Farnham, D., 1997. *Employee Relations in Context.* IPD, London.

Farnham, D. and Pimlott, J., 1995. *Understanding Industrial Relations.* 5th Edition. Cassell, London.

Fombrun, C.J., Tichy, N.M. and Devanna, M.A. (eds), 1984. *Strategic Human Resource Management.* Wiley, New York.

Fox, A., 1974. *Beyond Contract.* Faber and Faber, London.

Freeman, R. and Medoff, J., 1984. *What do Trade Unions Do?* Basic Books, New York.

Gallie, D., Penn, R. and Rose, M., 1996. *Trade Unionism in Recession.* Oxford University Press, Oxford.

Guest, D., 1987. Human Resource Management and industrial relations. *Journal of Management Studies* 24(5): 503–521.

Guest, D., 1989a. Human Resource Management: its implications for industrial relations and trade unions. In Storey, J. (ed.), *New Perspectives on Human Resource Management.* Routledge, London.

Guest, D., 1989b. Personnel and HRM: Can you tell the difference? *Personnel Management,* January, pp. 48–51.

Guest, D. and Hoque, K., 1994. The good, the bad and the ugly: employment relations in new non-union workplaces. *Human Resource Management Journal* 5(1): 1–14.

Herzberg, F., 1966. *Work and the Nature of Man.* Staples Press, London.

Hollinshead, G. and Leat, M., 1995. *Human Resource Management: An International and Comparative Perspective on the Employment Relationship.* Financial Times Pitman, London.

IPM, 1993. *Professional Education Scheme syllabus for Employee Relations,* London.

Legge, K., 1989. Human Resource Management: a critical analysis. In

Storey, J. (ed.), *New Perspectives on Human Resource Management.* Routledge, London.

Marchington, M. and Wilkinson, A., 1996. *Core Personnel and Development.* IPD, London.

Maslow, A.,1943. A theory of human motivation. *Psychological Review* 50: 370–396.

McGregor, D., 1960. *The Human Side of Enterprise.* McGraw-Hill, New York.

McLoughlin, I. and Gourlay, S., 1994. *Enterprise Without Unions.* Open University Press, Buckingham.

Metcalf, D., 1993. *Transformation of British Industrial Relations? Institutions, Conduct and Outcomes 1980–1990.* Centre for Economic Performance Paper No. 151, London School of Economics.

Millward, N., Stevens, M., Smart, D. and Hawes, W.R., 1992. *Workplace Industrial Relations in Transition.* Dartmouth, Aldershot.

Purcell, J., 1987. Mapping management styles in employee relations. *Journal of Management Studies* 24(5): 534–548.

Purcell, J. and Ahlstrand, B., 1994. H*uman Resource Management in the Multi-Divisional Company.* Oxford University Press, Oxford.

Purcell, J. and Ahlstrand, B., 1989. The impact of corporate strategy and the management of employee relations in the multi-divisional company. *British Journal of Industrial Relations* 27(3): 397–417.

Purcell, J. and Gray, A., 1986. Corporate personnel departments and the management of industrial relations: two case studies in the management of ambiguity. *Journal of Management Studies* 23(2), pp. 205–23.

Purcell, J. and Sisson, K., 1983. Strategies and practice in the management of industrial relations. In Bain, G.S. (ed.), *Industrial Relations in Britain.* Blackwell, Oxford.

Salamon, M., 1992. *Industrial Relations.* 2nd Edition. Prentice Hall, Hemel Hempstead.

Storey, J., 1987. Developments in the management of human resources: an interim report. Warwick Papers In Industrial Relations No. 17, IRRU, School of Industrial and Business Studies, University of Warwick, November.

Storey, J. (ed.), 1989. *New Perspectives on Human Resource Management.* Routledge London.

Storey, J., 1992. *Developments in the Management of Human Resources.* Blackwell, Oxford.

Torrington, D., 1989. HRM and the personnel function. In Storey, J. (ed.), *New Perspectives on Human Resource Management.* Routledge, London.

Undy, R. and Kessler, I., 1995. The changing nature of the employment relationship. IPD Annual Conference. Cited in Marchington, M. and Wilkinson, A., 1996. *Core Personnel and Development.* London.

Further reading

Fox, A., 1966. *Industrial Sociology and Industrial Relations.* Royal Commission Research Paper No. 3. HMSO, London.

Guest, D., 1989b. Personnel and HRM: can you tell the difference? *Personnel Management*, January, pp. 48–51.

Legislation

Trade Union and Labour Relations (Consolidation) Act 1992 (TULR(C)A 1992).

Part Four

The Organizational Context – Processes, Policies and Procedures

Chapter 9

Employee relations processes

Introduction

In the first chapter we concluded that at the heart of the subject matter of employee relations was the employment relationship and the interactions of the various parties to that relationship. These interactions may be between individuals, employee and employer, or between collective organizations representing and acting as agents for individuals or, indeed, a mix of the two, an individual interacting with an organization.

We noted that in this book the focus would be upon the collective interactions and regulation of this relationship but that this did not imply concern only with collective interactions involving trade unions and employers. We pointed out that there were different perspectives on and debates surrounding the nature of the employment relationship and that these would influence the perceived purpose of these interactions. Some, like the author, would argue that the relationship is:

- dominated by conflicting interests with regard to the price of labour and/or control of the labour process that are inherent, and that the purpose of the interactions should be the mutual reconciliation and regulation of these conflicts of interest, hopefully to the mutual satisfaction of the parties.

Others would argue that the relationship is:

- characterized by shared interests that would be looked after and furthered by management and that employees should acknowledge management's superior knowledge and expertise, acknowledge their right to manage and give them the loyalty and trust to which their position entitles them – a continuation of the master and servant relationship that does not acknowledge a legitimate role for collective organization and collective interaction and regulation, or
- characterized by some shared interests and that the purpose of the interactions is to ensure that these joint interests are pursued together in a spirit of cooperation and partnership with a degree of mutual and reciprocal commitment.

The interactions therefore may be adversarial or cooperative in nature and form. Whatever the perceived purpose of the interactions and the nature of the relationship, decision making may be unilateral, one of the parties makes the decision, or it may be joint, the parties make the decision together. Where the decisions are made by only one of the parties the process leading up to that decision-making point may still be participative in that the other parties may have an opportunity to input their view, with this view being listened to and taken into account, prior to the decision being made. Truly joint decision-making is where the parties make the decision together and where the decision is quite likely to take the form of an agreement.

However, you should not make the mistake of assuming that joint decisions are inevitably the product of cooperation or that it can only happen in a cooperative framework. Many joint decisions are the outcome of adversarial relations, are reached through a process of negotiation and are the product of compromises being made on all sides.

The subject matter of this chapter is the main collective processes through which employee relations are regulated, conflicts and issues are resolved. The outcome of the process may be substantive terms and conditions of employment, such as rates of pay and hours of work, it may be a new or revised policy or procedure for dealing with an issue such as equal opportunities or managing discipline, or it may be concerned to establish the rules and conventions that will govern the actual interaction of the parties, how this should work and what their respective rights and obligations are to be in particular sets of circumstances.

Some of the processes can be wide ranging in terms of the subject matter that can be dealt with, whereas others may be devised and intended to deal with specific issues. In examining these processes we will consider them in terms of:

- whether they provide employees with opportunities to participate in the decision-making process and thereby in the determination of outcomes, in the control and management of the labour process. The first section of the chapter examines the notion of employee participation and thereby provides a backdrop to the later consideration of whether the processes do or do not provide employees with participative opportunities
- whether they are adversarial or cooperative in nature
- whether they result in unilateral or joint decision-making.

In addition to producing the kind of traditional substantive or procedural outcomes referred to above the parties to these processes may perceive them as means of achieving other objectives and outcomes such as:

- enhanced employee involvement
- greater commitment on the part of employees to the goals and values of the organization as specified by management
- greater employee satisfaction and motivation
- production or service outcomes such as greater productivity or enhanced quality.

In the first two chapters on the employment relationship and the nature of work, technology and change, we examined the concepts of commitment and employee involvement and identified some of the main techniques and initiatives such as the quality circle and semi-autonomous team working, and how they relate to the achievement of these objectives as well as those of enhanced motivation and satisfaction, greater productivity and enhanced quality. We will not re-examine these arrangements here. In this chapter the emphasis is upon the following processes: collective bargaining, joint consultation, works and staff councils. In the following chapters we examine some of the specific policy and procedural outcomes of these processes.

Objectives

After studying this chapter you will be able to:

- Discuss the concept of employee participation and whether these processes may also enable employees to participate in management decision-making and control of the labour process
- Identify and distinguish the range of employee relations processes by which conflict may be resolved

- Explain the meaning and nature of collective bargaining
- Distinguish different models of joint consultation focusing upon the purposes of management and the degree of employee participation facilitated by them.

Employee participation

In capitalist systems ownership tends to confer upon the owners the right to direct and control the assets and activities of the organization, and the legal system supports this distribution of power. Owners often appoint managers as their agents and it is these managers that claim the right unilaterally to decide, resting their claim upon their appointment as the agent of the owner(s) and also increasingly upon their expertise in performing these functions.

Employee participation therefore, wherever and to the extent that it occurs, implies some diminution of these rights, some erosion of management's ability unilaterally to decide issues without consulting or paying any attention to the views or wishes of the labour force, a group who are after all one of the major stakeholders in the enterprise, its success and its future. Employee participation therefore implies an erosion of the traditional master–servant relationship.

Direct and indirect

Some forms of participation are direct and others indirect, the difference being in whether it is the employee him or herself that participates in the decision-making or whether this participation is achieved through representatives.

Direct participation is logistically difficult on issues other than those that affect only a relatively small number of employees. Examples of decisions that may lend themselves to determination through direct participation might be decisions concerning workgroup matters such as the allocation of work, output quality or job redesign where the group members make the decision between themselves. Decisions of a wider or more strategic nature are much more likely to be made through indirect or representative participatory mechanisms.

If we briefly examine some of the literature on the topic of employee participation and attempts at definition we once again become aware that there are different perceptions of what the term means and thereby the extent to which processes are participative. For example Walker (1974) argues that worker participation in management occurs when workers take part in 'the authority and managerial functions of the enterprise' indicating, as noted above, an erosion of managerial prerogative and change in the balance of power.

Some would see this as a relatively narrow definition and Strauss (1979) refers to three different participation models, each being distinguished on the dimension of the depth or the degree of workers' influence or control over management. Here management relates primarily to the function rather than the people but inevitably there is a relationship between the two:

- **consultative participation**: gives workers and/or their representatives the right (or opportunity) to be informed, to give a view or to raise objections but, crucially, the right to decide remains with management, their prerogative remains intact
- **co-management**: employees share the right to decide, they have joint decision-making powers with management and this may well translate into an effective right of veto, the consent of both parties being required before action can be taken
- **self-management by workers**: describes a scenario in which it is the employees either directly or through representatives that alone have the role of decision-making, this may be by virtue of the employees being the owners of the enterprise.

Part of the value of this concern with the depth or degree of influence or control is that it points up the significance of **power**, the ability to influence, and there are many potential sources of power and many influences upon them.

Traditionally employees and their representative associations have sought to gain power first of all through membership numbers and strength and then through a collective control over the supply of labour and thereby the job. Examples of the latter may be the pace of work, the degree of fragmentation, issues of quality and quality assurance and the allocation of work. Having obtained the power it has to be effectively exerted if employee objectives are to be realized and in the UK, the USA and many of the countries in the EU, the mechanism used to exert this power has most commonly been collective bargaining (which we examine in a subsequent section).

Both employees and employers sometimes resort to the use of industrial action and the imposition of sanctions upon the employer/employee as part of this power-based process.

In either event the depth of participation achieved through collective bargaining is likely to be a function, at least in part, of the relative power of the parties. Power is a factor in determining both the nature and extent of employee participation in any particular organization, country or time.

Further evidence of the range of definitions and interpretations can be detected from the work of Marchington *et al.* (1992). In this work they identify what they refer to as four paradigms or models of participation, each of which are distinguished on the basis of motive as well as on outcome in terms of the redistribution of power, and each of which can be seen to rest upon different underlying assumptions. The four paradigms are:

1 the control/labour process paradigm which perceives employee participation to result in a transfer of control of the labour process from management to employees
2 the cooperation/industrial relations paradigm links participation with conflict resolution, cooperation and with efficiency. Underpinning assumptions include a plurality of interests within organizations, conflict between them and the need to reconcile that conflict. Collective bargaining and consultation are perceived to be mechanisms through which employees can participate, conflict can be efficiently resolved and cooperation may also be enhanced
3 the satisfaction/QWL paradigm assumes a link between employee participation and job satisfaction, the assumption being that enhanced participation leads to enhanced satisfaction. This is a notion that has much in common with quality of working life programmes which focus upon job design and self-control of the task and immediate task environment. The participation envisaged in this paradigm is job- or task-centred with employees deriving satisfaction from an expansion or enrichment of their role, the latter yielding them greater responsibility and authority. We are not looking here at a model that implies an erosion of managerial authority or autonomy, or indeed one that has much to do with reconciling inherent conflicts of interests
4 the commitment/HRM paradigm, in which positive relationships are perceived to exist between employee participation and employee commitment to the goals and values of the enterprise, and between such commitment and enhanced performance and productivity. Committed employees work harder and are more productive.

1 Which of these Marchington *et al.* (1992) paradigms seem to you to be consistent with the notion of participation as defined by Walker above?
2 Try to work out whether Strauss's concept of employee participation and its forms or types fit with or are the same as Marchington *et al.*'s models and, if so, which?

We noted above that capitalist systems tend to support the rights and interests of employers and managers before those of the employees. Some of the arguments in favour of greater employee participation through employee relations processes such as collective bargaining, as well as through other methods, rest upon notions of morality and democracy; that as major stake-holders in the success of the enterprise employees have a moral right to participate in the managerial function, decision-making and control. In the context of this argument employee participation is a reflection of political democracy, that the governed have the right to exercise some control over those in authority.

If you look back to the article (**Figure 7.8**) by Ruth Lea and her comments on trade unions you see expressed there very much the alternative view, that businesses are not democracies and that management should be allowed to exercise their expertise on behalf of shareholder value.

Employee participation and employee involvement

Having said that the subject matter of this chapter is to be the employee relations processes that constitute collective interactions, that we will examine these in the context of whether they provide employees with participation in control and that we will not examine employee involvement initiatives since they tend to be different in nature and initiated for different reasons, it is perhaps necessary here to spend a little time just identifying clearly the differences between employee participation and involvement.

Some analysts and observers take the view that for all practical purposes employee participation and employee involvement (EI) can be treated as synonymous with each other whereas others, and the author of this text would fall into this camp, argue that while there may be overlap between them the concepts are different and can and should be distinguished from each other.

Some EI initiatives (**Figure 9.1**) may provide employees with the opportunity to participate in decision-making and thereby in the control and management of the assets, activities and direction of the enterprise. However, many of the initiatives associated with EI do no more than provide information; managements' hope being that through the provision of this information employees will feel more involved in and with the enterprise. There is also a common belief that if employees are more involved they will be more content, more motivated and more committed to the goals and values of the enterprise as determined by management and that this will also make them more productive.

Marchington *et al.* (1992) use the term 'employee involvement' to indicate the range of managerially inspired, designed and initiated processes at the level of the firm which 'are intended to improve communications with employees, to generate greater commitment, and enhance employee contributions to the organization'. Management motives in the introduction of such initiatives are clearly instrumental in nature and the objectives as specified do not include employee participation in decision-making and control.

Employee involvement (EI) initiatives and their frequency in the UK

Marchington and Wilkinson (1996) in drawing upon the literature, much of which is their own, conclude that EI initiatives can usefully be located into four main categories.

Downward communication

The principal purpose of these schemes, and there are many means available to management, is to educate and persuade employees of the value and merit of management initiatives and to inform about the performance of the organization or unit.

Team Briefing is perhaps the best known initiative new to the 1980s and regarded commonly as symptomatic of EI but there are other popular initiatives including house journals and newspapers and the use of video is becoming more popular. The 1998 WERS data show that 61 per cent of workplaces had a system of team briefing in operation.

There are very few grounds upon which it can legitimately be argued that this category of EI constitutes 'participation' by employees.

Upward problem solving

Here employees are involved in task-oriented issues and problems and either individually or as a group are invited to examine and propose remedies for work problems. The best known of these techniques is the quality circle (see Chapter 2) and others include attitude surveys, suggestion schemes and, in some instances, Total Quality Management (see Chapter 2). Management are seeking to use the knowledge and experience of employees and the assumption is that employees will not only contribute to the resolution of problems but also that they will feel more involved and, as such, the quality circle yields other benefits of enhanced commitment, productivity and quality etc.

The data from the 1998 WERS indicate that some 45 per cent of workplaces had conducted some form of staff attitude survey in the preceding five years and that 42 per cent had problem-solving groups such as quality circles.

Task participation

Many of these schemes can be seen to derive from and are consistent with the ideas of the Quality of Working Life movement, the essence of which is that employees derive satisfaction from manageable variety and complexity; such tasks provide intrinsic satisfactions and opportunities for self-fulfilment and self-actualization and that satisfied employees are likely to be more productive, etc.

Figure 9.1 EI initiatives

This form of EI then encompasses schemes such as job redesign, job enrichment, rotation and enlargement (see Chapter 2).

Financial involvement

There are a number of means by which employees can participate in the financial performance of the company. It may be through some form of bonus scheme linked to performance or it may be that they are encouraged to participate in the ownership of the organization through shareholding; these latter schemes often go under the banner of Employee Share Ownership Schemes (ESOPs). It is assumed that employees with some form of financial stake in the organization over and above their salary or wage will work harder and be more productive.

As shareholders employees can, in theory, participate in decision-making at a corporate level. However, in practice there have been very few schemes that provided employees with a sufficiently large stake in the ownership to enable them, even collectively, to exert a significant influence.

Again the 1998 WERS data show that 30 per cent of workplaces had a profit-sharing scheme for non-managerial employees but ESOPs were less common with 15 per cent of workplaces operating such schemes for non-managerial employees and even fewer workplaces operated individual performance related schemes for non-managerial employees. Cully *et al.* (1998) also make the point that these schemes appear to be complementary rather than substitute methods of financial involvement.

Figure 9.1 (*continued*)

As Poole and Mansfield (1992) discovered, 'Managers appear to support most employee involvement practices so long as these do not radically affect their control function within the firm. In other words they tend to prefer a unitary rather than a pluralist approach to employee participation in decision-making'. Even though the intentions may have nothing to do with participation, let alone democracy, it can be that a measure of enhanced participation, in the context of the 'depth' of influence in decision-making and control perceptions referred to above, is one of the outcomes, which is why we say that there may be overlap between the two notions.

The central role given in this definition to the generation of greater employee commitment locates EI as encompassing a set of practices and intentions that are consistent with models of Human Resource Management such as those of Beer *et al.* (1984) and Guest (1989a), which prescriptively place organizational commitment at the centre of the outcomes that should be achieved as a result of HRM initiatives (see Chapter 8).

EI processes are generally directed at individuals or work groups and tend to involve employees at this level. Generally they do not include a role for trade unions and it is sometimes suspected and/or alleged that the objectives for initiating the processes include the desire to bypass or weaken the trade unions by establishing that employees are valued for themselves and that the trade unions are not needed, that they are an anachronism.

Have another look at the four paradigms of participation identified by Marchington *et al.* (1992) and try to work out for yourself whether any of them are more consistent with notions of EI rather than participation.

1 Think back to Chapter 8, section on 'Managerial style(s)' and try to iden-tify the style(s) that would be consistent with managers pursuing EI initiatives.
2 With which of the main perspectives discussed in Chapter 1 does the EI concept fit?

Continuum of participation

As noted above, in some instances employee participation will extend to joint decision-making but in most, this is not what happens; management retains the right or ability to make the decision unilaterally, on their own, but employees play a participative role prior to the decision being made.

If we concentrate for a moment on this issue and if we view the various processes in terms of the extent to which they provide the participants with a full or partial share in decision-making and therefore in control, it is pos-sible to devise a continuum of participation (see **Figure 9.2**). This shows that at either end there is no sharing, only unilateral decision-making or complete autonomy for one of the actors and none for the other. Terms commonly used for each of these extreme positions are managerial prerog-ative, where management has complete or total autonomy, and workers control where there is no participation by management/employer. In between these extremes are a range of mechanisms and processes, each of which can be seen to demonstrate/exhibit different combinations of employee and employer autonomy and thereby different degrees of employee participation. As you can see from the figure there are different forms of consultation and each implies a different degree of employee par-ticipation.

We have included in the figure, for the purposes of comparison, a couple

PROCESS/TECHNIQUES

Employer control	Downward communication	Consultation cooperation	Co-decision/ Joint control	Self-management/ Employee control
1. Quality of Work Life Programmes that rotate or enlarge jobs	1. Company or Works Councils with rights to information only. 2. Team Briefing. 3. Newspapers. 4. Notice boards.	1. Company or Works Councils with rights to be consulted and raise objections. 2. Quality Circles with rights to recommend solutions to problems. 3. Worker Directors with less than equal voting right/share. 4. Attitude surveys. 5. Suggestion schemes. 6. Other upward problem-solving.	1. Collective bargaining 2. Works or Company Councils with rights to agree or veto. 3. Mechanisms for joint determination of objectives. 4. Worker Directors with equity of voting rights/power of veto.	1. Worker/Producer Cooperatives 2. Self-managed work groups with control of task-related matters such as the allocation and pace of work.

Low ←—————————————→ High

EMPLOYEE PARTICIPATION

Figure 9.2 Continuum illustrating degree or depth of employee participation in decision-making/control. Adapted from Leat 1998

of EI initiatives or processes that some might argue are participative but which in this context are demonstrably not.

What decisions?

We have been talking about participation in decision-making without yet addressing the important issue of 'what decisions?'. 'What areas of subject matter are we concerned with?' Perhaps inevitably there is a wide range of subject matter over which rights to autonomy are claimed by each side and there is often little consensus.

Many would argue that business decisions such as those concerning investment, location, expansion, competitive strategy, production systems and the technology to be employed should be the preserve of management. When it comes to issues specific to the management of labour, again many would suggest that management should retain prerogative over matters such as hiring and firing, promotions, transfers, discipline and the implementation of existing rules.

It is worth pointing out that in other countries within the European Union, and perhaps particularly in Germany, there are very different traditions and many of these latter decisions are actually subject to employee assent through the mechanism of the works council – see below. What this means in reality is that the works council has the ability, enshrined in legislation, to veto proposals in these areas; if they don't assent to the proposal it can't proceed.

Another interesting dimension of the situation in Germany is that the works council also has other legal rights, on some issues to be consulted and on others to be informed, and this distinction is indicative of different degrees and forms of employee participation to which we return also later in this section.

Are there any areas in which there are traditions in the UK of complete employee autonomy? In the past, and with some success in certain occupations such as printing, film and television technicians, trade unions have tried to control entry into particular occupations and jobs. However, since the effective outlawing of the closed shop this is now both more difficult and less common. They have also sought to control the pace of work and, in some cases, the allocation of work between the various members of a group, often through informal systems of control, and they have sought to control the work entitlements of certain trades or crafts so that certain types of work or tasks were to all intents and purposes 'owned' by a particular trade or group. Discipline has also been the subject of employee control in some circumstances, though it is probably more common that trade unions in particular have shied away even from joint decision-making in this area since they consider it inappropriate to take part in the decision to discipline, preferring to protect their 'independence' from the disciplinary decision so that they may more vigorously perform their representative role, taking up the case of someone who is the subject of such action.

In recent years a number of organizations have experimented with extending employee autonomy to issues concerned with the allocation and organization of work in the context of self-managing or semi-autonomous teams, though output targets generally remain the prerogative of management.

These are schemes that are often incorporated into EI initiatives and they usefully demonstrate the distinction between 'How?' and 'What?' decisions, with management arguably more willing to grant employees autonomy in decisions concerned with the How than with the What. The distinction here is between being able to determine the objectives (the What), for example production targets in terms of both quantity and quality, and decisions relating to the How in terms of the means of organizing, allocating and inspecting work so as to achieve the objectives set.

Activity 4

Look at the following list of subjects and ask yourself in each case whether you think employees should control or take part in the particular area of decision-making:

1   organizational structure
2   economic and financial state of company
3   probable developments in the business, production and sales
4   employment situation and trends
5   investment plans
6   organizational change
7   working methods and processes
8   transfers of production
9   mergers
10 cutbacks and closures
11 collective redundancies
12 employee transfers, promotions and dismissals
13 payment schemes and other substantive terms and conditions of employment
14 allocation and pace of work
16 discipline.

Collective bargaining

There are several definitions of collective bargaining, each slightly different (see **Figure 9.3**).

Activity 5

Look at the three definitions of collective bargaining in **Figure 9.3** and identify the common elements of the definitions and also how they differ.

The essence of the process is that employees and/or their representatives, and employers and/or their representatives negotiate with one another with a view to reaching an agreement on a range of issues, each of which may be perceived as a symptom of the inherent conflicts of interest that include both procedural and substantive matters. The scope and range of the possible subject matter is very wide and can encompass pretty well anything that concerns work and the employment relationship: terms and con-

---

The International Labour Office (1986, Convention No. 154) defines collective bargaining as encompassing:

> all negotiations between employers (or employers' organizations) and workers' organizations for the purpose of determining relations between them.

Gospel and Palmer (1993: 15) describe it as

> a process by which trades unions and similar associations representing groups of employees, negotiate with employers or their representatives with the object of reaching collective agreements.

Salamon (1992: 309) defines it as

> a method of determining terms and conditions of employment which utilizes the process of negotiation and agreement between representatives of management and employees.

Figure 9.3 Definitions of collective bargaining

ditions of employment and working conditions are certainly encompassed. The process need not be formal and it is a fallacy to assume that collective bargaining only occurs within the confines of formal institutional arrangements, experienced practitioners on both sides will usually readily acknowledge the value and frequency of informal negotiations and the agreements that are arrived at.

The single feature of the process that sets it aside from other joint employee relations processes is the intention to reach agreement. When parties enter into and engage in collective bargaining they are overtly or tacitly agreeing to share the decision-making on the particular issue, the outcome is to be subject to agreement. If there is not this intention to reach agreement then the process is not collective bargaining. Central also is the willingness to move and compromise, the willingness to negotiate. It is then a process that has as its intended outcomes jointly agreed decisions.

Students sometimes make the mistake of thinking that collective bargaining is the only employee relations process or scenario in which negotiations occur. This is not the case and it is quite common for management and employees and their respective representatives to negotiate in other circumstances, such as when an individual grievance is heard.

Collective bargaining as a process occurs for a number of reasons, one of which is the mutual dependence of the parties to the employment relationship; each of the parties needs the other and it is this mutual need that encourages them to try and reach agreement through negotiations. Each has something that the other needs and wants, for example the employee has his labour to sell and the employer needs to acquire and use that labour in the production or delivery of goods and services. However, the employee needs to try to obtain the best possible price for his labour whereas the employer's interest is to pay as little as possible for the labour resource.

In the UK there is a tradition of adversarial, rather than cooperative, bargaining in which each party seeks to exert pressure upon the other in order to persuade them to move towards a compromise position. It is for this reason that the process is sometimes referred to as being power-based and the concept of bargaining power is integral to the process and to an understanding of the outcomes.

We have noted in the chapter looking at ideology and the roles of government (Chapter 5) that collective bargaining was supported as part of the voluntarist tradition as the process that provided the means through which employees could collectively seek to remedy the imbalance of power between employer and individual employee that seems normally to exist in favour of employers (capital) in the labour market.

The tradition in the UK prior to 1980 was of main terms and conditions of employment being determined through collective bargaining and at a national or multi-employer level. The Donovan Commission Report (1968) had criticized employers in the private sector for abdicating their responsibilities for the conduct of industrial relations within their own companies and it had recommended a greater incidence of bargaining at the level of the firm, otherwise and commonly referred to as single employer bargaining.

We noted earlier in Chapter 7 on trade unions that the incidence and importance of collective bargaining as the mechanism through which rates of pay and other terms and conditions of employment were determined has declined since the election of a Conservative government in 1979. The percentage of workplaces in which a trade union was recognized for the purposes of collective bargaining having declined from 66 per cent in 1984 to 45 per cent in 1998. The provisions of the Employment Relations Act 1999, which give the unions some limited legal rights to recognition for collective bargaining, might be expected to halt this decline in the incidence and importance of collective bargaining.

In addition, a number of studies (for example, WIRS, 1990; Millward *et al.*, 1992; Brown, 1993) have demonstrated change in the dominant level at which the bargaining takes place.

There are also significant differences in both the extent and level of bargaining between the various sectors within the economy. Collective bargaining is still at its most extensive within the public sector and it still occurs at a national level in this sector to a greater extent than in other sectors. Manufacturing industry runs second to the public sector and the service sector demonstrates the least reliance upon collective bargaining for the determination of terms and conditions of employment and it is least likely to demonstrate national or multi-employer bargaining.

In addition to a shift from multi-employer to single employer bargaining there has been a shift downwards within large companies from bargaining at the level of the firm to bargaining at the level of the division or other business unit, region or establishment: a decentralization within organizations as well as decentralization from multi-employer to single employer (Purcell and Ahlstrand, 1994). This decentralization has been much more common in the private sector and, despite the open desire of government to achieve a measure of decentralization within the public sector, here it has been much less successful, partially because the unions have generally opposed the proposals. See **Figure 5.5**, which refers to union opposition to the decentralization of pay bargaining in the NHS.

There are many reasons why employers and government may prefer to decentralize the level at which collective bargaining takes place:

1 To achieve a greater congruence with the level of business decision-making. There has been a significant decentralization of this over the same period, a response often to the need to be more flexible and more responsive to the requirements of the customer. As an aid to the creation of a divisional or subsidiary identity.

2 To facilitate the introduction of local pay bargaining in the public sector to reflect the creation of new structures, the NHS probably provides the best-known example of this intent, and because the Conservative government in office until 1997 was convinced that local pay bargaining would

result in a lower overall pay bill. This latter rested on the assumption that in many parts of the country the nationally agreed rates of pay are greater than would be determined through the operation of the local labour market.

3 Contrary to 1 above, actually to separate the levels of collective bargaining and business decision-making, thereby giving management more freedom to act. If decisions to invest and locate are taken at corporate level it might be preferable to keep the unions away from this level so that they find it difficult to apply pressure at the appropriate level and time. This is sometimes known as a process of institutional separation.

Purcell (1989) produced an interesting catalogue of the issues that management should consider when deciding whether to decentralize collective bargaining or not and there are many combinations of circumstances. It is clear from his analysis that there are no common recipes for success; in some circumstances centralization at the level of the company may be the beneficial solution, in others it would be decentralization. He produced something akin to a checklist that management could use in the event of their considering a decentralization. He suggests that prior to making a decision on the issue management should consider:

1 the impact upon existing procedures and arrangements
2 the role, structure and staffing of the personnel function
3 the role of the first line supervisor and the impact of decentralized bargaining upon it
4 the impact upon the representatives of the trade unions, the shop stewards and the full-time officials
5 the impact of decentralization upon the integration of policy, strategy and practice
6 the impact of the change upon consistency across the company.

You must also beware of thinking that collective bargaining only occurs at one level within any particular industry, sector or organization. It has been common in this country that bargaining occurs at a number of different levels, so that within one industry you might have:

● bargaining at the level of the industry that dealt with certain subject matter, such as minimum rates of pay or national levels of holiday entitlement
● bargaining at the level of the firm where other subjects are dealt with, an example in this context might be the firm's occupational pension scheme or particular shift work pattern or, indeed, the interpretation and implementation of the national level agreement
● bargaining at the level of the division or at the level of the workplace where other matters might be dealt with, such as enhancements to national terms and conditions of employment to enable the firm to com-

pete in the local labour market and the implications of the introduction of new working methods or technology.

You should remember that the rules produced as the outputs of the system are both substantive and procedural and it is not uncommon to find procedures being agreed at national level which seek to determine how issues are to be dealt with at the various possible lower levels. If you have difficulty with the distinction between substantive and procedural agreements it might be helpful to think of substantive agreements and rules determining the What of terms and conditions of employment, for example rates of pay, hours of work and holiday entitlements etc. The procedures are concerned more with the How, and again examples might include the procedures to be followed in handling disciplinary issues or individual grievances or impending redundancies.

It has been suggested that the initial stimulus for collective bargaining tends to come from the trade unions rather than employers and that in the first instance it is matters of substance (some have labelled these as economic issues) that are the subject matter of the bargaining. However, while this is usually so, it is commonly not long before the parties realize that they need to agree between themselves just how they are going to conduct the bargaining: what is to be acceptable or not in terms of the behaviour of the parties, what rights and obligations they are to have to each other, whether industrial action is to be allowed and, if so, what constraints are to be imposed upon its use, how often they are to meet, are the agreements reached to be legally binding, for a fixed term? You begin to see the range of procedural issues that can be involved and the subject matter of agreement between the parties.

These procedural issues and agreements can be seen as the parties determining for themselves the rules within which they will operate and it is this which has encouraged the view that collective bargaining is at heart a rule-making process, the rules providing part of the context within which the parties to the employment relationship interact with each other. A process that in part results in a system, voluntarily agreed and implemented, of industrial governance, they form their own rules and conventions to govern their relationship. See Chamberlain and Kuhn (1965) who devised a model of collective bargaining in which they identify three forms or stages in the development of collective bargaining, one of which approximates to this perception of collective bargaining as a system of industrial governance.

In discussing this, Farnham and Pimlott (1995) suggest that 'Underlying the concept of collective bargaining as a process of industrial governance is the principle that those who are integral to the running of the enterprise should have some voice in determining the decisions of most concern to them'. Again, as mentioned above, we are confronted by the political and moral dimensions of employee participation.

As the area of subject matter (sometimes you will find the term 'scope' used in this context) that is subject to joint determination through collective bargaining expands, so also does the participation of the employees, through their trade union, in the management of the enterprise. As the scope of collective bargaining expands the area of managerial prerogative should logically diminish.

We noted in the earlier chapter on trade unions (Chapter 7) that the union movement in the UK has been engaged in a change of direction in terms of their objectives and their approach and that there has been a formal shift by the TUC in the direction of cooperation and the conclusion of partnership agreements. It is possible that such agreements may include a diminished or even negligible role for collective bargaining and its replacement by some form of consultation arrangement.

Figure 9.4 shows an article from *The Guardian*, giving some idea of what a partnership agreement might contain.

Activity 6

We have mentioned above that collective bargaining has been the dominant process in the UK and, indeed, it is also the case that it is the dominant process in many of the other countries in Europe. The structures may be different but the process has been common. What do you think may be the minimum requirements for collective bargaining to develop and continue?

Activity 7

In an earlier chapter (Chapter 1) we looked at the issue and relevance of perspective and we looked in some detail at three particular perspectives. Think back now to your understanding of those three perspectives and try to work out for yourself how each might view the process.

Joint consultation

Perhaps the first thing to say about joint consultation is that it is a category of process that includes the works council. Works councils have not been common in the UK but are common in the rest of the EU and it is likely that we will over the coming years become more used to them and more used to joint consultative arrangements being formally encompassed within works councils, the term is likely to be more widely used.

Works councils can take a number of forms and there is no one blueprint. The term is used in some countries in Europe to apply to groups of

Seumas Milne

Fourteen years ago, maverick electricians' leader Eric Hammond — now, in his retirement, leading the campaign to save the grammar schools — was heckled when he told the TUC in Brighton that partnership with employers was the way of the future. This week, scarcely a single TUC heavyweight will mount the same rostrum without paying homage to the "partnership agenda".

We are all partners now. The days of "them and us" confrontation are over, TUC general secretary John Monks, has declared. Partnership is the TUC's very own third way between what Monks calls "militant trade unionism and 80s-style macho management". Working together solves problems, adds value and "shapes change".

The new passion was given a ringing endorsement by a previously somewhat sceptical prime minister in May. Even employers — who, until the election, had shown precious little interest in unions as partners — are now rushing to join the bandwagon, with businessmen such as Niall Fitzgerald of Unilever and Sir Peter Middleton of Barclays Bank among true believers.

Under New Labour the political and industrial climate has changed. Stoppages are at an all time low — the table shows what causes the few there are. Next summer there is the prospect of a legally-enforceable right to union recognition under the employment relations act. No wonder then that partnership agreements with trade unions have taken on a new allure for employers. Tesco and Barclays, Littlewoods and Unisys, Legal and General and Go! are among the better-known firms to make such deals with unions in the past year or so, to add to earlier examples, such as Blue Circle and Rover. The TUC expects more, adding thousands to the TUC's already growing membership.

Not that the notion of union cooperation with employers is exactly a novelty in British industrial relations, stretching back as it does back through the new realism of the 80s and "Mondism" in the 20s to the TUC's founding conference in 1868, when two separate traditions — collaboration vs confrontation — were already well in evidence. Monks believes the TUC can embrace both: partnership for good employers and militancy for those who won't play ball.

Partnership can be a very elastic term indeed. Most union leaders hanker after the arrangement now under attack in Germany, complete with legally-underpinned structures of participation at company, industrial and national level. CBI president Sir Clive Thompson of Rentokil is all in favour of partnership but thinks it best achieved without any union involvement at all.

Most deals involve trading flexibility and a commitment to avoid industrial action with a measure of job security and scope for union recruitment. Genuine partnerships, according to the TUC, should include a joint commitment to the success of the organisation, recognition of the two sides' differing roles and interests, some guarantee of job security, a focus on the quality of working life, openness and clear gains for all.

But it is not only employers who have other ideas. Sir Ken Jackson of the Amalgamated

Reasons for disputes

UK, 12 months to June 1999

	Working days lost	Number of stoppages	Workers involved
Wage-rates & earnings levels	161,400	45	72,600
Redundancy questions	49,800	23	10,900
Working conditions & supervision	18,200	13	4,700
Dismissal & other disciplinary measures	14,900	22	6,400
Extra wage & fringe benefits	7,800	8	3,900
Manning & work allocation	3,300	26	2,800
Duration & pattern of hours worked	2,800	12	2,600
Trade union matters	1,500	5	1,200
All causes	259,700	154	105,200

Source: ONS, Labour Market Trends

Engineering and Electrical Union — successor to Eric Hammond and leader of Tony Blair's favourite union — has been stealing a march on his rivals and, under the banner of partnership, signing the kind of no-strike deals that got the electricians' union expelled from the TUC in the late 80s.

Not surprisingly, employers faced with the prospect of having to recognise trade unions under the new legislation are happy to be able to do business with such unions as the AEEU. A single-union deal, with the Western Mail and Echo in Cardiff, fixed up over the heads of the established journalists' and print unions' members, had threatened to spoil this week's party in Brighton until the AEEU staged a last-minute tactical retreat under TUC pressure.

Bill Morris, leader of the Transport and General Workers' Union — whose position is being undermined by the AEEU in the airline industry — says the "biggest threat to partnership comes from those who are running around offering sweetheart deals and saying to the employers, 'tell me what you want, boss, and we will call it partnership' ".

Earlier this summer, John Monks warned that unions needed to be "partners, not poodles" and even some employers fear Sir Ken's over-enthusiasm risks discrediting partnership altogether.

Yet the difficulties of trying to transplant industrial structures from the European mainland, where unions have undergone nothing like the pulverising treatment they have in Britain over the past 20 years, go wider than one rogue player. As the unlikely figure of Peter Mandelson reminded last year's TUC, the relationship between employer and employee is by its nature fundamentally unequal. Any partnership with employers is likely to be lopsided until more progress is made in recruiting in the new industries and workplaces.

Already, partnership is noticeably less popular lower down union hierarchies, where there are complaints about how much the deals deliver in practice. The much-vaunted Tesco agreement, for example, has already led to a loss of Sunday working premiums. The Rover deal's job guarantees have not proved as robust as some hoped. With evidence that other groups of workers — in the Post Office, rail and airline industries, for example — have benefited from a tougher approach, grumbling from the union side is likely to grow.

Seumas Milne is the Guardian's labour editor. Find useful links at www.newsunlimited.co.uk/analysis

Figure 9.4 *Source: The Guardian* 15 September 1999, p. 19

employee representatives only who meet together as the works council and also the council may then meet with management. In other countries the term 'works council' refers to the joint meeting of management and employee representatives and the council in these systems comprises both management and employee representatives. In a number of EU countries there are legal rights to form a works council, for that council to meet with management on a regular basis and for the meeting to have an agenda that is itself legally prescribed. It is also possible for the councils to have different legal rights in terms of the right to information, consultation and the right to agree or veto proposals, depending upon the subject matter under discussion.

Though there are pressures for change around the end of the century, the system that has dominated the post-war period in Germany (see **Figure 9.5**) is an example of one which is legally underpinned and which has traditionally encompassed these three sets of rights. Which right applies is dependent upon the subject matter.

Whilst not common perhaps there are examples of joint consultative arrangements in companies in the UK that also differentiate the rights of the employee representatives according to the subject matter. The following is an extract from the first section of an agreement in a manufacturing operation in the UK:

Function of the JCC.

1.1 For employee representatives and the Company's management to convey and discuss any legitimate concerns relating to performance efficiency, operating conditions and facts, and the general conditions of employment.

1.2 To receive, from the Company's management, information on the company's current trading position and future prospects.

This particular Company also requires that employee representatives agree in writing that they will abide by a secrecy agreement safeguarding company information.

Collective bargaining tends to be between recognized trade unions and employers' representatives. Joint consultation may involve trade unions representing the employees but it is also quite common for the process of consultation, even within formal structures, to include as representatives of the employees individual employees elected by their peers or selected and appointed by management.

We noted above the disputes in the early 1990s between the UK government and the EC as to whether the legislation implementing the directives concerned with the requirement for employers to consult on matters relating to collective redundancies and the transfer of an undertaking should specify employee representatives (the directives) or trade union officials (the UK legislation).

Joint consultation in its formal guise has not been as popular in the UK

The works council is the established and legislatively supported mechanism for achieving employee participation within the workplace.

The Works Constitution Acts of 1952 and 1972 constitute the major supporting legislation, although works councils have a history going back to the First World War. This legislation, in addition to requiring the establishment of works councils, also regulates the subject matter and nature of their role.

The works councils are not trade union bodies, the members of the council being elected from among employees with no requirement that they are trade union members.

The role of the councils varies according to the nature of the subject matter. Three distinct roles are identifiable, i.e. the right to give consent, the right to consultation and lastly the right to information.

The right to consent covers a range of economic and personnel issues including discipline, overtime and holiday allocations and schedules, payment systems, piecework rates, safety, welfare, employee performance, the pace of work, working environment, staff selection and training.

Rights to information and consultation relate to a range of production and business matters, although when it comes to business performance and prospects, the rights are limited to those of information only.

Overall, the role of the works council is to look after and protect the interests and safety of employees and in this latter respect in particular they have a monitoring role in respect of company compliance with appropriate legislation.

The nature of the relationship between the main actors is traditionally a consensual one and this is supported by the legislative requirement that they work together in a spirit of mutual trust and for their mutual benefit.

Figure 9.5 Works councils in Germany. Adapted from Hollinshead and Leat 1995, pp. 192–3

as elsewhere in Europe and it has not been as common as collective bargaining. The evidence of the WIRS 1990 (Millward *et al.*, 1992) was that there had been a decline in the incidence of formal joint consultative committees (JCC) arrangements in the private sector. The evidence of the more recent 1998 WERS (Cully *et al.*, 1998) is that the proportion of workplaces with a joint consultative committee in operation at 28 per cent was the same as in 1990. However, this more recent survey also identified that JCCs can and do occur at different levels within organizations; a further 25 per cent of organizations in the survey had a JCC at a higher level, even though there were no such arrangements at workplace level. They also highlight the relevance of size to the presence of JCCs and the level at which they occur. Workplace JCCs tend to occur in the larger workplaces and higher level arrangements tend to occur in the larger organizations. The researchers concluded that in all some 67 per cent of employees were employed in workplaces with joint consultative arrangements at the workplace or some higher level.

However, it must be remembered that there are other mechanisms through which management may seek to consult employees, such as attitude surveys, team briefings, quality circles and suggestion schemes.

There are different perceptions about the nature of joint consultation, what it is and what it should be. There are different versions and the parties may well have different motives, objectives and very different expectations of the outcomes. Managers will often consult with employees on an individual basis or collectively but outside formal joint consultative machinery, for example within the aegis of a team briefing. Our concern here is with the formal joint consultative machinery and the nature of the process. In examining the latter, the nature of the process, Farnham and Pimlott (1995) distinguish between:

1 **Pseudo-consultation**, this refers to the process whereby management or union are doing no more than passing information without giving the other party the opportunity to comment or without listening genuinely to the comments that are made. Commonly management is communicating a decision that is already firmly made. The intention is often not to consult but to give the impression that you are. In such circumstances the process can not be regarded as one in which employees and their representatives are given the opportunity to participate in decision-making.

2 **Classical consultation** describes the process when employees' representatives are given information often in the form of proposals or intentions and asked for their views. When received the views are considered prior to the decision being made. While the process differs from collective bargaining in that there is no commitment even of a moral nature that the process should end in agreement, it is nevertheless in such genuine circumstances possible for the employees' views to influence the decision eventually made and for the process therefore to be classified as a participative one. There is no obligation on either side that goes beyond listening and considering. Management does not give up any of its prerogative in entering into this process, it retains the right to unilaterally decide the issue, though there is the risk that the process will fall into disrepute if management are not seen over a period of time to at least sometimes take note of the views expressed and on occasion to modify its position prior to taking the decision.

3 **Integrative consultation** is described as a mechanism for furthering employee participation in management and it is presented as a process of

joint decision-making on a range of subject matter that is wider than the norm for collective bargaining. The process is commonly much more like a process of joint problem solving.

As noted in the earlier section the responsibility to encourage collective bargaining has been removed from ACAS's legislatively prescribed role and they have shown a preference for encouraging cooperation and partnership. As part of this they have been keen to promote the benefits, as they perceive them, of joint problem solving and joint consultation.

Marchington (1988) has identified four different models or faces of joint consultation and this typology is useful in that it identifies purpose and motive as variables. The four faces are the:

- **non-union model**. This is very similar to the pseudo form of consultation described above and has as its objective the prevention of unionism in the workplace by appearing to give employee representatives a role in decision-making but generally the process is little more than educative
- **competitive model**. Here the intention is to create a process that competes with collective bargaining and thereby to reduce the perceived value and need for collective bargaining
- **adjunct model**. The intent with this model is to distinguish collective bargaining from joint consultation by emphasizing and contrasting the high trust and open interactions of this process with collective bargaining, which tends to be less open and trusting and again it is argued that problem solving is common to this model
- **marginal model**. Here the intention is to keep employee representatives busy in the joint consultative machinery but at a low level, thereby hopefully dissipating any pressure that may have developed for more meaningful relations within either consultation or bargaining machinery.

As indicated by the WERS data joint consultation, like collective bargaining, can occur at a number of different levels within organizations. The subject matter of the consultation will probably vary from one level to another, with consultation at the level of the company much more likely to be on issues of company-wide significance, whereas consultation at the level of the workplace or workgroup is more likely to address issues more relevant to these levels.

It was noted earlier that the EWC directive applies at the level of the company, or at least the European headquarters of the organization, and we have also already indicated the nature of the process, information and consultation, and the range of mandatory subject matter (see Chapter 4). You should be aware that the EWC directive was motivated by both the desire to extend these rights to employees and their representatives but also by an awareness on the part of the EC and many of the member states that it was necessary to try to limit the otherwise unfettered power of the multinational to locate where it chooses and, if the mood takes it, to go regime shopping and play one member state off against another.

In many countries within Europe there is a legal requirement that employers consult with employee representatives on specified subject matters and at specified intervals. In this country the only legal requirements are for consultation with employee representatives in cases of collective redundancy, in the event of a Transfer of Undertaking and on matters relating to health and safety; in each case this is the product of EU legislation rather than as the result of the wishes of employers and the government in this country.

In many respects the attitude of government in the UK does not appear to have changed significantly with the election of New Labour in 1997. They have demonstrated already their preference for partnership and their unwillingness to see the EWC directive replicated at a national level. They have indicated their willingness to veto proposals that similar regulation requiring employees to be informed and consulted via formal machinery of a works council nature should be imposed upon companies at a national level as well as at the EU level.

Activity 8

Take a look back at the above material on joint consultation and collective bargaining and write down what you think it is that differentiates them.

Activity 9

Short answer questions:

1 What are the differences between employee participation and EI?
2 Which processes have gained in popularity in recent years and which have declined?

Summary

In this chapter we have established that there are a range of employee relations processes and that the various schemes and processes imply different degrees of employer autonomy and employee participation in management decision-making and control of the labour process. The point was made that employer autonomy or prerogative and employee participation are in some respects opposite sides of the same coin, in that enhancement of the latter tends to occasion an erosion of the former.

We introduced the notion of a continuum of participation.

The dominant process in the UK has been collective bargaining but, in recent years, the extent and coverage has declined. We have contrasted joint consultation with collective bargaining and have noted that there are different models of joint consultation which focus upon both the purposes of management and the degree of participation. In recent years managements in the UK have shown a preference for EI initiatives and in this chapter we have highlighted the fact that these may or may not be participatory.

Activity Answers

Activity 1

1 It is really only the first Marchington *et al.* model that has a degree of coincidence with the notion of participation as defined by Walker.

2 Strauss's (1979) concentration upon the depth of participation as the degree of control over, or influence in, managerial decision-making represents concern with a much narrower perception of participation than Marchington *et al.* (1992), and it is an interpretation much more consistent with that of Walker (1974). It is an interpretation consistent with only one of the Marchington *et al.* (1992) paradigms, the first one as listed above. You may have thought that there was some connection between Marchington *et al.*'s second model and that of Strauss since there is reference to both consultation and collective bargaining, but the intended outcomes are not employee participation in control and management, they are more concerned with conflict resolution, stability and efficiency.

Activity 2

It is arguable on a number of dimensions that numbers (3) and (4) of the Marchington *et al.* models are more appropriately described as involvement rather than participation paradigms.

Activity 3

1 EI initiatives are most likely to be pursued by managements that are in the sophisticated human relations or paternalist categories; in each case the emphasis is upon the individual and both are likely to seize upon opportunities to demonstrate to employees that they are valued and that they don't need a trade union to look after their interests. Both are also likely to be attracted by the assertion that involved employees will be committed employees, that committed employees will also be happier, happy or satisfied employees perform better and are therefore more productive and profitable. You will find some of these initiatives in unionized firms and therefore it is possible that where employers are using these techniques in the modern paternalist or sophisticated consultative styles categories, in some instances these initiatives have been introduced with the agreement or acquiescence of the unions.

2 Clearly the unitarist perspective is the one that is the most consistent. This perspective sees the organization as a team led by management whose authority should not be challenged and to whom employees should give loyalty. There is no need for joint decision-making but if there

are means that encourage employees to become more committed and productive, which at the same time do not dilute management prerogative, then they are to be seized, in essence this is part of the promise of EI.

Activity 4

There is no right or wrong answer to this question and you will find plenty of different viewpoints. Having said that, the list is not a completely random selection of topic areas, the first eleven are areas covered by the European Works Council Directive (see Chapter 4) and are areas of subject matter upon which the works council in organizations covered by the directive have legal rights to be both informed and consulted (see later for discussion of consultation as a process). Numbers12 and 13 are topics upon which works councils in Germany have a legal right to assent to and which they can therefore veto. The last two are topic areas about which there has periodically been debate and you will find some organizations in which employees do have a role in decision-making and others in which they don't.

Hopefully thinking about this activity has helped you to clarify in your own mind where some of the dividing lines may be and what you think about the legitimate role of employees and their representatives in regard to the question of autonomy and participation.

Activity 5

Common elements: each identifies it as a process involving negotiations, which are conducted between representatives of employees and employers.

Differences: subject matter: the ILO limits the subject matter to terms and conditions of employment and the regulation of relations between the parties. Salaman limits it to terms and conditions only. The Gospel and Palmer description does not seek to limit the subject matter of the process.

Objectives: both Salaman and Gospel and Palmer specify the objectives as one of agreement between the parties, the ILO makes no mention of it. Participants: none of the definitions fall into the trap of limiting the process to one necessarily involving trade unions, as not all employee organizations are trade unions.

Activity 6

There are a range of so-called minimum conditions or requirements which include:

1 freedom of association must at the least be lawful, it must at least be lawful for people to join trade unions and for them to function inside the law
2 employers must be willing to recognize the trade unions or alternatively required to do so by law. In the UK we haven't the same tradition of leg-

islative intervention and statutory rights with respect to trade union membership and recognition. However, there was legislation throughout much of the 1970s and 1980s which made it possible for employees to exert legislative pressure upon their employer to recognize and bargain and the Employment Relations Act 1999 restores some limited rights in this area

3 the parties must negotiate in good faith and adhere to the agreements reached, this is particularly crucial where the parties' participation is essentially voluntary.

Activity 7

The Marxist, or radical, sees it not as the process through which the natural imbalance of power between capital and labour is remedied but as a process through which the interests of capital secure the maintenance of the status quo, the maintenance of the supremacy of the interests of capital over those of labour.

The unitarist will see the process as unnecessary and the means through which employees seek to make an illegitimate attempt to intrude into areas of managerial prerogative, they are likely to view the imbalance of power in favour of capital as both desirable and legitimate.

The pluralist will see collective bargaining as the means through which the power imbalance can be remedied. They will see it as a legitimate conflict-resolving mechanism, the process through which conflict over the price of labour is determined, they may well consider its existence essential to the creation and maintenance of 'good' employee relations, they are likely to see it as a process that results in the joint determination of rules, a process of joint job regulation (Flanders, 1975).

Activity 8

The single feature of collective bargaining that sets it aside from other joint collective employee relations processes, of which joint consultation is probably the main one, is the intention to reach agreement. When parties enter into and engage in collective bargaining they are overtly or tacitly agreeing to share the decision-making, the outcome is to be subject to agreement. If there is not this intention to reach agreement then the process is not collective bargaining, though it may be joint consultation. Central to the reaching of agreement is the willingness to move and compromise, the willingness to negotiate and this is not a requirement of effective joint consultation. It is obviously possible that joint consultation may result in an agreed outcome but it is not central to the process whereas with collective bargaining it is.

Activity 9

1 Some EI processes may provide for employees to participate in managerial decision-making, control or ownership of the enterprise but other EI processes do not. There may be a degree of overlap between the two

concepts but they are not the same. EI processes are generally directed at individuals or work groups and tend to involve employees at this task or decentralized level, they do not generally include a role for trade unions and the objectives for initiating the processes may include the desire to bypass or weaken the trade unions.

2 The processes that have gained in popularity as measured by frequency of use are those that fall into the category of EI and the processes that can be described as unilateral managerial determination. Collective bargaining has been the main sufferer, though there is also some evidence that formal joint consultation has also declined

References

Beer, M., Spector, B., Lawrence, P.R., Quinn Mills, D. and Walton, R., 1984. *Managing Human Assets.* Free Press, New York.

Brown, W., 1993. The contraction of collective bargaining in Britain. *British Journal of Industrial Relations* 31(2): 189–200.

Chamberlain, N. and Kuhn, J.W., 1965. *Collective Bargaining.* McGraw-Hill.

Cully, M., O'Reilly, A., Millward, N., Forth, J., Woodland, S., Dix, G. and Bryson, A., 1998. *The Workplace Employee Relations Survey: First Findings.* DTI, ACAS, ESRC, PSI, London.

Donovan Commission Report, 1968. The Report of the Royal Commission on Trade Unions and Employers Associations. Command 3623, HMSO, London.

Farnham, D. and Pimlott, J., 1995. *Understanding Industrial Relations.* 5th Edition. Cassell, London.

Flanders, A., 1975. Collective bargaining: a theoretical analysis. In Flanders, A., *Management and Unions.* Faber & Faber, London.

Gospel, H. and Palmer, G., 1993. *British Industrial Relations.* Routledge, London.

Guest, D., 1989. Personnel and HRM: can you tell the difference? *Personnel Management,* January: 48–51.

Hollinshead, G. and Leat, M., 1995. *Human Resource Management: An International and Comparative Perspective on the Employment Relationship.* Financial Times Pitman, London.

ILO, 1986. Convention No. 154.

Marchington, M., 1988. The Four Faces of Employee Consultation. *Personnel Management,* May. London.

Marchington, M. and Wilkinson, A., 1996. *Core Personnel and Development.* IPD, London.

Marchington, M., Goodman, J., Wilkinson, A. and Ackers, P., 1992. *Recent Developments in Employee Involvement.* Employment Department Research Series No. 1, HMSO, London.

Millward, N., Stevens, M., Smart, D. and Hawes, W.R., 1992. *Workplace Industrial Relations in Transition.* Dartmouth, Aldershot.

Poole, M. and Mansfield, R., 1992. Managers' attitudes to Human Resource Management: rhetoric and reality. In Blyton, P. and Turnbull, P. (eds), *Reassessing Human Resource Management*. Sage, London.

Purcell, J., 1989. How to manage decentralised collective bargaining. *Personnel Management*, May. London.

Purcell, J. and Ahlstrand, B., 1994. *Human Resource Management in the Multi-divisional Company*. Oxford University Press, Oxford.

Salamon, M., 1992. *Industrial Relations: Theory and Practice*. 2nd Edition. Prentice Hall, Englewood Cliffs, NJ.

Strauss, G., 1979. Workers' participation: symposium introduction. *Industrial Relations* 18: 247–261.

Walker, K.F., 1974. Workers' participation in management: problems, practice and prospects. *Bulletin of the International Institute for Labour Studies* 12: 3–35.

Chapter 10

Employee relations procedures

Chapter
Outline

- Introduction
- Procedures – what are they and why have them?
- Disciplinary procedures
  The ACAS Code of Practice on Disciplinary Practice and Procedures
  The principles of natural justice
  Issues and considerations
  Stages and warnings, number and type
  Records
- Grievance procedures and handling
  Definitions
  Issues and considerations
  Information and representation
  Subject matter coverage/jurisdiction of the procedure
  Stages
  Time limits
- Grievance handling
  Negotiation
  The hearing/interview
- Chapter summary

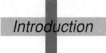

Introduction

In this section we examine in a little more detail the procedural dimension of employee relations, why organizations have procedures, the sorts of areas in which they do and the legal requirements for procedures. These procedures constitute outcomes of the interaction between the parties to the employment relationship that then also become part of the context within which that interaction takes place and that impose constraints upon it.

It used to be relatively common in the UK for employee relations procedures to have national as well as organizational structures. However, with the decline of national-level arrangements and interactions, it is probably the case that at the turn of the millennium the dominant level at which these procedures occur is that of the organization and this is the level upon which we concentrate in this chapter.

We are not able to examine all of the possible procedural areas in great depth, however in this chapter we do examine procedures for managing and handling discipline and grievances and in the following chapter we consider procedures relating to equality and discrimination. Firstly, however, we examine what procedures are and what they do and then we identify the reasons for having procedures.

Objectives

After studying this chapter you will be able to:

- Discuss the reasons for having employee relations procedures, including legislative requirements, and their implications for managerial prerogative
- Identify and discuss criteria against which the effectiveness of procedures may be assessed
- Explain why disciplinary procedures is one of the areas in which there has been the greatest degree of legal intervention and the quasi-legislative nature of the Code of Practice
- Identify and discuss the principles of natural justice
- Examine disciplinary procedures against the requirements of good practice and the law
- Explain the difference between a grievance and a dispute
- Identify and discuss issues and elements of good practice in the devising and drafting of grievance procedures
- Advise on some of the dos and don'ts, skills and aptitudes need to manage discipline and handle grievances effectively.

Procedures – what are they and why have them?

It was noted in Chapter 1 that among the outcomes of the industrial relations system (Dunlop, 1958) are both substantive and procedural rules. The procedural outcomes tend to govern the relationship between the parties to the employment relationship, how they deal with each other and with particular issues and situations. In a sense, the procedures provide the constitution, the set of principles and rules, within and by which the employment relationship should be conducted, but they are also operational mechanisms used by the parties in the day-to-day handling of issues. For example, as we see later in this chapter, a disciplinary procedure should inform and guide the parties as to the rights and obligations of both employee and management, the sanctions and options available to both parties as well as how the situation should be handled.

The industrial relations system of Dunlop (1958) tended to assume that these procedures would be the product of joint decision-making through the process of collective bargaining. However, they may equally well be the product of unilateral decision-making by management and/or the response to a legal requirement.

In advocating the joint determination of procedures Hawkins (1979) argued that agreed procedures can be seen as a voluntary code of behaviour encompassing restraints upon the use by the parties of their respective power, though it must be remembered that the parties are likely to have used this power in reaching the procedural agreement.

Examples of areas in which there is a legal requirement to have certain procedures in place or which has procedural implications, include:

- the formation of health and safety committees and the procedural and consultation rights of the safety representative
- the consultation of employee representatives in the event of collective redundancies and/or a transfer of undertaking
- there are implied legal requirements that an organization have in place some form of a grievance procedure and also a disciplinary appeals procedure
- there is legislation designed to ensure equality of access and treatment and an absence of discrimination on grounds relating to gender and racial or ethnic origin

and the Employment Relations Act 1999 contained provisions concerned to give individual employees rights to trade union representation on grievances and disciplinary issues and, in certain circumstances, giving trade unions a right to be recognized for the purposes of representation and collective bargaining (see Chapter 7).

It is not that unusual for a large organization to have a set of procedures that encompass most if not all of the following areas of subject matter and circumstances:

- trade union recognition, individual representation, negotiating and dispute resolution procedures
- joint consultative procedures and arrangements

- grievance procedures
- redundancy procedures
- discipline and/or dismissal procedures
- performance appraisal procedures
- the implementation and operation of payment systems
- job evaluation procedures
- promotion and transfer procedures
- equality of treatment, access and harassment etc.
- procedures governing the introduction of new technology.

However, before looking at specific procedural areas we should examine why it is a good idea for organizations and the respective parties to devise, develop and implement procedural rules. We need also to ask what are the criteria for the success of procedures.

The proceduralization of industrial/employee relations in the UK was given substantial encouragement by the Donovan Commission Report in 1968 and also by the subsequent work of the Commission on Industrial Relations, a third-party government agency established subsequent to the Donovan Report initially as a Royal Commission, and the 1971 Industrial Relations Act. The Donovan Commission felt that the lack of appropriate procedures was the cause of many disputes.

Marchington and Wilkinson (1996) identify a number of reasons why employers implement procedures in the area of employee relations:

1 they help to clarify the relationship between the parties within the organization
2 they should focus conflict within the agreed mechanisms and thereby help with its resolution, they can create a framework for good employee relations. Note that there are similarities here with the pluralist approach to the question of what constitutes good employee/industrial relations, see the earlier discussion of this in Chapter 1
3 they provide a mechanism for conflict resolution by identifying the position or person that has the role of, or responsibility to, deal with the issue in the first instance and also what the subsequent procedures may be, who deals with appeals against the original decision, how many stages there are to be etc.
4 they act as a safety valve and provide time during which the heat in a situation can be diffused
5 they help ensure that employees are treated consistently throughout the organization no matter who their first line manager may be and no matter which part of the organization they work in
6 they tend to lead to more adequate record keeping because of the formality of the procedure, because the parties know that their performance is likely to be judged against the requirements of the procedure so there is an incentive for records to be kept
7 procedures that are jointly agreed may yield benefits in terms of the work-

ing relationship between the parties to the process of negotiation, it may even be that this process takes on the nature of joint problem solving and is more cooperative/collaborative in nature.

The majority of these reasons can be viewed as reasons for management to want to have procedures and are, in that sense, of advantage to management. From the employees' viewpoint an advantage often claimed for devising and implementing procedures is that they provide a foundation for the achievement of fairness and equity in the treatment of employees and it is interesting that Marchington and Wilkinson (1996) do not include equity of treatment as a specific 'reason' in their list above. Consistency may be more important to managers and it may be argued that equity is achieved through consistent treatment.

We need also to bear in mind that agreed procedures do represent a further incursion into what would otherwise be an area of managerial prerogative. Therefore, the process of agreeing the procedures itself yields benefits to employees and their representatives, reinforcing the legitimacy of their participation in managerial decision-making within the organization.

While the list above contains a number of benefits to management we must not assume that all managements and all levels of management within an organization are going to share these views of the usefulness of procedures. In recent years the bargaining power of managements has increased and they have felt more able to voice their criticisms and uncertainties about the advantages of such procedural arrangements. Perhaps particularly we have seen managers and indeed government arguing that procedures introduce rigidity as well as constituting a brake upon their autonomy. It has been argued that the emphasis upon procedures, encouraged by the Donovan Commission and promoted by organizations such as the CIR and ACAS in its early days, acted as a brake upon the business need to be more flexible and responsive to changes in customer tastes and to the threats of global competition. Managers have criticized procedures for leading to long-drawn-out decision-making processes which are no longer appropriate; sometimes hard decisions have to be taken and they have to be taken quickly if the organization is to survive and prosper.

Other criticisms tend to come from the lower levels of line management who often see procedures, especially if they are the product of agreement with the trade unions, as a direct attack upon their right and ability effectively to manage their own particular group of employees. The provision of rights for employees to appeal against or raise grievances against first line supervision is perceived as a direct threat to their autonomy and also often as a weakening of support from more senior levels of management. The personnel function which tends to be involved in devising and agreeing the procedures is often the subject of criticism from other managerial functions for its role in the formulation of these rules and their nature.

Other criticisms of the procedural and collective approach emerge from the new emphasis upon individualism, individual contract, linking pay and individual performance and the future, compared with the perceived procedural emphasis upon the past and precedent, and consistency and equity. Many managers do not appreciate that there may be a relationship between equitable treatment and employee commitment, another of the much discussed 'new' objectives of management in the EI era, and employees may perceive flexibility as simply another word for arbitrary treatment.

We must also bear in mind that having a procedure doesn't necessarily mean that it will be used or implemented properly. There is commonly a degree of difference between the espoused policies and procedures in an organization and what actually happens in practice on the ground and there are many reasons why this may be so. Relationships at work can become very emotional and in such circumstances agreed procedures can be forgotten very easily, sometimes decisions do have to be taken on the spot and quickly and it may well be that there just isn't time to progress an issue through the agreed procedures, though this may say more about the organization and design of work and the appropriateness of the procedures than anything else. Sometimes you will find that procedures are not followed because the parties at ground level aren't sure of what they are and what they mean. There may be failings in the process by which they are communicated and it may be that the organization hasn't invested in the appropriate training for managers in how to implement them. It is also possible that non-adherence is deliberate on the part of either party.

One common event is for stages in procedures to be missed out or deliberately bypassed. Commonly the first line supervisor is missed out as a stage in the procedures either because it is their action that is the subject of the procedural complaint or because it has been realized that they don't have the power to make a decision and going through that procedural stage is simply a waste of time. This kind of bypassing is of course only possible if more senior management allow it to happen. To prevent it managers need to say 'no', and they often find this difficult when at the same time they claim to operate an open-door policy or have emphasized open communications.

When it comes to assessing the effectiveness of procedures there are obviously a number of criteria that one can use as the base for the assessment but, looking back at the above, maybe the main criterion is or should be whether they are used or not, the implication being that if the parties actually use the procedures it is likely to be because their experience leads them to the conclusion that they work:

- that they contain or provide a mechanism for the resolution of conflict
- that they do lead to greater consistency and equity, and/or
- that they do ensure that the organization doesn't become liable for legal action to be taken against them.

Many years ago now Marsh and McCarthy (1968) suggested that there were two main criteria for assessing the effectiveness or adequacy of procedures and these were **acceptability** and **appropriateness**.

Read the above again and devise lists of the advantages and disadvantages to both management and employees of having effective employee relations procedures.

Disciplinary procedures

Disciplinary procedures are not necessarily dismissal procedures, often these two concepts are used interchangeably and they should not be. One form of disciplinary action may be dismissal, but this should normally be an action of last resort being taken and implemented only when other options have been exhausted. There are also, of course, reasons for dismissal that have absolutely nothing at all to do with issues of discipline.

Nevertheless, it has to be admitted that much of the impetus for the development of disciplinary procedures and the legal significance of these procedures is due to the creation, via the Industrial Relations Act 1971, of the notion of legally fair and unfair dismissal. Subsequent to the creation of this concept of fair and unfair dismissal it was also decided that the absence of a disciplinary procedure, the existence of an inadequate one or the misapplication of an otherwise fair procedure all individually provide legal grounds for claiming and ruling a dismissal unfair. There is in effect a separation between substantive and procedural fairness and a dismissal can be adjudged unfair on either or both grounds.

The ACAS Code of Practice on Disciplinary Practice and Procedures

The other most significant development for disciplinary procedures was the publication in 1977 of the ACAS Code of Practice on Disciplinary Practice and Procedures (see **Figure 10.1** for the latest version of the Code). This document effectively spells out the minimum requirements for a disciplinary procedure to be regarded by the Industrial (recently renamed Employment) Tribunals and Courts as fair. The Code itself is not legally binding, it has a kind of quasi-legal status in that it can be taken into account by the relevant legal authorities when trying to judge whether a dismissal was fair. Over the years as the tribunals and courts have done this and through the device known as case law the code has acquired an authority that to all intents and purposes means: 'comply with the code or run the risk of the dismissal being found unfair'. Remember that the Code is concerned with discipline, not only dismissals.

The principles of natural justice

The Code of Practice asserts the importance of the principles of natural justice in the event of someone having an allegation made against them. The principles of natural justice would normally be considered to include the right to be:

- informed of the complaint against you
- given the opportunity to state your case before a decision is reached
- accompanied by a friend, trade union or legal representative
- given the outcome of the hearing in writing
- provided with and informed of your right of appeal.

Additionally, the Code recommends that:

- the procedures and rules should be in writing and specify to whom they apply
- the rules should clearly indicate the type of offence or failing that might render the individual liable to summary dismissal, such offences would normally fall into the category known as gross misconduct
- the procedures should ensure that employees are not normally dismissed for a first offence, unless the offence is considered to be gross misconduct
- the procedures should provide for matters to be dealt with quickly
- there should be a clear indication of the actions that may be taken
- the procedures should specify clearly those members of management that have the authority to dismiss
- the allegations are carefully investigated before any action is taken
- the procedures apply to all employees with no discrimination between them
- any period of suspension for the purposes of investigation is with pay unless the contract of employment specifically provides otherwise.

Generally, the actions taken should be appropriate to the circumstances and action should not be taken against an individual unless management feel that on the balance of probability the employee did in fact commit the alleged offence. The burden of proof is not as onerous as the criminal legal burden of proof when proof should be beyond a reasonable doubt.

The ACAS Code of Practice on disciplinary practice and procedures in employment

This revised Code from pages 7 to 15 [pp.37–43] revises the *ACAS Code of Practice on Disciplinary Practice and Procedures in Employment* which came into effect on 20 June 1977 and was issued under section 6 of the Employment Protection Act 1975 (now section 199 of the Trade Union and Labour Relations (Consolidation) Act 1992 ("the 1992 Act")).

This revised Code is issued under section 201 of the 1992 Act and was laid before both Houses of Parliament on 28 October 1997. This code comes into effect by order of the Secretary of State on 5 February 1998.

In accordance with section 201, this revised Code makes minor changes only to the earlier Code in order to bring it into conformity with statutory provisions subsequent to that Code.

Effect of failure to comply with Code

A failure on the part of any person to observe any provision of this Code of Practice does not of itself render that person liable to any proceedings.

In any proceedings before an industrial tribunal or the Central Arbitration Committee any Code of Practice issued under sections 199 and 201 of the Trade Union and Labour Relations (Consolidation) Act 1992 is admissible in evidence, and any

provision of the Code which appears to the tribunal or Committee to be relevant to any question arising in the proceedings is required to be taken into account in determining that question. (Trade Union and Labour Relations (Consolidation) Act 1992, section 207).

Introduction

1. This document gives practical guidance on how to draw up disciplinary rules and procedures and how to operate them effectively. Its aim is to help employers and trade unions as well as individual employees – both men and women – wherever they are employed, regardless of the size of the organisation in which they work. In the smaller establishments it may not be practicable to adopt all the detailed provisions, but most of the features listed in paragraph 10 could be adopted and incorporated into a simple procedure.

Why have disciplinary rules and procedures?

2. Disciplinary rules and procedures are necessary for promoting fairness and order in the treatment of individuals and in the conduct of industrial relations. They also assist an organisation to operate effectively. Rules set standards of

37

Figure 10.1 The ACAS Code of Practice on Disciplinary Practice and Procedures

conduct at work; procedure helps to ensure that the standards are adhered to and also provides a fair method of dealing with alleged failures to observe them.

3. It is important that employees know what standards of conduct are expected of them and the Employment Rights Act 1996 requires employers to provide written information for their employees about certain aspects of their disciplinary rules and procedures.[1]

4. The importance of disciplinary rules and procedures has also been recognised by the law relating to dismissals, since the grounds for dismissal and the way in which the dismissal has been handled can be challenged before an industrial tribunal. Where either of these is found by a tribunal to have been unfair, the employer may be ordered to reinstate or re-engage the employees concerned and may be liable to pay compensation to them.

Formulating policy

5. Management is responsible for maintaining discipline within the organisation and for ensuring that there are adequate disciplinary rules and procedures. The initiative for establishing these will normally lie with management. However, if they are to be fully effective, the rules and procedures need to be accepted as reasonable both by those who are to be covered by them and by those who operate them. Management should therefore aim to secure the involvement of employees and all levels of management when formulating new or revising existing rules and procedures. In the light of particular circumstances in different companies and industries, trade

[1] *The Employment Rights Act 1996, section I requires employers to provide employees with a written statement of particulars of their employment. Such statements must also specify any disciplinary rules applicable to them and indicate the person to whom they should apply if they are dissatisfied with any disciplinary decision or wish to seek redress of any grievance. The statement should explain any further steps which exist in any procedure for dealing with disciplinary decisions or grievances. The employer may satisfy certain of these requirements by referring the employees to a reasonably accessible document which provides the necessary information. The requirements relating to disciplinary rules and procedures do not apply in the case of an employee where on the day when the employee's employment began the total number of employees employed by his employer and any associated employer was less than twenty.*

[2] *The Employment Rights Act 1996, section III (2)(a) specifies that a complaint of unfair dismissal has to be presented to an industrial tribunal before the end of the 3-month period beginning with the effective date of termination.*

38

Figure 10.1 (*continued*)

union officials[3] may or may not wish to participate in the formulation of the rules but they should participate fully with management in agreeing the procedural arrangements which will apply to their members and in seeing that these arrangements are used consistently and fairly.

Rules

6. It is unlikely that any set of disciplinary rules can cover all circumstances that may arise: moreover, the rules required will vary according to particular circumstances, such as the type of work, working conditions and size of establishment. When drawing up rules, the aim should be to specify clearly and concisely those necessary for the efficient and safe performance of work and for the maintenance of satisfactory relations within the workforce and between employees and management. Rules should not be so general as to be meaningless.

7. Rules should be readily available and management should make every effort to ensure that employees know and understand them. This may be best achieved by giving every employee a copy of the rules and by explaining them orally. In the case of new employees this should form part

of an induction programme.

8. Employees should be made aware of the likely consequences of breaking rules and, in particular, they should be given a clear indication of the type of conduct which may warrant summary dismissal.

Essential features of disciplinary procedures

9. Disciplinary procedures should not be viewed primarily as a means of imposing sanctions. They should also be designed to emphasise and encourage improvements in individual conduct.

10. Disciplinary procedures should:

(a) Be in writing;

(b) Specify to whom they apply.

(c) Provide for matters to be dealt with quickly.

(d) Indicate the disciplinary actions which may be taken.

(e) Specify the levels of management which have the authority to take the various forms of disciplinary action, ensuring that immediate superiors do not normally have the power to dismiss without reference to senior management.

[3] *Throughout this Code, trade union official has the meaning assigned to it by section 119 of the Trade Union and Labour Relations (Consolidation) Act 1992 and means, broadly, officers of the union, its branches and sections, and anyone else, including fellow employees, appointed or elected under the union's rules to represent members.*

39

Figure 10.1 (*continued*)

(f) Provide for individuals to be informed of the complaints against them and to be given an opportunity to state their case before decisions are reached.

(g) Give individuals the right to be accompanied by a trade union representative or by a fellow employee of their choice.

(h) Ensure that, except for gross misconduct, no employees are dismissed for a first breach of discipline.

(i) Ensure that disciplinary action is not taken until the case has been carefully investigated.

(j) Ensure that individuals are given an explanation for any penalty imposed.

(k) Provide a right of appeal and specify the procedure to be followed.

The procedure in operation

11. When a disciplinary matter arises, the supervisor or manager should first establish the facts promptly before recollections fade, taking into account the statements of any available witnesses. In serious cases, consideration should be given to a brief period of suspension while the case is investigated and this suspension should be with pay. Before a decision is made or penalty imposed, the individual should be interviewed and given the opportunity to state his or her case and should be advised of any rights under the procedure, including the right to be accompanied.

12. Often supervisors will give informal oral warnings for the purpose of improving conduct when employees commit minor infringements of the established standards of conduct. However, where the facts of a case appear to call for disciplinary action, other than summary dismissal, the following procedure should normally be observed:

(a) In the case of minor offences the individual should be given a formal oral warning or, if the issue is more serious, there should be a written warning setting out the nature of the offence and the likely consequences of further offences. In either case the individual should be advised that the warning constitutes the first formal stage of the procedure.

(b) Further misconduct might warrant a final written warning which should contain a statement that any recurrence would lead to suspension or dismissal or some other penalty, as the case may be.

(c) The final step might be disciplinary transfer, or disciplinary suspension without pay (but only if these are allowed for by an express or implied condition of the contract of

40

Figure 10.1 (*continued*)

employment), or dismissal, according to the nature of the misconduct. Special consideration should be given before imposing disciplinary suspension without pay and it should not normally be for a prolonged period.

13. Except in the event of an oral warning, details of any disciplinary action should be given in writing to the employee and if desired, to his or her representative. At the same time the employee should be told of any right of appeal, how to make it and to whom.

14. When determining the disciplinary action to be taken, the supervisor or manager should bear in mind the need to satisfy the test of reasonableness in all the circumstances. So far as possible, account should be taken of the employee's record and any other relevant factors.

15. Special consideration should be given to the way in which disciplinary procedures are to operate in exceptional cases. For example:

(a) **Employees to whom the full procedure is not immediately available:**
Special provisions may have to be made for the handling of disciplinary matters among nightshift workers, workers in isolated locations or depots or others who may pose particular problems, for example because no-one is present with the necessary authority to take disciplinary action or no trade union representative is immediately available.

(b) **Trade union officials:**
Disciplinary action against a trade union official can lead to a serious dispute if it is seen as an attack on the union's functions. Although normal disciplinary standards should apply to their conduct as employees, no disciplinary action beyond an oral warning should be taken until the circumstances of the case have been discussed with a senior trade union representative or full-time official.

(c) **Criminal offences outside employment:**
These should not be treated as automatic reasons for dismissal, regardless of whether the offence has any relevance to the duties of the individual as an employee. The main considerations should be whether the offence is one that makes the individual unsuitable for his or her type of work or unacceptable to other employees. Employees should not be dismissed solely because a charge against them is pending or because they are absent through having been remanded in custody.

Appeals

16. Grievance procedures are sometimes used for dealing with disciplinary appeals though it is normally more appropriate to

41

Figure 10.1 (*continued*)

keep the two kinds of procedure separate since the disciplinary issues are in general best resolved within the organisation and need to be dealt with more speedily than others. The external stages of a grievance procedure may, however, be the appropriate machinery for dealing with appeals against disciplinary action where a final decision within the organisation is contested or where the matter becomes a collective issue between management and a trade union.

17. Independent arbitration is sometimes an appropriate means of resolving disciplinary issues. Where the parties concerned agree it may constitute the final stage of procedure.

Records

18. Records should be kept, detailing the nature of any breach of disciplinary rules, the action taken and the reasons for it, whether an appeal was lodged, its outcome and any subsequent developments. These records should be carefully safeguarded and kept confidential.

19. Except in agreed special circumstances, breaches of disciplinary rules should be disregarded after a specified period of satisfactory conduct.

Further action

20. Rules and procedures should be reviewed periodically in the light of any developments in employment legislation or industrial relations practice and if necessary, revised in order to ensure their continuing relevance and effectiveness. Any amendments and additional rules imposing new obligations should be introduced only after reasonable notice has been given to all employees and, where appropriate, their representatives have been informed.

42

Figure 10.1 (*continued*)

Issues and considerations

The Code is accepted as a statement of good practice but it does not answer all the questions that practitioners have with respect to the design and development of appropriate procedures for their own particular organizational circumstances. Many of these other issues are referred to in the later document (ACAS, 1987), which encompasses the original Code but is also an advisory document. In this latter document there are sections on handling disciplinary matters, conducting a disciplinary interview, record keeping and some particular cases and issues such as absence, sub-standard work and dealing with the particular problem of disciplinary action against a trade union official. There isn't space here to examine all of these issues or particular problem situations, nevertheless it is worth mentioning some of the more common areas of difficulty.

Stages and warnings, number and type

The Code suggests a procedure with up to four stages comprised of an initial and informal oral warning which it is suggested may not form part of the formal deciphering procedure, followed by up to two more warning stages, the first of which might be a formal oral or first written warning, with the second a final written warning, to be followed by a fourth stage which might be dismissal. Depending upon the seriousness of the case the procedure might start at any stage and in cases of gross misconduct the first action taken may be the final stage of dismissal.

The original Code raised some issues concerning the difference between an informal and formal oral warning and some analysts have argued that a formal oral warning is a misnomer if a written record is to be made and retained as advised in the Code. The point has also been made that if a written record is to be kept of the oral warning what is the point of distinguishing between the two types of warning when they both end up as written notes or records on the individual's personal file.

This difficulty is partially addressed by the advisory document (ACAS, 1987). The Code remains unchanged but in an Appendix to the document a model procedure is preferred which no longer refers to an informal oral warning as the first stage of the procedure; the first stage becomes the formal oral warning, to be followed by two written warning stages before the last stage, which may be dismissal. However, the later advice doesn't significantly address the issue of 'difference' between formal oral and first written and arguably, once you decide that disciplinary action is necessary why bother with something so complex and indecisive as a formal oral warning which you then keep a record of, surely it is simpler to move straight to a first written warning?

Records

Allied to the above is the question of what you do with the records once you've got them and, perhaps even more important, what do you do with them once the warnings recorded been effectively spent. The essence of the advice in the Code is that records should be kept of all disciplinary action taken and also that the action taken should be accompanied by or include a statement to the individual concerned specifying the duration of the warning as an active entity. In other words, when given a warning of any kind the employee should be told for how long it will remain effective in the context of it being a factor to be taken into account with regard to future disciplinary action. The Code suggests that breaches of disciplinary rules should be disregarded after a specified period of satisfactory conduct/time but doesn't indicate what this should be.

Again this issue is addressed in the later advisory document and, in section six of that advice, the suggestion is made that the length of effectiveness of the action should increase with the severity of the offence; for first warnings it might be appropriate for the warning to remain effective for six months whereas for final warnings a period of twelve months satisfactory conduct might be appropriate. Neither of the documents is really clear as to what should happen to the records once the warning is 'spent'; there is mention of the warning being 'disregarded' and in section six of the later document there is even one mention of 'removed'.

There is also the problem that even if the warning is removed from a file it may not be removed from management's mind and there can hardly ever be incontrovertible proof that prior disciplinary action has been disregarded. In practice there are plenty of examples of warnings remaining on file long after the 'spent' date and there are also examples of records being removed from one file only to be relocated in another file and not necessarily for sinister reasons, many employers feel that they have a duty to keep comprehensive records of and for employees and that the physical destruction of records is not to be countenanced.

See **Figure 10.2** for an example of a disciplinary procedure.

Try to answer without re-reading the text.
The ACAS Code of Practice rests upon the principles of natural justice. What are they? Think of the rights of someone suspected of a criminal offence and if this doesn't help think of the rights you would want to have if the person charged with the criminal offence was you.

DISCIPLINARY PROCEDURE

PURPOSE AND SCOPE

PRINCIPLES

PROCEDURE

GROSS MISCONDUCT

APPEALS

<u>APPENDICES:</u>

1.   **Rights of Staff**

Figure 10.2 An example of a disciplinary procedure. Adapted from one produced for a NHS Trust.

1.   **PURPOSE AND SCOPE**

This procedure is designed to help and encourage all employees to achieve and maintain the highest possible standards of conduct, attendance and job performance. The aim is to ensure consistent fair treatment for all.

2.   **PRINCIPLES**

2.1   No disciplinary action will be taken against an employee until the case has been fully investigated by an independent Manager not in direct line management of the individual concerned. There are three categories of misconduct – Minor Misconduct, Serious Misconduct and Gross Misconduct. (For examples of Gross Misconduct, see para. 4)

2.2   At the onset of disciplinary proceedings a copy of Rights Of Staff (Appendix 1) will be given to the individual concerned. The employee will be advised at every stage in the procedure of the nature of the complaint and will be given the opportunity to state his/her case before any decision is made. All relevant information should be made available to the individual concerned prior to the hearing.

2.3   At all stages the employee will have the right to be accompanied by a trade union representative or work colleague not acting in a legal capacity during the disciplinary interview.

2.4   No employee will be dismissed for a first breach of discipline except in the case of gross misconduct, when the penalty will be dismissal without notice or payment in lieu of notice.

2.5   An employee will have the right to appeal against any disciplinary penalty imposed.

2.6   The procedure may be implemented at any stage if the employee's alleged misconduct warrants such action.

Figure 10.2 *(continued)*

3.   **PROCEDURE**

Minor faults will be dealt with informally, to identify the problem and to resolve it, but where the matter is more serious, the following procedure will be used:

Stage 1 – Spoken warning
If conduct or performance does not meet acceptable standards, the employee will normally be given a formal SPOKEN WARNING. He/she will be advised of the reason for the warning; that it is the first stage of the disciplinary procedure; and that he/she has a right of appeal. A brief note of the spoken warning will be filed but will be removed after a period of between one to three months defined at the starting date and subject to satisfactory conduct and performance.

Stage 2 – Written warning
If the offence is a serious one, or if a further offence of a like nature occurs, a WRITTEN WARNING will be given to the employee. This will give details of the complaint, the improvement required and the timescale. It will warn that action under Stage 3 will be considered if there is no satisfactory improvement and will advise of the right of appeal. A copy of this written warning will be kept but it will be disregarded for disciplinary purposes after a period of between three to six months defined at the starting date and subject to satisfactory conduct and performance.

Stage 3 – Final written warning
If there is still a failure to improve conduct or performance is still unsatisfactory, or if the misconduct is sufficiently serious to warrant only one written warning, (in effect both first and final written warning) but insufficiently serious to justify dismissal, a FINAL WRITTEN WARNING will normally be given to the employee. This will give details of the complaint, will warn that dismissal will result if there is no satisfactory improvement and will advise of the right of appeal. A copy of this final written warning will be kept but it will be spent after a period of between six to twelve months (the period may be longer in exceptional cases) defined at the start date and subject to satisfactory conduct and performance.

Stage 4 – Dismissal
If conduct or performance is still unsatisfactory and the employee still fails to reach the prescribed standards, DISMISSAL will normally result. The employee will be provided with written reasons for dismissal, the date on which employment will terminate and the right of appeal.

Figure 10.2 *(continued)*

4. **GROSS MISCONDUCT**

The following list provides examples of offences which would be regarded as gross misconduct:

Theft; fraud; deliberate falsification of records;
Physical assault or threatening behaviour on another person;
Sexual harassment;
Deliberate damage to Trust property;
Incapability due to being under the influence of alcohol or drugs;
Negligence which causes unacceptable loss, damage or injury;
Serious act of insubordination.

If you are accused of an act of gross misconduct, you may be suspended by your Manager from work on full pay (normally for not more than ten working days), while the Trust investigates the alleged offence.

5. **APPEALS**

An employee who wishes to appeal against a disciplinary decision should inform the Manager who made the decision within 14 working days. The Senior Manager (the next level of management from the Manager concerned) will hear the appeal and his/her decision is final on behalf of the Trust.

Figure 10.2 *(continued)*

Appendix 1
to Disciplinary Procedure

<u>RIGHTS OF STAFF</u>

In disciplinary matters, each member of staff has the right:

1   to be represented by an accredited trade union representative or a colleague in the Disciplinary Procedures from the outset, when sufficient time shall be allowed for the representative to advise the member and to prepare the case. Management will give the maximum assistance in securing this representation promptly so that the matter may be resolved without unnecessary delay, and will make arrangements for the release from normal duties of accredited staff representatives.

2.   to professional legal representation but this may only be employed at the appeal stage subject to the Trust being notified 3 working days prior to the hearing.

3.   to be advised of the details of the alleged misconduct.

4.   to look at the records of any disciplinary action which are retained on his/her personal file.

5.   to be informed in writing of his/her right of appeal in matters involving Serious and/or Gross Misconduct.

6.   to be informed in writing on whose authority he/she may be dismissed.

Figure 10.2 *(continued)*

Examine the copy of a disciplinary procedure in **Figure 10.2** and assess it against the Code of Practice (**Figure 10.1**) and other guidance given above. The procedure is from an NHS Trust and those who drew it up did so intent upon devising a procedure that complied with the requirements of the Code.

Your task is to identify areas in which the procedure might be considered deficient. Look at it from the viewpoint of management's interests and objectives as well as from the viewpoint of whether you are going to be legally safe.

Short answer questions:

1 Identify some of the criticisms of the procedural approach that have been expressed more freely in recent years.
2 Which of the various alternatives would you choose to use as a measure of the effectiveness of procedures and why?
3 Explain the legal status and relevance of the Code of Practice on Disciplinary Practice and Procedures.

Grievance procedures and handling

The first thing to do is to define what a grievance is in this context and to distinguish it from what we might refer to as a dispute.

Definition

A **grievance** is an expression of dissatisfaction or a complaint by an individual that usually concerns the application, interpretation, implementation of or change to a statutory right or existing procedure, rule, custom, working practice or agreement. It may be that the complaint or dissatisfaction is concerned with the consistency of implementation, interpretation, with the failure to apply or with the application etc. in inappropriate circumstances of one or more of what are often referred to as rights, rights not necessarily in terms of legislative rights but in the context of the agreement, procedure or custom and practice. Many grievances are occasioned by management introducing change to existing working arrangements and methods.

Commonly, the individual alleges that management are not treating him/her fairly, not giving them their due or that they have been disadvantaged in some way or other, often in comparison with the way that it is perceived management have treated someone else. Another of the distinguishing features of a grievance is that it is commonly a complaint against a member of management, often the immediate supervisor.

Disputes, on the other hand, tend to be collective and concern rates of pay or some other substantive element of the terms and conditions of employment. Commonly a dispute concerns dissatisfaction with the terms and conditions status quo, the existing situation, rather than the employees' rights under existing rules and regulations and tends to surface as a request to improve or in some other way amend the status quo. The most obvious example is a dispute concerning the employees' request for an increase in pay. A dispute concerning the recognition of a trade union for collective bargaining purposes, where employees are collectively seeking such recognition, may not be substantive in the traditional and accepted sense but it is certainly about change to the existing situation, the status quo, rather than the interpretation etc. of an existing rule or custom and it is change that is being initiated by employees rather than by management. The dividing line between the two is sometimes blurred and it is not uncommon for something that starts off as an individual grievance to escalate into a collective dispute.

Issues and considerations

In this case, unlike in the case of disciplinary procedures, there is no code of practice to rely on, though there is plenty of advice around to guide the parties to any negotiation or those charged with the task of devising appropriate procedures.

Information and representation

Employees generally have a legal right to be informed of the person or officer of the organization to which they can take a grievance and, under the proposals in the 1999 Employment Relations Act, all employees will have a right to be accompanied by a trade union official if they wish at a grievance as well as at a disciplinary hearing. In this latter case it is perhaps to be expected that this new right will put greater pressure upon employers and managers to deal with employee grievances fairly and reasonably and it may indeed lead to some initial increase in the raising of grievances as employees realize that they no longer need to be quite so afraid of raising a grievance as perhaps they have been in the past.

What then are the common issues that arise and need to be resolved in the devising and drafting of such procedures?

Subject matter coverage/jurisdiction of the procedure

Management or the parties to an agreed procedure might not want to comprehensively list the kinds of grievances that can be dealt with via the procedure but they would need to decide whether some issues are to be excluded and dealt with differently or separately; examples of such might include appeals against disciplinary action and sexual harassment. An individual might well feel that the existing disciplinary procedure has been applied inappropriately or unfairly and this might constitute a legitimate grievance in the terms of the definition above, something that could arguably be dealt with within the grievance procedure. However, the disciplinary procedure should contain provision for the individual on the receiving end of the action to appeal against that action and in such circumstances it might be advisable, in order to reduce uncertainty and support the authority of the disciplinary as well as the grievance procedure, to stipulate explicitly that such matters can not be dealt with in the grievance procedure.

The issue of sexual harassment and its relationship to the grievance procedure is different in nature but still important in that grievances are generally perceived as complaints against management about the way in which management has treated an employee. An allegation of sexual harassment can fall into this category but it may also have nothing to do with management directly and the allegation may well be that the harassment was committed by another employee or employees. In these latter circumstances it might lead to confusion as to the purpose of the grievance procedure if such matters were dealt with that way and it would seem appropriate to deal with issues of sexual harassment in a completely separate procedure that provides for informality and counselling in the early stages as well as providing mechanisms through which the matter can be resolved and the harassment stopped.

Distinct procedures can sometimes be usefully linked at certain points and an example of this would be the linking of harassment and disciplinary procedures at the point at which the harassment constitutes a disciplinary offence, though a personal view would be that the integrity of procedures is best preserved by keeping them separate and distinct from each other.

Stages

As with disciplinary procedures decisions have to be made about how many stages there are to be and who is to preside at each of these stages. To some extent these issues will be dependent upon the size and structure of the organization and also whether there are bargaining structures within the industry that extend beyond the level of the firm. For example, if you are looking at a small firm then there may only be room for one or two stages internally, whereas if you were looking at the National Health Service where there are still some national negotiations on terms and conditions of employment as well as nationally agreed procedural arrangements then it would not be surprising perhaps if the procedure allowed for more stages to ensure consistency of treatment across the service and that some of these stages were outside the particular Trust or health unit.

There is no right number of stages but generally the advice would be that there should be more than one and that the final stage should be at a level that does facilitate consistency and fairness of treatment across the organization. It is also important that the first stage should involve the person about whom the allegation is made, the individual who is the subject of the grievance. Often such a first stage may not result in resolution but it is important that the subject of the grievance is not bypassed in the procedure, that they are given the opportunity to reconsider the way in which they have interpreted a particular rule or procedural provision. Line managers should be required to manage their staff and this involves dealing with their grievances as well as discipline.

As organizational structures have been flattened and de-layered in recent years many existing grievance procedures have had to be altered to fit with the new structure. The reduction in the number of layers in the organizational structure and hierarchy has sometimes meant that restructuring has encouraged the shortening of grievance procedures.

One of the questions often raised is whether the final stage in the procedure should be within or external to the organization, is management's decision to be final or is there to be recourse to an organization like ACAS for conciliation or arbitration? As noted in Chapter 5, conciliation is a process that seeks to obtain an agreed solution to a problem whereas arbitration is more judicial in nature, a process whereby you give the power of decision to a third party. Some people argue that agreeing to go to arbitration is a dereliction of management's responsibility and duty to manage and runs too many risks in terms of an outcome that is not consistent with other decisions taken within the organization, that it may create more problems than it solves. Conciliation, on the other hand, may be a much more acceptable option given that the parties retain the decision-making power and can accept or reject any suggested solution or outcome.

Time limits

It is fair to try and deal with a grievance within a reasonable period of time and certainly employees should not be left wondering just how long it is going to take for their grievance to be dealt with. These pressures have often led organizations to introduce into grievance procedures time limits on the holding of a grievance hearing after the lodging of the grievance, the giving of an answer, the advising of intent to appeal and progression to the next stage. The most important advice on this issue is that the limits, if necessary, should be realistic and not too optimistic, they should also be fair to both sides and they should be adhered to. Speed should not be at the expense of fairness and the ability to deal with the issue raised in a constructive manner. All too often organizations have devised procedures with time limits that cannot be kept and the danger is that because the time limits are not adhered to the whole procedure falls into disrepute and other means are taken to secure resolution of the grievance.

Grievance handling

Negotiation

There is a temptation for managers to think that in dealing with a grievance they can preserve their managerial prerogative, their unilateral right to manage, to decide issues. However, the reality is that grievance hearings are usually characterized, at the end if not at the beginning, by a process of searching for compromise, for a solution that sufficiently meets the needs and interests of both parties for it to be acceptable to both. It is relatively rare for the right to all be on the one side and often the process of dealing with a grievance yields evidence that there are other problems which need to be resolved and again these are often to be resolved through the process of negotiation. A reasonably common example would be the realization that existing rules etc. are not fair or sufficiently precisely drafted or that there are inconsistencies within or between them which need to be ironed out and which may result in the formation of some form of joint working party or problem solving group.

The hearing/interview

In most grievance procedures there is provision for a hearing or interview in which the complainant outlines the grievance, its nature and the circumstances in which it occurred. As noted above the first of these should normally be with the employee's immediate supervisor, who is quite likely to also be the individual who is the subject of the allegation. As also noted above it is advisable that there is at least one further stage, which may be regarded as an appeal stage since it is only likely if the first raising of the grievance results in a failure to agree a satisfactory outcome.

Whatever the precise format and however many people attend it would be normal for the hearing to be conducted by management even though it has been initiated by an employee.

The importance of preparation and conducting as full an investigation as possible, allowing the employee to put their case, considering this input and being consistent and fair are just as great as they are in the case of disciplinary hearings.

Figure 10.3 contains some simple but important guidelines on conducting a grievance interview.

It is important that the parties to the hearing remain calm, that they keep as open a mind as possible, that they listen and question when they don't understand something, and that efforts are made to establish the facts where this is possible.

Nevertheless a grievance hearing is very different from a disciplinary hearing in that at the end of the day management are being asked to conclude that a member of their own ranks made a mistake or deliberately did something that occasioned the employee to feel aggrieved that one or more of their rights were being infringed or violated. In this context there is obviously the danger that management will require a great deal of convincing

---

Listen

Keep an open mind

Question

Collect facts: keep in mind the 5 'Ws'

☐ What

☐ When

☐ Where

☐ Who

☐ Why

Check understanding with employee

Figure 10.3 The grievance interview. Adapted from Gennard and Judge (1997 pp. 211–12)

before they are prepared to acknowledge the grievance to be genuine, there may well be a natural desire to side with their management colleague. In these circumstances a scrupulously open and fair approach is even more of a necessity if an acceptable solution is to be found.

1 Explain the difference between a grievance and a dispute.
2 Outline the main points of difference between managing discipline and managing grievances.

Examine the grievance procedures displayed in **Figure 10.4** and identify and discuss the ways in which the issues identified above are illustrated and dealt with in the two procedures.

Procedure 1

GRIEVANCE PROCEDURE

Introduction

1. Every employee has the right to seek redress for grievances relating to his/her employment, and it is important that every individual should understand the correct procedure for doing this.

2. It is very important that grievances are settled fairly, promptly, and as near as possible to the point of origin.

Procedure

Stage 1: The employee with the grievance must first raise it with his or her immediate Team Leader/Manager.

Stage 2: If the matter has not been satisfactorily resolved during Stage 1, then arrangements will be made for the employee to see the next level of management.

Stage 3: If the grievance remains unresolved after the above meeting, then arrangements will be made for the employee to attend an interview with the Head of Department and, if necessary, the Company Personnel Manager.

Stage 4: If the grievance is still unresolved then a meeting will be called to give the employee an opportunity to discuss his/her grievance with a Director of the Company. In attendance will be the Senior Manager responsible in the department and the Company Personnel Manager.

Notes:

1. Up to and including Stage 2, the grievance may be verbal or written, but should it not be resolved during Stage 2, then the employee will be asked to put his/her grievance in writing before Stage 3.

   In addition to this, the level of management involved at Stage 2 will be required to put in writing the points discussed and the decision made so far, if any.

   These 2 documents should be passed to the Company Personnel Manager who will arrange for Stage 3 of the procedure.

2. If the grievance is not resolved at Stage 1, then the employee may, if he or she so wishes, request that a colleague be present at any subsequent meetings held under Stages 2, 3 or 4.

3. Stage 4 represents the Appeal Stage.

Figure 10.4 Examples of grievance procedures. Procedure 1 is adapted from a private sector manufacturing company, while Procedure 2 is a fairly typical public sector procedure.

Procedure 2

GRIEVANCE PROCEDURE

1. PURPOSE

To enable individual employees to seek redress for grievances relating to their employment.

This procedure is not to be used for grievances relating to a disciplinary decision where the appeals procedure contained within the Disciplinary and Capability Procedure must be utilised. Where an issue relates to a decision regarding grading the normal grading appeals procedure would be utilised.

Employees may also utilise the procedure contained within the Harassment Policy where this is more appropriate to the nature of the grievance.

2. SCOPE

All established and temporary employees who work under a contract of employment.

3. POLICY STATEMENT

The authority acknowledges its responsibility and the responsibility of all employees, managers and supervisors to develop a working relationship where:

- employees are to be treated first and foremost as people with individual needs and expectations; and

- any individual's problems should be dealt with promptly and fairly.

Most issues should be discussed and dealt with satisfactorily within the course of normal working relationships where employees should feel that their problems and opinions can be discussed frankly and freely with their manager or supervisor. Employees need not fear that they will suffer a detriment due to their raising a grievance.

1

Figure 10.4 (*continued*)

Where an employment problem is considered to be of a sufficiently serious nature to be termed as a grievance, the Grievance Procedure provides a framework for dealing promptly and fairly with the matter. It is not an appropriate procedure for resolving differences in opinion of a professional judgement. Where grievances concerning employment exist employees must:

- be given a fair hearing on any grievance by their immediate manager or supervisor; and

- have the right to take the issue to higher management where appropriate; or

- if still not satisfied they have the right to appeal.

Any grievance must be settled as quickly as is reasonably practicable and as near to its source as possible.

4.   PROCEDURE

The following procedure is designed to achieve the objectives referred to in the above policy statement in an effective and efficient manner.

4.1   Stage One

Any employee who has a personal grievance or problem should first of all raise the issue with his or her immediate supervisor/manager.

Whether the approach is written or oral the employee must clearly state that the formal grievance procedure is being utilised.

Providing the above procedure is followed the supervisor/manager must arrange a meeting with the employee as soon as is reasonably practicable. Even if the first meeting is of an exploratory nature it should normally take place within five working days of the notification of the grievance. A written summary of the contents of the meeting must be made by the manager, signed by both parties and a copy kept confidentially on file.

The employee may wish to be accompanied or represented by a workplace colleague or fellow employee or a recognised departmental trade union representative.

Where the employee chooses not to be accompanied it is advisable to note in the written summary that representation was offered and declined.

4.2   Stage Two

If the employee is not satisfied with the progress made after the first meeting, disagrees with the decision that was made at that meeting or cannot accept the proposed period before action is to be taken he/she may decide to refer the matter to Stage Two of the procedure.

2

Figure 10.4 (*continued*)

Alternatively an employee may consider that the issue is not appropriate to raise with his/her own immediate supervisor/manager. In this event the employee may submit his/her grievance at Stage Two without utilising Stage One. To submit a grievance at this level it must be put in writing to the manager and/or chief officer to whom the employee's immediate supervisor/manager reports. The manager will arrange a meeting within ten working days of receipt of the grievance. Where the issues are complex this initial meeting may again be of an exploratory nature. The manager may also choose to have a representative from the Personnel Services Unit present and the employee may again choose to be accompanied or represented by a fellow employee or a recognised trade union representative. When necessary any further meetings will be arranged within five working days. Any decisions/responses will be confirmed in writing.

4.3   Final Stage – Appeal

Where the employee is not satisfied with the result(s) of Stage Two of the procedure he/she may appeal against the decision, in writing, within ten working days, to the Director of Personnel. Again a meeting will normally be arranged within ten working days of receipt of the appeal or as soon as is practicable thereafter. Confirmation of the outcome will be given in writing. The employee may be accompanied or represented by a fellow employee or trade union representative. The decision of this meeting is final unless either party consider the grievance concerns a difference regarding the application of a decision reached by the National or Provincial Council.

5.   ADVICE AND CONFIDENTIALITY

At any stage an employee or manager may seek advice on this procedure from the Personnel Services Unit. When seeking advice the employee should request a confidential interview and refer to this provision of the Grievance Procedure. The representative from the Personnel Services Unit who attends the interview will not become involved in any forward stages of the procedure if the issue is then progressed.

Due regard will be given throughout the procedure to the maintenance of confidentiality.

6.   THE IMPACT OF CHANGE

In the event of any grievance arising concerning a change in working practice, arrangements or agreements and where the grievance cannot be resolved immediately, it may be necessary to implement such a change pending a settlement of the grievance. This may be necessary, for example, where to do otherwise would have a detrimental impact on safety, security or service provision.

3

Figure 10.4 (*continued*)

7. **RESPONSIBILITY**

Employees covered by this procedure must understand that this procedure is also incorporated into their contract of employment.

Individual managers are responsible for ensuring that this procedure is applied within their own area.

Any queries on the application or interpretation of this procedure must be discussed with the Personnel Services Unit. Where differences in the interpretation of this procedure exist, the matter should be referred to the Director of Personnel. Subject to consultation with the appropriate trade union representative, the ruling of the Director of Personnel will be final.

The Personnel Services Unit has the responsibility for ensuring the maintenance, regular review and updating of this procedure.

4

Figure 10.4 (*continued*)

Summary

There is a potentially wide range of procedural outcomes and they tend to provide the parties to the employment relationship with a constitution as well as being operational mechanisms. Procedures may be the product of joint decision-making between the employee's representatives and management or they may be the outcome of unilateral decisions by management. Some procedures are required by law. There are a number of reasons why it is a good idea to have a comprehensive portfolio of procedures and these include: clarifying the relationships between the parties, focusing and resolving conflict, encouraging consistency and equity in the treatment of staff, encouraging a more collaborative approach and relationship between the parties, and providing a safety valve and additional means by which managerial prerogative may be curtailed.

The tests for the effectiveness of procedures include that they are used and that they are accepted and appropriate.

Disciplinary procedures have been significantly influenced by the publication in 1976 of the Code of Practice which has acted as a template of best practice. Even so, there are issues not addressed and questions not answered in the Code. The Code's notion of fairness rests upon the principles of natural justice, clarity and transparency.

We have distinguished a grievance from a dispute and you have been made aware of some of the procedural issues that must be resolved in the devising and drafting of a grievance procedure:

- the coverage of the procedure and its relationship to certain others
- the importance of ensuring that employees have the opportunity to be informed, accompanied and represented
- the question of how many stages there should be in the procedure
- whether the final stage(s) should be within or external to the organization
- the issue of time limits and the advisability of not engaging in the quest for speed at the expense of fairness and obtaining a solution satisfactory to both parties.

In the latter part of the chapter we have emphasized the importance of seeing a grievance hearing and the quest for a solution in terms of negotiating and achieving compromise, rather than simply asserting management's prerogative, and we have pointed out the importance of certain interpersonal and communication skills along with keeping an open mind and establishing the facts.

Activity Answers

Activity 1
Management.
Advantages: clarity, consistency, guidance, prevention of unwittingly acting unlawfully, base for more adequate record keeping, a mechanism for providing early warning, taking the heat out of and resolving

conflict, provide a safety valve, may enhance the quality of employee relations.

Disadvantages: rigidity and inflexibility in decision-making and responding to competitive pressures, limitation upon managerial prerogative and freedom, the cost of devising, communicating and training.

Employees.

Advantages: the main advantages for employees are in the area of order and consistency, fairness, openness, providing a means for redressing perceived unfairness, appealing against arbitrary decisions and as a brake upon the otherwise unfettered right of management to act autonomously, as a mechanism for conflict resolution. May provide a base for enhancing their influence within the organization.

Disadvantages: the main ones are that procedures also limit the opportunity for employees to act autonomously. This is perhaps particularly an issue where the procedures have been jointly agreed and where therefore they share some of the responsibility for ensuring that the procedures are complied with.

Activity 2
The principles of natural justice would normally be considered to include the right to be:

- informed of the complaint against you
- given the opportunity to state your case before a decision is reached
- accompanied by a friend, trade union or legal representative
- given the outcome of the hearing in writing
- provided with and informed of your right of appeal.

Activity 3
The first thing to say is that there are obviously similarities between this procedure and the requirements and guidance contained within the Code. Nevertheless, there are also points of difference and some provisions which may be both unwieldy and in some instances questionable from management's point of view.

I would question the complete absence of reference to sanctions in the opening section on purposes and scope, certainly the purpose is not simply to punish but to omit all reference to the possibility of sanctions being imposed seems to me to be potentially misleading on the one hand and unlikely to convince employees on the other.

In the section 'Principles', paragraph 2.1, I don't think that the assertion that all cases be investigated by an independent manager is necessary or desirable. An implication of this is that line managers are incapable of being fair and, perhaps more importantly, such a provision removes from line managers one of their main roles, managing and where necessary disciplining staff. Such a provision may have greater merit in respect of serious cases but as it is written it would appear to cover all disciplinary action including the formal 'spoken warning'. Under normal circumstances one would expect such an oral warning to be delivered by the line manager or supervisor. Here it is not clear who issues the spoken warning.

I like the idea in paragraph 2.2 that employees should be given a clear statement of their rights in disciplinary proceedings and this would seem to be relatively rare. The right specified to examine his/her personal file for records of disciplinary action is particularly unusual and to be applauded.

Paragraph 2.4. I would want to make clear at this early stage in the document that dismissal may (not will) be the consequence of gross misconduct. Use of the word 'may' provides management with the opportunity to dismiss for gross misconduct but does not imply that this is the only solution appropriate and available in such cases.

Paragraph 2.5. As indicated in the text there are concerns about oral warnings as part of the formal procedure. However, the Code advises it and so most procedures contain such a provision. Nevertheless, I do find the notion of an appeal against an oral warning somewhat difficult since the recipient of the warning will find it difficult to present a case at appeal against action when the events leading up to its imposition and the reasons for it may not be recorded in any meaningful form.

In the section 'Procedure', Stage 1, see above and, more specifically, I think there is a certain ambivalence about the provision to remove the note of the warning, presumably from the employee's personal file. The procedure does not indicate that the note will be destroyed nor does it say that the action taken in this event will be disregarded for the purpose of any future disciplinary action after the period of time mentioned.

Stage 2. First sentence – I think the word 'Will' limits management's discretion unnecessarily and there is ambiguity about the reference to a further offence of a like nature, what is and why need it be?, and presumably the intention in this instance is to refer to further offences inside the time period of satisfactory conduct required and specified in the first action, this is not what is said. Again there is no mention of what happens to the copy of the warning once removed from the file but here in this stage we do have specific reference to the warning being disregarded for disciplinary purpose after the appropriate time period. A similar statement should be incorporated at all stages if this is what is intended.

Stage 3. Again saying that 'dismissal will result' may be unnecessarily limiting to management. 'May' would be better. One of the issues also with this stage is that the employee is given no clear idea of what kind of an offence qualifies.

Stage 4. Here we have qualification of the 'Will' and I would suggest that this example is used throughout.The procedure could here specify who normally would have the right/role to discuss.

General points would also include the absence of any reference to how the Trust is to deal with the 'special cases' referred to in the Code – trade union officials, criminal offences outside work, etc.

Overall the procedure is reasonably close to that recommended but as noted there are issues and some potential difficulties.

Activity 4

1 Procedures have been criticized for acting as a brake upon the business need to be more flexible and responsive to changes in customer tastes and to the threats of global competition. Managers have criticized procedures for leading to long-drawn-out decision-making processes which are no longer appropriate; sometimes hard decisions have to be taken and they have to be taken quickly if the organization is to survive and prosper.

Lower levels of line management often see procedures as a direct attack upon their right and ability effectively to manage their own particular group of employees, a direct threat to their autonomy and a weakening of support from more senior levels of management.

Other criticisms of the procedural and collective approach emerge from the new emphasis upon individualism and the future, compared with the perceived procedural emphasis upon the past, precedent, consistency and equity.

2 I don't know which you chose or your reasons but it is likely that your choice was either whether they are used or not, which implies an acceptability or whether they work, which implies a degree of appropriateness; for example do they:

- contain or provide a mechanism for the resolution of conflict
- lead to greater consistency and equity
- ensure that the organization doesn't become liable for legal action to be taken against them.

3 The Code effectively spells out the minimum requirements for a disciplinary procedure to be regarded by the employment tribunals and courts as fair. It is not legally binding but it has a kind of quasi-legal status in that it can be taken into account by the relevant legal authorities when trying to judge whether a dismissal was fair and, over the years as the tribunals etc. have done this, the Code has acquired an authority that to all intents and purposes means that if an organization does not comply with it, the organization runs the risk of the dismissal being found unfair.

Discipline represents one of the areas in which there has been the greatest degree of legal intervention and the quasi-legislative Code of Practice provides an informative blueprint of how such procedures should look and what they should contain.

Activity 5

1 A grievance is a complaint by an individual usually against management whose actions or behaviour have infringed one or more of his or her rights under an existing rule, law, agreement, custom, practice etc. An allegation by an employee that management have acted unfairly. A dis-

pute is much more likely to be collective and concerned with the pursuit of change, for example to existing terms and conditions of employment.

2 The main points of difference occur because, in managing discipline, management are investigating an allegation against an employee, management are the complainant and initiate the process whereas in managing grievances the issue is usually a complaint against management and the process is initiated by the employee. In the first instance management are much more likely to act in a judicial role, deciding an issue and imposing a sanction, in the second instance management are much more likely to be defending a colleague, seeking solutions acceptable to both parties, looking for compromise.

Activity 6

If we look at the public sector procedure first we can see that many of the issues referred to above have been identified as issues that need to be addressed. In the first couple of sections we see that the organization is keen to determine which matters may appropriately be dealt with through this procedure and perhaps more crucially which should be addressed through other means, e.g. disciplinary appeals, grading of jobs and sexual harassment complaints.

The policy statement makes clear the importance the organization attaches to treating employees fairly and dealing with any grievance promptly. However, as indicated later in the procedure this prompt dealing is not allied to rigid time limits even though indicators of appropriate times are given.

The procedure makes it absolutely clear that in the first instance a grievance should be raised with the immediate supervisor, though there is an unspecified area of exemption from this which allows for the first stage to be bypassed. It seems as if this is to be at the discretion of the employee and this does seem to be a weakness in the system since there is no attempt to indicate what might be considered as appropriate in these circumstances; there seems to be no requirement for management to agree that the circumstances are exceptional. There is the obvious danger in such a situation for employees to bypass the first line supervisor because they think they will obtain a more favourable response at stage two than they are likely to obtain at stage one or simply as a means of speeding up the process.

The right of the individual to be accompanied or represented is also clearly stated and is to apply at all stages. The procedure contains only three internal stages and this is relatively few for an organization employing thousands rather than hundreds of people. At the final stage there is also a limited right to take the grievance outside the organization to the provincial council conciliation machinery.

The personnel department is there to advise both parties but the Director of Personnel also constitutes the final internal stage and there may well be some potential and interesting conflicts of interest in these arrangements even though provision is made that the individual advising should not be party to any subsequent stage in the procedure.

The employer has also been careful to retain their 'right' to implement change pending the outcome of any grievance raised.

Moving on to look at the procedure in the manufacturing organization, the first thing to say is that the new legislative proposals regarding individual trade union representatives may well have an impact upon this non-union company. The existing procedure incorporates very similar principles to those in the public sector organization: fairness and promptness and there is reference to employees' rights to seek redress for grievances.

The first stage is to be with the first line supervisor but there is no provision in this procedure for bypassing this stage and starting at stage two. There is provision for four stages (the fourth of which is described as the appeal stage, which presumably means that it is also the final stage), none of which are to be external to the organization. The role of the personnel function is not quite so clear but it would appear that it is to advise management and to make the arrangements for the later stages of the procedure. It may also be that the provision for the presence and involvement of the Personnel Function in the procedure is perceived as a safeguard for employees. In both cases also there is a requirement that the grievance be put in writing prior to the latter stages of the procedure, even if it starts off verbally.

There is no attempt to impose time limits to the various stages or to even give an indication of what might be appropriate. The employee is given the right to be accompanied by a colleague only at the second and subsequent stages. There is no discussion or definition in this document of the relationship between the grievance procedure and other procedures such as the disciplinary or harassment procedures, there is also no attempt to define what a grievance is.

Generally speaking the public sector procedure and documentation is very much more comprehensive and detailed.

References

Advisory Conciliation and Arbitration Service, 1976. *Code of Practice 1 on Disciplinary Practice and Procedures.* HMSO, London.

Advisory Conciliation and Arbitration Service, 1987. *Discipline At Work.* HMSO, London.

Donovan Commission Report, 1968. *The Report of the Royal Commission on Trade Unions and Employers Associations.* Command 3623, HMSO, London.

Dunlop, J.T., 1958. *Industrial Relations Systems.* Holt, New York.

Gennard, J. and Judge, G., 1997. *Employee Relations.* IPP, London.

Hawkins, K., 1979. *A Handbook of Industrial Relations Practice.* Kogan Page, London.

Marchington, M. and Wilkinson, A., 1996. *Core Personnel and Development*. IPD, London.

Marsh, A.I. and McCarthy, W.J., 1968. *Disputes Procedures in Britain*. Donovan Commission Research Paper No.2 Part 2. HMSO, London.

Further reading

Fowler, A., 1996. How to conduct a disciplinary interview. *People Management* November, pp. 40–2.

Chapter 11

Equal
opportunities

Introduction

We have already noted in earlier chapters on the role of government, the legislative context and the European Union that there is a legal dimension to the issue of equal opportunities at work. Individuals have been given certain limited rights to be not discriminated against and to equal pay, access to and treatment at work and employers have had statutory obligations imposed upon them. In the UK rights and obligations of this kind have been granted in respect of equality on the grounds of race, sex, marital status and more recently in respect of disability.

In many respects equality and discrimination are opposite sides of the same coin, with a right to equality of opportunity or treatment implying at the same time a right not to be discriminated against.

These legal rights become implied terms of individual contracts of employment and specific provision has in the main been made for allegations of infringement of rights to be dealt with via an application to an employment tribunal. In the section looking at the work of ACAS we noted that there are still thousands of applications per year on the grounds that individual rights to equal pay, opportunity and treatment have been infringed. This is an indication that equality in these areas has not yet been achieved despite the fact that much of the legislation has been in existence in the UK for periods exceeding twenty years. Other indicators, for example on pay, participation and activity rates and on the proportion of women and ethnic minorities in senior positions in organizations, are all consistent with the observation that inequality and discrimination continue in employing organizations.

Figure 11.1 demonstrates that employers are likely to be held legally responsible for the actions of their employees whilst at work and it also raises the issue of institutional racism.

As with other individual rights, effective prosecution of the law may provide the aggrieved employee with financial compensation but other remedies are extremely difficult to enforce, even in situations where a national independent organization has been established to encourage: positive action and remedies, the promulgation of information and good practice and compliance with the law.

There is a tendency to concentrate upon the legal dimensions of the issue of equality but we must bear in mind that there are moral, political, social, economic, ethical and business dimensions to the matter as well. We have noted in Chapter 4 on the EU that from early in the existence of the Union the ECJ took the view that equality between the sexes was a fundamental human right, they did not apply the same logic to issues of racial or ethnic equality.

The focus in this chapter is not so much upon the legislative background as upon the origins and causes of inequality and discrimination and the policies and practices that employers can develop and implement. For policies and procedures to be effective in addressing and resolving particular issues and problems they must be devised in the context of an awareness of their origins and causes. Therefore in the early part of this chapter we discuss some of the more common explanations that have been identified before we discuss the policies and procedures that employers might usefully follow to achieve the objective of equal opportunities and treatment.

Asian Ford worker's years of torment

Company accepts full liability for racial abuse at Dagenham plant

Seumas Milne
Labour Editor

An Asian worker at Ford's Dagenham factory in Essex yesterday broke down as he described years of abuse and humiliation, threats of assault and sabotage of his work, after the company admitted racial discrimination, harassment and victimisation at an east London employment tribunal.

Ford accepted full liability at the Stratford hearing for the treatment meted out to Sukhjit Parma, 34, an engine plant worker who has been off sick since August. A superviser was sacked last Friday and a foreman demoted for their role in the campaign — 19 months after the transport union demanded Ford carry out an internal investigation.

Along with systematic verbal abuse, Indian food was kicked out of Mr Parma's hands, graffiti was scrawled on his pay packet, the words "Ku Klux Klan" were daubed on the toilet block next to where he worked, he was set up for dismissal and warned he would have his legs broken if he named any of his tormentors.

Mr Parma was also confined in an area known as the "punishment cell" — where oil mist is sprayed over engine parts — without protective equipment, making him violently sick. He had to be accompanied to work by colleagues and has now had to take extra security measures on police advice.

Bill Morris, the Transport and General Workers' Union leader, yesterday said Mr Parma's was the worst case of racist intimidation the union had ever had to deal with and called for urgent talks with Ford's world president, Jac Nasser, to tackle institutional racism at Dagenham.

The tribunal was adjourned until February while the company and union discussed a settlement.

But Mr Morris said this was merely the latest example of institutional racism at Dagenham, which had "consistently been seen to fail their black workers". What was needed was an external inquiry, as the "local workforce do not have confidence in the management to deal adequately with this situation".

This is the third recent racist scandal involving Ford. Three years ago, the company was forced to apologise and pay compensation to four black workers after white faces were imposed on their photographs in a sales brochure.

The following year, Ford had to pay out more than £70,000 compensation to seven Asian and Afro-Caribbean workers at Dagenham who were turned down for jobs in the truck fleet, where pay is roughly double the shopfloor average, but fewer than 2% of workers are from ethnic minorities — compared with 45% across the factory.

Under pressure from the TGWU, Ford also agreed to introduce independent recruitment procedures, but two years later there has been no significant progress and the commission for racial equality is understood to have launched an investigation.

Union officials say that unlike the Dagenham body and assembly plants, there have been persistent problems of racism in the engine plant which the company has refused to address. Steve Turner, the TGWU's regional organiser for Dagenham, said yesterday the company had to act now to introduce effective procedures for dealing with racial discrimination at the factory.

Ford yesterday apologised for Mr Parma's treatment and said it had a "zero tolerance policy against discrimination or harassment of any kind".

Figure 11.1 *Source: The Guardian,* 24 September 1999

Objectives

After studying this chapter you will be able to:

- Outline the specific legal context surrounding the issues of equality and discrimination including harassment
- Understand the various origins and explanations of inequality and discrimination, the relevance of stereotyping, economic and other explanations
- Discuss the evidence of inequality and discrimination
- Advise on the management of inequality and the elimination of discrimination at the workplace
- Draft an equal opportunities policy statement.

Equality of what – opportunity, treatment, outcome?

In order to develop effective policies and procedures on equality it is important that employers and employees clarify their objectives. In the introduction we have already referred to equality in terms of **access to opportunity**, **treatment** and **pay** and, while we need to acknowledge that the distinctions between these concepts are often blurred and unclear, we also need to be clear as to which of them the policies and procedures are designed to achieve and deal with.

Jewson and Mason (1986) distinguished between equality policies that were liberal in that they sought to ensure that everyone was treated equally (including opportunity) and those that were concerned to achieve equality of outcome, which they term radical. Examples of each might include:

- treatment incorporating opportunity. Pre-work experience and circumstance, including educational experience, the provision of training and development opportunities as well as opportunities to compete for employment and advancement within a particular employing organization, the allocation of tasks, working conditions, selection for redundancy, issues of harassment and conditions governing dismissal
- outcome. Pay, which may include much more than the money received directly in return for work, such as pension contributions and entitlements, as well as some other substantive terms and conditions of employment, hours of work, holiday entitlement etc. Also included in this category would be the intent to achieve quotas in respect of the workforce, for example pursuing policies on recruitment and selection which had as their objective a labour force comprising 50 per cent men and 50 per cent women.

Liff (1995), on the other hand, argued the advantages of an alternative objective, to try to ensure or create the conditions in which people can compete on equal terms, an objective she finds preferable to both the liberal and radical approaches of Jewson and Mason, though you might take the view that here again it is equality of opportunity that is the objective, the opportunity to compete on equal terms. An example of the kind of measure or change that might facilitate the achievement of this objective is the amendment of the requirements of or conditions attached to jobs, for example the (unnecessary) requirement that jobs be worked on a full-time basis when the alternative of job sharing might well be feasible; the implication here is that insisting upon full-time working actually discriminates against women.

Discrimination

It is patently the case that the sexes and the many different racial and ethnic groups in the UK that make up what is now a multicultural society are not homogeneous, there are differences. We must not therefore assume that all differences in employment opportunity, or workplace treatment and outcome between the sexes and between racial and ethnic groups are necessarily the result of (unfair) discrimination, some of the differences in opportunity or treatment or outcome may be both objective and justified. As Adnett (1996) points out: 'the existence of a gender wage gap need not indicate labour market discrimination since women may possess different labour market characteristics or tastes'. Nevertheless it is also the case that some such differential workplace experience, treatment and outcomes may be the product of discrimination, which Adnett (1996) defines as something that occurs when some superficial personal characteristic (*such as colour of skin, ethnic origin, nationality and sex*) is used to restrict an individual's opportunity to achieve economic or social development and advancement. Adnett also seeks to distinguish different types or categories of labour market discrimination and these are:

- pre-entry discrimination
- employment or occupational discrimination
- wage discrimination.

The law

The legal rights and obligations of the parties to the employment relationship in this area of equal opportunity, treatment and outcome are contained within four main pieces of legislation:

The Equal Pay Act 1970
The Sex Discrimination Act 1975
The Race Relations Act 1976
The Disability Discrimination Act 1995

It might be reasonable to assume that all acts of discrimination are unlawful but this is not so. There are two main areas in which discrimination at work is lawful. One relates to the concept of positive action or discrimination and the other to the notion of a Genuine Occupational Qualification (GOQ) which enables the preferential employment of a member of a particular sex, race or ethnic group on grounds such as those of dramatic performance, authenticity and privacy or decency. An example of a GOQ might be an insistence on the employment of a particular sex or race to play a role in a play or film for the purposes of physiological or racial authenticity, and another might be the employment of a particular sex in circumstances where to do otherwise might offend public decency or serve to embarrass customers or clients, as in public toilets or single-sex hostels or prisons. The test in such circumstances is whether the need is genuine.

The Race Relations Act defines 'racial grounds' as 'colour, race, nationality or ethnic or national origins'.

Positive action or discrimination

The law allows certain kinds of discriminatory practice and initiative so long as the preferential treatment is to a member of a disadvantaged or under-represented group and it has the objective of promoting equality of opportunity. So that, for example, the provision of training opportunities to women currently out of work but wishing to re-enter the workforce can be lawful even though the same opportunities are not provided for men. Similarly, recruitment or selection practices which promote the employment of members of disadvantaged or under-represented groups can be lawful even though they discriminate against members of other groups. There has been a considerable amount of controversy and debate about such practices and in particular which were lawful and which not.

The EU Treaty agreed at Amsterdam in 1997 tries to determine this issue in respect of discrimination on the grounds of sex by inserting the provision that member states could adopt measures allowing for specific advantages to be provided to members of the under-represented sex if they make it easier for the members of that sex to pursue a vocational activity or if the measures are geared towards preventing or compensating for disadvantages in professional careers.

It is to some extent still unclear whether lawful discrimination of this kind can extend to the creation and maintenance of rigid quotas.

It seems as if quotas are acceptable, for example the intent to recruit women to a particular category of job until they constitute 50 per cent of those in occupancy, as long as it is actually possible for men to apply, compete and be offered a position if they prove to be the best qualified candidate. Another example of lawful discrimination would be the statement in a job advertisement that applications are particularly welcomed from members of particular (disadvantaged or under-represented) ethnic groups.

The law on discrimination in the UK encompasses both direct and indirect discrimination and the notion of victimization.

Direct discrimination

Direct discrimination involves less favourable treatment of an individual or group (directly) because of their sex or on the grounds of their race, skin colour, etc. An example might be stating in a job advertisement that only men need apply.

Indirect discrimination

Indirect discrimination relates to circumstances in which there may have been no intent to discriminate against a group but nevertheless the reality is that discrimination occurs, one group being disadvantaged in comparison with another. An example might be an insistence that successful applicants for a position are over 6 feet tall, 'able to speak the Queen's English' or, as noted above, that applicants must be able to work full-time, when the conditions cannot be justified by the requirements of the job. The impact of the condition is to disadvantage one group, women or members of particular nationalities or ethnic groups, in comparison with another and it is an indirect consequence of the conditions attached to the vacancy. Selection tests, assessment centres and job evaluation and classification schemes can easily incorporate criteria and methods that result in indirect discrimination and the EC has highlighted the dangers of job evaluation schemes discriminating against women in terms of the values attached to job and personal characteristics (EC Code of Practice on The Implementation of Equal Pay for Work of Equal Value for Women and Men COM (96) 336).

Governments have also been found to be guilty of indirect discrimination in their legislation, an example in the UK being the legislation which imposed upon part-time workers more stringent qualification rules regarding entitlement to claim unfair dismissal than were imposed upon full-time workers. It was decided by the courts that because the vast majority of part-time workers were women this legislation was in fact indirectly discriminatory against women, they were disadvantaged in comparison with men and such discrimination was held to be unjustified.

Victimization

This type of discrimination occurs when an employer treats an employee less favourably than another because the victim has taken a step in connection with proceedings under the EPA, SDA, or RRA. The purpose of including victimization as discrimination is patently geared towards the prevention of reprisals being taken against complainants.

Vicarious liability

This is the legal principle which allows employees or prospective employees who feel they have been discriminated against by other employees as well perhaps as by management to take or include in the action the employing organization. An example of this in practice is shown in **Figure 11.1**. This liability does not extend to the criminal actions of employees but it certainly covers civil wrongs, known as torts. Commonly, an action under the legislation will include both the employees and the employer irrespective of whether the employer knew of the discrimination being practised by their employees.

Harassment as discrimination

In order for harassment to be treated as discrimination and therefore for the appropriate legislation to apply it is necessary that the individual can be shown to have been treated less favourably and that this less favourable treatment is on racial grounds or on the grounds of the individual's sex.

The European Commission definition of sexual harassment has been adopted as the standard: 'unwanted conduct of a sexual nature or other conduct based on sex affecting the dignity of men and women at work'.

The principle of vicarious liability applies to cases of sexual harassment as much as to other discriminatory practices.

Harassment is not only a civil offence. The Criminal Justice and Public Order Act 1994 made intentional harassment a criminal offence for which imprisonment is a possible outcome. Harassment on the grounds of sex, race, disability and sexual orientation would all appear to be covered by this legislation. In order for the offence to be committed there has to be intent to cause a person harassment, alarm or distress and the Act covers using threatening, abusive or insulting language, threatening behaviour, disorderly behaviour or displaying writing, a sign or other visible representation.

It is clear that harassment can be the product of a range of actions and behaviours including touch, verbal abuse and insults, pornographic pictures and pin-ups, graffiti, suggestive remarks or innuendoes and unwanted comments about dress or appearance.

Examine the sample advertisements in **Figure 11.2** and try to work out whether they are each lawful or not in the context of existing legislation or Equal Opportunities and the prevention of discrimination.

Evidence that employers infringe employees' rights to equality and to not be discriminated against can be derived from the ACAS caseload referred to in the earlier chapter. The ACAS annual report for 1998 includes the following statistical evidence on the number of claims received in the year under review:

> The company is a leader in the retail sector and our recent rapid expansion means that we now need to recruit a number of new store managers. We recruit on a national basis and successful applicants may be appointed to a store anywhere in the country. Promotion for exceptional candidates can be rapid and you should expect to be mobile.
>
> Applications should be made to . . .

> **Refuse Operatives Required.**
>
> The company has a number of refuse collecting contracts in multi-ethnic and cultural communities and we are looking to recruit more refuse operators.
>
> We particularly want our refuse collection crews to reflect the ethnic and cultural diversity of the communities in which they operate and therefore preference will be given to applicants that will help us to achieve this objective. Applicants should ring . . .

> We are looking for production line operatives. Currently approximately 60% of our operatives are women and we want to have a roughly equal sex mix among the operative labour force, therefore on this occasion we are only interested in applications from men. Men who are interested should ring . . .
>
> We are an Equal Opportunities Employer

Figure 11.2

Are you aged 25–35 with 10 years relevant experience? We are a young go getting software company that needs to employ more salespersons. We offer a substantial benefits package for on target performance including a company car that fits the young and thrusting image that we want you to present as our representative. If you think you fit the bill apply to . . .

The company welcomes applicants from all sectors of the community and is an equal opportunities employer.

Figure 11.2 (*continued*)

- sex discrimination – 6882 (+4 per cent on 1997)
- race discrimination – 3173 (+10 per cent)
- equal pay – 3447 (+50 per cent)
- disability discrimination – 2758 (nearly double)

A total of 16,260 applications from individuals that one of their statutory rights to equal treatment and pay under existing legislation had been infringed by employers. This accounts for 14.3 per cent of the total ACAS caseload received during the year 1998.

Patterns of participation and pay – the evidence

We have already noted in the chapters on demography and the EU that there is evidence that the sexes and racial and ethnic groups experience differential opportunities, participation in and outcomes of the labour market in the UK. We noted that demographic developments were leading to change in the age–sex composition not just of the population but also of the labour force. We noted that there were persistent wage and earnings gaps between men and women with the gender gap averaging 25–35 per cent in favour of men. There is a gap irrespective of educational attainment level and pre-motherhood. The gap seems to open at around the age of 20 years and remains for life thereafter, though there is also evidence that motherhood tends to make the gap larger.

More recently, towards the end of 1999, some evidence began to emerge that among the impacts of the introduction of the minimum wage might be a slight narrowing of this gender pay gap. This is a reasonable likelihood given the preponderance of women among the ranks of the lowest paid and as long as those on higher wages don't insist upon the maintenance of existing differentials. The Office for National Statistics data released in October 1999 assert that the gender pay gap, in terms of annual hourly rates of pay, decreased by 1 per cent between April 1998 and April 1999. It seems as if the greatest beneficiary occupations were hairdressing and waiting.

The proportion of the female population of working age that are economically active is lower than that of men, women make up a relatively small proportion of the total self-employed, however, more women work part-time and on a temporary basis and they dominate employment in the service sector. Women also tend to dominate the secretarial, clerical, personal services and health associate professionals markets, whereas males dominate the skilled trades, management, science and engineering professions. In a report in 1999 the Equal Opportunities Commission confirmed that men dominate employment in the following sectors: construction (87 per cent), engineering and water supply (89 per cent) and mining and quarrying (89 per cent), whereas women dominate in health and social work (83 per cent), education (70 per cent) and public administration (70 per cent). This labour market segregation is also apparent in the take-up of the new modern apprenticeships (DfEE, 1999).

Women tend to suffer less from unemployment, or at least the unemployment rate for women is consistently lower than for men. Unemployment among ethnic minority groups tends to be higher than it is for comparable categories of 'white' citizens, this is particularly the case among the young and long-term unemployed. Members of ethnic minority groups stay unemployed longer, they find it more difficult to find work even where they have superior academic qualifications, they are likely to stay in a job for a shorter period of time and there was some evidence of ethnic pay gaps.

Berthoud (1999), in a report that looks at the incomes, including social security payments and benefits, of ethnic minority groups, concludes that the evidence of ethnic pay gaps is inconsistent and that some ethnic minority groups do better than others. He concludes that Pakistani and Bangladeshi families are almost four times as likely as white families to be living on low incomes and there is a greater propensity for men in this group to be unemployed. The wages of Caribbean men are also likely to be below those of white counterparts, the incomes of Africans are low and yet Indian and Chinese minority groups tend to have high levels of employment with earnings on a par with those of their white counterparts.

These findings are in main consistent with an European Foundation for the Improvement of Living and Working Conditions (EFILWC; 1996) report which concluded that the migrant and visible (visible because of racial and ethnic difference) minority population in the EU were disproportionately represented in poor and insecure work and amongst the unemployed and that this also applied to the second- and third-generation migrant descended population who had been born and raised in the EU. The EFILWC report also concluded that in the UK the statistical information available supports the conclusion that only a small portion of the discrepancy between the unemployment rates of white nationals and ethnic minority groups can be accounted for by the level of education and other differences. The conclusion drawn is that racial discrimination is the variable that most likely explains the differences in employment experience.

When it comes to participation in education and training and the relationship between qualifications and employment experience we also see evidence of differential experience and opportunity. Men still stay longer in education but the gap has narrowed. We reported that women tend to be more qualified than men for the jobs that they do and that many of the women with poor educational attainment levels never enter the labour force at all.

Traditionally, the lifetime employment patterns of women in the UK have shown a decline in participation in the early 20-year age group that then continued through into the mid-30s age range, after which participation rates tended to rise again. McGivney (1999) points out that women returners, as this group are often called, accounted for over one-third of Britain's workforce. This pattern has been changing and the scale and duration of this decline or dip in female participation rates have themselves been in decline. There are associations between this pattern and the factors of marriage and childbirth as well as with the age of the youngest child. Other common characteristics of female employment are that females are less likely to achieve managerial status than are men.

It is relatively easy to obtain statistical evidence of the above trends and rates, it is much more difficult to obtain evidence of discrimination or inequality at the level of and within the firm and in respect of aspects of treatment such as career development opportunities, training provision, recruitment and selection, opportunities for promotion and participation in organizational decision-making.

Over the years there has been a great deal of debate as to what may be the major causes of the differences and general trends identified above and, indeed, the extent to which they are symptoms of inequality or discrimination. It is extremely difficult in most of the areas of apparent inequality and discrimination identified to establish causal relationships and it is common that a number of factors serve to explain each of the phenomena identified. We now examine some of the more common of these explanations.

Origins and explanations of discrimination and inequality

Socialization and stereotypes

At least some discrimination is due to perceived, rather than actual, differences between the sexes, racial and ethnic groups and these perceptions often reflect popular norms regarding socially appropriate and socially acceptable roles. These norms are an outcome of the process known as socialization.

As we grow up in a particular society we acquire values and attitudes which influence both our perceptions of others and our behaviour. These values and attitudes are acquired or learned from others, they tend to be shared and they provide a base upon which group cohesion is developed. As they provide a base for the formation and reinforcement of groups they also provide a base upon which groups are distinguished from each other; each group having a shared set of values and attitudes that are to some extent distinct from those of other groups. We then tend to develop stereotypes of these other distinct groups that of course may or may not be accurate, which we tend to ascribe to all members of that group as if they were one and which, as noted above, are likely to include perceptions of appropriate and acceptable roles for members of the other group.

In this context it isn't just different racial and ethnic groups that are likely to be distinguished and stereotyped, men and women are also likely to be in different groups and one outcome is likely to be sexual or gender stereotyping.

In his work on cultures Hofstede (1991) refers to culture as: 'collective programming of the mind which distinguishes the members of one group or category of people from another' (p. 5), and asserts that 'The (mental) programming starts within the family; continues within the neighbourhood, at school, in youth groups, at the workplace, and in the living community' (p. 4). In elaborating upon this notion of culture he suggests that in any society

there is a men's culture and a different women's culture and that women are often not considered suitable for jobs traditionally filled by men, not because they are technically unable to perform the jobs but because they don't carry the symbols, do not correspond to the hero images, do not participate in the rituals or foster the values dominant in the men's culture; and vice versa.

Similar comments could be made about different racial and ethnic groups.

In discussing gender roles within societies Hofstede suggests that stereotypically men are supposed to be assertive, tough and competitive, whereas women are supposed to be more concerned with taking care of the home, the children and people in general; the contrast is between the achieving male and the caring female. There are differences between societies in the degree to which these gender roles are separated and in the degree to which the attitudes and behaviour of the sexes actually conform to them. Nevertheless, his work does suggest that there are common and pervasive sexual stereotypes. He identifies a number of attitudes and behaviours that might be considered as symptoms or indicators of the extent to which a particular society is structured in a manner in which these dominant sexual and gender stereotypes prevail. Indicators of consistency with the dominant stereotype might be:

- boys and girls studying different subjects at school and dominant social values that favour competition, the achievement of success and a concern with materialism

whereas indicators of a society in which the dominant gender stereotypes are less prevalent might include:

- boys being taught that it is okay for them to cry and the dominant values include caring and a concern for equality and the quality of working life.

The existence of racial and gender stereotypes and the nature of them therefore are likely to influence perceptions of appropriate work roles and this includes occupations and sectors. They are likely to play a part in, be a cause of, discrimination and the existence of inequality and there is evidence that in the UK these stereotypes are well established before students leave school. The DfEE report (DfEE,1999) on modern apprenticeships referred to above asserts that gender stereotypical attitudes are well entrenched by the time children (both sexes) reach year 11 and that these stereotypical attitudes are the product of the influence of parents and teachers.

Activity 2

Examine **Figure 11.3** and conclude whether the survey reported does or does not confirm the existence of gender stereotypes and, if so, what are the characteristics, behaviours and values associated with each.

Economic explanations

We noted above the observation of Adnett (1996) that differential experience, treatment and outcome are not necessarily the product of discrimi-

Study shows women make best managers

Jamie Wilson

Women are more efficient and trustworthy, have a better understanding of their workforce and are more generous with their praise. In short they make the best managers, and if men are to keep up they will have to start learning from their female counterparts, a report claims today.

The survey of 1,000 male and female middle and senior managers from across the UK is an indictment of the ability of men to function as leaders in the modern workplace.

A majority of those questioned believed women had a more modern outlook on their profession and were more open minded and considerate. By way of contrast, a similar number believe male managers are egocentric and more likely to steal credit for work done by others.

Management Today magazine, which conducted the research, said that after years of having to adopt a masculine identity and hide their emotions and natural behaviour in the workplace, women have become role models for managers.

The findings tally with a survey of female bosses carried out in the US. A five year study of 2,500 managers from 450 firms found that many male bosses were rated by their staff of both sexes to be self-obsessed and autocratic. Women on the other hand leave men in the starting blocks when it comes to teamwork and communicating with staff.

In Britain more than 61% of those surveyed said men did not make better bosses than women. Female managers use time more effectively, with many of those surveyed commenting that juggling commitments is a familiar practice for women with a home and a family.

Female managers also appear to make good financial sense for penny-pinching companies: most people, of either sex, would rather ask for a rise from a man.

"If men want to be successful at work they must behave more like women," said the magazine's editor, Rufus Olins. "Businesses need to wake up to the fact that so-called feminine skills are vital for attracting and keeping the right people. In the past women who aspired to management were encouraged to be more manly. It looks now as if the boot is on the other foot."

Figure 11.3 *Source: The Guardian*, 27 September 1999

nation and that some such differences may be the appropriate outcome or reflection of differences in labour market characteristics or tastes. In other words, women and members of ethnic minority groups earn less because their labour is worth less in market terms. In terms of the conventional competitive model there are differences in the value of the marginal product. This may indeed be the case and, to the extent that women and members of ethnic minorities have lower levels of educational and skills attainment, then we should expect this to be the outcome of a competitive and efficient market. Where this is true, then the differences in outcome are not the product of discrimination they are the product of the market working efficiently and effectively.

It may be that here we are confronting outcomes that are the indirect product of discrimination in that the differences in educational and skills attainment levels are themselves the product of discrimination; however they may be the product of perfectly rational decisions of the individuals and their families. For example, in the case of women it may be rational for families to invest less in education and training for women and concentrate their scarce resources in investment in the human capital of husbands and sons. Why? – well, there may be an expectation that women will experience discontinuous employment because of their role in childbirth, the absence of adequate and convenient childcare facilities and dominant social attitudes and social customs with regard to the distribution of family responsibilities and which frown upon mothers working. However, the expectation of a lower rate of return may also be influenced by an expectation of discrimination and where this occurs we may have an expectation of inequality or discrimination which then becomes self-perpetuating.

We noted above that outcomes and workplace experience may be the product of tastes and tastes may result in discrimination against particular categories of labour. Becker (1957) saw discrimination as a taste of the employer, which is itself the result of prejudice. There are profit consequences for employers who discriminate in this way, they may not be willing to employ labour whose marginal product is greater than the wage that would have to be paid and in this sense they can be perceived to be willing to pay a price to exercise and practise their prejudices. A further consequence of such a policy on the part of the employer is that competition in the labour market is restricted and the categories of labour that have preferential status gain or earn a wage that is higher than it would be if the categories of labour that are discriminated against were active competition for the work available.

A further consequence of such discrimination on the part of employers is a segmented labour market in which there are categories of labour that do not compete with one another even though there may be competition within each segment. Under competitive conditions such discrimination would be removed by employers not prepared to pay the price of discriminating, they would be more efficient and their costs would be lower.

A further explanation of employers' willingness to discriminate may be in their unwillingness to upset their existing labour force and employment structures. For example, if insiders are racist (see **Figure 11.1**) or unwilling for whatever reason to work with women it is unlikely the employers will voluntarily make decisions on hiring that threaten existing relationships. In this scenario outsiders are doomed to remain so and therefore are doomed to remain within the secondary employment sectors characterized by poorer terms and conditions of employment, fewer opportunities, less training and investment, less security and lower expectations. The inequality and discrimination practised in such firms also then tends to confirm existing stereotypes and inequality and discrimination are perpetuated.

So, differential workplace experiences and outcomes may be the product of the market working efficiently and effectively, reflecting differences in educational and skills attainment, but they may also be the product of employers being willing to pay the price of their own prejudices or they may be the product of employers being unwilling to upset their existing workforce. The former is not an instance of discrimination whereas the latter two are.

The Marxist analysis of the consequences of capitalism suggests that not only does capitalism result in the exploitation of labour it also results in male domination and exploitation of women who serve the interests of capital by providing a cheap way of ensuring that the well-being of the labour resource is taken care of and that the next generation of labour is produced and raised. Additionally the Marxist analysis suggests that certain sections of the population of working age constitute a 'reserve army of labour' and women and ethnic minorities and their treatment in the labour market can be viewed in these terms. What this means is that they constitute a pool of labour that will be drawn into the labour market only periodically and in periods of tight labour supply. The prime examples of this would be the treatment of women in the two World Wars of the twentieth century, in these circumstances special measures are taken and facilities provided to enable the reserve army to work but as soon as they are no longer required they are effectively returned to reserve status; to use a sporting analogy they are on the bench and to be used only in emergency.

This frame of mind and attitude may result in crèches and family-friendly work practices when labour supply is insufficient but also in gender or ethnic origin being a criteria for selection for redundancy when necessary; the reserve army is quickly returned to the bench when no longer needed. Associated with this analysis is the notion that women only work for pin money, that the main breadwinner is the male in the household, that the female's earnings are not really necessary and so they don't have to be paid so much.

Other explanations of differential participation, treatment and outcome

So far we have identified a number of potential explanations of the differential participation rates, treatment in and outcomes of employment experienced by the genders and by racial and ethnic minorities in comparison with 'white males'. We have mentioned the acquisition of values and attitudes that may result in stereotyping, the productivity and value of the labour that is affected by educational and skills attainment, employers' and insider employees' preferences and prejudices and the influence of expectations of discrimination. In addition to these there are a number of other partial explanations and influences.

We noted earlier that female labour tends to dominate employment in the service sector, certain caring, clerical and secretarial occupations and employment of a part-time and temporary nature. To the extent that these sectors continue to expand and there is a continuation of the emphasis upon numerical and temporal flexibility, we might reasonably expect the demand for female labour and its participation in the labour force to also continue the trends of recent years.

Opportunity for and participation of female labour may also be a product of the nature of the technological environment. The increase in opportunities and participation in recent decades may be a reflection of technological change de-emphasizing the strength aspects of much work and emphasizing attributes and abilities allegedly possessed by women to a greater extent than men.

The degree and nature of regulation in the labour market may also have an impact upon female participation rates as well as upon labour market outcomes and it has been suggested that regulations such as those imposing:

- a minimum wage, which should narrow wage gaps (see the first evidence available and mentioned above which confirms this expectation) and attract more female and ethnic minority labour into the market
- employment rights for part-time and other atypical contract workers that are equivalent on a pro rata basis to those provided for full-time workers
- employment rights for pregnant workers, the right to return, the right to maternity leave and pay, the right not to be dismissed when pregnant, etc.

might all serve detrimentally to influence the demand for female labour and therefore the opportunities available.

Activity 3

Take a few moments now to think through how and why this might be the consequence.

Another viewpoint is that since managements have demonstrated a considerable capacity to circumvent regulations geared towards the achievement of greater equality of opportunity, treatment and outcome there is no reason to imagine that further regulation will have the desired impact. Also, where demand is significantly influenced by prejudicial attitudes on the part of employers and they have demonstrated their willingness to pay the price of prejudice it is unlikely that the passage of legislation will have much impact; it is notoriously difficult to change values and attitudes through the passage of legislation.

So far we have skirted around the issue of childbirth and its implications as an explanation of differential opportunities, treatment and outcomes. We have implied that the impact of childbirth as a source of discontinuity of employment may influence decisions regarding investment in human capital, education and training; we have referred to the relevance of dominant social attitudes regarding the role of women in child rearing; we have noted that lifetime working patterns for women do tend to show a decline in labour force participation associated with childbirth, which is then partially redeemed as the children grow up; and we have discussed the potential impact of regulation geared towards ensuring that pregnant women are not discriminated against simply because they are or are liable to become pregnant.

However, associated with this are the issues of childcare and the availability and cost of childcare facilities. Those countries in Europe that have high female participation rates tend also to have plentiful childcare provision in the right place and at an affordable price, in many cases involving considerable amounts of state or employer subsidy. A particularly good example of the relevance of availability of affordable childcare occurred with the reunification of East and West Germany at the beginning of the 1990s. The collapse of the state childcare service in the East after reunification certainly contributed to a rapid and marked decline in the ability if women to take up work outside the home and female unemployment soared.

Additionally, the number of children that a woman has, the age of the youngest child and whether the family is a two-parent family appear to be influential factors.

The discontinuity of employment associated with the female role in childbirth tends also detrimentally to affect opportunities for career advancement and also labour market outcomes in terms of pay. This is particularly likely to be the case where salary scales are incremental with length of service.

One of the differences between the experience of racial and ethnic minority groups compared with that of women is that the experience of discrimination may be that it is much more robust if not violent. We have already noted that there are wage gaps and that the rate of unemployment tends to be higher amongst these minority groups but it also seems to be the case that the incidence and intensity of racial discrimination tends to be positively associated with the degree of hardship or perceived threat to those who are not in the racial or ethnic minority groups.

There are positive relationships between unemployment, economic and social exclusion among the indigenous population and the expression of racism by that population. The overt and often violent indications of that racism may become more apparent with higher and longer unemployment and as the incidence of social and labour market exclusion increases. While the worst and most violent expression of racism and discrimination is perhaps most likely to come from other 'outsiders', we have already noted the role of insiders in encouraging employers to discriminate and in practising discrimination and harassment themselves; this also seems to be positively associated with perceived threat and hardship. In the case referred to in **Figure 11.1** there was evidence that the expression of racism and discrimination on these grounds intensified with the intensification of pressures upon other workers and perceived threats of difficult times ahead. The case reported in **Figure 11.4** also illustrates this, as well as providing further useful evidence of the importance and resilience of traditional attitudes and stereotypes.

There is evidence here that members of the white male majority perceive members of racial and ethnic minorities as a reserve army in much the same way as they do women.

So far we have concentrated upon evidence of discrimination and inequality, its origins and causes at a level external to the organization. Now, and for the remainder of the chapter, we concentrate upon the policies, procedures and practices pursued within organizations.

See how many of the following you can answer briefly without re-reading the earlier sections of this chapter.

1 Is all discrimination unlawful?
2 What does the principle of vicarious liability imply for employers?
3 Explain briefly the difference between direct and indirect discrimination.
4 In what respects is it appropriate to see discrimination as the expression of taste?
5 Why might an expectation of inequality or discrimination be self-fulfilling?
6 How can harassment be discrimination?

Managing equality in the workplace

As we noted in the Introduction, policies and measures aimed at reducing discrimination and promoting equality, whether it be opportunity, treatment or outcome, should be based in and upon the evidence available as to

Hidden racism triggered by hard times

The faces on the shop floor were all colours and the jokes on the evening shift were friendly. But when an economic downturn brought redundancies to a famous old firm in Sheffield, buried attitudes and racial stereotypes re-emerged.

So says a significant industrial tribunal judgment published last week, which is already circulating in boardrooms where the primitive hazards of "sack because they're black" were thought to belong to vanished decades. The solicitor and his two specialist advisers who formed the tribunal reveal how genuine goodwill formed the feeblest of barriers to gut assumptions when the axe had to fall in a hurry.

A century old this year, the Abbey Glen laundry has a good reputation in Sheffield for employing ethnic community workers, busy all hours with hotel and restaurant orders, including one for an international chain.

Evening shift supervisor Dean Cefferty was also an appropriately relaxed and encouraging line manager; when he took on six young Afro-Caribbeans last summer, he followed his usual policy of promoting good work by constant praise.

"There was an amicable and fruitful relationship," records the tribunal judgment, which looks in vain for malice or personal clashes when the six got their cards in September last year.

The sort of crude racist remarks common on countless shop floors didn't happen at Abbey Glen; the six workers were efficient and a good team; and outside work, they were all buddies together at the New Testament Church of God in Nursery Road.

But it wasn't enough. When workers had to go, the six were chosen - the only redundancies on the evening shift, whose white workers with worse time-keeping and attendance records were kept on. Searching vainly through a haphazard, almost non-existent system of appraisal for redundancy, the tribunal found that managers had simply assumed the four men and two women were "less reliable and more than their 200 colleagues because they were Afro-Caribbean.

"This affair shows the absolute requirement for personnel systems which rule out stereotypes or make them very difficult," says Val Rowlands of the Northern Complainants Aid Fund, the Bradford-based specialists in fighting race discrimination tribunals who took on the group's case. "It isn't enough to be nice and matey when jobs can be at risk."

She points to tribunal references to Mr Cefferty's "innocence and naivety" which allowed a constant friendliness with the workers - including talk of casual re-employment as soon as possible - to co-exist with this deadly lack of proper personnel procedure which allowed subconscious stereotyping to thrive. The tribunal shredded the firm's defence as the sacked six turned out to be far more punctual and dedicated to their work than almost all their colleagues who were kept on.

The judgment, which is being studied as a landmark exercise by the Commission for Racial Equality, also shows how the lack of systems led Abbey Glen into a worse mess when it became clear that the Chattoo brothers - Marlon and Kenneth - partners Kingsley and Diane Paul, and their mates Devon Myrie and Gavin Gordon were not going to take dismissal lying down.

Managers fatally made another stereotypical assumption, says the tribunal: that these sunny, Christian Afro-Caribbeans would turn the other cheek and come back for jobs when the laundry business picked up again. In the tribunal's words: "The group did not "roll over" quietly and when the firm had to justify its decision, it found the task much more difficult than it had imagined."

"The plain truth is that the firm lumped these Afro-Caribbeans together, having rather intuitively and hastily surmised that they were less reliable and perhaps less likely to complain."

Abbey Glen is considering an appeal. But the firm will be discouraged by the tribunal's anger at the way the laundry's legal defence led to "juggling and doctoring" as the flimsiness of mere goodwill became clear.

"We were good workers. We were sacked because we were black. Justice has been done," says 19-year-old Gavin Gordon. For all the decency at the laundry that is the sad truth, says Ms Rowlands. And systematic personnel regulations are her answer.

Martin Wainwright

Figure 11.4 *Source: The Guardian*, 17 July 1999. Jobs and Money p. 21.

the origins and causes of the inequality that exists. Some issues can be addressed at a national level through legislation and the creation of statutory rights and obligations, through exhortation, the production of advice and codes of good practice and the financial support provided for various initiatives. Similarly, government can influence the content and context of the education received by children in the state system, they can determine the curriculum and they can provide funding for educational and training initiatives directed at influencing the values and attitudes acquired through the socialization process.

However, in the end, the reality of equality will also depend upon the policies, practices and procedures created by management and the rigour with which they are pursued and implemented, as well as upon the attitudes of management, the workforce and their representative organizations.

One of the difficulties associated with the achievement of equality at the workplace involves persuading managers and employees that there are good reasons why equality should be pursued. To some extent a legal obligation will assist with this persuasion, as will the presence of a visible enforcing agency such as the Equal Opportunities Commission (EOC) and the Commission for Racial Equality (CRE) but it is notoriously difficult to change people's attitudes and values and there is no easy route to this through the passage of legislation.

From the perspective of the economy as a whole there is a potential inefficiency in the use of resources if, as a result of prejudice-based discrimination, people from minority groups are either unemployed or underemployed, for example because they are employed in jobs that are below their skill and aptitude capacity or because they are unable to obtain as much work as they would like: a waste of talent and the human resource. It is also the case from the national perspective that social exclusion resulting from discrimination and inequality can lead to social division and unrest, violence and destruction of property, and there are inevitably social costs associated with such behaviour.

Probably the most effective way of persuading employers to take the pursuit of equality seriously is if it is possible to demonstrate that the organization will become more competitive as a result. This may, for example, be due to cost reductions, to quality improvements or to enhanced capacity for innovation and development. This is sometimes referred to as the business case for equality.

Some of the points to be made here are similar to those above; inequality and discrimination can lead to a waste of resources and talent within the organization, it can also lead to poor motivation and performance and, where talent and resources are being wasted and motivation is low, we must expect that productivity, quality and innovation are all likely to be detrimentally affected. Where this happens there should be scope for improvements to be obtained as a result of pursuing policies and practices that serve to achieve greater equality.

Further points and possibilities include the image of the company and the damage that may be done to the company's relationships with customers and suppliers if it becomes apparent that the organization is one in which inequality and unlawful discrimination are rife. Inevitably, as indicated in the Ford case referred to earlier (**Figure 11.1**), there is also the possibility of internal conflict and disruption to production as groups discriminate against and argue with each other. The public knowledge of discrimination and inequality, harassment and bullying in a particular company may also make it difficult to recruit a labour force of the appropriate quality and quantity.

Policies and practices

There are many different ways in which employers can seek to ensure that inequality is minimized within the organization that they control. Perhaps first and foremost they should produce a clear and unambiguous statement of their commitment to the principle of equality and this might be expressed as a statement of intent or policy. However, such statements are insufficient in most cases to ensure that equality is achieved; other measures need to be taken which are linked to the known causes and characteristics of inequality in the workplace and if an organization is to take the pursuit of equality seriously they should in the early stages audit their existing policies and practices to establish the extent to which these are currently consistent with the objective of achieving equality. Examples of the kinds of areas of policy and practice that should be included in such an audit are:

- the organization of work schedules and work practices and the employment contracts on offer, in particular the utilization of family-friendly options such as term-time contracts, job sharing and working at home
- recruitment, selection, appraisal, promotion, selection for redundancy, grievance, discipline and dismissal practices and procedures
- training and development opportunities and the procedures used for the determination of training and development needs
- job evaluation schemes and terms and conditions of employment generally.

Having undertaken such an audit employers should then consider, in the light of the findings of the audit, what initiatives or improvements they should adopt in order to remedy shortcomings. Examples might well include:

- specific training for recruiters and line management in the meaning and understanding of equality issues and the prevention of discrimination
- anti-discrimination and equality awareness training through which cultural and self-understanding and attitudinal change may be encouraged

- the utilization of opportunities for the implementation of positive action, such as recruitment, selection and training programmes geared towards women returners or members of specific ethnic minorities
- the creation of workforce targets for women and ethnic minorities
- the provision of specific family-friendly facilities such as crèche facilities or after-school clubs
- information gathering and mechanisms for the regular monitoring of the implementation of the policies and operation of the procedures, so that the incidence and nature of inequality can be ascertained and appropriate remedial measures taken
- encouraging an enhanced role for women and ethnic minorities in the various decision-making processes and mechanisms
- the creation of specific confidential procedures to deal with allegations of sexual or racial harassment and the clear and unambiguous declaration that harassment is a disciplinary offence
- mechanisms to ensure that there is no victimization as a result of a complaint being made.

There is relatively little research evidence available as to the extent to which policies and practices of this kind are in place and being implemented. Cully *et al.* (1998), in the first findings from the WERS 1998, present some findings but the number of practices investigated was relatively small. Nevertheless, in the survey, which covers workplaces with twenty-five or more employees and encompasses the responses of 1906 managers, it was discovered that:

- 64 per cent of workplaces were covered by formal written equal opportunities policies specifically addressing the issues of equality of treatment or discrimination
- of those workplaces with a formal written policy nearly all covered the areas of race, sex and disability
- approximately half of those workplaces without a formal written policy said that they had an unwritten one or otherwise claimed to be an equal opportunities employer. There was a relationship with size of labour force and in the main those without a policy were relatively small organizations in terms of labour force size
- those workplaces with a formal written policy were much more likely to have a range of practices in place promoting equality of treatment
- the practices referred to are in the main concerned with the recording of information such as ethnic origin of employees, the collection of statistics and the monitoring of activities such as promotions and selection procedures.

Trade unions and equality

The trade union movement in the UK has come only lately to the issue of equality. The history of the movement in the UK is of a movement seeking social change but only relatively recently have the objectives of the movement included the pursuit of sex and racial equality in the workplace and indeed inside the movement itself. In part this is a product of the origins of the movement and the traditional membership base, the heavy manufacturing, extractive and utility industrial sectors that were dominated by male manual workers, but it is also a reflection of ignorance and selfishness encompassing the concern to protect and further the interests of those in work at the expense of those who are not, insiders at the expense of outsiders. In many instances earlier in the twentieth century women and ethnic minority groups were perceived by many in the union movement as the enemy competing for jobs that were rightly the preserve of the white male majority.

There is little doubt that the change of heart was promoted as much by membership decline in the 1980s as by a desire to further the interests of female and ethnic minority groups. Economic, industrial and labour-force trends of recent decades (see Chapter 6) have led to an increase in the proportion of the labour force who are women and members of ethnic minorities and, as the industries and trades that were the traditional base of trade union membership have declined, the union movement has realized that women and ethnic minority members and the service sector are among the prime opportunities for recruitment and membership growth.

We noted in the earlier chapter on trades unions (Chapter 7) that when the TUC gave evidence to the Donovan Commission on the objectives of the movement, there was no mention whatever of the pursuit of equality. Now equal rights are very much part of the trade union movement's agenda and the TUC General Council has, since 1983, had a number of earmarked or reserved seats for women and since 1989 there have also been a number of seats on the Council reserved for coloured members. Some trade unions are now in the forefront of the battle for equality in the workplace but progress has by no means been universal and, as has been indicated in the figures above, there are still plenty of situations for the unions to address. In part, the problems that trade unions face are compounded by the democratic nature of their organization and government. If a majority of the membership are concerned to protect and further their own interests as insiders it is difficult for the leadership to adopt policies that may promote the interests of outsiders, even where these outsider groups may constitute the union's main source of potential membership.

In **Figure 11.5** we have included a copy of an equal opportunities policy statement. Critically appraise this statement in the light of the contents of this chapter.

Now draft out for yourself an equal opportunities policy statement that meets the above criticisms as well as being consistent with the guidance given in the text of the chapter.

Equal Opportunity

The Company is unreservedly opposed to any form of discrimination being practised against its members because of their sex, marital status, disability or on the grounds of race, colour, creed and ethnic or national origin.

Company policy therefore requires entry to the Company and progression within it to be based upon objective criteria and personal merit. If you feel you have been discriminated against on any of these grounds you should complain to your manager, who is required to instigate a thorough investigation of such complaints.

Figure 11.5

We began this chapter by pointing out that there are several different equality objectives: are we concerned about achieving equality of opportunity, treatment or outcome? There is a legal context to these issues and we briefly identified its main elements, including the concepts of positive action, direct and indirect discrimination, victimization, vicarious liability and harassment as discrimination.

Having located the issues in their legal context we examined the evidence of inequality in terms of outcome and participation in the labour market and concluded that there are gender and ethnic wage gaps, that there are differential participation rates, that ethnic minority groups tend to experience greater and longer unemployment and that while there may be an association between educational attainment level and achievement in the labour market there is nevertheless evidence that women and ethnic minority groups tend to be better qualified for the jobs they do than are white males.

We then identified some of the main explanations for discrimination, including the impact of socialization and the formation of stereotypes. We pointed out as we did so that not all discrimination is unlawful and that some differential treatment is likely to be the product of genuine differences between the genders or racial and ethnic groups, in terms of the value of the product of their labour and their value within the labour market. Nevertheless, much of the difference in treatment and outcome is also due to discrimination that is not a reflection of a difference in value, much of which may be unlawful.

Childbirth is still a major explanatory variable for the differential labour market participation rates and experiences of women compared with men.

There are a range of policies and initiatives that can be taken at national as well as workplace level in order to reduce inequality and discrimination. At the workplace level employers may generally comply with the law, though there is also plenty of evidence of individual rights being infringed. However, the promotion of positive measures at this level will depend in part on the business case for equality and there are a range of ways in which this can be demonstrated.

Our discussion of equal opportunities policy statements at workplace level illustrated many of the ways in which employers can seek to ensure equality of opportunity, treatment and outcome.

Finally we briefly commented upon the role of trade unions in the pursuit of equality and the removal of discrimination.

Activity Answers

Activity 1

1 Here there are at least two issues or grounds upon which the ad may be considered discriminatory in an unlawful manner. In the context of equality of opportunity or access the term manager may be held to imply maleness and that the company is really looking to appoint men rather than women. This could be remedied by the use of a term such as managers/manageresses or a statement which emphasizes that the company would welcome applications for these positions from both sexes. If the ad were found to be discriminatory on these grounds would we be looking at an example of direct or indirect discrimination? Arguably the ad implies that mobility on a national basis is a condition for both appointment and promotion and this may also be indicative of a preference both for male applicants and also perhaps for unmarried applicants (discrimination against marriage is also unlawful) since mobility is likely to pose greater difficulties for those who are married and for women, especially where children are concerned. Here we are looking at the issue of discriminatory treatment and whether the tribunals or courts found for or against the company in this case would depend in part upon how genuine and real a requirement this was, or was it just a device through which the company could indirectly discriminate against women and perhaps particularly those who are married and who have children.

2 Here the issues concern both genuine occupational qualifications and

positive action and whether the case described fits with the circumstances in which such discrimination or expressed preference for members of particular ethnic or racial groups may be lawful. Here we are not looking at the issue of authenticity, dramatic performance or decency and it seems unlikely that we are confronted with a set of circumstances that would persuade tribunals that the employer's preference is a GOQ.

On the question of positive action the employer is not saying that other applicants need not apply or that they will only appoint from particular ethnic groups and so it again would seem unlikely that the ad is discriminatory on these grounds.

3   Here we seem to be confronted with a relatively straightforward example of positive action as unlawful discrimination. The company is not in these circumstances justified in stating that only men need apply, there is no GOQ and no lawful grounds for refusing to accept applications from and/or appoint a woman. In this instance the company is clearly not acting as an equal opportunities employer.

4   A more complex case here. The company says it is an equal opportunities employer etc. and has used some gender neutral terminology such as salesperson but the combination of the age and experience specifications could be held to be indirectly discriminatory against women who are arguably less likely to be able to comply given the incidence of childbirth. It might also be held that the use of the phrase 'young and thrusting' is indirectly discriminatory in that in the context of gender stereotypes it implies maleness.

Activity 2

The survey would appear to confirm the existence of gender stereotypes; men and women are being compared as if all men are the same and all women are the same and we have the comment 'If men want to be successful at work they must behave more like women'.

The characteristics, behaviours and values identified as associated with each gender are pretty much consistent with those that Hofstede identifies as symptoms of the stereotypes and include:

- men – egocentric, competitive, self-obsessed, autocratic, more likely to be dishonest
- women – trusting, understanding, generous, considerate, open minded, efficient, capable of managing multiple commitments.

Activity 3

The main arguments usually put forward suggest that regulation of these kinds might have the opposite effect from that intended because they serve to increase both direct and indirect costs, the price of employing women and because they hamper the ability of management to use labour flexibly. Whether these are indeed the consequences will at least in part depend upon the reasons for employing female/ethnic minority labour currently, if these categories of labour are being employed as a cheap and flexible alternative then it might be realistic to envisage consequences of this kind.

Activity 4

1 Definitely not. Discrimination can be lawful, for example if it occurs as a result of there being a GOQ, e.g. for reasons of authenticity or decency or where discrimination takes the form of positive action, giving preference to the members of an underrepresented group.
2 The principle of vicarious liability means that employers can be held liable for the civil wrongs, such as unlawful discrimination and harassment, committed by their employees at the workplace, even if the employer knew nothing of the behaviour concerned.
3 Direct discrimination tends to be upfront and obvious, such as when an employer states in a job advertisement 'only white males need apply'. Indirect discrimination occurs when a condition is attached to a job or to an employment practice or law which indirectly discriminates against a particular group or category of labour and which cannot be justified by the requirements or circumstance of the job. Examples would include stating in a job advertisement that candidates should be in their early 30s and have fifteen years continuous employment experience when these are not actually requirements of the work to be done.
4 Discrimination that is due to the prejudice of an employer, for example against particular ethnic groups or against women or men can, in terms of an economic analysis, be seen as the employer being prepared to pay for his/her tastes. This of course does not make such discrimination lawful.
5 Where families and individuals expect inequality or to be discriminated against this may result in their taking quite rational decisions not to invest scarce resources in further education and training or, in some cases, not to seek employment of a particular type or indeed at all. Given that there is an association between educational attainment and labour force participation and outcome it can be argued that such expectations becomes self-fulfilling.
6 Harassment becomes discrimination at the point at which it results in an individual or group being treated less favourably and that this less favourable treatment is on racial grounds or on the grounds of the individual's sex.

Activity 5

This statement contains almost the least it could get away with and has a negative tone, the emphasis being upon preventing and dealing with discrimination rather than the promotion of equality. Other than as a heading the word 'equality' is not used in the statement. There is no explanation of why the company is 'unreservedly opposed' to any form of discrimination and no attempt to persuade the labour force that the pursuit of equality might have advantages for them and for the company, let alone any mention of moral or human rights explanations. An employee might well feel that the company is saying the right words but that genuine commitment to the pursuit of equality is at the least questionable. The areas or grounds of discrimination referred to are those specified by the law and no more. There is reference to entry into and progression within the company but no reference to equal treatment and/or harassment or indeed to equality of outcome. There is no indication that employees might have a role to play in the promotion of equality or indeed that they have any responsibility in this area. There are no definitions to assist the employee in deciding whether they think they have been discriminated against, e.g. the inclusion of indirect as well as direct discrimination, no indication that the policy encompasses harassment as discrimination, no mention of positive action or the promotion of an equality culture. If we move on to the procedural element of the statement, there is no indication of what to do if it is the manager that is the source of the perceived discrimination.

Activity 6
The first thing to say is that, as with any policy statement or procedure, you should think through what is practicable, what you can actually achieve or control. There is no point in saying you are going to do something that you are unable to since this may eventually lead to scepticism and disaffection, not only with this policy statement but with all. Once it becomes apparent to staff that promises are not being delivered or even pursued there will be a negative impact upon trust and this can have wide-ranging implications.

The statement should be positive in tone and emphasis, stressing the company's commitment to the principles of achieving equality, and contain material on:

- the reasons for pursuing equality and the main responsibilities, advantages and roles of management, employees and trade unions
- the coverage in terms of sex, race, disability, etc. – and treatment, opportunity and outcome
- definitions of direct and indirect discrimination and you may also include definitions of victimization, GOQ and harassment
- particular areas in which the company is determined to achieve equality, such as recruitment and selection, training and development, appraisal, the determination of terms and conditions of employment with particular attention paid to the criteria and mechanics of any job evaluation scheme in use
- what to do if you as an employee feel that you are being discriminated against, victimized or harassed, referring employees to the appropriate procedural mechanisms
- a clear and unambiguous statement of the consequences for individuals found to have committed acts of discrimination, harassment or victimization

- a guarantee that progress towards the achievement of equality will be monitored and shortcomings identified and addressed.

The above may not be as comprehensive as the statement that you have drafted but if you have included all of these points you won't go far wrong.

References

Adnett, N., 1996. *European Labour Markets: Analysis and Policy*. Longman, Harlow.

Becker, G., 1957. *The Economics of Discrimination*. The University of Chicago Press, Chicago, IL.

Berthoud, R., 1999. *The Incomes of Ethnic Minorities*. Institute for Social and Economic Research, ISER Report 98-1.

Cully, M., O'Reilly, A., Millward, N., Forth, J., Woodland, S., Dix, G. and Bryson, A., 1998. *The Workplace Employee Relations Survey: First Findings*. DTI, ACAS, ESRC, PSI. Crown, London.

DfEE, 1999. *Modern Apprenticeships and Gender Stereotyping*. Crown, Sheffield.

Equal Opportunities Commission, 1999. *Facts about Women and Men 1998*. Manchester.

European Commission, 1997 *Annual Report from the Commission. Equal Opportunities for Women and Men in the European Union – 1996*. Luxembourg.

European Foundation for the Improvement of Living and Working Conditions, 1996. *Preventing Racism at the Workplace*. EFILWC, Dublin.

Hofstede, G., 1991. *Cultures and Organizations: Software of the Mind*. McGraw-Hill, London.

Jewson, N. and Mason, D., 1986. The theory and practice of equal opportunities policies: liberal and radical approaches. *Sociological Review* 34(2): 307–334.

Liff, S., 1995. Equal opportunities: continuing discrimination in a context of formal equality. In Edwards, P. (ed.), *Industrial Relations Theory and Practice in Britain*. Blackwell, Oxford.

McGivney, V., 1999. *Returning Women: Their Training and Employment Choices and Needs*. NIACE Publications, Leicester.

Chapter 12

Recent and future directions

A central strand running through this book has been change and adaptations to it. The last twenty-five years of the twentieth century have been witness to significant and ongoing change in the environment and contexts of employee relations in the UK, in the nature of the employment relationship, in the means used to resolve conflict and secure employee participation and involvement, and in the outcomes of the interactions between the various participants.

The following is not intended to be an exhaustive list but includes the more important of these changes:

- a shift in the balance of power in society in the direction of capital and a reassertion of managerial prerogative
- the massive development of the MNC as a worldwide phenomenon as part of the process of globalization and the liberalization of trade and with significant power to influence the nature of the employment relationship, the direction and content of employee relations
- enhanced pressures upon organizations to be competitive in a global rather than national economy and market
- the continuing erosion of the ideology of liberal collectivism, and in Europe of corporatism and their replacement with liberal individualism
- the emergence of potentially significant new political and economic structures in Europe with significant implications for structures of industrial ownership, the scale and nature of employment and social protection and the distribution of power between labour and capital
- a re-emphasis of the significance of the market as a contextual influence and constraint and its impact upon the structure of industry and thereby the demand for labour and, perhaps in particular, labour flexibility
- the emergence of the model of the flexible firm and its impact upon management thinking and policies
- change in the quality and composition of labour supply influenced at

least in part by the demographic influence towards an aging population and labour force

- technological change at an increasing rate and the development of new information and electronic technologies that have significant implications for the organization and nature of work as well as for the demand for labour
- the adoption of new competitive imperatives and strategies and consequential working practices such as those associated with Total Quality Management and lean production
- the emergence of different dominant values such as individualism and enterprise and the apparent demise of collectivism and the search for consensus
- change in the psychological contract and increased levels of stress and anxiety amongst the workforce
- an increasingly interventionist role for government as legislator and the significant modification of the legal environment within which employee relations are conducted
- removal from ACAS of the responsibility to promote the improvement of employee relations through collective bargaining
- removal of the public sector from its position as model for the private sector and a reversal of this relationship; the public sector being exhorted by successive governments to adopt private-sector ethics and practices such as performance management and the use of market forces as an internal mechanism for determining resource allocation
- decline in the size and influence of the trade union movement both in the workplace and in society generally, including its influence with government, forcing the movement to reappraise its objectives and strategies
- the decline of collective bargaining as the dominant conflict-resolving mechanism and means of achieving employee participation; the emergence of a newly strong management unilateralism embodied in different managerial styles and a preference for managing without trade unions
- the emergence of the notion of partnership as a new paradigm for the relationship between the interests and organizations of employees and employers
- a decline in the use of conciliation and arbitration for collective disputes allied to a significant increase in individual recourse to the judicial system to resolve grievances and obtain statutory entitlements and thereby to the ACAS caseload for individual conciliation.

These changes were accompanied by the development of a new model or paradigm for employee relations in the UK which, in many respects, may be seen as an adaptation to some of these changes, a model which arguably had as its central features:

- rejection of the principles of social protection
- deregulated labour markets and an emphasis upon labour flexibility and cost reduction
- a reassertion of management's right to manage and control the labour process
- a revised psychological contract in which stress, anxiety and insecurity play a more significant role
- weakened trade unions, greater legal constraints upon industrial action and less employee protection
- an emphasis upon individualism, individual contract and employee commitment to organizational goals
- devolution and decentralization of decision-making and the dismantling of national/sectoral industrial relations institutions
- less collective bargaining and joint decision-making, less employee participation and an emphasis instead upon employee involvement schemes and initiatives
- an emerging interest in partnership as cooperation and joint problem solving.

One of the inevitable debates among observers of and active participants in the system concerns the extent to which these trends seem set to continue and the impact that they may have in the future or are we likely to see twists and turns in the direction and nature of change?

It is impossible to give definite answers to this and similar questions and there isn't space here to examine the future in any detail. Nevertheless we can identify some elements of the environment and other trends mentioned above that seem likely to continue and maybe also some that do not.

There would appear to be little reason to imagine that there will be any diminution of the pressures from globalization, liberalization, galloping increases in the scale of FDI and the influence of the MNC and, indeed, from technological change. These and other competitive pressures for labour and labour markets to become more flexible seem set to continue and also set to continue to influence government policy.

New Labour

However, there are some signs of countervailing influences in the New Labour government's legislative interventions and proposals that employees are to have a measure of greater protection at work, for example rights to individual union representation in grievance and disciplinary hearings and the reduction of the qualifying time before employees become eligible for statutory rights regarding unfair dismissal. Protections of this kind are commonly criticized for reducing the scope for employers to use labour flexibly and thereby it is argued that they hamper job creation and the achievement of full employment. These latter rights to representation or accompaniment may also act as an incentive for employers/managers to introduce formal and fair procedures, possibly through negotiations or partnership arrangements with trade unions, within the organization thereby signalling less reliance upon the judicial resolution of grievances.

The proposals regarding trade union recognition for collective bargaining may go some way to halting or even reversing the trend of decline in the incidence of both collective bargaining and recognition and to the extent that there is increased use of collective bargaining it may be that employee participation will also benefit.

There is presumably also some cause for optimism that these proposals will encourage individuals to join trade unions; visibility, presence and demonstrable achievement appear to influence joining decisions. Even though the TUC thinks that the support thresholds are too high they nevertheless seem to envisage an increase in membership over the next few years.

The new government's attitude to membership of the European Union, the speedy decision at Amsterdam in the summer of 1997 to agree to proposals for a new Social Chapter in the Treaty and retrospectively to implement in the UK those measures that had been adopted under the Maastricht Protocol Procedures, may also signify the beginnings of a new period of support for employees at work. However, the other member states are subject to many of the same external pressures related to technology, globalism and competitiveness as is the UK and it is arguable that many of the member states are beginning to contemplate the gradual and variable adoption of something close to the model that has emerged in the UK. So far their responses may not have been as expensive to employees in terms of rights and protections as were the responses of the Conservative governments in the UK between 1979 and 1997, nevertheless there are some similar trends apparent such as the trends towards decentralization of collective bargaining, deregulation to enhance employers' ability to utilize labour more flexibly and higher levels of unemployment than are historically common. The labour movements in the other member states have also in the main been experiencing decline. It is also clear that there is a new commitment within the EU to the agreement at that level of only basic principles which are to be fleshed out at local–national level and in accordance with local tradition.

The election of New Labour in 1997 seemed to present an opportunity for a shift of ideological emphasis away from liberal individualism and unitarism in the direction of social partnership and greater employee participation. However, it was also clear early in the new governments' period of office that there was no intention to return to a form of social partnership that implied a return to corporatism. The social partners were likely to be involved more in consultations with government but there was no indication that the new government intended to devolve or cede decision-making to the social partners or to mechanisms of a tripartite nature.

A government that is so publicly committed to the retention of labour market flexibility is unlikely to take notions of partnership to the point where it allows the partners the ability to agree requirements and regulations that might be inconsistent with the flexibility imperative.

The new Labour government in the UK seems to want to pursue a kind of middle or hybrid course emphasizing:

- the need for labour flexibility and flexible labour markets
- the avoidance of onerous labour market regulation and other burdens upon business
- a determination to impose greater barriers to the continuing receipt of unemployment and other social security and disability benefits as part of a package of measures designed to provide incentives for the unemployed to join/rejoin the working population
- greater expenditure upon education and vocational training as a means of improving the quality of the labour force and dealing with shortfalls of skills
- an emphasis upon social partnership as cooperation rather than participation
- the replacement of the notion of a right to work with that of a duty to work.

Flexibility and competitiveness at the same time as a more limited concept of social justice and protection.

Partnership in this New Labour context seems to have more in common with adopting a cooperative approach and attitude than with sharing decision-making or power. This notion of social partnership, where partnership is perceived as a preferable alternative to conflict rather than as joint decision-making or power sharing, seems to offer employees little more than is offered by the EWC directive, the opportunity to receive information and express a view.

We may be witnessing the emergence of a new perspective on employee relations, one in which trade unions are recognized as having a limited right to recognition as representatives of employees' interests but where they are also expected to be team players, a form of unitarism that encompasses collective organization and in which employees and their representatives are expected to subjugate their interests to those of the organization in which they are partners.

There are those who are sceptical of the objectives of New Unionism and the TUC's own adoption of a partnership approach and they, like Claydon among others, suspect that such an approach simplifies the task of management in preserving the status quo of unilateralism and managerial prerogative in pursuit of the interests of capital and shareholders.

There would appear to be little reason to suppose that employee relations in small firms are on the threshold of improvement since they are to remain exempt from the main thrust of legislative support for employees.

Glossary

A-Gs	Advocates-General
ACAS	Advisory, Conciliation and Arbitration Service
AEEU	Amalgamated Engineering and Electrical Union
ASLEF	Associated Society of Locomotive Engineers and Firemen
BIFU	Banking, Insurance and Finance Union
CBI	Confederation of British Industry
CCT	Compulsory Competitive Tendering
CEEP	European Centre of Public Enterprises
CFDT	Confederation Française Democratique du Travail
CFTC	Confederation Française des Travailleurs Chretien
CGT	Confederation Generale du Travail
CRE	Commission for Racial Equality
CROTUM	Commissioner for the Rights of Trade Union Members
CVS	The Chinese Value Survey
DfEE	Department for Education and Employment
EC	European Commission
ECHR	European Court of Human Rights
ECJ	European Court of Justice
EcoSoc	Economic and Social Committeee
ECSC	European Coal and Steel Community
EEA	European Economic Area
EEC	European Economic Community
EFILWC	European Foundation for the Improvement of Living and Working Conditions
EFTA	European Free Trade Association
EIB	European Investment Bank
EIC	European Industry Committee
EIF	European Industry Federation
EIF	European Investment Fund
EIRR	European Industrial Relations Review
EMU	European Monetary Union
EOC	Equal Opportunities Commission
EP	European Parliament
EPA	Equal Pay Act
EPA	Employment Protection Act 1975

ER	Employee Relations
ESF	European Social Fund
ESOP	Employee Share Ownership Scheme
ETUC	European Trade Union Confederation
ETUI	European Trade Union Institute
EU	European Union
EURES	European Employment Services
EWC	European Works Council
FDI	Foreign Direct Investment
FO	Confederation Generale du Travail–Force Ouvriere
GCHQ	Government Communications Headquarters
GDP	Gross Domestic Product
GNP	Gross National Product
GNVQ	General National Vocational Qualification
HASAW	Health and Safety at Work Act 1974
HASTE	European Health and Safety Database
HCN	Host Country National
HRM	Human Resource Management
ICFTU	International Confederation of Free Trade Unions
IDS	Incomes Data Services
IEC	International European Committees
IGC	Inter-Governmental Conference
ILO	International Labour Organisation
IMF	International Monetary Fund
IPD	Institute of Personnel and Development
ITBs	Industrial Training Boards
JIT	Just-in-Time
LFS	Labour Force Survey
LTU	Long-term Unemployed/Unemployment
MEPs	Members of the European Parliament
MNC	Multinational Corporation
MNE	Multinational Enterprise
NAFTA	North American Free Trade Agreement
NCVQ	National Council for Vocational Qualifications
NEC	National Executive Committee
NHS	National Health Service
NJC	National Joint Councils
NOW	New Opportunities for Women
NVQ	National Vocational Qualification
OECD	Organisation for Economic Cooperation and Development
ONS	Office of National Statistics
PCN	Parent Country National
PEPPER	Promotion of Employee Participation in Profits and Enterprise Results
PSBR	Public Sector Borrowing Requirement
QC	Quality Circle

QMV	Qualified Majority Voting
QWL	Quality of Work Life
RRA	Race Relations Act 1968
RSI	Repetitive Strain Injury
SAC	Social Affairs Council
SAP	Social Action Programme
SDA	Sex Discrimination Act 1975
SEA	Single European Act 1986
SEDOC	Systeme European de Diffusion des Offres et Demandes d'emploi en Compensation.
SMEs	Small and Medium-size Enterprises
SMIC	Salaire Minimum Interprofessional de Croissance (French minimum wage)
SPASP	Social Protocol Agreement on Social Policy
TCN	Third Country National
TEC	Training and Enterprise Councils
TEN	Trans European Network
TEU	Treaty on European Union
TGWU	Transport and General Workers Union
TNC	Transnational Corporation
TQM	Total Quality Management
TULRA	Trade Unions and Labour Relations Act 1974
UEFA	Union of European Football Associations
UN	United Nations
UNCTAD	United Nations Conference on Trade and Development
UNICE	Union of Industrial and Employers Confederations of Europe
URTU	The United Road Transport Union
WCL	World Confederation of Labour
WERS	1998 Workplace Employee Relations Survey
WFTU	World Federation of Trade Unions
WHO	World Health Organisation
WTO	World Trade Organisation

Acts of Parliament and EU initiatives/ legislation

Acts of Parliament in chronological order

The Contracts of Employment Act 1963
The Industrial Training Act 1964
The Redundancy Payments Act 1965
The Trades Disputes Act 1965
The Race Relations Act 1968
The Equal Pay Act 1970
The Industrial Relations Act 1971
The Health and Safety at Work Act 1974
The Trade Unions and Labour Relations Act 1974
The Employment Protection Act 1975
The Sex Discrimination Act 1975
The Race Relations Act 1976
The Employment Protection (Consolidation) Act 1978
The Employment Act 1980
The Transfers of Undertakings Regulations 1981
The Employment Act 1982
The Trades Union Act 1984
The Equal Value Regulations 1984
The Sex Discrimination Act 1986
The Wages Act 1986
The Remuneration of Teachers Act 1987
The Employment Act 1988
The Employment Act 1989
The Employment Act 1990
The Trades Union Reform and Employment Rights (TURER) Act 1993
The Criminal Justice and Public Order Act 1994

The Collective Redundancy and Transfer of Undertakings (Amendment) Regulations 1995
The Disability Discrimination Act 1995
The Employment Rights Act 1996
The Employment Relations Act 1999

EU initiatives/legislation

The Directive on the Establishment of a European Works Council or a Procedure in Community Scale Undertakings and Community Scale Groups of Undertakings for the Purposes of Informing and Consulting Employees 94/45.

The Directive on Collective Redundancies 75/129, extended by 92/56 and amended by 98/59.

The Directive on the Transfer of Undertakings 77/187 amended by 98/50.

The Draft Vth Directive on the Harmonisation of Company Law/Company Structure and Administration in the EC COM (83) 185, revised by COM (90) 629 and COM (91) 372.

The Draft Directive Accompanying/Complementing the European Company Statute on the Involvement of Employees in the European Company COM (89) 168, revised by COM (91) 174.

The Draft Vredeling Directive. Draft Directive on Procedures for Informing and Consulting Employees in Undertakings with Complex Structures COM (80) 423, revised by COM (83) 292.

The Health and Safety Framework Directive 89/391.

The Directive on Parental Leave 96/34. Introduced pursuant to an agreement between the social partners in accordance with Article 2.2 of the Social Policy Agreement.

The Directive on the Adaptation of Working Time 93/104.

Equal Pay Directive 75/117.

Equal Treatment Directive 76/207.

Directive 97/81 EC concerning the Framework Agreement on Part-time

Work concluded by UNICE, CEEP and ETUC.

Directive 99/70 EC concerning the Framework Agreement on Fixed Term Work concluded by ETUC, UNICE and CEEP.

The Directive on the Protection of Pregnant Workers (92/85).

Non-binding instruments

Recommendation 92/443 on Equity Sharing and Financial Participation.

Community Charter of the Fundamental Social Rights of Workers (The Social Charter) 1989.

Code of Practice on The Implementation of Equal Pay for Work of Equal Value for Women and Men COM (96) 336.

Council Recommendation 92/241 concerned with childcare.

Council Resolution on Balanced Participation of Men and Women in Decision-making 95/C168/02.

Code of Practice on the Dignity of Women and Men at Work.

Bibliography

ACAS, 1997. *Annual Report for 1996.* HMSO, London.

ACAS, 1998. *Annual Report 1997.* HMSO, London.

ACAS, 1999. *Annual Report for 1998.* HMSO, London.

Adnett, N., 1996. *European Labour Markets: Analysis and Policy.* Longman, Harlow.

Advisory Conciliation and Arbitration Service, 1976. *Code of Practice 1 on Disciplinary Practice and Procedures.* HMSO, London.

Advisory Conciliation and Arbitration Service, 1987. *Discipline At Work.* HMSO, London.

Baldry, K., 1995. Changes in the Management of Employee Relations in Royal Mail. M.Phil. Thesis, Unpublished. University of Plymouth.

Bamber, G. and Lansbury, R.D., 1993. *International and Comparative Industrial Relations.* 2nd Edition. Routledge.

Barrell, R. and Pain, N., 1997. EU: an attractive investment. Being part of the EU is good for FDI and being out of EMU may be bad. *New Economy* 4(1): 50–4.

Bartlett, C.A. and Ghoshal, S., 1989. *Managing Across Borders: The Transnational Solution.* Harvard Business School Press, Harvard, Cambridge, Massachusetts.

Bassett, P. and Cave, A., 1993. *All for One: the Future of the Unions.* Fabian Society, London.

Bean, R., 1985. *Comparative Industrial Relations: an Introduction to Cross-National Perspectives.* Croom Helm, London.

Beaumont, P., 1992. *Public Sector Industrial Relations.* Routledge, London.

Becker, G., 1957. *The Economics of Discrimination.* The University of Chicago Press, Chicago, IL.

Beer, M., Spector, B., Lawrence, P.R., Quinn Mills, D. and Walton, R., 1984. *Managing Human Assets.* Free Press, New York.

Berthoud, R., 1999. *The Incomes of Ethnic Minorities.* Institute for Social and Economic Research, Report 98-1.

Black, J. and Upchurch, M., 1999. Public sector employment. In Hollinshead, G., Nicholls, P. and Tailby, S. (eds), *Employee Relations.* FT Pitman Publishing, London.

Blackburn, R., 1967. *Union Character and Social Class.* Batsford.

Blyton, P. and Turnbull, P., 1994. *The Dynamics of Employee Relations.* (2nd Edition 1998) Macmillan, Basingstoke.

Boyer, R., 1993. *The Convergence Hypothesis Revisited: Globalisation but still the Century of Nations?* Couvertures Oranges de CEPREMAP, No 9403, Paris.

Braverman, H., 1974. *Labour and Monopoly Capital.* Monthly Review Press, New York.

Brown, W., 1993. The contraction of collective bargaining in Britain. *British Journal of Industrial Relations* 31(2): 189–200.

Carley, M., 1993. Social dialogue. In Gold, M. (ed.), *The Social Dimension – Employment Policy in the European Community.* Macmillan, Basingstoke.

Certification Office for Trade Unions and Employers Associations 1999. Annual Report of the Certification Officer 1998. Crown, London.

Chamberlain, N. and Kuhn, J.W., 1965. *Collective Bargaining.* McGraw-Hill.

CIR, 1972. *Study No. 1 Employers Organizations and Industrial Relations.* HMSO, London.

Claydon, T., 1996. Union derecognition: a re-examination. In Beardwell, I. (ed.), *Contemporary Industrial Relations: A Critical Analysis.* Oxford.

Colling, T., and Ferner, A. 1995. Privatisation and marketisation. In Edwards, P. (ed.), *Industrial Relations Theory and Practice in Britain.* Blackwell, Oxford, pp. 491–514.

Crouch, C., 1982. *The Politics of Industrial Relations.* 2nd Edition. Fontana.

Crouch, C., 1993. *Industrial Relations and European State Traditions.* Clarendon, Oxford.

Cully, M. and Woodland, S., 1997. Trade union membership and recognition. *Labour Market Trends.* June pp. 23–9.

Cully, M., O'Reilly, A., Millward, N., Forth, J., Woodland, S., Dix, G. and Bryson, A., 1998. *The Workplace Employee Relations Survey: First Findings.* DTI, ACAS, ESRC, PSI. Crown Copyright, London.

Denny, C., 1999. Employers renege on New Deal Training. *The Guardian* 28 July 1999.

Devanna, M.A., Fombrun, C.J. and Tichy, N.M., 1984. A framework for strategic Human Resource Management. In Fombrun, C.J., Tichy, N.M. and Devanna, M.A. (eds), *Strategic Human Resource Management.* Wiley, New York.

DfEE Skills and Enterprise Network, 1999. *Labour Market Quarterly Report,* August. Sheffield.

DfEE, 1999. *Modern Apprenticeships and Gender Stereotyping,* Crown, Sheffield.

Dickens, L. and Hall, M., 1995. The state: labour law and industrial relations in Edwards, P. (ed.), 1995 *Industrial Relations: Theory and Practice in Britain.* Blackwell, Oxford.

Donovan Commission Report, 1968. *The Report of the Royal Commission on Trade Unions and Employers Associations.* Command 3623. HMSO, London.

Dolvik, J.E., 1997. *Redrawing Boundaries of Solidarity? ETUC, Social Dialogue and the Europeanisation of Trade Unions in the 1990s.* Arena and FAFO, Oslo.

Dowling, P. and Schuler, R., 1990. *International Dimensions of Human Resource Management.* PWS-Kent.

Due, J., Madsen, J.S. and Jensen, C.S., 1991. The social dimension: convergence or diversification of industrial relations in the Single European Market. *Industrial Relations Journal* 22(2): 85–102.

Dunlop, J.T., 1958. *Industrial Relations Systems.* Holt, New York.

Edwards, P., 1995. The employment relationship. In Edwards, P. (ed.), 1995 *Industrial Relations: Theory and Practice in Britain.* Blackwell, Oxford.

Edwards, P. (ed), 1995. *Industrial Relations: Theory and Practice in Britain.* Blackwell, Oxford.

Edwards, P., *et al.*, 1992. Great Britain, still muddling through. In Ferner, A. and Hyman, R. (eds), *Industrial Relations in the New Europe.* Blackwell, Oxford.

Edwards, P., Armstrong, P., Marginson, P. and Purcell, J., 1996. Towards the transnational company? The global structure and organisation of multinational firms. In Crompton, R., Gallie, D. and Purcell, K. (eds), *Changing Forms of Employment.* Routledge, London.

Equal Opportunities Commission, 1999. *Facts about Women and Men 1998.* Manchester.

Etzioni, A., 1975. *A Comparative Analysis of Complex Organisations.* Free Press, New York.

European Commission, 1996. *The Demographic Situation in the European Union 1995.*

European Commission, 1997. *Annual Report from the Commission. Equal Opportunities for Women and Men in the European Union 1996.* Brussels.

European Commission, 1999. *Employment in Europe 1998.* Luxembourg.

European Foundation for the Improvement of Living and Working Conditions, 1996. *Preventing Racism at the Workplace.* EFILWC, Dublin.

European Works Council Bulletin Issue 3, May/June 1996, Indutrial Relations Research Unit.

Farnham, D., 1993. *Employee Relations.* IPM, London.

Farnham, D., 1997. *Employee Relations in Context.* IPD, London.

Farnham, D. and Horton, S., (eds), 1993. *Managing the New Public Services.* Macmillan, Basingstoke.

Farnham, D. and Pimlott, J., 1995. *Understanding Industrial Relations.* 5th Edition. Cassell, London.

Felstead, A., Burchell, B. and Green, F., 1998. Insecurity at work. *New Economy* 5(3) pp. 180–4.

Flanders, A., 1968. *Management and Unions.* Faber & Faber, London.

Flanders, A., 1975. Collective bargaining: a theoretical analysis. British Journal of Industrial Relations. Vol vi, No. 1, pp. 1–26.

Flanders, A., 1974. The tradition of voluntarism. *British Journal of Industrial Relations* 12(3): 352–70.

Fowler, A., 1996. How to conduct a disciplinary interview. *People Management* November, London.

Fox, A., 1966. *Industrial Sociology and Industrial Relations.* Royal Commission Research Paper No. 3. HMSO, London.

Fox, A., 1974. *Beyond Contract.* Faber & Faber, London.

Gallie, D., Penn, R. and Rose, M., 1996. *Trade Unionism in Recession.* Oxford University Press, Oxford.

Gallin, D., 1994. *Drawing the Battle Lines Inside the New World Order.* International Union of Food and Allied Workers, Geneva.

Gennard, J. and Judge, G., 1997. *Employee Relations.* IPD, London.

Gold, M., 1993. Overview of the social dimension. In Gold, M. (ed.), *The Social Dimension – Employment Policy in the European Community.* Macmillan, Basingstoke.

Gold, M. and Hall, M., 1992. *Report on European Level Information and Consultation in Multinational Companies – An Evaluation of Practice.* The European Foundation for the Improvement of Living and Working Conditions, Dublin.

Goldthorpe, J.H. (ed.), 1984 Order and Conflict in Contemporary Capitalism. Clarendon, Oxford.

Gospel, H.F., 1992. *Markets, Firms and the Management of Labour in Modern Britain.* Cambridge University Press, Cambridge.

Gospel, H. and Palmer, G., 1993. *British Industrial Relations.* 2nd edition Routledge, London.

Grahl, J. and Teague, P., 1991. Industrial relations trajectories and European Human Resource Management. In Brewster, C. and Tyson, S. (eds), *International Comparisons in Human Resource Management.* Pitman, pp. 67–91.

Guest, D., 1987. Human Resource Management and industrial relations. *Journal of Management Studies* 24(5): 503–521.

Guest, D., 1989a. Human Resource Management: its implications for industrial relations, and trade unions. In Storey, J. (ed.), *New Perspectives on Human Resource Management.* Routledge, London.

Guest, D., 1989b. Personnel and HRM: can you tell the difference? *Personnel Management,* January pp. 48–51.

Guest, D., 1992. Employee commitment and control. In Hartley, J.F. and Stephenson, G.M. (eds), *Employment Relation.* Blackwell, Oxford.

Guest, D., 1995. *Why do People Work?* A Presentation to the IPD National Conference, cited in Marchington, M. and Wilkinson, A., 1996 IPD, London.

Guest, D.E. and Conway, N., 1999. *Fairness at Work and the Psychological Contract.* IPD, London.

Hall, M., 1994. Industrial relations and the social dimension. In Hyman, R. and Ferner, A. (eds), *New Frontiers in European Industrial Relations.* Blackwell, Oxford.

Hamill, J., 1983. The labour relations practices of foreign owned and indigenous firms. *Employee Relations* 5(1): 14–16.

Hamill, J., 1984a. Multinational corporations and industrial relations in the UK. *Employee Relations* 6(3): 12–16.

Hamill, J., 1984b. Labour relations decision making within multinational corporations. *Industrial Relations Journal* 15(2): 30–34.

Hawkins, K., 1979. *A Handbook of Industrial Relations Practice.* Kogan Page.

Heery, E., 1996. The new New Unionism. In Beardwell, I. (ed.), *Contemporary Industrial Relations: A Critical Analysis.* Oxford.

Hendry, C., 1994. *Human Resource Strategies for International Growth.* Routledge.

Herzberg, F., 1966. *Work and the Nature of Man.* Staples Press, London.

Hirsch-Weber, W., quoted in Van der Vall, M., 1970. *Labour Organisations.* Cambridge University Press, p. 53, and cited in Salamon, M., 1992. Industrial Relations, 2nd edition. Prentice Hall. Hemel Hempstead.

Hodgetts. R.M. and Luthans, F., 1997. *International Management.* 3rd Edition. McGraw-Hill, London.

Hofstede, G., 1991. *Cultures and Organisations: Software of the Mind.* McGraw-Hill, London.

Hollinshead, G. and Leat, M., 1995. *Human Resource Management: An International and Comparative Perspective on the Employment Relationship.* Pitman Publishing, London.

Hollinshead, G., Nicholls, P. and Tailby, S., 1999. *Employee Relations.* Financial Times Pitman Publishing, London.

Hyman, R., 1995. Industrial relations in Europe: theory and practice. *European Journal of Industrial Relations.* 1(1): 17–46.

Hyman, R., 1995. The Historical Evolution of British Industrial Relations in Edwards, p. (ed.), 1995. *Industrial Relations: Theory and Practice in Britain.* Blackwell, Oxford.

Hyman, R., 1999. National industrial relations systems and transitional challenges: an essay in review. *European Journal of Industrial Relations* 5(1): 90–110.

IDS Focus No. 91, Autumn 1999.

Ietto-Gillies, G., 1997. Working with the big guys: hostility to transnationals must be replaced by co-operation. *New Economy* 4(1): pp. 12–16.

Inman, P., 1999. 35% of New Dealers leave for unknown destination. *The Guardian* 13 August 1999.

IPM, 1993. *Professional Education Scheme Syllabus for Employee Relations.*

Jewson, N. and Mason, D., 1986. The theory and practice of equal opportunities policies: liberal and radical approaches. *Sociological Review* 34(2): 307–334.

Keller, B.K., 1991. The role of the state as corporate actor in industrial relations systems. In Adams, R.J. (ed.), *Comparative Industrial Relations, Contemporary Research and Theory.* Harper Collins, London, p.83.

Kelly, J. and Kelly, C., 1991. Them and Us: social psychology and the new industrial relations. *British Journal of Industrial Relations* 29(1): 25–48.

Kennedy, T., 1980. *European Labour Relations.* Lexington Books, Lexington, Massachusetts.

Kochan, T.A., Katz, H.C. and McKersie, R.B., 1986. *The Transformation of American Industrial Relations.* Basic Books, New York.

Kodz, J., Kersley, B. and Strebler, M., 1999. *Tackling a Long Hours Culture.* Institute for Employment Studies, Sussex University.

Leat, M., 1998. *Human Resource Issues of the European Union.* Financial Times Pitman Publishing, London.

Leat, M., 1999. Multi-nationals and employee relations. In Hollinshead, G., Nicholls, P. and Tailby, S., *Employee Relations*. Financial Times Pitman Publishing, London.

Leat, M., 1999. The European Union. In Hollinshead, G., Nicholls, P. and Tailby, S., *Employee Relations*. Financial Times Pitman Publishing.

Lecher, W.E. and Platzer, H.-W. (eds), 1998. *European Union – European Industrial Relations? Global Challenges National Developments and Transnational Dynamics*. Routledge, London.

Lecher, W.E. and Rub, S., 1999. The constitution of EWCs: from information forum to social actor? *European Journal of Industrial Relations* 5(1): 7–25.

Legge, K., 1995. *Human Resource Management: Rhetorics and Realities*. Macmillan, Basingstoke.

Liff, S., 1995. Equal opportunities: continuing discrimination in a context of formal equality. In Edwards, P. (ed.), *Industrial Relations Theory and Practice in Britain*. Blackwell.

Main, B.G.M., 1996. The union relative wage gap. In Gallie, D., Penn, R. and Rose, M. (eds), *Trade Unionism in Recession*. Oxford.

Marchington, M., 1988. *The Four Faces of Employee Consultation*. Personnel Management, May. London.

Marchington, M. and Wilkinson, A., 1996. *Core Personnel and Development*. IPD, London.

Marchington, M., Goodman, J., Wilkinson, A. and Ackers, P., 1992. *New Developments in Employee Involvement*. Employment Department Research Series No. 2, HMSO, London.

Marginson, P. and Sisson, K., 1994. The structure of transnational capital in Europe: the emerging Euro-company and its implications for industrial relations. In Hyman, R. and Ferner, A., (eds), *New Frontiers in European Industrial Relations*. Blackwell, Oxford.

Marginson, P. and Sisson, K., 1996. Multi-national companies and the future of collective bargaining: a review of the research issues. *European Journal of Industrial Relations*. 2(2): 173–197.

Marsh, A.I. and McCarthy, W.J., 1968. *Disputes Procedures in Britain*. Donovan Commission Research Paper No.2 Part 2. HMSO, London.

Maslow, A., 1943. A theory of human motivation. *Psychological Review* 50: 370–396.

Maurice, M., Silvestre, J.-J. and Sellier, F., 1980. Societal differences in organising manufacturing units: a comparison of France, West Germany and Great Britain. *Organisational Studies* 1: 59–86.

McCarthy, W.E.J. (ed.), 1992. *Legal Intervention in Industrial Relations*. Blackwell, Oxford.

McGivney, V., 1999. *Returning Women: Their Training and Employment Choices and Needs*. NIACE Publications.

McIlroy, J., 1995. *Trades Unions in Britain Today*. Manchester University Press, Manchester.

McLoughlin, I. and Gourlay, S. 1994. *Enterprise Without Unions*. Open

University Press, Buckingham.

Metcalf, D., 1993. *Transformation of British Industrial Relations? Institutions, Conduct and Outcomes 1980–1990.* Centre for Economic Performance, Paper No. 151. LSE, London.

Michels, R., 1966. *Political Parties.* Free Press, New York.

Miliband, R., 1969. *The State in Capitalist Society.* Weidenfeld & Nicholson.

Millward, N., Stevens, M., Smart, D. and Hawes, W.R., 1992. *Workplace Industrial Relations in Transition.* Dartmouth, Aldershot.

Mowday, R.T., Steers, R.M. and Porter, L.W., 1982. *Employee–Organisation Linkages: The Psychology of Commitment, Absenteeism and Turnover.* Academic Press, New York.

Mueller, F. and Purcell, J., 1992. The Europeanisation of manufacturing and the decentralisation of bargaining multinational management strategies in the European automobile industry. *International Journal of Human Resource Management* 3(1) 15–34.

Nakano, S., 1999. Management views of European Works Councils: a preliminary survey of Japanese multinationals. *European Journal of Industrial Relations* 5(3): 307–26.

Nicholls, P., 1999. Context and theory in employee relations. In Hollinshead, G., Nicholls, P. and Tailby, S. (eds), *Employee Relations.* Financial Times Pitman Publishing, London.

Office of National Statistics, 1999. *Social Focus on Older People.* The Stationery Office, London.

Ohmae, K., 1990. *The Borderless World: Power and Strategy in the Interlinked Economy.* Harper, New York.

Organization for Economic Co-operation and Development, 1999. *Annual Employment Outlook 1999.* OECD.

Peel, J., 1979. *The Real Power Game.* McGraw-Hill.

Perlmutter, H., 1969. The tortuous evolution of the multi-national corporation. *Columbus Journal of World Business* 4(1): 9–18.

Poole, M. and Mansfield, R., 1992. 'Managers' attitudes to Human Resource Management: rhetoric and reality. In Blyton, P. and Turnbull, P. (eds.), *Reassessing Human Resource Management.* Sage, London.

Prahalad, C.K. and Doz, Y.L., 1987. *The Multinational Mission.* Free Press, New York.

Prasad, S.B., 1995. *International Management; A Reader.*

Purcell, J. and Gray, A. 1986. Corporate Personnel Departments and the management of industrial relations: two case studies in the management of ambiguity. *Journal of Management Studies* 23 (2): 205–23.

Purcell, J., 1987. Mapping management styles in employee relations. *Journal of Management Studies* 24(5): 534–548.

Purcell, J., 1989. How to manage decentralised collective bargaining. *Personnel Management* May, London.

Purcell, J. and Ahlstrand, B., 1989. The impact of corporate strategy and the management of employee relations in the multi-divisional company. *British Journal of Industrial Relations* 27(3): 397–417.

Purcell, J. and Ahlstrand, B., 1994. *Human Resource Management in the Multi-Divisional Company*. Oxford University Press, Oxford.

Purcell, J. and Sisson, K., 1983. Strategies and practice in the management of industrial relations. In Bain, G.S. (ed.), *Industrial Relations in Britain*. Blackwell, Oxford.

Rivest, C., 1996. Voluntary European Works Councils. *European Journal of Industrial Relations*. 2(2): 235–253.

Roethlisberger, F.J. and Dickson, W.J., 1939. *Management and the Worker*. Harvard University Press, Cambridge, Massachusetts.

Ronen, S. and Shenkar, O., 1985. Clustering countries on attitudinal dimensions: a review and synthesis. *Academy of Management Journal*, September, pp. 435–454.

Salamon, M., 1992. *Industrial Relations: Theory and Practice*. 2nd Edition. Prentice Hall, Englewood Cliffs, NJ.

Salamon, M., 1999. The state in employee relations. In Hollinshead, G., Nicholls, P., and Tailby, S. (eds), *Employee Relations*. FT Pitman Publishing.

Schein, E., 1988. *Organisational Psychology*. Prentice Hall, Englewood Cliffs, NJ.

Schregle, J., 1981. Comparative industrial relations: pitfalls and potential. *International Labour Review* 120(1): 15–30.

Schulten, T., 1996. European Works Councils: prospects of a new system of European industrial relations. *European Journal of Industrial Relations* 2(3): 303–324.

Smith, J., 1999. New Deal needs some figuring out. *The Guardian* 2 August 1999.

Stewart, M., 1994. *Union Wage Differentials in an era of Declining Unionisation*. University of Warwick.

Storey, J., 1992. *Developments in the Management of Human Resources – An Analytical Review*. Blackwell, Oxford.

Storey, J. and Sisson, K., 1993. *Managing Human Resources and Industrial Relations*. Open University, Buckingham.

Strauss, G., 1979. Workers' participation: symposium introduction. *Industrial Relations* 18: 247–261.

Treu, T. (ed.), 1987. *Public Service Labour Relations: Recent Trends and Future Prospects: A Comparative Survey of Seven Industrialised Market Economy Countries*. ILO, Geneva.

TUC, 1997. *European Works Councils*.

TUC, 1995. *General Council Report for 1995*.

TUC, 1999. *British Trade Unionism – the Millennial Challenge*.

Turner, H.A., 1962. *Trade Union Growth, Structure and Policy*. Allen and Unwin, London.

Turner, L., 1996. The Europeanisation of labour: structure before action. *European Journal of Industrial Relations*. 2(3): 325–344.

Undy, R. and Kessler, I., 1995. The changing nature of the employment relationship. IPD Annual Conference, Harrowgate. Cited in Marchington, M. and Wilkinson, A., 1996. *Core Personnel and Development*. IPD, London.

United Nations Conference on Trade and Development, 1999. Report on World Investment 1998. UNCTAD, Geneva.

Visser, J. and Ebbinghaus, B., 1992. Making the most of diversity? European integration and transnational organisation of labour. Greenwood, J., Grote, J.R. and Ronit, K. (eds.), *Organised Interests and the European Community.* pp. 206–237.

Waddington, J. and Whitston, C., 1995. Trade unions: growth, structure and policy. In Edwards, P. (ed.), *Industrial Relations Theory and Practice in Britain.* Blackwell, Oxford, pp. 151–202.

Waddington, J. and Whitston, C., 1997. Why do people join trade unions in a period of membership decline? *British Journal of Industrial Relations* December.

Wakelin, K., Girma, S. and Greenaway, D., 1999. *Wages, Productivity and Foreign Ownership in UK Manufacturing.* Centre for Research on Globalisation and Labour Markets, University of Nottingham.

Walker, K.F., 1974. Workers' participation in management : problems, practice and prospects. *Bulletin of the International Institute for Labour Studies* 12: 3–35.

Waterman, P., 1998. The second coming of proletarian internationalism? A review of recent resources. *European Journal of Industrial Relations* 4(3): 349–377.

Webb, S. and Webb, B., 1894. *The History of Trade Unionism.* Reprinted by Augustus Kelly, New York, 1965.

Webb, S. and Webb, B., 1920. *Industrial Democracy.* Longman.

Whitston, C. and Waddington, J., 1994. Why join a union? *New Statesman and Society* 18 November pp. 36–38.

Wilkinson, A., Marchington, M., Ackers, P. and Goodman, J., 1992. Total Quality Management and employee involvement. *Human Resource Management Journal* 2(4): 1–20.

Winchester, D. and Bach, S., 1995. The state: the public sector. In Edwards, P. (ed.), *Industrial Relations Theory and Practice in Britain.* Blackwell, Oxford, pp. 304–334.

Index

Tutor
Support
Material is
available....

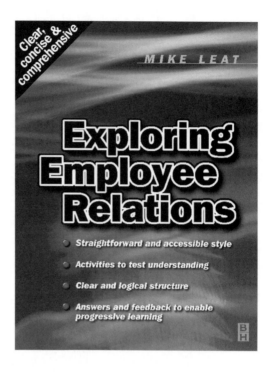

A free Tutor Resource Pack for *Exploring Employee Relations*, providing extra support material for lecturers and tutors in the form of discussion questions and answers, will be available on our web site from Spring 2001. Please contact our Management Marketing Department, quoting ISBN 075065032X, for your password on:

Tel: 01865 314459
Fax: 01865 314455
E-mail: bhmarketing@repp.co.uk